Novel Research and Development Approaches in Heterogeneous Systems and Algorithms

Santanu Koley
Haldia Institute of Technology, India

Subhabrata Barman
Haldia Institute of Technology, India

Subhankar Joardar
Haldia Institute of Technology, India

A volume in the Advances in Systems Analysis,
Software Engineering, and High Performance
Computing (ASASEHPC) Book Series

Published in the United States of America by
IGI Global
Engineering Science Reference (an imprint of IGI Global)
701 E. Chocolate Avenue
Hershey PA, USA 17033
Tel: 717-533-8845
Fax: 717-533-8661
E-mail: cust@igi-global.com
Web site: http://www.igi-global.com

Library of Congress Cataloging-in-Publication Data

Names: Koley, Santanu, 1981- editor. | Barman, Subhabrata, 1974- editor. |
   Joardar, Subhankar, 1969- editor.
Title: Novel research and development approaches in heterogeneous systems
   and algorithms / edited by Santanu Koley, Subhabrata Barman, Subhankar
   Joardar.
Description: Hershey, PA : Engineering Science Reference, [2023] | Includes
   bibliographical references and index. | Summary: "Novel Research and
   Development Approaches in Heterogeneous Systems and Algorithms addresses
   novel research and developmental approaches in heterogenous systems and
   algorithms for informationcentric networks of the future. Covering
   topics such as image identification and segmentation, materials data
   extraction, and wireless sensor networks, this premier reference source
   is a valuable resource for engineers, consultants, practitioners,
   computer scientists, students and educators of higher education,
   librarians, researchers, and academicians"-- Provided by publisher.
Identifiers: LCCN 2022057058 (print) | LCCN 2022057059 (ebook) | ISBN
   9781668475249 (h/c) | ISBN 9781668475256 (s/c) | ISBN 9781668475263
   (eISBN)
Subjects: LCSH: Heterogeneous computing. | Image steganography. |
   Diagnostic imaging. | Cyberbullying. | Wireless sensor networks.
Classification: LCC QA76.88 .N68 2023 (print) | LCC QA76.88 (ebook) | DDC
   004/.35--dc23/eng/20230109
LC record available at https://lccn.loc.gov/2022057058
LC ebook record available at https://lccn.loc.gov/2022057059

This book is published in the IGI Global book series Advances in Systems Analysis, Software Engineering, and High Performance Computing (ASASEHPC) (ISSN: 2327-3453; eISSN: 2327-3461)

British Cataloguing in Publication Data
A Cataloguing in Publication record for this book is available from the British Library.

For electronic access to this publication, please contact: eresources@igi-global.com.

Advances in Systems Analysis, Software Engineering, and High Performance Computing (ASASEHPC) Book Series

Vijayan Sugumaran
Oakland University, USA

ISSN:2327-3453
EISSN:2327-3461

MISSION

The theory and practice of computing applications and distributed systems has emerged as one of the key areas of research driving innovations in business, engineering, and science. The fields of software engineering, systems analysis, and high performance computing offer a wide range of applications and solutions in solving computational problems for any modern organization.

The **Advances in Systems Analysis, Software Engineering, and High Performance Computing (ASASEHPC) Book Series** brings together research in the areas of distributed computing, systems and software engineering, high performance computing, and service science. This collection of publications is useful for academics, researchers, and practitioners seeking the latest practices and knowledge in this field.

COVERAGE

- Computer Graphics
- Virtual Data Systems
- Software Engineering
- Parallel Architectures
- Performance Modelling
- Distributed Cloud Computing
- Engineering Environments
- Enterprise Information Systems
- Human-Computer Interaction
- Network Management

IGI Global is currently accepting manuscripts for publication within this series. To submit a proposal for a volume in this series, please contact our Acquisition Editors at Acquisitions@igi-global.com or visit: http://www.igi-global.com/publish/.

Titles in this Series

For a list of additional titles in this series, please visit: www.igi-global.com/book-series

Quantum Computing and Quantum Cryptography in Future Computers
Bhawana Rudra (National Institute of Technology, Karnataka, India)
Engineering Science Reference • ©2023 • 300pp • H/C (ISBN: 9781799895220) • US $270.00

Developing Linear Algebra Codes on Modern Processors Emerging Research and Opportunities
Sandra Catalán Pallarés (Universidad Complutense de Madrid, Spain) Pedro Valero-Lara (Oak Ridge National Laboratory, USA) Leonel Antonio Toledo Díaz (Barcelona Supercomputing Center, Spain) and Rocío Carratalá Sáez (Universidad de Valladolid, Spain)
Engineering Science Reference • ©2023 • 266pp • H/C (ISBN: 9781799870821) • US $215.00

New Approaches to Data Analytics and Internet of Things Through Digital Twin
P. Karthikeyan (National Chung Cheng University, Chiayi, Taiwan) Polinpapilinho F. Katina (University of South Carolina Upstate, USA) and S.P. Anandaraj (Presidency University, India)
Engineering Science Reference • ©2023 • 307pp • H/C (ISBN: 9781668457221) • US $270.00

Futuristic Trends for Sustainable Development and Sustainable Ecosystems
Fernando Ortiz-Rodriguez (Tamaulipas Autonomous University, Mexico) Sanju Tiwari (Tamaulipas Autonomous University, Mexico) Sailesh Iyer (Rai University, India) and José Melchor Medina-Quintero (Tamaulipas Autonomous University, Mexico)
Engineering Science Reference • ©2022 • 320pp • H/C (ISBN: 9781668442258) • US $270.00

Emerging Technologies for Innovation Management in the Software Industry
Varun Gupta (Universidad de Alcalá, Madrid, Spain) and Chetna Gupta (Jaypee Institute of Information Technology, Noida, India)
Engineering Science Reference • ©2022 • 282pp • H/C (ISBN: 9781799890591) • US $270.00

Technology Road Mapping for Quantum Computing and Engineering
Brojo Kishore Mishra (GIET University, India)
Engineering Science Reference • ©2022 • 243pp • H/C (ISBN: 9781799891833) • US $250.00

Designing User Interfaces With a Data Science Approach
Abhijit Narayanrao Banubakode (MET Institute of Computer Science, India) Ganesh Dattatray Bhutkar (Vishwakarma Institute of Technology, India) Yohannes Kurniawan (Bina Nusantara University, Indonesia) and Chhaya Santosh Gosavi (MKSSS's Cummins College of Engineering, India)
Engineering Science Reference • ©2022 • 325pp • H/C (ISBN: 9781799891215) • US $270.00

701 East Chocolate Avenue, Hershey, PA 17033, USA
Tel: 717-533-8845 x100 • Fax: 717-533-8661
E-Mail: cust@igi-global.com • www.igi-global.com

Table of Contents

Chandan Koner, Dr. B.C. Roy Engineering College, Durgapur, India

Solanki Pattanayak, Haldia Institute of Management, India
Sabyasachi Samanta, Haldia Institute of Technology, India
Dipankar Dey, Global Institute of Science and Technology, India
Abhijit Sarkar, Haldia Institute of Technology, India
Souvik Bhattacharyya, University Institute of Technology, Burdwan, India

Soumya Roy, Haldia Institute of Technology, India
Yuvika Vatsa, Haldia Institute of Technology, India
Moumita Sahoo, Haldia Institute of Technology, India
Somak Karan, Haldia Institute of Technology, India

Kuntal Mukherjee, Haldia Institute of Technology, India
Syed Saif Ahmed, Haldia Institute of Technology, India
Mohammad Aasif, Haldia Institute of Technology, India
Sumana Kundu, Dr. B.C. Roy Engineering College, India
Soumen Ghosh, Haldia Institute of Technology, India

Prasenjit Dey, Coochbehar Government Engineering College, India
Arnab Gain, Coochbehar Government Engineering College, India

Detailed Table of Contents

Chapter 1

Tarun Kumar Ghosh, Haldia Institute of Technology, India
Krishna Gopal Dhal, Midnapore College, India
Sanjoy Das, University of Kalyani, India

Grid computing has emerged as an intelligent distributed computing paradigm due to the huge improvements in performance of wide-area network and powerful yet low-cost computers. Computational grids accumulate and share the power of heterogeneous, geographically dispersed, and multi-domain-administered computational resources to offer high performance or high-throughput computing. To realize the promising potential of computational grids, an effective and efficient task scheduling system is primarily important. Task scheduling in computational grid is one of the most challenging and complex tasks. In other words, the task scheduling in computational Grid is considered as NP-hard problem due to the problem complexity and intractable nature of the problem. Such a problem could be solved using meta-heuristic algorithms. In this chapter, several nature-inspired meta-heuristics are compared with respect to the parameters (i.e., minimization of makespan and flowtime) for scheduling tasks in computational grids. The nature-inspired meta-heuristics involved in this chapter are genetic algorithm (GA), particle swarm optimization (PSO), ant colony optimization (ACO), and cuckoo search (CS) algorithms. Experimental results show that the GA outperforms the other methods in terms of average makespan and the PSO algorithm performs best among all 4 algorithms in terms of average flowtime.

Chapter 2

Vishalakshi G. R., Dayananda Sagar College of Engineering, India
Gopala Krishna, SJB Institute of Technology, India
Hanumantha Raju, BMS Institute of Technology and Management, India

In today's world, smartphones are ubiquitous and feature high-quality cameras and video recording capabilities. The camera shake, shadows, or other environmental factors lead to poor video, even in low-lighting situations with a high-end camera. To preserve and enhance low-light mobile video, a wavelet energy-based adaptive retinex algorithm is proposed. The first step in the method is to extract frames from the composite video before it is fed into the algorithm in HSV space. The authors then apply the wavelet energy-based adaptive retinex algorithm to the dynamic range-extended value channel. Lighting conditions that cause video degradation are restored adaptively to their natural brightness. A color restoration technique that improves the conventional retinex method fixes the gray world violation problem. Wavelet energy is used as a metric in concurrence with the retinex algorithm to objectively validate image enhancement quality. An experimental work of more than 300 still images and videos show that the proposed technique outperforms the current state of the art.

Chapter 3

To make human life easy and compact, XAI has developed a lot with more innovations and contributed its own share. To make a suitable treatment while diagnosed with brain tumour, one needs to classify the tumour and detect it in a proper way where the explained result is most important. With the help of different analysis processes where marker-based approaches can help in proper segmentation and noise reduction analysis, numerous imaging modalities exist for tumour detection that are utilized to identify tumours in the brain. One of the most important issues of XAI system is medical diagnosis through ML in medical image processing. In this chapter, the authors present a modified marker-controlled watershed transformation approach to detect brain tumour with XAI and machine learning approaches. They include CNN and data augmentation algorithms. Image pre-processing takes the main area to detect and diagnose disease and diagnose properly. The statistical measurements have been introduced to get the mathematical abstractions of different approaches for result analysis.

Chapter 4

Visual impairment, such as cataract, if not detected and treated early, might lead to blindness. Cataract detection still takes a long time and is quite subjective, depending on ophthalmologist's preference. To expedite cataract screening procedure, an automated cataract detection system should be developed. Fundus image analysis for automatic categorization and grading of cataracts has the potential to reduce the burden of competent ophthalmologists while also assisting cataract patients in learning about their diseases and getting treatment suggestions. The optic disc and blood vessel data play a significant role in the detection and grading of cataracts. Normal, mild, moderate, and severe cataract stages are differentiated based on texture, colour, size, and contrast. Classification and severity rating are carried out using random forest classifier, an ensemble machine-learning method. The accuracy discovered is equivalent to prior study in the literature. This study is expected to help doctors detect cataracts early and prevent cataract-related suffering.

Chapter 5

Gunjan Mukherjee, Brainware University, India

Arpitam Chatterjee, Jadavpur University, India

Bipan Tudu, Jadavpur University, India

Sourav Paul, Ramakrishna Mission Vidyamandira, India & Swami Vivekananda Research Centre, India

Aerial views of the scenes captured by UAV or drone have become very familiar as they easily cover the wide view of the scene with different terrain types and landscapes. The detection of the scene images captured by drone and their subparts have been done on the basis of simple image processing approach involving the pixel intensity information. Many computer vision-based algorithms have successfully performed the tasks of segmentation. The manual approach of such segmentation has become time consuming, resource intensive, and laborious. Moreover, the perfection of segmentation on the irregular and noisy images captured by the drones have been lowered to greater extents with application of machine learning algorithms. The machine learning-based UNet model has successfully performed the task of segmentation, and the performance has been enhanced due to optimization. This chapter highlights the different variations of the model and its optimization towards the betterment of accuracy.

Chapter 6

Cynthia Jayapal, Kumaraguru College of Technology, India

Clement Sudhahar, Karunya Institute of Technology and Sciences (Deemed), India

Centralized and decentralized systems are prone to security breaches while storing private data. It is challenging to establish trust when an administrator is not known. Blockchain-based technologies use distributed ledgers that can be trusted, audited, validated, and verified by network nodes. The assets stored in a blockchain are immutable, timestamped, and cannot be tampered because of the integrated cryptographic mechanisms. Consensus algorithms are used to validate the transactions and blocks stored in a blockchain. Multiple research reviews focus either on various application domains of blockchain or comparative study of consensus algorithms or security aspects. This chapter aims at providing a comprehensive review on blockchain technologies, performance metrics, and guidelines for choosing a blockchain technology and consensus algorithm based on an organization's requirements and protocols. This chapter also captures concepts on blockchain types, consensus algorithms, and typical applications of blockchain with its features.

Chapter 7

Minakshi Sarkar, Haldia Institute of Technology, India

Indrajit Banerjee, Indian Institute of Engineering Science and Technology, Shibpur, India

Tarun Kumar Ghosh, Haldia Institute of Technology, India

Anirban Samanta, Haldia Institute of Technology, India

Anirban Sarkar, Guru Nanak Institute of technology, India

Technologies related to the internet of things (IoT) have been extensively employed in business operations, military research, networking technologies, etc. With the proliferation of the IoT, data theft and leakage have gradually increased because the data communication system is public. Various novel steganography algorithms have been proposed for data hiding. But in this process, the quality of the hidden image decreases badly. We want to give an accurate color to the image instead of severe color changes. To change it, we have to perform a colorization process by mapping the original image to the stego image. It gains more characteristics according to the actual embodiment. Here, the objective is to improve the appearance by calculating the loss function. The stego image can withstand steganalysis by using the authors' proposed scheme by maintaining its integrity while to some extent improving the quality of the image. The experimental results confirmed the proposed method outperforms the existing methods (SGAN and CycleGAN) for information hiding with enhanced image transmission quality.

Chapter 8

AI-Based DBMS Controlled Speech Recognition Model for Some Common Computing

Mrinmoy Sen, Haldia Institute of Technology, India
Sunanda Jana, Haldia Institute of Technology, India
Swarnajit Bhattacharya, Haldia Institute of Technology, India
Gitika Maity, Dr. Meghnad Saha Institute of Technology, India

Speech recognition has become an important part of the AI model. It plays a vital role in the correct function of different AI enabled devices that we see today. Many automobile industries use this voice recognition technology in their AI to develop modern voice enabled cars. To that end we have implemented a deep learning-based voice recognition model in the MySQL database to execute various DBMS command automatically through speech recognition by using intelligent Google Speech API and match-LSTM model. Our proposed model accept speech as input and by using intelligent Google Speech API service we construct MySQL database and perform training using match-LSTM. The latency rate and data transfer speed of this model is very fast because of its prior training approach. This type of methodical approach can be made in any DBMS systems to make it more convenient, smart and easy to use for normal user.

Chapter 9

Priyatosh Jana, Haldia Institute of Technology, India
Pranab Roy, Institute of Engineering and Technology, J. K. Laxmipat University, Jaipur,
  India
Sarit Chakraborty, Government College of Engineering and Leather Technology, India
Tanmoy Biswas, Shyamaprasad College, India
Soumen Ghosh, Haldia Institute of Technology, India

Digital microfluidic biochips (DMFB), a newly developed lab-on-chip device, has evolved in recent years as a significant miniaturized platform for applications in the area of point-of-care investigations, DNA sequencing, and further biomedical detection and analysis. By means of rapid escalation in scalability, complexity, and requirements of more accurate control and accuracy, a novel DMFB-based architecture known as microelectrode dot array (MEDA) has been introduced. Due to its higher complexity and parallel execution of multiple bioassays, conventional testing methods used for DMFBs may not be adequate for fault diagnosis and detection in such devices. In this chapter, the authors proposed new techniques compatible with higher complexity and applicable for structural testing of MEDA-based biochips. The proposed testing methods provide detection of faults or failure (if any) within a given layout using minimal resources with minimal test completion time. The testing simulations are carried out with specified layout dimensions and variable droplet size.

Chapter 10

Abhijit Sarkar, Haldia Institute of Technology, India
Sabyasachi Samanta, Haldia Institute of Technology, India

The internet has grown to be widely used by billions of individuals in our digital age. The internet is required for a variety of platforms, online apps, and standalone applications. Numerous methods, including cryptography, encryption/decryption, and data concealment algorithms, are developed for this goal. However, the employment of these methods was not very secure, making it simple for hackers to get the secret message. A new method called "steganography" was developed to offer the highest level of protection for sensitive data. Steganography's primary goal is to conceal the presence of concealed messages. Additionally, it seeks out concealed messages using factors like the kind of embedding method, the message's length, its content, or the carrier's secret key. At this point in the chapter, a single bit of data has been embedded into edge-based pixel positions with arbitrary bit positions. The authors have compared their method to three standard edge detection algorithms for a more comprehensive assessment. Different statistical measures also have been made for the uniqueness of the technique.

Chapter 11

Uday Kumar Banerjee, Dr. B.C. Roy Engineering College, Durgapur, India
Anup Kumar Das, Dr. B.C. Roy Engineering College, Durgapur, India
Rajdeep Ray, Dr. B.C. Roy Engineering College, Durgapur, India
Chandan Koner, Dr. B.C. Roy Engineering College, Durgapur, India

A chaotic cryptographic method and bit shuffle methodology for image encryption and decoding have both been suggested. In order to evaluate the encryption's effectiveness and determine whether it met the desired standard, a number of performance analysis tools were also used. These included the number of pixel change rate (NPCR), the unified average changing intensity (UACI), the entropy analysis, which is a component of an encryption scheme that shows how random the image is, and the correlation coefficient. These results reveal the safety of the suggested cryptographic technique.

Chapter 12

Solanki Pattanayak, Haldia Institute of Management, India
Sabyasachi Samanta, Haldia Institute of Technology, India
Dipankar Dey, Global Institute of Science and Technology, India
Abhijit Sarkar, Haldia Institute of Technology, India
Souvik Bhattacharyya, University Institute of Technology, Burdwan, India

Sleuthing images that conceal information has continuously been a stimulating and difficult problem in cyber security. Finding hidden data in nursing image is called steganalysis. In this chapter, the authors explore the method employed in the study. The investigational results are have included followed by a discussion with prospect analysis. Several 2×2 blocks are recycled to implant the data bits within the stego-image, and using the Arnold Map, four quadrants of the pixels of each block is selected to embed the data in nonlinear bit position. Different measures with the change of BPP (bits per pixel) are also worked out.

Chapter 13

Soumya Roy, Haldia Institute of Technology, India
Yuvika Vatsa, Haldia Institute of Technology, India
Moumita Sahoo, Haldia Institute of Technology, India
Somak Karan, Haldia Institute of Technology, India

Technology is now playing a critical role in many industries to overcome challenges and get better and optimum results. The farming industry in India significantly affects the country's economy. The agricultural sector continues to employ half of the nation's workforce. The majority of agricultural activities in the nation still use outdated methods, and technical advancement is modest. Effective technology can be applied to this industry to maximize yield and minimize difficulties. Thus, based on the weather, moisture, and season, the machine learning-based farming solution may provide a crop recommendation system that aids farmers in selecting the appropriate crop to sow in their field. This work used six classifiers to recommend best fitted crop depending on soil as well as environmental parameters. It has been observed that the highest accuracy score has been achieved by Naïve Bayes followed by SVM – SVC, decision tree, KNN, SVM – NuSVC, and logistic regression classifier.

Chapter 14

Kuntal Mukherjee, Haldia Institute of Technology, India
Syed Saif Ahmed, Haldia Institute of Technology, India
Mohammad Aasif, Haldia Institute of Technology, India
Sumana Kundu, Dr. B.C. Roy Engineering College, India
Soumen Ghosh, Haldia Institute of Technology, India

Finding a house for rent in a new city within the budget is a major issue especially for new college students and employees. In this scenario, an effective house rent prediction algorithm will be extremely beneficial. The rent for a house is affected by certain aspects such as number of rooms, distance from the market, region, availability of transport, and many more. With the help of different machine learning algorithms, the authors try to analyze, predict, and visualize the rent of a house. In this chapter, the authors have implemented multiple linear regression models and other ensemble learning methods like Adaboost regressor, random forest regressor, gradient boost regressor, and XGboost regressor to tune the overall model performance. The authors self-surveyed data set contains records of a city in West Bengal, India. So far, almost no work has been done in this context for Haldia. The authors' proposed house rent prediction model predicts rent with an accuracy of 98.20%.

Chapter 15

Prasenjit Dey, Coochbehar Government Engineering College, India
Arnab Gain, Coochbehar Government Engineering College, India

Wireless sensor network (WSN) consists of sparsely distributed, low energy, and bandwidth sensor nodes that collect sensed data. In WSNs, these data are initially converted from analog to digital signals and transmitted to base stations. Routing in WSNs is the process of determining the most efficient path for data transmission among various sensor nodes. In routing, small sensor nodes use limited network bandwidth and energy to capture and transmit a limited amount of data. However, with the advancement of big data and IoT, large-scale sensors are used to route massive amounts of data. Routing with this huge data consumes a lot of network bandwidth and energy and thus reduces the lifespan of the network. Thus, for energy-efficient routing (EER), there is a need for data optimization that can be achieved by many machine learning (ML) algorithms. Many researchers have devised various noteworthy works related to ML to have an EER in WSNs. This chapter reviews the existing ML-based routing algorithms in WSNs.

Foreword

It gives me pleasure to say few words regarding this book titled *Novel Research and Development Approaches in Heterogeneous Systems and Algorithms* and its editors. This book focuses on the most recent advancements in research and uses of algorithms created for applications in engineering and IT. It focuses on a range of methods and systems as well as practical applications. For scientists, biological engineers, academics, students, and researchers who are interested in learning how natural models have influenced the modern technology-centric world, this book is appropriate. A record-breaking increase in interest in machine learning has occurred in recent years as a result of the accessibility of massive datasets, advancements in algorithms, and exponential development in computing power. Machine learning techniques are now successfully used to perform tasks such as classification, regression, clustering, and dimensionality reduction on huge datasets with particularly high-dimensional input data. Machine learning has actually demonstrated superhuman powers in a number of domains (such as playing go, self driving cars, image classification, etc.). Large portions of our daily lives are now powered by machine learning algorithms, including image and speech recognition, web searches, fraud detection, email/spam filtering, credit ratings, and many more.

In some disciplines, including image identification, machine learning algorithms have already revolutionised. The development of deep convolutional neural networks, however, from the first perceptron up to the present, was a difficult and drawn-out process. One must utilise machine learning techniques to their full potential as well as the knowledge gained from previous research in other domains in order to achieve meaningful results.

The editors are widely experienced in this area with long research and teaching experiences.

I feel extremely happy to see the topics of applications of superbly efficient technological systems for the benefit of human civilisations. I hope the editors will be very successful in their great effort and students, teachers and professionals will find this book very useful.

Debasis Giri
Department of Information Technology, Maulana Abul Kalam Azad University of Technology, India

Preface

The explosion of data science and AI wouldn't have been possible without advances in computer power and specialist hardware and software. We need to continue to adapt and refine computer technology in order to meet the needs of the next generation of algorithms and data scientists.

We are focused on addressing new research and development solutions in heterogenous systems and algorithms for next generation information-centric networks. Computing has dramatically changed nearly every aspect of our lives, from business and agriculture to communication and entertainment. As a nation, we rely on computing in the design of systems for energy, transportation, and defense; and computing fuels scientific discoveries that will improve our fundamental understanding of the world and help develop solutions to major challenges in health and the environment. Computing innovations "at the high end" tend to "trickle down," leading to increased performance and new applications of computing throughout the entire performance spectrum. These advances have relied on computing innovations in the broadest sense: faster algorithms, new mathematical and statistical models, powerful programming abstractions, ubiquitous high-performance networks, and computing systems that have become smaller, faster, cheaper and more accessible over time.

We are concentrating on novel research and development approaches in heterogeneous systems and algorithms for information-centric networks of the future. Almost every element of our life, from commerce and agriculture to communication and entertainment, has been profoundly altered by computing. As a country, we depend on computing for the creation of systems for energy, transportation, and military, as well as for the advancement of science and the creation of answers to the world's most pressing health and environmental problems.

Algorithms existed long before computers. Algorithms, which are at the core of computing, are increasingly more prevalent thanks to computers. This book offers a thorough introduction to the current field of computer algorithm research. It introduces numerous algorithms, discusses them in great detail, and nevertheless makes their design and analysis understandable to people of different reading levels. We have made an effort to keep explanations simple without losing mathematical rigour or depth of content.

A distinct aspect of an algorithm, a design method, an application field, or a related topic is presented in each chapter. The pseudocode used to describe algorithms is written in English and is intended to be readable by anyone who has done some programming. Many of the figures in the book, many of which have many components, show how the algorithms operate. We focus on efficiency as a design parameter; thus, we carefully analyse each of our algorithms and describe the results.

This book focuses on the most recent advancements in research and uses of algorithms created for applications in engineering and IT. This book is an important resource for graduate students, decision makers, and researchers in the public and private sectors who are looking for research-based methodologies for modelling uncertain real-world issues. It focuses on a range of methods and systems as well as practical applications. For scientists, biological engineers, academics, students, and researchers who are interested in learning how natural models have influenced the modern technology-centric world, this book is appropriate.

The following research topics are well covered in this book:

- Nature-inspired meta-heuristics algorithms
- Algorithms for image and video processing
- Algorithms for machine and deep learning
- Cryptographic algorithms
- Algorithms for natural language processing
- Algorithms for VLSI design

The book is organized into 15 chapters. A brief description of each of the chapters is as follows:

Chapter 1: This chapter provides an overview of several nature inspired meta-heuristics are compared with respect to the parameters, viz., minimization of makespan and flow time, for scheduling tasks in computational Grids. The nature inspired meta-heuristics involved in this chapter are Genetic Algorithm (GA), Particle Swarm Optimization (PSO), Ant Colony Optimization (ACO) and Cuckoo Search (CS) algorithms. Grid computing has emerged as an intelligent distributed computing paradigm, due to huge improvements in performance of wide-area network and powerful yet low-cost computers. Computational Grids accumulate and share the power of heterogeneous, geographically dispersed and multi-domain administered computational resources to offer high performance or high-throughput computing. To realize the promising potentials of computational Grids, an effective and efficient task scheduling system is primarily important. Task scheduling in computational Grid is one of the most challenging and complex tasks. Such a problem could be solved using meta-heuristic algorithms.

Chapter 2: The aim of this chapter is to propose a new method based on wavelet energy based adaptive retinex algorithm to the dynamic range extended value channel. Lighting conditions that cause video degradation are restored adaptively to their natural brightness. A color restoration technique that improves the conventional retinex method fixes the gray world violation problem. Wavelet energy is used as a metric in concurrence with the retinex algorithm to objectively validate image enhancement quality. An experimental work of more than 300 still images and videos show that the proposed technique outperforms the current state-of-the-art.

Chapter 3: This chapter focuses on a modified marker-controlled watershed transformation approach to detect brain tumour with XAI and machine learning approaches where we include CNN and data augmentation algorithm for image pre-processing takes main area to detect and diagnose disease and diagnose properly. The statistical measurements have been also introduced to get the mathematical abstractions of different approaches for result analysis.

Chapter 4: This chapter expedites cataract screening procedure, an automated cataract detection system should be developed. Fundus image analysis for automatic categorization and grading of cataracts has the potential to reduce the burden of competent ophthalmologists while also assisting cataract patients in learning about their diseases and getting treatment suggestions. The optic disc and blood vessel data play a significant role in the detection and grading of cataracts. Normal, mild, moderate, and severe cataract stages are differentiated based on texture, colour, size, and contrast. Classification and severity rating are carried out using Random Forest classifier, an ensemble machine-learning method. The accuracy discovered is equivalent to prior study in the literature. This study is expected to help doctors detect cataracts early and prevent cataract-related suffering.

Chapter 5: This chapter deals with the detection of the scene images captured by drone on the basis of simple image processing approach involving the pixel intensity information. Many computer vision-based algorithms have successfully performed the tasks of segmentation. The manual approach of such segmentation has become much time consuming, resource intensive and laborious. Moreover the perfection of segmentation on the irregular and noisy images captured by the drones have been lowered to greater extents with application of machine learning algorithms. Machine learning based UNet model has successfully performed the task of segmentation and the performance has been enhanced due to optimization. This review paper highlights the different variation of the model and its optimization towards the betterment of accuracy.

Chapter 6: This chapter aims at providing a comprehensive review on blockchain technologies, performance metrics and guidelines for choosing a blockchain technology and consensus algorithm based on an organization's requirements and protocols. This chapter also captures concepts on blockchain types, consensus algorithms and typical applications of blockchain with its features.

Chapter 7: This chapter deals with various novel steganography algorithms which have been proposed for data hiding. The authors give an accurate color to the image instead of severe color changes. To change it, a colorization process is performed by mapping the original image to the stego image. It gains more characteristics according to the actual embodiment. Here, the objective is to improve the appearance by calculating the loss function. The stego image can withstand steganalysis by using our proposed scheme by maintaining its integrity while to some extent improving the quality of the image. The experimental results confirmed the proposed method outperforms the existing methods (SGAN and CycleGAN) for information hiding with enhanced image transmission quality.

Chapter 8: In this chapter a trained voice recognition model has been implemented in the MySQL database to perform various DBMS command automatically through speech recognition. A deep learning model has been implemented here. The latency rate and data transfer speed of this model is very fast because of its prior training approach. This type of methodical approach can be made in any DBMS systems to make it more convenient, smart and easy to use.

Chapter 9: This chapter proposes new techniques compatible with higher complexity and applicable for structural testing of MEDA based biochips. The proposed testing methods provide detection of faults or failure (if any) within a given layout using minimal resources with minimal test completion time. The testing simulations are carried out with specified layout dimensions and variable droplet size.

Chapter 10: In this chapter, the authors propose a new steganographic method to offer the highest level of protection for sensitive data. A single bit of data has been embedded into edge-based pixel positions with arbitrary bit positions. However, the authors compare the proposed method to three standard edge detection algorithms for a more comprehensive assessment. Different statistical measures also have been made for the uniqueness of the technique.

Chapter 11: In this chapter, a chaotic cryptographic method and bit shuffle methodology for image encryption and decoding have both been suggested. In order to evaluate the encryption's effectiveness and determine whether it met the desired standard, a number of performance analysis tools were also used. These included the number of pixel change rate (NPCR), the unified average changing intensity (UACI), the entropy analysis, which is a component of an encryption scheme that shows how random the image is, and the correlation coefficient. These results reveal the safety of the suggested cryptographic technique.

Chapter 12: In this chapter, the authors have deliberated a new steganographic method. Here several 2×2 blocks are recycled to implant the data bits within the stego-image and using the Arnold Map, four quadrants of the pixels of each blocks is selected to embed the data in nonlinear bit position. Different measures with the change of BPP (Bits per Pixel) also have worked out in this chapter.

Chapter 13: This chapter highlights the use of machine learning based farming solution to provide a crop recommendation system that aids farmers in selecting the appropriate crop to sow in their field. These classifiers recommend best fitted crop depending on soil as well as environmental parameters. It has been observed that the highest accuracy score has been achieved by Naïve Bayes followed by SVM – SVC, Decision tree, KNN, SVM – NuSVC and Logistic Regression classifier.

Chapter 14: In this chapter, the authors try to analyze, predict, and visualize the rent of a house using different Machine learning algorithms. The authors have implemented multiple linear regression models and other ensemble learning methods like Adaboost regressor, Random Forest Regressor, Gradient Boost regressor and XGboost regressor to tune the overall model performance. The self-surveyed data set of authors contains records of a city in West Bengal, India. The proposed house rent prediction model predicts rent with an accuracy of 98.20%.

Chapter 15: In this chapter, the authors perform a comprehensive review of over 20 papers on the topic of automatic cyberbullying detection. Analyses of published articles have shown that the proposed cyberbullying detection methodology has limited real-world use. There is still a problem with limited datasets, inconsistent annotation, overfitting difficulties, and the inherent imbalance of datasets. For future systems to have a practical and substantial application, their study hopes to guide future research in this area. Also included are recommendations for future research based on the limits that have been identified.

We have designed this book to be both versatile and complete. You should find it useful for a variety of courses, from an undergraduate course in data structures up through a graduate course in algorithms. Because we have provided considerably more material than can fit in a typical one-term course, you can consider this book to be a "buffet" or "smorgasbord" from which you can pick and choose the material that best supports the course you wish to teach.

Santanu Koley
Haldia Institute of Technology, India

Subhabrata Barman
Haldia Institute of Technology, India

Subhankar Joardar
Haldia Institute of Technology, India

Acknowledgment

We would like to thank everyone who provided inspiration and worked with us to get the book published. The book connects many persons both subtly and overtly. IGI Global Publishing deserves our gratitude for stepping up to host the publication of this book. We are grateful to the entire distinguished Editorial Board for their assistance in ensuring the high standards of the book. We would like to extend our sincere gratitude to our reviewers for their ongoing assistance and priceless recommendations for improving this book. We are grateful to all the esteemed authors for providing us with chapters containing their insightful research. The authors served as the project's cornerstones, and the quality and scope of their contributions inspired us to continue focusing on the project's qualitative components in addition to its quantitative ones. All of the reviewers have worked hard to uphold the chapters' calibre by offering meticulous judgement and rigorous evaluation. They are deserving of our sincere gratitude. We would like to take this opportunity to thank our co-workers and peers for contributing their scholarly insights and practical advice to enhance the book. Finally, we would like to extend our sincere gratitude to the audiences who served as the inspiration for our project. The enormous applications of algorithms for the next generation of information-centric networks will only be useful to students, researchers, academicians, and other personnel if they gain something from this book.

We also acknowledge the love and support of our wives, Sukanya Koley, Jayashri Deb Sinha, and Sangita Joardar, who helped us edit this book. This endeavour was made possible by our families' patience and support. This book is lovingly dedicated to them.

Chapter 1
Comparative Study of Some Nature–Inspired Meta–Heuristics for Task Scheduling in a Computational Grid System

Tarun Kumar Ghosh

(iD) https://orcid.org/0000-0003-4685-5381

Haldia Institute of Technology, India

Krishna Gopal Dhal

(iD) https://orcid.org/0000-0002-6748-0569

Midnapore College, India

Sanjoy Das

(iD) https://orcid.org/0000-0002-8331-5168

University of Kalyani, India

ABSTRACT

Grid computing has emerged as an intelligent distributed computing paradigm due to the huge improvements in performance of wide-area network and powerful yet low-cost computers. Computational grids accumulate and share the power of heterogeneous, geographically dispersed, and multi-domain-administered computational resources to offer high performance or high-throughput computing. To realize the promising potential of computational grids, an effective and efficient task scheduling system is primarily important. Task scheduling in computational grid is one of the most challenging and complex tasks. In other words, the task scheduling in computational Grid is considered as NP-hard problem due to the problem complexity and intractable nature of the problem. Such a problem could be solved using meta-heuristic algorithms. In this chapter, several nature-inspired meta-heuristics are compared with respect to the parameters (i.e., minimization of makespan and flowtime) for scheduling tasks in computational grids. The nature-inspired meta-heuristics involved in this chapter are genetic algorithm (GA), particle swarm optimization (PSO), ant colony optimization (ACO), and cuckoo search (CS) algorithms. Experimental results show that the GA outperforms the other methods in terms of average makespan and the PSO algorithm performs best among all 4 algorithms in terms of average flowtime.

DOI: 10.4018/978-1-6684-7524-9.ch001

1. INTRODUCTION

The Grid computing is a distributed environment where sharing and synchronized use of heterogeneous resources are ensured at run-time (Foster et al. 1999). The main module of a Grid system is the resource scheduling and management component. Primary roles of this component are to accept tasks from valid users and distribute the tasks to suitable existing Grid resources (Krauter et al. 2002). An efficient task scheduling algorithm which utilizes all available resources optimally is essential for a good Grid computing system.

The computational Grid consists of many computing resources which are geographically dispersed under different ownerships each having their own access policy, cost and various constraints. Therefore, the task scheduling in such complex systems is a challenging problem. In other words, the task scheduling in computational Grid is considered as NP-hard problem. Therefore the use of meta-heuristics is the de facto mechanism in order to cope in practice with its difficulty. The problem is generally treated as a multi-objective, the two main important objectives being the minimization of makespan and flowtime of the system. Makespan refers to the time when Grid completes the latest task and flowtime refers to the sum of finalization times of all the tasks.

In this chapter, some popular nature inspired meta-heuristics such as Genetic Algorithm (GA), Particle Swarm Optimization (PSO), Ant Colony Optimization (ACO) and Cuckoo Search (CS) are compared with respect to the parameters, viz., minimization of makespan and flowtime.

This chapter is organized as follows. Section 2 briefly outlines the relevant past works done on task scheduling in computational Grid environment. In Section 3, the framework of Grid task scheduling problem has been defined. Section 4 presents the GA. Section 5 describes the PSO. Section 6 outlines the ACO. Section 7 presents the CS algorithm. Section 8 exhibits the results obtained in this study. Finally, Section 9 concludes the chapter.

2. RELATED WORKS

The task scheduling in computational Grids is proven as NP-hard problem due to complexity and intractable environment of the problem. This type of problem can be answered using meta-heuristic methods. These methods make realistic assumptions based on a priori knowledge of the concerning environment and of the system load characteristics. The most frequently used meta-heuristic algorithms are Genetic Algorithm (GA), Particle Swarm Optimization (PSO), Ant Colony Optimization (ACO) and Cuckoo Search (CS) algorithms.

The GA is a very popular algorithm to solve various types of combinatorial optimization problems. Task scheduling in computational Grid using GA has been addressed by Buyya et al. (2000), Braun et al. (2001), Zomaya and Teh (2001), Martino and Mililotti (2004), Page and Naughton (2005), Gao et al. (2005), Xhafa et al. (2008) and Aggarwal and Kent (2005). Prakash and Vidyarthi (2015) have proposed a new mechanism to maximize the availability of resources for task scheduling in computational Grid using GA. Enhanced Genetic based scheduling for Grid computing is proposed in (Kolodziej and Xhafa, 2011). Task scheduling in computational Grid using PSO has been studied by Izakian et al. (2009), Zhang et al. (2008) and Salman et al. (2002). Abraham et al. (2010) proposed an approach for scheduling tasks on computational Grids using fuzzy PSO algorithm. Goswami et al. (2011) have proposed a local search-based approach using Simulated Annealing (SA) as a periodical optimizer to other dynamic, space shared and schedule based scheduling policies.

Ghosh et al. (2020) have proposed a hybrid algorithm that intelligently combines the GA with Particle Swarm Optimization (PSO) for the Grid task scheduling. Wang et al. (2010) have proposed a Genetic-Simulated Annealing (GSA) algorithm which combines GA with Simulated Annealing (SA) algorithm for Grid task scheduling.

An Ant Colony Optimization (ACO) implementation of the problem has been given by Ritchie (2003). Lorpunmanee et al. (2007) have also implemented an ACO algorithm for dynamic task scheduling in Grid environment. Tiwari and Vidyarthi (2014) have examined the effect of inter process communication in auto controlled ACO based scheduling on computational Grid. Task scheduling in computational Grid using Cuckoo Search (CS) algorithm has been investigated by Prakash et al. (2012), Rabiee and Sajedi (2013), and Ghosh et al. (2017). A large number of researches have been carried out using hybrid methods which combine two or more meta-heuristic algorithms in order to achieve a result that is not achievable using a single algorithm (Xhafa et al., (2009); Ghosh and Das, (2016)).

Ghosh & Das (2018) have applied a very recent evolutionary heuristic algorithm known as Wind Driven Optimization (WDO) for efficiently allocating tasks to resources in a computational Grid system so that makespan and flowtime are minimized. Ghosh & Das (2022) have proposed Teaching Learning Based Optimization (TLBO) for solving the task scheduling problem in computational Grid system with minimization of makespan, processing cost and job failure rate, and maximization of resource utilization criteria.

3. PROBLEM DEFINITION

A computational Grid system consists of a pool of decentralized heterogeneous resources and a large number of tasks. Let $T = \{T_1, T_2, ..., T_n\}$ denote the set of n tasks that are independent of each other to be scheduled on m resources $R = \{R_1, R_2, ..., R_m\}$ within the Grid system. In this chapter, we consider the problem of scheduling n tasks on m computing resources with objectives of minimizing the makespan and flowtime. If the number of tasks is less than the number of resources in the Grid, then the tasks can be allocated on the appropriate resources.

If the number of tasks is more than the number of resources, then an efficient scheduling algorithm is required for allocation of tasks. So, we consider the number of tasks is more than the number of computing resources in this work. Since one task cannot be assigned to different resources, no task migration is allowed. Also, we have assumed that tasks submitted to the Grid are independent and are non-preemptive (they cannot change the resource they have been assigned to once their execution is started, unless the resource is dropped from the Grid).

An estimation of the computational load of each task and the computing capacity of each resource in the system is assumed to be available a priori. This formulation is practically applicable as the computing capacity and computational needs can be known from user specifications, historic data or prediction. This information can be contained in an Expected Time to Compute (ETC) matrix where each entry $ETC(T_i, R_j)$ specifies the expected time to compute task T_i on resource R_j. The size of the ETC matrix is *no_of_tasks* x *no_of_resources*. For the simulation studies, characteristics of the ETC matrices are varied in an attempt to represent a series of possible heterogeneous environments.

The performance parameters used to compare the algorithms are makespan and flowtime. These performance parameters are defined below.

Makespan: It is probably the most popular and widely used optimization criterion in the given subject. The objective of any scheduler is to minimize it, since lesser values of makespan signify that the scheduler is producing good and proficient planning of tasks to resources. Makespan is a sign of the common productivity of the Grid system. Thinking makespan as a separate criterion not essentially implies optimization of other objectives. As mentioned previously, optimization of makespan may produce adverse results for other optimization criteria. The makespan is the total application execution time. The total application execution time is measured from the time the first task is sent to the Grid system until the last task comes out of the Grid. The makespan is given by

$$Makespan = max \{RT(R_j)\}, \forall j \in m \tag{1}$$

Here, m is the number of available resources and the ready time $RT(R_j)$ of resource R_j is calculated by

$$RT(R_j) = \sum_{i=1}^{n} ETC(T_i, R_j) \tag{2}$$

where, n is the number of tasks submitted to the resource R_j and $ETC(T_i, R_j)$ specifies the expected time to compute task T_i on resource R_j.

Flowtime: It is another popular and significant optimization criterion and is also to be minimized. The flowtime is known as the response time of the user's task submitted to the system for execution. In other words, the flowtime is the sum of finalization times of all the tasks. Thus, it is easy to understand that reducing the value of flowtime implies reducing the average response time of the Grid system. Formally it can be defined as:

$$Flowtime = \sum_{j=1}^{m} RT(R_j) \tag{3}$$

It can be noted that makespan is unaffected by any specific execution order of tasks for a particular resource; however, all submitted tasks must be sorted in ascending order of their estimated workload (completion time) before execution in the case of minimization of flowtime.

It is worth mentioning that in reality, makespan and flowtime are contradictory criteria. The flowtime has a higher magnitude order compared to the makespan and their difference increases as more tasks and resources are used. For this reason, the value of mean flowtime is used to evaluate flowtime. Besides, both values are weighted in order to balance their importance. Fitness value of a given solution S is thus calculated as:

$$fitness(S) = \lambda \times makespan(S) + (1 - \lambda) \times mean\,flowtime(S) \tag{4}$$

where,

Algorithm 1*: Genetic Algorithm (GA)*

An initial population $P(t = 0)$ of n individuals (chromosomes) is generated.
Fitness of each individual of the population is evaluated. Evaluate ($P(t)$).
While (terminating condition or maximum number of iterations is not reached) **do**
Begin
  A subset of x pairs from $P(t)$ is selected. Let $P_1(t) = \text{Select}(P(t))$.
  Each of the x chosen pairs is crossed with probability P_c. Let $P_2(t) = \text{Cross}(P_1(t))$ be the set of off-springs.
  Each offspring in $P_2(t)$ is mutated with probability P_m. Let $P_3(t) = \text{Mutate}(P_2(t))$.
  Fitness of each offspring is evaluated. Evaluate ($P_3(t)$).
  A new iteration from individuals in $P(t)$ and $P_3(t)$ is created. Let $P(t + 1) = \text{Replace}(P(t); P_3(t))$; $t = t + 1$.
End
Post process results and visualization.

$$mean\ flowtime(S) = \frac{flowtime(S)}{no.\ of\ resources}$$

and λ is used to control the efficacy of parameters used in this equation. In this study, λ is taken as 0.7 because the makespan is considered as the primary objective.

4. GENETIC ALGORITHM (GA)

Developed in 1975 by John Holland, Genetic Algorithm (GA) is a stochastic search optimization technique that mimics the evolutionary processes in biological systems. The main idea behind the GA is to combine exploitation of best solutions from previous searches with the exploration of new areas of the solution space. The GA for scheduling problem can be formulated as: First, an initial population of chromosomes is generated either randomly or using other heuristic algorithm. A chromosome in the population specifies a possible solution. As far as our scheduling problem is concerned, a solution is a mapping sequence between tasks and resources. Next, each chromosome is evaluated for a fitness value associated with it. The fitness value measures degree of goodness of individual chromosome compared to others in the population. A new iteration is created next by using the genetic operators, namely selection, crossover and mutation; in other words, the population evolves (Haupt and Haupt (2004)). Lastly, the fitness value of each chromosome from this newly evolved population is assessed again. This way one iteration of the GA is completed. When a predefined number of iterations is met or all chromosomes have converged to the same mapping, the algorithm stops. The major steps of GA can be summarized as pseudo code in Algorithm 1:

5. PARTICLE SWARM OPTIMIZATION (PSO)

The PSO algorithm is a population-based optimization technique that tries to find the optimal solution using a population of particles (Zhao et al., 2005). Each particle is an individual and the swarm is composed of particles. In PSO, the solution space of the problem is formulated as a search space. Each position of a particle in the search space corresponds to a potential solution of the problem. Particles cooperate to find the best position (best solution) in the search space (solution space). Each particle moves according to its velocity. At each iteration, the particle movement is computed as follows:

$$v_{id}(t + 1) = wv_{id}(t) + c_1 r_1 (pbest_{id} - x_{id}(t)) + c_2 r_2 (gbest_d - x_{id}(t)) \tag{5}$$

$$x_{id}(t + 1) = x_{id}(t) + v_{id}(t + 1) \tag{6}$$

$V_i = (v_{i1}, v_{i2}, \ldots\ldots, v_{id})$ and $X_i = (x_{i1}, x_{i2}, \ldots\ldots, x_{id})$ represent the velocity and position of the i-th particle along d-dimensions at iteration t respectively. $pbest_{id}$ is the best position found by i-th particle itself so far and $gbest_d$ is the best position found by the whole swarm so far. w is the inertia weight which regulates the impact of the previous velocity value on the current velocity value. It is observed that a larger value of inertia weight supports global exploration while a small one encourages local exploration. Appropriate choice of inertia weight w usually gives a balance between the global and local exploration and decreases the average number of iterations to trace the optimum solution. To reach a high performance, we linearly reduce the value of inertia weight from about 0.9 to 0.4 during a run. c_1 and c_2 are two acceleration coefficients that scale the influence of the best personal position of the particle ($pbest_{id}$) and the best global position ($gbest_d$), and r_1 and r_2 are random numbers in the interval (0, 1).

Now let us assume that the swarm consists of n particles and the objective function f is used to calculate the fitness of the particles with a minimization task. Assuming $i \in \{1, 2, \ldots, n\}$, the personal best ($pbest_{id}$) and global best ($gbest_d$) values are updated at iteration t as

$$pbest_{id}(t+1) = \begin{cases} pbest_{id}(t), & \text{if } f(best_{id}(t)) \leq f(x_{id}(t+1)) \\ x_{id}(t+1), & \text{otherwise} \end{cases} \tag{7}$$

$$gbest_d(t + 1) = \min \{f(y), f(gbest_d(t))\}, \tag{8}$$

where $y \in \{pbest_{0d}(t), pbest_{1d}(t), \ldots\ldots, pbest_{nd}(t)\}$

The major steps of PSO can be summarized as pseudo code in Algorithm 2.

6. ANT COLONY OPTIMIZATION (ACO)

Proposed by Dorigo, et al. (Dorigo and Maniez, (1991)), Ant Colony Optimization (ACO) algorithm has been used as a discrete optimization technique. ACO is inspired by the real ants' foraging behavior. Real ants are capable of finding the shortest path from their nest to a food source without using any visual signal. Instead, they communicate information about the food source through depositing a chemical substance called pheromone on the paths. The following ants are attracted by the pheromone. Since the shorter paths have higher traffic densities, these paths are having higher concentration of pheromones. Hence, the probability of ants following these shorter paths would be higher than that of those following the longer ones. As time passes, the oldest pheromone-paths evaporate and at some time, only the shortest path will remain with a good amount of pheromones.

Algorithm 2: *Particle Swarm Optimization (PSO)*

Initialize a population of particles with random positions and velocities in the search space.
While (terminating conditions are not met) **do**
Begin
    For each particle *i* **do**
    Begin
    Update the velocity of particle *i* according to Eq. (5).
    Update the position of particle *i* according to Eq. (6).
    Map the position of particle *i* in the solution space and calculate its fitness
    value according to the fitness function.
    Update *pbest*$_{id}$ and *gbest*$_d$ according to Eqs. (7) and (8).
    End
End

The quantity of pheromone is stored into a matrix which specifies the probability for each decision to lead to a good solution. All the decisions are initialized with a uniform probability. Then a certain number of routines (ants) are started to construct different solutions (paths) iteratively. At each decision point, a probability is generated for each of the admissible choices as follows:

$$P_{x,y} = \frac{[\tau_{x,y}]^\alpha [\eta_{x,y}]^\beta}{\sum_{l \in \Omega_x} [\tau_{x,l}]^\alpha [\eta_{x,l}]^\beta} \qquad (9)$$

where x is the present point in the decision process, and y is the possible destination, η is a problem-related local heuristic (i.e., calculated every time a probability is generated), while τ is the global heuristic determined by the pheromone. Both contributions, weighted through α and β, control the decision of the ant. Ω_x contains all the choices at the present point x. At the end of each iteration, the results are evaluated and the pheromones are updated using the following:

$$\tau_{x,y} = (1 - \rho) * \tau_{x,y} + \sum_{l=1}^{m} \Delta\tau^{(l)}_{x,y} \qquad (10)$$

where $0 < \rho < 1$ is the evaporation rate and the deltas are computed as $\Delta\tau^{(l)}_{x,y} = R/S$, if the path from x to y was in the solution, 0 if not, with R as pheromone delivery rate and S as the cost of the result. The number of ants at point x is m. After each iteration, some pheromones evaporate on all the paths. This allows forgetting paths explored and never revisited, avoiding early convergence to local minima.

In Grid task scheduling, the ACO algorithm can be summarized as Algorithm 3. Termination criteria of the search can be a maximum number of iterations or convergence to a sub-optimum.

7. CUCKOO SEARCH (CS) ALGORITHM

Yang and Deb in 2009 have proposed the Cuckoo Search (CS) algorithm based on the Lévy flight behavior and brood parasitic behavior (Yang and Deb (2009)). The CS has been shown to produce very good results in constrained optimizations. The cuckoo birds follow an aggressive reproduction process.

Algorithm 3: *Ant Colony Optimization (ACO)*

Initially associate each path connecting task-source (x) to resource-destination (y) with a pheromone path $\tau_{x,y}$.
While (terminating conditions are not met) **do**
Begin
    Put m ants on an initial point (task-source).
    Each ant constructs its own path. The probability of going from the present point x to the destination point y is calculated using Eq. no. (9).
    Evaluation of the quality of the result.
    Update of the pheromones using Eq. no. (10), firstly evaporating the pheromone-paths on all the paths and then incrementing it by a factor proportional to the quality of the result found.
End

Female birds take control and lay their fertilized eggs in other birds' nests. If the host bird realizes that the egg is not its own, it either throws the alien egg away or rejects the nest and constructs a new one at other place.

Every single egg in a nest indicates a probable solution and each cuckoo egg indicates a new solution. Here, purpose is to find out new and possibly superior solutions (cuckoos) to substitute old solutions in the nests. For simplicity, it is assumed that each nest has one egg. In (Yang and Deb (2009), (2010)), it is proved that the CS can be stretched further to more complex situations when each nest contains multiple eggs representing a set of solutions. The CS can be summarized by following three important rules:

- A single egg is laid by each cuckoo at a time and is disposed in a haphazardly selected nest.
- Most promising nests carrying excellent quality of eggs (solutions) will switch to the next iterations.
- There are a fixed number of available host nests and a host-bird can recognize a foreign egg with probability $p_a \in (0, 1)$. In this situation, the host-bird can either eliminate the foreign egg from the nest or dump the nest to erect an entirely new nest in a new place (Yang and Deb (2009)).

In practice, the third hypothesis can be estimated by a probability p_a of the n nests being substituted by new ones, having new arbitrary solutions. In the case of an optimization problem, the superiority or fitness of a solution is directly related with the objective function.

In CS, the walking steps of a cuckoo are determined by the Lévy flights. Following Lévy flight is computed to generate new solutions $x_i(t + 1)$ for the *ith* cuckoo:

$$x_i(t + 1) = x_i(t) + a \oplus \text{Lévy(1)} \tag{11}$$

where $\alpha > 0$ symbolizes the step length that must be correlated to the degree of the problem concerned. The product symbol $\oplus$ specifies entry-wise multiplications (Yang and Deb (2010)). This chapter has considered a Lévy flight where step-lengths are scattered as per the probability distribution given as:

$$\text{Lévy } u = t^\lambda, \ 1 < \lambda \leq 3 \tag{12}$$

which has an unlimited variance. The successive steps of a cuckoo effectively constitute a random walk procedure obeying a power-law step-length distribution with a heavy tail. On the basis of previously cited rules, the main ideas of the CS are summed up as pseudo code in Algorithm 4.

Algorithm 4: *Cuckoo Search (CS) Algorithm*

Fitness function $f(x)$, $x = (x_1, ..., x_d)^T$ is determined.
An initial population of n host nests x_i $(i = 1, ..., n)$ is generated.
While (terminating condition or maximum number of iterations is not met) **do**
Begin
  A cuckoo (say, i) is obtained arbitrarily and a new solution by Lévy flights is generated.
  Quality / fitness of the new solution is evaluated. Let it be F_i.
  A nest among n (say, j) is chosen arbitrarily.
    if $(F_i > F_j)$
      Nest j is replaced by the new solution.
    end if
  A fraction (p_a) of worse nests is abandoned and new ones are constructed at new sites using Lévy flights.
  Most promising solutions (or nests having higher quality solutions) are recorded.
  All available solutions are graded and the current best solution is determined.
End

---

8. EXPERIMENTS AND RESULTS

As mentioned earlier, 4 popular meta-heuristics namely, Genetic Algorithm (GA) (Ghosh et al. (2015)), Particle Swarm Optimization (PSO) (Ghosh & Das (2016)), Ant Colony Optimization (ACO) (Lorpunmanee et al. (2007)) and Cuckoo Search (CS) (Ghosh et al. (2015)) are considered for the task scheduling problem in computational Grids. All algorithms have common set of objectives, viz. minimization of both makespan and flowtime. Tests are performed on a Pentium IV 2.6 GHz, 4GB RAM, and the algorithms are implemented using MATLAB Release 2013A. To enhance the performances 4 algorithms, fine tuning is made and best values for their parameters are selected which are given in Table 1. Also the benchmark by Ali et al. (2000) is used for realistic simulations in this work.

In the simulation model proposed by Ali et al. (2000), expected time to compute (ETC) matrix is used for 512 tasks and 16 resources. To evaluate the algorithms for different mapping scenarios, the characteristics of the ETC matrix were varied based on three metrics: task heterogeneity, resource heterogeneity and consistency. The amount of variance among the execution times of tasks for a given resource/machine is defined as task heterogeneity. Resource heterogeneity represents the variation that is possible among the execution times for a given task across all the machines. An ETC matrix is said to be consistent if whenever a machine m_j executes any task j_i faster than machine m_k, then machine m_j executes all tasks faster than machine m_k. Consistent matrices are generated by sorting each row of the ETC matrix independently, with machine m_0 always being the fastest. In contrast, inconsistent matrices characterize the situation where machine m_j may be faster than machine m_k for some tasks and slower for others. These matrices are left in the unordered, random state in which they are generated. Partially consistent matrices are inconsistent matrices that include a consistent sub-matrix of a predefined size. Following four cases were considered in this simulation for the consistent matrices.

Case-1: Low task heterogeneity and low resource heterogeneity
Case-2: Low task heterogeneity and high resource heterogeneity
Case-3: High task heterogeneity and low resource heterogeneity
Case-4: High task heterogeneity and high resource heterogeneity.

Table 1. Parameter settings for the algorithms

Algorithm	Parameter Name	Parameter Value
GA	Population size	25
	Maximum number of iterations	500
	Crossover probability (P_c)	0.8
	Mutation probability (P_m)	.07
	Scale for mutations	0.1
PSO	Population size	25
	Maximum number of iterations	500
	$c_1 = c_2$	1.49
	$r_1 = r_2$	0.8
	Inertia weight ω	$0.9 \rightarrow 0.4$
ACO	Number of iterations	1000
	Evaporation rate (ρ)	0.015
	Weight for local heuristic (α)	1
	Weight for global heuristic (β)	1
CS	Number of nests	20
	Number of iterations	1000
	Mutation probability value (p_a)	0.25
	Step size (α)	1.5

The makespan and flowtime obtained using GA, PSO, ACO and CS are presented in Tables 2 and 3 respectively. The results are averaged over 10 independent runs. In Table 2, the first column indicates the case number, the second, third, fourth and fifth columns specify the mean makespan (in second) obtained by GA, PSO, ACO and CS algorithms respectively. The results show that the GA has minimized makespan than other algorithms for all 4 cases. The performances based on average flowtime (in second) of all the algorithms are tabulated in Table 3. Table 3 depicts the minimum average flowtime for the CS algorithm in the first 3 cases, while the minimum average flowtime for the PSO algorithm in the fourth case only. The statistical results of all algorithms in terms of the mean makespan and flowtime for the four cases are summarized in Figures 1 and 2 respectively. From the figures, it can be seen that the GA produces reduced average makespan and the PSO algorithm has minimized average flowtime values. Therefore, the GA outperforms the other algorithms in terms of average makespan and the PSO algorithm performs best among all 4 algorithms in terms of average flowtime.

Irrespective of the problem sizes, CS usually takes the smaller completion time to execute all the tasks on the Grid nodes compared to other algorithms (Ghosh et al. (2015), Ghosh & Das (2016)). It is to mention that ACO has to spend maximum time to complete the scheduling. Therefore, when compared among 4 algorithms, an important advantage of the CS algorithm is its ability to obtain faster and feasible schedules.

Table 2. Comparison of statistical results for average makespan (in second) obtained by GA, PSO, ACO and CS algorithms

Case No.	GA	PSO	ACO	CS
1	**6102**	7567	8599	7673
2	**426122**	464149	695200	612466
3	**215654**	225412	259730	215403
4	**12507697**	14660686	19582148	17415884

9. CONCLUSION

Task scheduling in computational Grid is an NP-hard problem. Therefore, using meta-heuristic techniques is an appropriate approach in order to cope with its difficulty in practice. This chapter investigates the task scheduling algorithms in Grid environments as optimization problems. This chapter implements and compares 4 popular meta-heuristics such as GA, PSO, ACO and CS algorithm to schedule the tasks in computational Grids. The goal of the scheduler in this paper is minimizing makespan and flowtime as a multi-objective problem. The performances of the 4 methods are compared through carrying out exhaustive simulation tests on different settings. Experimental results show that the GA outperforms the other methods in terms of average makespan and the PSO algorithm performs best among all 4 algorithms in terms of average flowtime.

Table 3. Comparison of statistical results for average flowtime (in second) obtained by GA, PSO, ACO and CS algorithms

Case No.	GA	PSO	ACO	CS
1	127528	135698	127355	**100924**
2	8302547	8245587	10245686	**7969268**
3	4635376	3635254	3863741	**3356139**
4	238630142	**205944724**	288625550	251333495

Figure 1. Mean makespan (in second) comparison among GA, PSO, ACO and CS algorithms

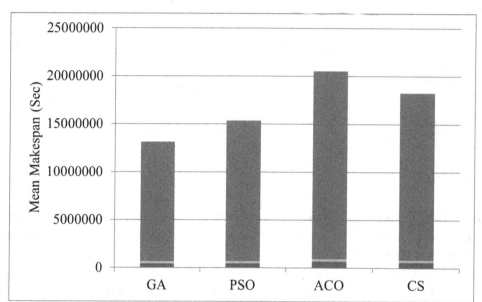

Figure 2. Mean flowtime (in second) comparison among GA, PSO, ACO and CS algorithms

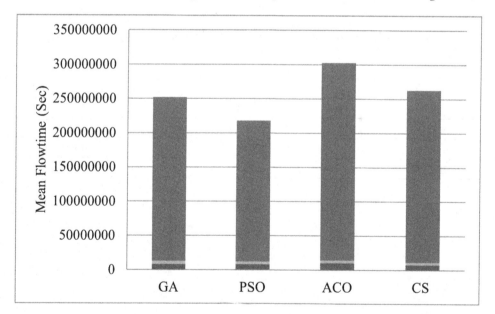

REFERENCES

Abraham, A., Liu, H., Zhang, W., & Chang, T. (2010). Scheduling jobs on computational grids using a fuzzy particle swarm optimization algorithm. *Future Generation Computer Systems, 26*(8), 1336–1343. doi:10.1016/j.future.2009.05.022

Aggarwal, M., & Kent, R. (2005). Genetic Algorithm Based Scheduler for Computational Grids. *Proceedings of the 19th International Symposium on High Performance Computing Systems and Applications (HPCS '05)*. 10.1109/HPCS.2005.27

Ali, S., Siegel, H. J., Maheswaran, M., Hensgen, D., & Ali, S. (2000). Representing Task and Machine Heterogeneities for Heterogeneous Computing Systems. *Tamkang Journal of Science and Engineering, 3*(3), 195–207.

Braun, T. D., Siegel, H. J., Beck, N., Boloni, L. L., Maheswaran, M., Reuther, A. I., Yao, B., & ... . (2001). A comparison of eleven static heuristics for mapping a class of independent tasks onto heterogeneous distributed computing systems. *Journal of Parallel and Distributed Computing, 61*(6), 810–837. doi:10.1006/jpdc.2000.1714

Buyya, R., Abraham, A., & Nath, B. (2000). Nature's heuristics for scheduling jobs on computational grids. In *Proceedings of 8th IEEE International Conference on Advanced Computing and Communications (ADCOM2000)* (pp. 45-52). IEEE.

Dorigo, C. A., & Maniez, M. (1991). *Distributed optimization by ant colonies*. Elsevier Publishing.

Foster, I., & Kesselman, C. (Eds.). (1999). *The Grid: blueprint for a new computing infrastructure*. Morgan Kaufmann Publishers Inc.

Gao, Y., Rong, H., & Huang, J. Z. (2005). Adaptive Grid job scheduling with genetic algorithms. *Future Generation Computer Systems, 21*(1), 151–161. doi:10.1016/j.future.2004.09.033

Ghosh, T. K., & Das, S. (2016). A hybrid algorithm using genetic algorithm and cuckoo search algorithm to solve job scheduling problem in computational grid systems. *International Journal of Applied Evolutionary Computation, 7*(2), 1–11. doi:10.4018/IJAEC.2016040101

Ghosh, T. K., & Das, S. (2016). A Modified Binary PSO Algorithm for Scheduling Independent Jobs in Grid Computing System. *International Journal of Next-Generation Computing, 7*(2), 144–154.

Ghosh, T. K., & Das, S. (2018). Efficient Job Scheduling in Computational Grid Systems Using Wind Driven Optimization Technique. *International Journal of Applied Meta-Heuristic Computing, 9*(1), 49-59.

Ghosh, T. K., & Das, S. (2022). Teaching Learning Based Optimization for Job Scheduling in Computational Grids. *International Journal of Advanced Intelligence Paradigms, 21*(1/2), 72–86. doi:10.1504/IJAIP.2022.121030

Ghosh, T. K., Das, S., Barman, S., & Goswami, R. (2017). Job Scheduling in Computational Grid Based on an Improved Cuckoo Search Method. *International Journal of Computer Applications in Technology, 55*(2), 138–146. doi:10.1504/IJCAT.2017.082864

Ghosh, T. K., Das, S., & Ghoshal, N. (2020). Job Scheduling in Computational Grid Using a Hybrid Algorithm Based on Genetic Algorithm and Particle Swarm Optimization. In *Proceedings of International Conference on Information Technology and Applied Mathematics (ICITAM 2019)*. Springer. 10.1007/978-3-030-34152-7_66

Ghosh, T. K., Das, S., Goswami, R., & Barman, S. (2015). A Comparison Between Genetic Algorithm and Cuckoo Search Algorithm to Minimize the Makespan for Grid Job Scheduling. In *Proceeding of International Conference on Computational Intelligence (ICCI, 2015)*. Springer. 10.1007/978-981-10-2525-9_14

Goswami, R., Ghosh, T. K., & Barman, S. (2011). Local search based approach in grid scheduling using simulated annealing. In *Proceedings of IEEE International Conference on Computer and Communication Technology (ICCCT)* (pp. 340-345). 10.1109/ICCCT.2011.6075112

Haupt, R. L., & Haupt, S. E. (2004). *Practical Genetic Algorithms*. John Wiley & Sons.

Izakian, H., Abraham, A., & Snášel, V. (2009). Metaheuristic Based Scheduling Meta-Tasks in Distributed Heterogeneous Computing Systems. *Sensors (Basel)*, *9*(7), 5339–5350. doi:10.339090705339 PMID:22346701

Kolodziej, J., & Xhafa, F. (2011). Enhancing the Genetic-Based Scheduling in Computational Grids by a Structured Hierarchical Population. *Journal of Future Generation Computer Systems*, *27*(8), 1035–1046. doi:10.1016/j.future.2011.04.011

Krauter, K., Buyya, R., & Maheswaran, M. (2002). A taxonomy and survey of Grid resource management systems for distributed computing. *Software, Practice & Experience*, *32*(2), 135–164. doi:10.1002pe.432

Lorpunmanee, S., Sap, M. N., Abdullah, A. H., & Chompooinwai, C. (2007). An Ant Colony Optimization for Dynamic Job Scheduling in Grid Environment. *International Journal of Computer, Electrical, Automation, Control and Information Engineering*, *1*(5), 1343–1350.

Martino, V. D., & Mililotti, M. (2004). Sub-optimal scheduling in a grid using genetic algorithms. *Parallel Computing*, *30*(5-6), 553–565. doi:10.1016/j.parco.2003.12.004

Nabrzyski, J., Schopf, J. M., & Weglarz, J. (Eds.). (2004). *Grid Resource Management: State of the Art and Future Trends*. Kluwer Academic Publication. doi:10.1007/978-1-4615-0509-9

Page, J., & Naughton, J. (2005). Framework for task scheduling in heterogeneous distributed computing using genetic algorithms. *AI Review*, *24*(3-4), 415–429. doi:10.100710462-005-9002-x

Prakash, M., Saranya, R., Jothi, K. R., & Vigneshwaran, A. (2012). An optimal job scheduling in grid using cuckoo algorithm. *International Journal of Computer Science and Telecommunications*, *3*(2), 65–69.

Prakash, S., & Vidyarthi, D. P. (2015). Maximizing Availability for Task Scheduling in Computational Grid using GA. *Concurrency and Computation*, *27*(1), 197–210. doi:10.1002/cpe.3216

Rabiee, M., & Sajedi, H. (2013). Job Scheduling in Grid Computing with Cuckoo Optimization Algorithm. *International Journal of Computers and Applications*, *62*(16).

Ritchie, G. (2003). *Static multi-processor scheduling with ant colony optimization and local search* [Master Thesis]. School of Informatics, University of Edinburgh.

Salman, A., Ahmad, I., & Al-Madani, S. (2002). Particle swarm optimization for task assignment problem. *Microprocessors and Microsystems*, 26(8), 363–371. doi:10.1016/S0141-9331(02)00053-4

Tiwari, P. K., & Vidyarthi, D. P. (2014). Observing the effect of inter process communication in auto controlled ant colony optimization based scheduling on computational grid. *Concurrency and Computation*, 26(1), 241–270. doi:10.1002/cpe.2977

Wang, J., Duan, Q., Jiang, Y., & Zhu, X. (2010). A New Algorithm for Grid Independent Task Schedule: Genetic Simulated Annealing. *World Automation Congress (WAC)*, 165–171.

Xhafa, F., Duran, B., Abraham, A., & Dahal, K. P. (2008). Tuning struggle strategy in genetic algorithms for scheduling in computational grids. *Neural Network World*, 18(3), 209–225.

Xhafa, F., Gonzalez, J. A., Dahal, K. P., & Abraham, A. (2009). A GA(TS) Hybrid Algorithm for Scheduling in Computational Grids. *Proceedings of the 4th International Conference on Hybrid Artificial Intelligence Systems*, 285-292. 10.1007/978-3-642-02319-4_34

Yang, X. S., & Deb, S. (2009), Cuckoo Search via Levy Flights. *Proceedings of World Congress on Nature & Biologically Inspired Computing*, 210-225. 10.1109/NABIC.2009.5393690

Yang, X. S., & Deb, S. (2010). Engineering Optimization by Cuckoo Search. *Int. J. Mathematical Modeling and Numerical Optimization*, 1(4), 330–343.

Zhang L., Chen Y., Sun R., Jing S. & Yang B. (2008). A task scheduling algorithm based on PSO for grid computing. *International Journal of Computational Intelligence Research, 4*.

Zhao, B., Guo, C. X., & Cao, Y. J. (2005). A Multi-agent based Particle Swarm Optimization Approach for Optimal Reactive Power Dispatch. *IEEE Transactions on Power Systems*, 20(2), 1070–1078. doi:10.1109/TPWRS.2005.846064

Zomaya, A. Y., & Teh, Y. H. (2001). Observations on using genetic algorithms for dynamic load-balancing. *IEEE Transactions on Parallel and Distributed Systems*, 12(9), 899–911. doi:10.1109/71.954620

Chapter 2
Wavelet Energy–Based Adaptive Retinex Algorithm for Low Light Mobile Video Enhancement

Vishalakshi G. R.
Dayananda Sagar College of Engineering, India

Gopala Krishna
 https://orcid.org/0000-0001-5410-0144
SJB Institute of Technology, India

Hanumantha Raju
BMS Institute of Technology and Management, India

ABSTRACT

In today's world, smartphones are ubiquitous and feature high-quality cameras and video recording capabilities. The camera shake, shadows, or other environmental factors lead to poor video, even in low-lighting situations with a high-end camera. To preserve and enhance low-light mobile video, a wavelet energy-based adaptive retinex algorithm is proposed. The first step in the method is to extract frames from the composite video before it is fed into the algorithm in HSV space. The authors then apply the wavelet energy-based adaptive retinex algorithm to the dynamic range-extended value channel. Lighting conditions that cause video degradation are restored adaptively to their natural brightness. A color restoration technique that improves the conventional retinex method fixes the gray world violation problem. Wavelet energy is used as a metric in concurrence with the retinex algorithm to objectively validate image enhancement quality. An experimental work of more than 300 still images and videos show that the proposed technique outperforms the current state of the art.

INTRODUCTION

An important and challenging component of video processing is video enhancement. The enhancement

DOI: 10.4018/978-1-6684-7524-9.ch002

of video and reconstruction of images have always proven useful in astronomy, forensics, and medical imaging. Enhancing video results not only improves visual quality but also eases the performance for subsequent tasks. Moreover, video enhancements aim to improve the overall appearance of videos or provide a better representation of the transform for future automated video processing, such as analysis, detection, segmentation, recognition, tracking, and surveillance. For specific purposes, the video enhancement problem can be described as follows: given an input video of low quality yields an output video of high quality. Digital videos have become an integral part of everyday life. The primary goal of video enhancement is to reveal invisible details in the video.

Digital recording technology has improved over the years, but there are still several situations where recorded images or video sequences may suffer significant degradation. The poor quality of recorded video sequences can be attributed to low lighting conditions, camera shakes, and uncontrolled recording. Therefore, video enhancement on mobile device remains as challenging problem for researchers. Mobile phone used to record dramatic events, naturally jiggles. Therefore, the placement of the subject and approach used to record the video can lead to a better output. Furthermore, since most mobile video evidence is shot freehand on a smartphone camera, there is no guarantee that it will be of decent quality.

EXISTING WORK

In the earlier work, (Yunbo et.al., 2012) presented a survey on video enhancement techniques. (Chongyi et.al., 2021) proposed a comprehensive survey to cover various aspects ranging from algorithm taxonomy to unsolved open issues. To examine the generalization of existing methods, the author proposed a low-light image and video dataset, in which the images and videos are taken by different mobile phones, cameras under diverse illumination conditions. To reconstruct high-resolution videos from low resolution ones (Hongying et.al., 2022) proposed a comprehensive survey on video super-resolution based on deep learning.

(Singh et.al., 2015) used a recursive histogram equalization algorithm to enhance low-exposure images. The author claims that technique works well for images captured under common light conditions, such as underwater sequences or night vision images. However, the inappropriate sub-divisions may not give natural-looking output images. Furthermore, the algorithm's performance is dependent on number of iterations. (Wang et.al., 2020) proposed an experiment-based review of low-light image enhancement methods and summarises their principals and characteristics. Finally compared the outcome of the algorithms.

(Pizer et.al., 1987) proposed contrast limited histogram equalization (CLAHE) to overcome the adaptive histogram equalization (AHE) problem by clipping the obtained histograms, which limits the maximum slope of the transformations computed for each tile. (Shaochen et.al., 2022), proposed a low-illuminance image enhancement by converting RGB images into YUV color space. It comprises the luminance (Y) and two-color difference (U, V) components. (Qian et.al., 2022) proposed an adaptive image enhancement method based on visual saliency as an attribute of image enhancement, that improves brightness and contrast of low-illumination color images by avoiding over-enhancement. (Yadong et.al., 2022) proposed a novel variational enhancement model to overcome earlier challenges. This method focuses on enhancing the visibility of low-illumination images while preserving the details and the texture information.

The retinex-based image enhancement algorithms rely on the logarithmic domain, that works on the illumination-reflection model. In the following paragraphs we present the basic and advanced retinex algorithms that form the basis to our approach. (Jobson et.al.,1997) proposed the first version of the retinex algorithm to fill the gap between color images and human observations of the scene. Numerous researchers contributed to retinex algorithms have used the retinex method as a benchmark. This scheme works well for most of the color images and videos. However, the color images enhanced in this method suffer from gray world violation, and sometimes over-enhance the appearance of an image. The additional color restoration step presented in this scheme restores the lost naturalness due to the RGB domain processing of the retinex algorithm, But the reconstruction is ineffective for low-light videos.

To mitigate the above problem existing in the earlier works, (Chenet.al.,2022) proposed retinex low-light image enhancement network based on the attention mechanism. An attention mechanism function is embedded in the convolutional layer, which is the second part of the network. This method adaptively adjusts the illumination's luminance information and preserves the image structure's consistency. In recent work on the retinex algorithm, researchers exploited the adoption of deep neural networks based retinex algorithms (Guo et al.,2023) (Hai et al., 2023) (Li et al.,2018). Although, there is a substantial improvement in the quality of reconstructed images, computational complexity increases for high-resolution input images.

In the following sections, the basic retinex model, our proposed approach, experimental results of our method, comparative study and conclusion on the overall idea is discussed.

RETINEX MODEL

The physics origin of the retinex model was proposed by (Edwin Land,1977) as the justification for the color variations in real scenes. Artificial or natural light, also called ambient light, illuminates objects, producing light wavelengths to vary, sometimes slightly, sometimes severely, thereby changing the visual appearance of the color. The main part of the retinex algorithm is the design of the Gaussian surround function shown in Equation (1) with various surround space constants, specifically, 80, 120, 250.

$$G_n(x,y) = K_n \times e^{\frac{\left(-\left(x^2+y^2\right)\right)}{2\sigma^2}} \tag{1}$$

The K_n is selected such that it satisfies Equation (2)

$$K_n = \frac{1}{\sum_{i=1}^{M}\sum_{j=1}^{N} e^{\frac{\left(-\left(x^2+y^2\right)\right)}{2\sigma^2}}} \tag{2}$$

where x and y denote the spatial coordinates, σ denotes the Gaussian surround space constant, M×N represent the image resolution in pixels, and n is preferred as 1, 2, and 3 since the three Gaussian scales are used for each R, G, and B component of the image.

In single scale retinex (SSR) method proposed by (Jobson et.al.,1997) the illumination $l_i(x,y)$ is estimated by applying a linear low-pass filter for an input color image. The output color image $R_i(x,y)$ is obtained by subtracting the log signal of the determined illumination, which is the 2D convolution of the Gaussian surround function and therefore, the original image of the ith component is presented by Equation (3):

$$R_{SSR_i}(x,y) = log_2\left[I_i(x,y)\right] - log_2\left[G_n(x,y) \otimes I_i(x,y)\right]$$ (3)

where $i \in \{R,G,B\}$, $R_{SSR_i}(x,y)$ is the SSR output for channel 'I', $I_i(x,y)$ is the image value for ith channel, $\otimes$ denotes convolution operation, and $G_n(x,y)$ is a Gaussian surround function. The convolution operation $\left[G_n(x,y) \otimes I_i(x,y)\right]$ represents illumination estimation obtained by convolving the Gaussian surround function with the original image. The convolution operation in time domain can be replaced by multiplication operation in frequency domain. The frequency domain multiplication operation significantly reduces computation complexity.

Multiplying SSR output with the weighting factor, W_n and summing up for all three channels accomplishes multiscale retinex (MSR) operation. The MSR operation on a 2D image is carried out by using Equation (4)

$$R_{MSR_i}(x,y) = \sum_{n=1}^{N} W_n \times R_{SSR_{ni}}(x,y)$$ (4)

where $R_{MSR_i}(x,y)$ indicates the MSR output, W_n is a weighting factor that is assumed as $\frac{1}{3}$ and N indicates the number of scales. The multiscale retinex color restoration (MSRCR) output is given by Equation (5):

$$R_{MSRCR_i}(x,y) = C_i(x,y) \times R_{MSR_i}(x,y), i \in R,G,B$$ (5)

The value of $C_i(x,y)$ is given by Equation (6)

$$C_i(x,y) = \beta \times \left\{ log_2\left[\alpha I_i(x,y)\right] - log_2\left[\sum_{x=1}^{M} \sum_{y=1}^{N} I_i(x,y)\right]\right\}$$ (6)

where β is the gain constant and α controls the strength of nonlinearity. The final version of the MSRCR is given in Equation (7)

$$R_{MSRCR_i}(x,y) = G \times \left[C_i(x,y)\left\{log_2 I_i(x,y) - log_2\left[G_n(x,y) \otimes I_i(x,y)\right]\right\} + b\right]$$ (7)

where G indicates gain and b represents the offset value.

In a nutshell, the conventional retinex method is summarized as follows:

1. Read the original image/video in RGB color space.
2. Separate composite image/video into R, G, and B channels.

3. Initial settings: N, $[\sigma_1, \sigma_2, \sigma_3]$, Gain (G), offset (b), α, β, Wn where N = 3, σ = [80, 120, 250], G=192, b=-30, α=125, β=46, Wn=$_{1/}$3

4. Design Gaussian function with various surround space constants [Equation (1) and (2)].

5. Convolve each of the R, G, and B color channel with three Gaussian surround functions while retaining the central part of the convolution.

6. Apply single scale retinex algorithm on R, G, and B color channels in the logarithmic domain [Equation (3)].

7. Apply the multiscale retinex algorithm on three channels [Equation (4)].

8. Restore the colors lost due to gray world violation using the color restoration technique [Equation (5) through (7)].

9. Combine the three channels to generate composite RGB images/video.

PROPOSED METHOD

Low-light images (LLI) (Liu et al.,2023) typically suffer from two problems. First, their pixel values are small, which means they have low visibility. Due to an inadequate signal-to-noise ratio (SNR), the image content is also degraded due to substantial noise. Nevertheless, most existing LLI enhancement methods (Ren et al.,2019) use noisy datasets. Well-trained photographers can only take photographs with minimal noise. In reality, most low-light images are not like this. Even though improving low-light photos (Shen at al.,2017) simultaneously with removing their noise is ill-posed, we find that noise exhibits different levels of contrast in different frequency layers, making detecting noise in the lower frequencies much more accessible than in the higher frequencies.

The proposed method addresses the problems mentioned in the earlier paragraph. The workflow of our approach is presented in Figure 1. First, the low-light image or video is applied as an input to our algorithm. The poor-quality images are directly used as input; however, the composite videos are transformed into individual frames before applying as input. Finally, to avoid the color distortion problem in RGB color space, we transfer images or frames into the HSV domain.

The hue from the HSV domain is preserved since it is a color-dependent parameter while the saturation and value components are processed. We apply the proposed adaptive retinex algorithm to the value channel since the value is a luminance component. Luminance or brightness enhances details as well as overall visual appearance of an image.

Before applying our retinex algorithm, the contrast of the value channel is stretched using Equation (8):

$$X'(x,y) = \frac{I(x,y) - I_{min}}{I_{max} - I_{min}} \times 255 \tag{8}$$

where $X'(x,y)$ is the contrast stretched image, $I(x,y)$ is the value component of the original input image, I_{min} is the minimum pixel value, and I_{max} is the maximum pixel value channel. Equation (8) is scaled up by 255 to translate the pixel values in the display range.

Figure 1. The Flowchart of the Proposed Adaptive Retinex Method

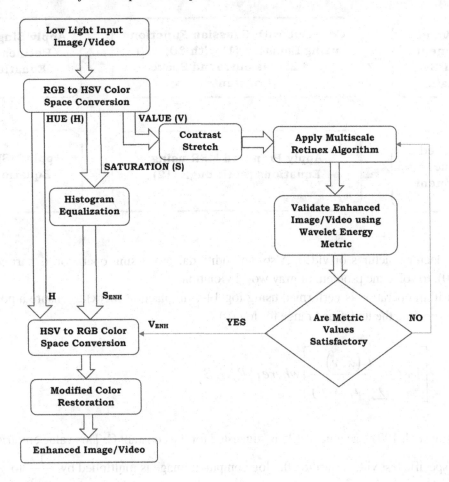

Adaptive Retinex Algorithm

The proposed modified retinex algorithm presented in Figure 2 is applied to the contrast stretched value channel. The enhancement equations presented in Equations (1) to (4) remain similar to that of the conventional retinex algorithm. However, from Equation (4) onwards, we adopt the proposed MSR technique defined as in Equation (9). The operational sequence of the overall modified retinex algorithm is determined using the following equations (9) through (12):

$$R'_{MSR_i}(x,y) = R_{MSR_i}(x,y) \times 28.44 + 128 \tag{9}$$

where $R'_{MSR_i}(x,y)$ shows the new retinex, $R_{MSR_i}(x,y)$ represents the conventional MSR scheme, 28.44 is the gain, and 128 indicates the offset value.

The proposed MSR algorithm, $R'_{MSR_i}(x,y)$ defined in Equation (9) translates image pixel values of traditional multiscale retinex scheme from ±4.5 range to [0, 255], which is appropriate for obtaining

Figure 2. Flow Sequence of the Proposed Modified Retinex Algorithm with Color Restoration

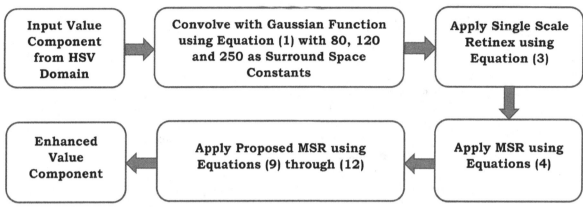

visually satisfactory pictures or video. Also, an additional processing operation is carried out using Equation (10). to solve the problem of gray world violation.

The logarithm operation is performed using log(1+x) in place of log(x) to ensure a positive result and also to overcome the undefined range for log (0).

$$I_i'(x,y) = log\left[1 + C\frac{I_i(x,y)}{\sum_{i=1}^{3}I_i(x,y)}\right] where\, i\{R, G, B\} \tag{10}$$

In Ref. (Jobson et.al.,1997), a value of 125 is suggested for the constant C. This value empirically settles to 100 for a specific test video. Further, the log computed image is multiplied by $\frac{1}{255}$ to maintain the value of the image in the range of 0 to 255 using Equation (11).

$$R''_{MSR_i}(x,y) = \frac{I_i'(x,y) \times R'_{MSR_i}(x,y)}{255} \tag{11}$$

The final version of the MSR is given by equation (12)

$$R_{MSR_i}^E(x,y) = \left[G \times R''_{MSR_i}(x,y)\right] + b \tag{12}$$

where G and b represent the final gain and offset value, respectively.

The $R''_{MSR_i}(x,y)$ values result in positive and negative values, and the histogram can generally have giant tails. Thus, a final gain offset has been applied to get an enhanced image. The gain of 2.25 and an offset value of -30 is used here to obtain satisfactory results. The choice of the scale is application dependent, but for most applications, three scales are required.

The next step is to validate the enhanced value component of our modified retinex algorithm. We have chosen the full reference quality assessment (QA) metric, wavelet energy (WE) (M. C. Hanumantharaju et.al.,2013), to validate the enhanced value component of the modified retinex algorithm. The WE depict the sub-band characteristics in the wavelet domain. Enhanced image QA is achieved by applying multi-level wavelet decomposition on both the original and the improved image. Next, the WE and vector are computed to obtain the energy percentage corresponding to the approximation and the details.

Wavelet Energy

The wavelet domain is a powerful and efficient technique for analysing, decomposing, denoising and compressing signals. In particular, the Discrete Wavelet Transform (DWT) breaks a signal into several time-frequency components that enable extracting features desired for signal identification and recognition. The DWT and wavelet theory has been developing rapidly over the past few years. The DWT and its energy computation are exploited for visual quality assessment of an enhanced color image. Extracting detailed WE coefficients from an image provides information about image details, and extracting approximate WE coefficients provides an image's global contrast information.

Generally, the two-dimensional wavelet transform (WT) is used to examine the time-frequency realm most suited for non-stationary signals. The WT has been used to capture the localized features of the signal. A continuous wavelet transforms (CWT) maps a given function from the time domain into two-dimensional functions of s and t. The parameter s is called the scale corresponding to the frequency in the Fourier transform, and t is the transformation of the wavelet function. The CWT is defined by

$$CWT(x,y) = \frac{1}{\sqrt{s}} \int S(T)\varphi\left(\frac{T-t}{s}\right)dt \tag{13}$$

where S(T) is the signal, $\varphi(T)$ is the basic wavelet, and $\frac{1}{\sqrt{s}}\varphi\left(\frac{T-t}{s}\right)$ is the wavelet basis function.

The DWT is generally used for short-time analysis. The DWT for a signal is given by

$$DWT(m,n) = \frac{1}{2^m} \sum_{i=1}^{N} S(I,i)\varphi\left[2^{-m}(i-n)\right] \tag{14}$$

Wavelet energy (WE) is a method for finding energy for 1-D wavelet decomposition. The WE computation of 1-D wavelet decomposition of a signal provides the percentage of energy corresponding to the approximation. The vector containing the rate of energy corresponds to details. The WE is expressed as follows

$$WE = \frac{1}{2^{\frac{-m}{2}}} \sum_{i=1}^{N} S(I,i)\varphi\left[2^{-m}(i-n)\right] \tag{15}$$

The WE is an efficient metric to assess the quality of the enhanced image. The higher the averaged detailed coefficients, the global image appearance is better. In most quality assessment metrics, high-frequency information of a picture is not sensitive to more prominent features to distinguish diverse objects in an image.

The enhanced value component of the image is verified using the WE metric. The v is computed using a linear combination of high-frequency coefficients after a Daubechies wavelet transform. The enhanced image details look better if the detailed WE coefficients are more significant than the original image. The approximate WE coefficients are used as a metric to improve the global information of the picture. Higher approximate WE coefficients than the original image; globally, the enhanced image appears to be better. Once the details and overall visual quality metrics are satisfactory, the images are fed into the HSV to RGB color space converter, followed by the modified color restoration.

Modified Color Restoration

This section presents the modified color restoration adopted in our scheme. Generally, the retinex algorithm undergoes various operational sequences (Zhao et al., 2021). This leads to the loss of naturalness in the enhanced images. Therefore, an improved version of images is subjected to the color restoration function. As a result, the color consistency between the original image and the enhanced image can be obtained by using the equations (16) through (18):

$$R_{enh}(x, y) = \frac{I_{enh}(x, y)}{I(x, y)} \times R(x, y) \tag{16}$$

$$G_{enh}(x, y) = \frac{I_{enh}(x, y)}{I(x, y)} \times G(x, y) \tag{17}$$

$$B_{enh}(x, y) = \frac{I_{enh}(x, y)}{I(x, y)} \times B(x, y) \tag{18}$$

where $I(x,y)$ is given by $Max[R,G,B]$, $I_{enh}(x,y)$ is the enhanced intensity image and $R_{enh}(x,y)$, $G_{enh}(x,y)$, and $B_{enh}(x,y)$ are the restored color components of the original colors R, G, B.

However, the color constancy obtained from this method is application specific. Further, the color restoration is accompanied by equations (19) through (21).

$$R_{enh}(x, y) = \left[\frac{I_{enh}(x, y)}{I(x, y)} \right]^{\gamma} \times R \tag{19}$$

$$G_{enh}(x,y) = \left[\frac{I_{enh}(x,y)}{I(x,y)}\right]^{\gamma} \times G \tag{20}$$

$$B_{enh}(x,y) = \left[\frac{I_{enh}(x,y)}{I(x,y)}\right]^{\gamma} \times B \tag{21}$$

γ is a constant which may be assumed as 0.77.

EXPERIMENTAL WORK AND COMPARATIVE STUDY

This section presents experimental results on various test images downloaded from popular databases. First, we present the initial settings of our experiments, followed by various datasets used in the testing. We compare the decomposition and enhancement results with other retinex-based enhancement methods to evaluate the decomposition performance of the proposed method. Following this, the enhanced images are compared with other low-light image enhancement models taking subjective and objective factors into an account. Next, with extreme dark image enhancement, various environmental results were presented to show the performance of our algorithm. Finally, we discuss our methods and their advantages over existing research methods in enhancement. The proposed method to enhance low-light images was coded in Matlab (Ver. R2021a) software installed on a PC with an Intel core i5-11400 CPU and 16 GB RAM. The low-light videos from the database are converted into frames and then transformed into the HSV domain before applying to our algorithm. It is easier to process images in .jpg, .bmp, .png, and .tiff formats if we apply them directly to our system in RGB format. We have used standard, freely available, and widely used databases to check the performance of our algorithm. Experiments are conducted on images downloaded from the LIME, DCIM, ExDARK, and LLIV-Phone databases. The images in these databases are available in numerous sizes, file formats, and environmental conditions. The quality of images varies from low to moderate. Mobile videos and low-light images are used to test the proposed work. Figure 3 presents a sample of images from the standard databases mentioned earlier and selected for our experimental work

Figure 4 presents the comparison of decomposition and corresponding enhancement results of the models (Fu et.al.,2016), (Li et.al.,2018) and the proposed method. As we can observe from the results presented, the illumination estimation of other models uses either l_2 prior to the illumination gradient or l_1 prior to the reflection gradient. As seen from the experimental results of Figure 4, the illumination of most natural low-light images is not uniformly distributed. This generates observable halo artifacts. This is because that l_2 norm causes blurred boundaries around areas where the illumination changes dramatically, which is quite common in low-light images. The top portion of an image shown in Figure 4 is clipped. It is presented separately in Figures 5 and 6 to show that the illumination and reflections of our method are based on Gaussian surround space constant convolution with the input image, maintaining overall structure images and presenting better visual quality. The enhancement and the details preserved are evident from the enhancement results.

Figure 3. Sample Test Images used in our Experiments: Denoted from 1 to 17.

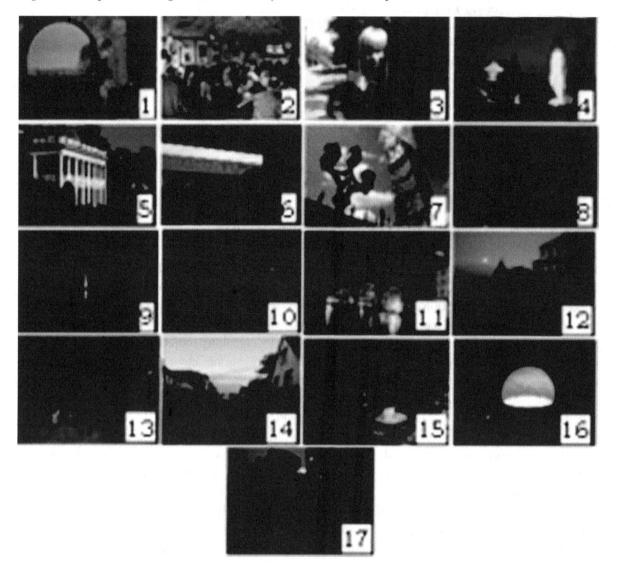

The proposed model is compared with the three classical models, namely, (Kimmelet.al.,2003), (Fu et.al.,2016), (Li et.al.,2018) and other models available in the literature. For a fair comparison, the constraints used in all the methods are set to be optimal. In addition, a few models use RGB color space to enhance the images. In our approach, we have used HSV color space to achieve enhancement to avoid color distortion problems in the RGB domain. We only process the value and saturation channel and convert the processed image to the RGB domain.

The results of (Kimmel et.al.,2003), (Xueyang Fu et.al.,2016), (Li et.al.,2018) and, (Guoet.al.,2017) presented in Figures 7 and 8 are generated by the code downloaded from the authors' websites, with recommended experiment settings. Figure 7 shows the natural low-light images with different environmental conditions. However, in Figure 8 we have shown few closed room and open space pictures. The proposed method shows a substantial improvement in both the environments.

Figure 4. Comparisons of Decomposition and Corresponding Enhancement Results.
From top to bottom: Results of Fu et.al.,2016, Li et.al.,2018, and the Proposed Method.

In Figure 9, we have used extremely dark images downloaded from dark dataset and tested on our algorithm. As it is evident from the results presented that our method is able to preserve the naturality without introducing distortions. Specifically, when the extreme dark images are tested on (Kimmel et.al., 2003), (Fu et.al., 2016), (Li et.al.,2018), and (Guo et.al.,2017) methods, introduces halo artifacts and distortions. Therefore, the techniques mentioned earlier works well for moderate darkness and low light.

We have tested our method using foggy images downloaded from NASA dataset in order to show the performance of our technique. Figure 10 shows the foggy image enhancement results. The enhancement of foggy images is more challenging compared to other images. There are algorithms specifically developed to improve the quality of these images. Nevertheless, (Fu et.al., 2016) and our method have provided moderate result while enhancing the foggy images. Although the fog exists in the enhanced image but few details such as houses & tree (first row) train light & rail (second row), fire fighter & background (third row) are visible in our enhanced results.

An important objective in the low light enhancement is to supress the noise. Therefore, we have tested our method using noisy images. We have added additive white Gaussian noise (AWGN) 'n' with $\sigma=5$. Figure 11 shows the performance of low light image denoising using LIME (Guo et.al.,2017), SRIE (Fu et.al.,2016) and our method. Two clean test images from standard dataset, namely, 'palace' and 'statue' are shown in the first column of Figure 11. Histograms are shown below these images that provide the pixel distribution of an image with reference to the intensity value.

Second column shows the noisy image. The gamma correction and enhancement results using (Guo et.al.,2017), and (Fu et.al.,2016) models are shown in third and fourth column, respectively. It is clear from the enhancement results that these methods amplify the noise after enhancement. However, the proposed method effectively handles Gaussian noise, particularly in the dark region. The performance

Figure 5. Comparison of the Clipped Portion of Figure 4
Column 1: Input Image, Column 2: Illumination, Column 3: Reflection, Column 4: Enhanced Results. Results from Top to
Bottom: Fu et.al.,2016, Li et.al.,2018, and the Proposed Method.

evaluation of these models is shown in Table 1 using peak signal to noise ratio (PSNR) and structure
similarity index (SSIM). A low-light image's noise suppression is evaluated by objective metrics such as
PSNR and SSIM. As the MSE approaches zero, the PSNR value approaches infinity; therefore, a higher
PSNR value results in a better image and vice versa.

$$MSE(f,g) = \frac{1}{M \times N} \sum_{i=1}^{M} \sum_{j=1}^{N} \left(f_{ij} - g_{ij}\right)^2 \tag{22}$$

$$PSNR(f,g) = 10 \times log_{10} \left[\frac{255^2}{MSE(f,g)} \right] \tag{23}$$

where f is the reference image, g is the test image, $M \times N$ is the total number of pixels.

The SSIM is defined as

Figure 6. Comparison of the Clipped Portion of Figure 4
Results from Top to Bottom: Fu et.al.,2016, Li et.al.,2018, and the Proposed Method Column 1: Input Image, Column 2: Illumination, Column 3: Reflection, Column 4: Enhanced Results

$$SSIM(f,g) = l(f,g) \times c(f,g) \times s(f,g) \tag{24}$$

where $l(f,g)$, $c(f,g)$, and $s(f,g)$ is given by

$$l(f,g) = \frac{2\mu_f \mu_g + C_1}{\mu_f^2 + \mu_g^2 + C_1} \tag{25}$$

$$c(f,g) = \frac{2\sigma_f \sigma_g + C_2}{\sigma_f^2 + \sigma_g^2 + C_2} \tag{26}$$

$$s(f,g) = \frac{\sigma_{fg} + C_3}{\sigma_f \sigma_g + C_3} \tag{27}$$

In Equation (25), the luminance comparison function measures how close the mean luminance of the two images are (μf and μg). The factor is maximal and equal to 1 if $\mu f = \mu_g$. The second term is the comparison of contrast, which measures how close the two images are to one another. The contrast is calculated based on the standard deviations σf and σg. This term is maximal and equal to 1 only if $\sigma f = \sigma g$. The correlation between the two images is determined by the structure comparison. Note that σfg is the covariance between f and g. The positive values of the SSIM index are in [0,1]. A value of 0

Figure 7. Comparison of Enhancement Results with Other Models
Column 1. Inputs Column 2. Kimmel et.al., 2003 Column 3. Fu et.al.,2016 Column4. Li et.al., 2018 Column 5. Ours

Figure 8. Comparison of Enhancement Results with Other Models
First Column: Original Input Images, Second Column: Kimmel et.al.,2003, Third Column: Guo et.al.,2017, Fourth Column: Li et.al.,2018, Fifth Column: Proposed Method

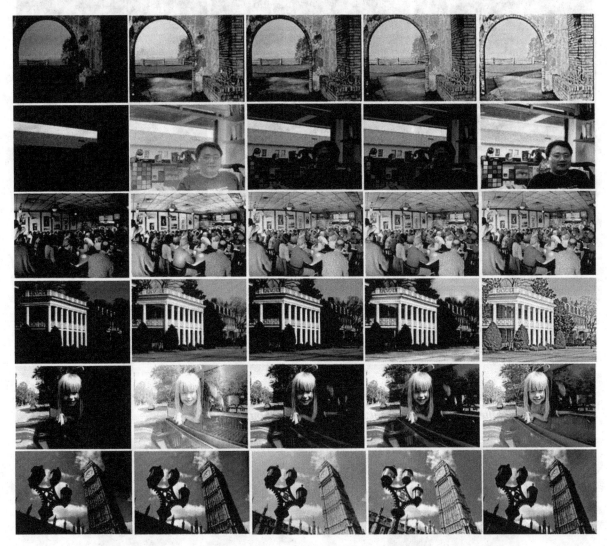

means no correlation between images, and 1 means that f=g. The positive constants C1, C2, an$_d$ C3 are use$_d$ to avoid a null denominator.

The PSNR and SSIM shows that the proposed method not only supresses noise and meanwhile improves the image quality.

Subjective Comparison

Numerous researchers have developed the derivative of the traditional retinex algorithm. A variational framework for classical retinex algorithm based on the centre/surround function was proposed by(Kimmel et.al.,2003). The gamma correction is processed in the HSV domain to preserve color information. Though this method is able to overcome the color distortion problem by applying retinex in HSV domain, over

Figure 9. Top row: dark images, bottom row: enhanced results of our method

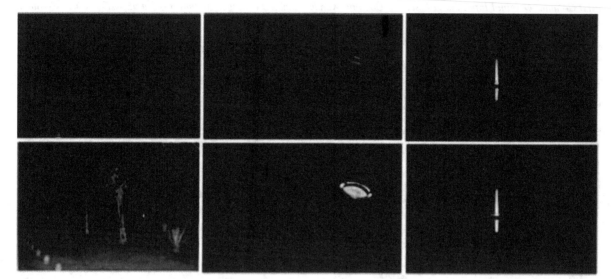

enhanced the bright regions of the image which loses the naturality of the image. As can be seen from the results presented, (Kimmel et.al., 2003) can effectively enhance details and contrast with color correction. However, the proposed method has better natural performance, such as dark regions in Figure 7 and 8 are enhanced much better than the MSRCR methods.

Figure 10. Foggy image enhancement results: first column is the original image (1024×768 pixels), second column is the Fuet.al.,2016 results, third column is our results

Figure 11. Comparison of noise suppression and enhancement
First column: 'palace' and 'statue' (512×768 pixels) clean image, second column: noisy image (σ = 5), third column: Guo et.al.,2017), fourth column: Fu et.al.,2016) and fifth column: our results

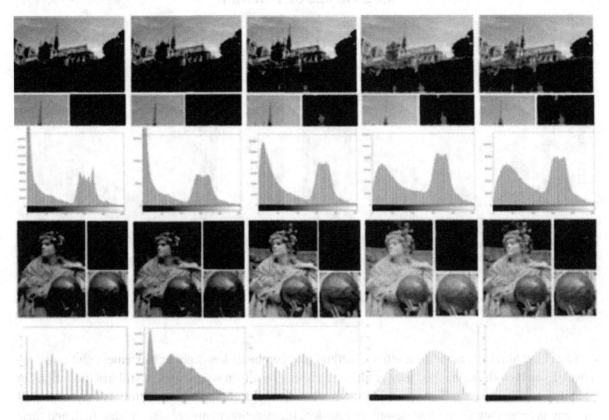

(Fu et.al.,2016) separately estimates the reflection and illumination component, achieving image enhancement and correction by evaluating the solution in an alternate minimization scheme. SRIE is the first of its kind to introduce a weighted variational model that is significantly different from previous models. However, this model achieves unsatisfactory performance and generality due to the poor representing capacity. (Fu et.al., 2016) is a complicated optimization model due to its neural architecture design. (Fu et.al., 2016) provides satisfactory results for a few images but introduces halo-artifacts in some pictures. Also, noise is evident in few enhanced versions and hence cannot sufficiently improve the visual quality of the input image.

Table 1. PSNR and SSIM metric values of Figure 11

Image	Metric	Noisy Image	Guo et. al., 2017	Fu et. al., 2016	Ours
First Row	PSNR	16.12	15.02	17.66	19.48
	SSIM	0.76	0.85	0.59	0.56
Second Row	PSNR	15.02	11.93	13.53	16.60
	SSIM	0.85	0.67	0.67	0.66

Figure 12. NIQE Values of Figure 7

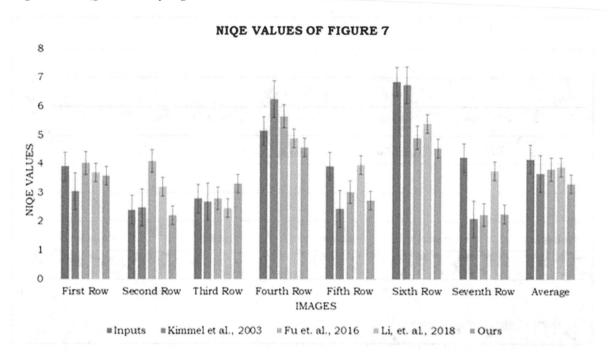

The (Li et.al.,2018) model is a retinex method that combines low-light enhancement and noise removal. Even though this method may produce promising results in some cases, it still has limitations in its ability to decompose reflectance and illumination. Image decomposition constraints that work well for various scenes are difficult to design. In addition, illumination maps are also handcrafted, and their performance is typically dependent on careful parameter tuning. As a result of this method, the details are over-smoothed, whereas other baselines produce color deviations and amplify the noise.

Figure 8 shows the images with low lighting conditions, the face of the person, a group of people and various shades in the picture. (Kimmel et.al., 2003) model over enhance in almost all the images. The results of (Fu et.al.,2016) and (Li et.al.,2018) are somewhat better for a few images. (Guo et.al.,2017) shows brilliant performance in lighting up dark regions. However, this method can easily over-enhance areas with relatively high intensities. Comparatively, the proposed method produces more natural results while successfully enhancing low-light images visibility.

BASELINE EVALUATION

Due to the unavailability of the ground truth of the enhanced image, a blind image quality assessment of Ref. (Mittal et.al.,2012) is used to evaluate the improved results. This metric is the Natural Image Quality Evaluator (NIQE) (Mittal et.al.,2012) based on statistical regularities from realistic and undistorted images.

A lower NIQE value indicates a higher image quality. In addition, we have used the quality image score of Ref. (Mittal et.al., 2012) to assess our enhanced results. The score typically has a value between 1 and 10 (10 represents the best quality, and one is poor quality). NIQE values obtained for the image enhancement results presented in Figure 7 are graphically plotted in Figure 12. Figure 13 presents the

Figure 13. NIQE Values of Figure 8

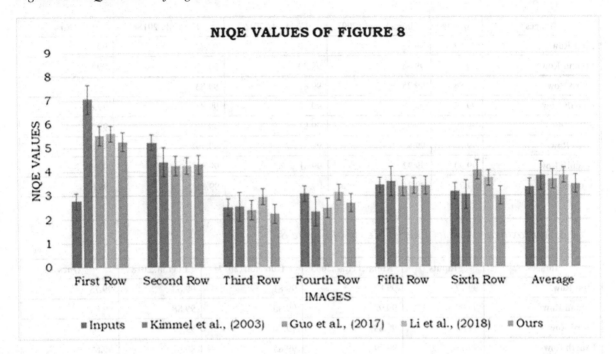

graphical plot of NIQE values of Figure 8. We have used the wavelet energy metric adopted in our retinex model to assess the other low light enhancement models. The two components of wavelet energy, namely, approximate and detailed energies are computed for the image enhancement results. Approximate wavelet energies (AWE) must be close to the input image. Higher the AWE value indicates, better is the global enhancement.

Table 2 and 3 shows the approximate wavelet energies for the image enhancement results shown in Figure 7 and 8, respectively. The values shown in bold represents the enhancement results are satisfactory. In the first row of Table 2, the AWE value of our method is 99.76 which has greater AWE value compared to other models. This shows that our method has a better global enhancement. Similarly, in the third row of Table 2, the global enhancement of Ref. (Li et.al., 2018) is good.

Table 4 and 5 shows the detailed wavelet energies (DWE) for the image enhancement results shown in Figure 7 and 8, respectively. Detailed wavelet energies (DWE) must be closer or greater than the input image. Higher the DWE value indicates, better is the detail enhancement. In the first row of Table 4, our method has a DWE of 0.240 which is greater than the input image DWE value of 0.235. Therefore, our method is able to provide more details compared to other models

CONCLUSION

This paper presents Wavelet Energy based Adaptive Retinex Algorithm for Low Light Mobile Video Enhancement. As a result of the camera problem and environmental concerns, the proposed research addresses the limitations of image acquisition. First, we discussed the issues associated with conventional retinex algorithms and their impact on image quality. Compared with the traditional retinex algorithm,

Table 2. Approximate Wavelet Energy Metric of Figure 7

Images	Inputs	Kimmel et.al., 2003	Fu et. al., 2016	Li et. al., 2018	Ours
First Row	99.77	99.75	99.70	99.72	**99.76**
Second Row	99.89	**99.88**	99.80	99.82	99.85
Third Row	99.84	99.75	99.81	**99.83**	99.82
Fourth Row	99.75	99.79	99.85	99.87	**99.89**
Fifth Row	99.79	**99.82**	99.81	99.80	99.79
Sixth Row	99.78	99.82	99.81	99.79	**99.89**
Seventh Row	99.90	**99.92**	99.81	99.85	99.86
Average	99.81	99.81	99.79	99.81	**99.83**

Table 3. Approximate Wavelet Energy Metric of Figure 8

Images	Inputs	Kimmel et.al.,2003	Guo et.al.,2017	Li et.al.,2018	Ours
First Row	99.77	99.82	99.81	99.83	**99.75**
Second Row	99.89	99.92	99.80	**99.88**	99.84
Third Row	99.84	**99.88**	99.80	99.81	99.82
Fourth Row	99.75	99.79	99.85	99.87	**99.89**
Fifth Row	99.79	99.82	99.77	99.83	**99.85**
Sixth Row	99.78	99.82	**99.84**	99.82	99.75
Average	99.80	**99.84**	99.81	99.84	99.82

the proposed work requires fewer operations. The retinex algorithm is iterative and is made adaptive by utilizing the wavelet energy metric. A combination of approximate and detailed energy computations produces an image with superior quality and enhanced details. The hue component is preserved during enhancement operations, and the value and saturation components are processed in HSV color space. In this algorithm, the value component is modified based on the adaptive retinex algorithm, while the saturation component histogram is stretched by applying histogram equalization. RGB color distortions

Table 4. Detailed Wavelet Energy Metric of Figure 7

Images	Inputs	Kimmel et.al., 2003	Fu et. al., 2016	Li et.al., 2018	Ours
First Row	0.235	0.192	0.230	0.238	**0.240**
Second Row	0.221	0.219	0.222	0.228	**0.229**
Third Row	0.245	0.185	0.232	**0.239**	0.238
Fourth Row	0.257	0.218	0.231	0.248	**0.249**
Fifth Row	0.235	**0.230**	0.201	0.227	0.225
Sixth Row	0.291	0.287	0.275	0.281	**0.290**
Seventh Row	0.287	**0.251**	0.242	0.231	0.242
Average	0.253	0.226	0.233	0.241	**0.244**

Table 5. Detailed Wavelet Energy Metric of Figure 8

Images	Inputs	Kimmel et.al.,2003	Guo et.al., 2017	Li et.al., 2018	Ours
First Row	0.241	0.239	0.231	**0.240**	0.232
Second Row	0.183	0.127	0.125	0.145	**0.171**
Third Row	0.281	0.149	0.153	**0.172**	0.164
Fourth Row	0.298	0.267	0.245	0.256	**0.291**
Fifth Row	0.187	0.141	0.169	0.165	**0.175**
Sixth Row	0.152	0.141	0.145	**0.149**	0.147
Average	0.223	0.177	0.178	0.187	**0.196**

are avoided by using the HSV space. To restore the naturalness of the enhanced image, color restoration is carried out in RGB space on the enhanced image. Finally, we have compared the proposed method with other prominent research methods. The experimental results and evaluation techniques show that the proposed work outperforms other low-light enhancement techniques.

REFERENCES

Chen, Li, & Hua. (2022). Retinex Low-Light Image Enhancement Network based on Attention Mechanism. *Multimedia Tools Application.* . doi:10.1007/s11042-022-13411-z

Fu, Zeng, Huang, Zhang, & Ding. (2016). A Weighted Variational Model for Simultaneous Reflectance and Illumination Estimation. In *Proceedings of the IEEE conference on computer vision and pattern recognition* (pp. 2782-2790). 10.1109/CVPR.2016.304

Guo, Li, & Ling. (2017, February). LIME: Low-Light Image Enhancement via Illumination Map Estimation. IEEE Transactions on Image Processing, 26(2), 982-993. doi:10.1109/TIP.2016.2639450

Guo, X., & Hu, Q. (2023). Low-light Image Enhancement via Breaking Down the Darkness. *International Journal of Computer Vision, 131*(1), 48–66. doi:10.100711263-022-01667-9

Hai, J., Xuan, Z., Yang, R., Hao, Y., Zou, F., Lin, F., & Han, S. (2023). R2rnet: Low-light image enhancement via real-low to real-normal network. *Journal of Visual Communication and Image Representation, 90*, 103712. doi:10.1016/j.jvcir.2022.103712

Hanumantharaju, Ravishankar, Rameshbabu, & Manjunath Aradhya. (2013). Novel Full-Reference Color Image Quality Assessment Based on Energy Computation in the Wavelet Domain. *Journal of Intelligent Systems, 22*(2). 155-177.doi.org/10.1515/jisys-2012-0026

Jobson, D. J., Rahman, Z., & Woodell, G. A. (1997, July). A Multiscale Retinex for Bridging the gap between Color images and the human observation of scenes. *IEEE Transactions on Image Processing, 6*(7), 965–976. doi:10.1109/83.597272 PMID:18282987

Kimmel, Elad, Shaked, Keshet, & Sobel. (2003). A Variational Framework for Retinex. International Journal of Computer Vision, 52(1), 7–23.

Land, E. (1977, December). The Retinex Theory of Color Vision. *Scientific American*, *236*(6), 108–128. doi:10.1038cientificamerican1277-108 PMID:929159

Li, Guo, Sun, & Sun. (2022). A Low-Illuminance Image Enhancement Method in YUV Color Space. *14th International Conference on Measuring Technology and Mechatronics Automation (ICMTMA)*, 286-291. 10.1109/ICMTMA54903.2022.00062

Li, C., Guo, C., Han, L., Jiang, J., Cheng, M.-M., Gu, J., & Loy, C. C. (2022, December 1). Low-Light Image and Video Enhancement using Deep Learning: A Survey. *IEEE Transactions on Pattern Analysis and Machine Intelligence*, *44*(12), 9396–9416. Advance online publication. doi:10.1109/TPAMI.2021.3126387 PMID:34752382

Li, C., Guo, J., Porikli, F., & Pang, Y. (2018). LightenNet: A convolutional neural network for weakly illuminated image enhancement. *Pattern Recognition Letters*, *104*, 15–22. doi:10.1016/j.patrec.2018.01.010

Li, M., Liu, J., Yang, W., Sun, X., & Guo, Z. (2018, February). Structure-Revealing Low-Light Image Enhancement via Robust Retinex Model. *IEEE Transactions on Image Processing*, *27*(6), 2828–2841. doi:10.1109/TIP.2018.2810539 PMID:29570085

Liu, H., Ruan, Z., Zhao, P., Dong, C., Shang, F., Liu, Y., Yang, L., & Timofte, R. (2022). Video Super-Resolution based on Deep Learning: A Comprehensive Survey. *Artificial Intelligence Review*, *55*(8), 5981–6035. doi:10.100710462-022-10147-y

Liu, X., Ma, W., Ma, X., & Wang, J. (2023). LAE-Net: A locally-adaptive embedding network for low-light image enhancement. *Pattern Recognition*, *133*, 109039. doi:10.1016/j.patcog.2022.109039

Mittal, A., Soundararajan, R., & Bovik, A. C. (2012). Making a Completely Blind Image Quality Analyzer. *IEEE Signal Processing Letters*, *20*(3), 209–212. doi:10.1109/LSP.2012.2227726

Pizer, Amburn, Austin, Cromartie, Geselowitz, Greer, Romeny, Zimmerman, & Zuiderveld. (1987). Adaptive Histogram Equalization and Its Variations. *Computer Vision, Graphics, and Image Processing, 39*(3), 355-368,

Qian, S., Shi, Y., Wu, H., Liu, J., & Zhang, W. (2022). An Adaptive Enhancement Algorithm Based on Visual Saliency for Low Illumination Images. *Applied Intelligence*, *52*(2), 1770–1792. doi:10.100710489-021-02466-4

Rao & Chen. (2012). A Survey of Video Enhancement Techniques. *Multimedia Signal Processing*, *3*(1), 71–99.

Ren, W., Liu, S., Ma, L., Xu, Q., Xu, X., Cao, X., Du, J., & Yang, M. H. (2019). Low-light image enhancement via a deep hybrid network. *IEEE Transactions on Image Processing*, *28*(9), 4364–4375. doi:10.1109/TIP.2019.2910412 PMID:30998467

Shen, L., Yue, Z., Feng, F., Chen, Q., Liu, S., & Ma, J. (2017). *Msr-net: Low-light image enhancement using deep convolutional network*. arXiv preprint arXiv:1711.02488.

Singh, K., Kapoor, R., & Sinha, S. K. (2015, October). Enhancement of Low Exposure Images via Recursive Histogram Equalization Algorithms. *Optik (Stuttgart)*, *126*(20), 2619–2625. doi:10.1016/j.ijleo.2015.06.060

Wang, W., Wu, X., Yuan, X., & Gao, Z. (2020). An Experiment-Based Review of Low-Light Image Enhancement Methods. *IEEE Access: Practical Innovations, Open Solutions*, *8*, 87884–87917. doi:10.1109/ACCESS.2020.2992749

Xu & Sun. (2022). A Novel Variational Model for Detail-Preserving Low-Illumination Image Enhancement. *Signal Processing, 195*, 108468. ISSN0165-1684.doi.org/10.1016/j.sigpro.2022.108468

Zhao, Z., Xiong, B., Wang, L., Ou, Q., Yu, L., & Kuang, F. (2021). Retinexdip: A unified deep framework for low-light image enhancement. *IEEE Transactions on Circuits and Systems for Video Technology*, *32*(3), 1076–1088. doi:10.1109/TCSVT.2021.3073371

Chapter 3
Identification and Segmentation of Medical Images by Using Marker–Controlled Watershed Transformation Algorithm, XAI, and ML

Tahamina Yesmin
https://orcid.org/0000-0002-5931-793X
Haldia Institute of Management, India

Pinaki Pratim Acharjya
https://orcid.org/0000-0002-0305-2661
Haldia Institute of Technology, India

ABSTRACT

To make human life easy and compact, XAI has developed a lot with more innovations and contributed its own share. To make a suitable treatment while diagnosed with brain tumour, one needs to classify the tumour and detect it in a proper way where the explained result is most important. With the help of different analysis processes where marker-based approaches can help in proper segmentation and noise reduction analysis, numerous imaging modalities exist for tumour detection that are utilized to identify tumours in the brain. One of the most important issues of XAI system is medical diagnosis through ML in medical image processing. In this chapter, the authors present a modified marker-controlled watershed transformation approach to detect brain tumour with XAI and machine learning approaches. They include CNN and data augmentation algorithms. Image pre-processing takes the main area to detect and diagnose disease and diagnose properly. The statistical measurements have been introduced to get the mathematical abstractions of different approaches for result analysis.

DOI: 10.4018/978-1-6684-7524-9.ch003

INTRODUCTION

AI has become a progressively flooded topic for various scientific journals now a day's including medical image processing. In Explainable AI (XAI) domain the procedures are developed to experiments the predictions which made usually made up by AI systems and the features and the characteristics of a human nature and their activities in day-to-day life. It can work with the images of medical field data to precise and the effective diagnosis of medical images to better treatment and identification of problems. ML algorithms which are based on XAI applications have experienced a tremendous breakthrough over last decades in some field like computer vision, signal processing, image processing etc. Mostly the medical sectors have taken the maximum of advantages of applications in XAI that gets most of the images use in medical field which made automation of clinical support systems easy and machine depended.

Recently ML applications and their tools have become fit enough to satisfy clinical necessities and, in this manner, research and clinical groups, as well as organizations are cooperating to foster clinical XAI arrangements. Today, we are nearer than any time in recent memory to the clinical execution of AI and, consequently getting to know the essentials of this innovation turns into a "must" for each expert in the clinical field. Helping the clinical material science local area to gain such strong foundation information about XAI and learning techniques, including their development and present status of the craftsmanship, will surely bring about more excellent examination, work with the initial steps of new scientists in this field, and motivate novel exploration headings (Singh, R., et.al, 2020; Wang, M., et.al, 2020; Wang, C., et.al, 2019. Wang, T., et.al, 2021; Thompson, R.F., et.al, 2018; Morra, L., et.al, 2019; Li, C., et.al, 2013; Ranschaert, E.R., et.al, 2019).

It is additionally utilized for the motivations behind problem-solving within the domain of progress of medical care frameworks so successful therapy can be provided. In prior days, medical care data were similarly little compared to present situation. Indeed, owing the massive headway within the domain of picture procurement gadgets, there is a critical need of the techniques which can investigate even the big data. Without a doubt, picture examination is an exhausting and interesting task. The ML and AI empower the doctor to analyse and figure unequivocally and quickly the illnesses so it very well may be rectiðed inside the specified time (Pandey, et.al, 2019)

In this chapter it is discussed how machine learning algorithm (CNN) is going to use with the morphological reconstruction approaches with the help of pre-processing procedures where we can detect the disease with more efficient way and automatically by the means of artificial intelligence. This chapter thoroughly explains all the steps involves in methodology along with the algorithms and mathematical equations.

LITERATURE REVIEW

J. Welina, et.al, (2022), Introduce a XAI in an indispensable component while implementing AI as clinical equipment's on medical care related works. This paper explains some doubtful questions related to field ML and existing XAI methods by conducting clinical requirements ground and systematic evaluation to answers the questions with clinical image explanations and computational works. Author proposed XAI algorithm on brain tumor. This work sheds light into the reducing of risk factors lies of directly applying XAI methods on some models (Jin, W., et.al 2022).

H.M. Das, et.al, (2022), presents an overview of XAI which is used in deep learning based medical analysis. More 220 papers on medical image analysis XAI techniques has surveyed and a framework of XAI criteria is introduced and categorized according to the framework and anatomical location. Mainly the paper focused on current critique on XAI, evaluation of XAI and future perspective of XAI (Bas, H.M., et.al, 2022).

Suganyadevi, S., (2021), introduceda model clinical picture handling techniques and examination, basic data and cutting-edge approaches with profound learning. The paper presents research on clinical picture handling as well as to characterize and execute the key rules that are distinguished and tended to. Through CNN network model additionally the paper enlightened the present status of the crafts-manship in light of the new logical writing which might be valuable to radiologists around the world (Suganyadevi, S., 2021).

Montero. A and Javaid. U et al (2021),Presented a survey on the essential innovative mainstays of AI alongside the cutting-edge AI techniques and their application to clinical imaging likewise examined the recent fads and future examination bearings. It will be useful to comprehend the people groups how AI strategies are currently turning into a universal device in any clinical picture examination work process and prepare for the clinical execution of AI-based arrangements [13].

P. Muralikrishna, et.al, (2021), paper presents the advancement of counterfeit brain organizations, extensive examination of DLA (Deep Learning Approach), which conveys promising clinical imaging applications. The vast majority of the DLA executions focus on the X-beam pictures related to medical care and computerized the images for grouping, recognition, and division of clinical pictures in view of DLA. The audit of exploration papers directs the specialists to consider fitting changes in clinical picture examination in view of DLA (Puttagunta, M., et.al, 2021).

Maier, A., et.al, 2018, explain in their paper that XAI can be utilized to make the AI-generated ex-periment results to be more explained and traceable and generalize. This domain is to be explained the predictions made by the AI systems and can used in analysis and diagnosis of medical data with data accountability, transparency, model improvement and result tracing (Maier, A., et.al, 2018).

XAI AND MACHINE LEARNING

There are many challenging fields which is remain complicated to be solved or explainable like safety and accountability standard explanation, quality and performance implementations, models of stockholders and the degree in which it will differentiate, complicated clinical and IT workflows integrations etc. AI models and its assisted decision-making systems can run very efficiently with the applications of explain-able AI models with high priority values in the field of medical care. Machine Learning is an expandable application or to be focused area where ML models and the hardware infrastructures, processes that is related to the explain ability. Mostly XAI helps in decision making precisely with the help of justifying outputs of the system or processes predictions of outputs and the reasoning process as well which is very much important to accountability of a system. In XAI the response of recipient explanation is very important because it works with the multidisciplinary research approaches influenced by many fields like sociology, education, psychology, human-computer interactions and philosophy. XAI actually works with the definitions of explanation of any reasons or outcomes of the work ability of any models to be summarizing the reasons, behaviours and the trust ability of users to produce the cause of any insights of a particulardecision-makingprocess. The several desired facts that to be explained like consistency, stability, accuracy, comprehensibility, relevancy and certainty etc. A good explanation always needs to be responsible and evaluated rigorously proceed in nature. (Aurangzeb, A. M., et.al, 2018; Gilpin, L. H., et.al, 2018; Molnar, C. 2020; Ferreira, J.J., et.al, 2020).

XAI (ML) is a use of AI that can have the option to work without being explicitly modified, that gain from data and pursue expectations or choices in light of past data. Machine Learning Processes incorporate the extraction of information from any model and the choice of reasonable highlights for a particular problem. The most recent outcome of AI has been made potential on account of enormous developments of both computational power and information accessibility. Specifically, AI applications in view of machine learning (ML) algorithms have encountered exceptional. The area of medical care field taken benefits of the phenomenal improvements toconstruct XAI applications get a large portions of critical care images and robotizing various strides of the clinical choices (Erickson, B.J. 2017).

This chapter focuses on the multi-model working process of medical images which are needed for critical medical decision-making support in MRI, CT scans different pathological works etc with the XAI evaluations in medical image processing works with the combinations of modified marker-controlled watershed transformation algorithm. The interpretation of the medical data is the most difficult and complex process where the data augmentation techniques helped to executions of data's properly with the explanation of XAI. To make a powerful Explainable AI tool the attribution methods of CNN tools to be apply for the medical image classification tasks without any further modifications in architectures to make them convenient. The main focus to develop an explainable model with the help of CNN and augmentation techniques which are more likely to be trusted the users of medical data analysis field. CNN is used to produce the disease predictions and early detections along with their explanations in term of similar images and common images. As ML is driven by information, fundamental advances are to separate and choose important elements from information, or at least, quantitative qualities that sum up data conveyed by information into vectors or clusters. Then, at that point, this data is taken care of two nonexclusive prescient models, similar to classifiers, which figure out how to play out a specific errand (Ana, B.M., et.al, 2021; Lambin, P., et.al, 2017). Figure1 showing the XAI and ML major applications of heath care activities which goes more easy and helpful to monitor health activities.

IMPORTANCE OF XAI AND ML IN MEDICAL IMAGE PROCESSING/ SEGMENTATION

Medical imaging assumes a huge part in various clinical applications, for example, medical strategies utilized for early recognition, checking, determination, and treatment assessment of different medical circumstances. ML is a utilization of AI that can have the option to work without being explicitly customized, that gain from information and pursue forecasts or choices in light of past information. Segmentation of medical images arises by use of DLA as a quickly developing exploration field. DLA (Deep Learning Approaches) has been broadly utilized in process of medical image to recognize the presence or nonattendance of the sickness (Lambin P, et.al, 2021).

Various ML and DL models have been advanced which are incorporated with programmed recognition and disease identifications. A portion of these strategies incorporate staggered limits, deep CNN, Bayesian methodologies, SVM, district developing procedures, brain networks, and some more. Alongside that, deep learning likewise furnishes an immense region to manage medical image segmentation.

Figure 1. XAI and ML applications in healthcare

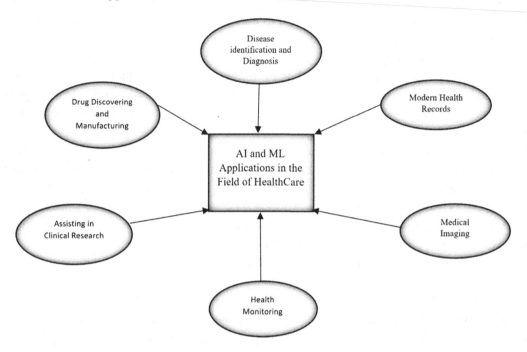

It has acquired a ton of fame lately. Different models have been advanced which concentrate includes and perform order consequently (Puttagunta, M., et.al, 2021).

Current medical-imaging datasets are a lot more modest than those that got leap forwards computer vision. Albeit a balanced examination of sizes can't be made, as computer vision datasets have many classes with high variety (contrasted with not many classes with less variety in medical imaging), arriving at better speculation in medical imaging might require gathering essentially bigger datasets, while keeping away from predispositions made by crafty information assortment, as portrayed underneath (Anum, K., et.al, 2020).

XAI mostly using in research fields to be explained and describe observe the output or result of algorithms they had used. It gives a good explanation of how a process to be done and explained to take a decision perfectly. XAI algorithms mainly explain the already deployed or trained models by providing the algorithm model parameters for input-output process pairs.

METHODOLOGY

This chapter introduced a XAI based modified marker-controlled watershed transformation algorithm which is going to execute step-by-step procedure and shown in Figure 2. We took two MRI images to go through the Enhanced marker-controlled Watershed Segmentation calculation method for segmentation alongside the sifting system to pre-interaction of images prior to applying marker base and subsequent to obtain the portioned outcome some pre-processing procedures will apply and after that we had proposed some Machine Learning calculation to handle an image with all the more instructively and come by the arranged outcome. We have utilized just MRI images which are sorted by the proposed strategy. Machine

Figure 2. Flow chart of the proposed methodology

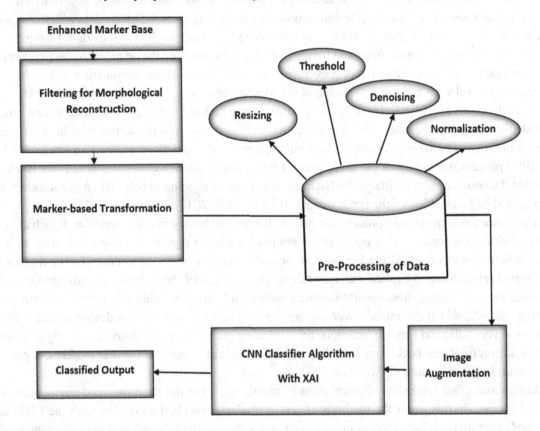

learning has high layered highlights which can be valuable in such circumstances. This won't just assistance in expanding exactness yet in addition assist the specialists with relieving the patient inside the necessary time. The mathematical tool used to complete our examinations in MATLAB R2021a. Being a unique device with many implicit capabilities as well as libraries, it is an easy-to-use instrument and directs all tests successfully with the XAI explanation for justify, control, discover and to improve the data authentication which is most important to be explained in every aspect of process to get a proper error free output.Figure 2 explain the full process of methodology in graphical way.

The two essential morphological administrators are widening and disintegration, from which numerous activities can be determined. This will likewise help in morphological remaking. For gray scale picture f and organizing component A, expansion and disintegration are characterized as follows:

Dilation: $\delta_A(f)_{(m,n)} = \max \{f(m - p, n - t) + A(p, t) \mid m - p), (n - t) \in D_f; (p, t) \in D_A\},$ (1)

Erosion: $\varepsilon_A(f)_{(m,n)} = \min \{f(m + p, n + t) - A(p, t) \mid (m + p), (m + p) \in D_f; (p, t) \in D_A\},$ (2)

Where, for image f and organizing component A, (m, n) and (p, t) are the respective co-ordinates sets and D_f and D_a are the respective domains.

Filtering process is depended on the nature of the image. If we think an image as a function (is an inherited properties of images and the technical process use to manipulate the image data which comprised of separate pixel values) mapping locations in any image to count the pixel values then filtering is the technique that represent a new enhanced image from a combination of the original image pixel values. The commonly used filtering is moving average filter and image segmentation filter where first one replaces each pixel with average pixel value of it and a neighbourhood window of adjacent pixels. This step actually involves with neighbourhood operations, in which the value of each pixel in one process is recalculate based on the value of surrounding pixels. Similar spectral properties with high frequency patterns in order to harmonize an area brings out clearer and details information of an image, the low-pass filter process use to reduce the noise present on an image and edge enhancement filter is used to highlight the boundaries of an image. So basically, this process is going to help with noise removal, blur removal and edge detection of the taken images. (Gu, Z., et.al, 2019).

In watershed transformation process the marker is used for binary image operations which are consisting of either a separate marker points or a combination marker region which is also known as larger region where every connected marker point is placed within an object of interest. Every marker has coordinated relationship to explicit watershed districts. The limit of the watershed segmentation is then organized on ideal edges, subsequently isolating each item from its neighbour's image is sectioned by utilizing MCWS, which diminishes over segmentation. The modified process demonstrated which is going to be very solid and flexible technique for sectioning curios with shut frames, with edges showing the limits. Forefront and background markers are lined up with inner and outside markers, separately (Bhishman, D. 2020; Sivagami, M., et.al, 2003).

Marker-controlled watershed segmentation is mostly used for the detection and segmentation of medical images. In this paper the methods of use of marker-controlled algorithm with the CNN base approach to get image information in more proper and accurate way where it will help in image quality improve. From the input image we can extract the marker image or from a separately available marker image using some feature detection algorithms. It can also be defined manually. The detailed approach of the Marker Controlled Watershed Algorithm (Ghaderi, S., et.al, 2021) is given below:

1. First the step the variety image is perused then trades it to dark scale.
2. Further develop inclination images by means of the utilization of appropriate edge identification task.
3. Mark the very front items the use of morphological remodel (proficient than the initial image with an end).
4. Figure the neighbourhood maxima and minima to accomplish the ideal ahead markers.
5. Lay over the closer view marker image on the native image.
6. Perfect the closures of the markers the use of finishes reconstructing.
7. Computing the childhood markers.
8. Computing the watershed change of the utility.

Pre-processing is basic and required for computer vision and mainly medical image segmentation where any mistaken information can cause to create any issue to a successful classifier. In data pre-processing phase many processes are going to execute like resizing, thresholding, denoising and normalization. To get legitimate information from divided watershed images assigned where pre-processing stages includes for examination. Datasets which process medical images are generally with much noise and mess up with a huge amount of unwanted data. Maximum of time it is required to pre-processed the image to get rid of the unwanted information from the image. Most important thing is to collect exact and needful data from the unprocessed images so that next processing part does not effect. Many pre-processing techniques are there to process the image like thresholding, histogram equalization and contrast stretching etc. These steps also improve the image attributes which enhances the image and increase the contrast etc. In this chapter we had applied thresholding and many other processes like denoising, normalization, resizing to pre-process the images for image augmentation process.

De-Noising is generally a relic of the image sensor, however not consistently. There are a few extra curios that might be available in image. The objective of error expulsion is to eliminate the error not to twisting the original one and the main aim to eliminating ancient rarities is comparable. Contingent upon the sort of noise or ancient rarity, various strategies might be utilized for pre-processing. The most fundamental methodology is to eliminate anomalies, and different methodologies are taken, including thresholding and neighborhood locale based factual channels like the position channel and middle channel. Weighted image averaging is likewise at some point utilized for eliminating error, it can function admirably. Despite the fact that deblurring or Gaussian smoothing convolution bits are some of the times to remove errors such strategies may cause spreading and not be the proper methodology (Essa, Z. M., et.al, 2020).

Thresholding strategy parcels the original imageinto two different parts whereintensity of pixels values that are less than the threshold values and intensity values of pixels that are more than threshold values.Theprocess of multi steps thresholding process is important for variety image segmentation in numerous implementations. To section the variety parts Red, Green and Blue, beyond what two ideal limits can be required. In future a more noteworthy number of limits is fundamental. In any case, a more prominent number of limits can diminish the presentation of segmentation process (Krig, S., 2014).

A threshold image$h (a, b) = \{1$, if $f (a, b) > T$ 0, if $f (a, b) < T$,where 1 is object and 0 is background.

Multi-level Thresholding:
$h (a, b) = \{p$, if $f (a, b) > T2$
q, if $T1 < f (a, b) < T2$
r, if $f (a, b) < T1$

Standardized cuts focus on ideal parting by decreasing number of regions. This strategy depends on chart hypothesis. Loads on the edge are relegated by closeness, distance, variety, dim level or surfaces, etc between two comparing pixels (Heming, J. (2019).

Machine learning comprise of element extraction module that separate the significant highlights like edges, surfaces and a characterization module which group in view of component removed. Yet, there are a few restrictions of image grouping utilizing machine learning it can remove just specific arrangement of elements on images and it can't separate from highlights, not quite the same as prepared data. CNN can be treated as an element extractor. Regularly talking, acknowledgment algorithms in light of CNNs utilize the result from last phase as an element portrayal. In any case, the information in this layer is excessively coarse for thick expectation. Going against the norm, prior layers might be exact in restriction, yet they won't catch semantics. To outdo the two benefits, they characterize the hyper segments use for vector of initiations of all phases of CNN. The algorithm advances straightforwardly from image data so there is no need of manual component extraction. It enjoys fundamentally three benefits, for example, boundary sharing, comparable portrayal and scanty communications (Nida, M., et.al, 2015; Liu, X., et.al, 2019).

Figure 3. CNN Algorithm Process

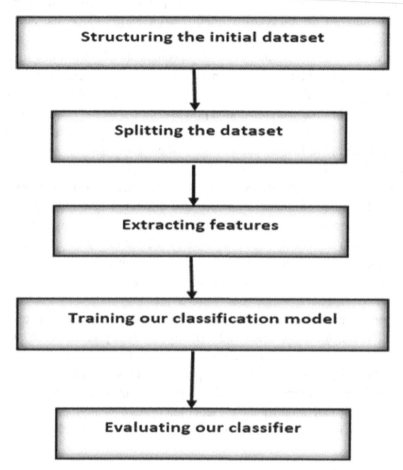

CNN approves three distinct ideas connected with ML framework that are-

1. Inadequate Communication
2. Boundary Sharing
3. Symmetric Spaces.

Lack of interconnection is utilized to identify little and significant highlights, for example, edges by making the bit more modest than the info. We can likewise allude to it as the scanty availability or same weight. Boundary Sharing, on the same process we imply that each element map is having similar loads, thus the quantity of boundaries is diminished. The boundary sharing makes the layer that has the equity called as simplistic and interpretation. Each step is associated with the past layer by a channel (Priyanka. P., et.al, 2020). In figure 3 the CNN algorithm process is explained with the help of flow chart from structuring the initial dataset to evaluating the classifier.

Convolutional Neural Networks (CNNs) is introduced, for image recognition. Neural Network is an artificial neural network which combines the mathematical method of convolution and neural network. The convolutional neural network (CNN) with the help of gradient attracted considerable attention because of its successful application in target detection, image classification, knowledge acquisition, and image semantic segmentation.

The detailed Algorithm of gradient descent for a CNN(LeCun, Y., 1998) is given below

Step 1: function GDCNN (a, b, θ, type, α)
Step 2: a1 ← a
Step 3: for m∈ {1, . . ., n} do
Step 4: an+1 = c (a; θ)
Step 5: xm ← Ψim (cm (ym, am))
Step 6: am+1 ← Φ(xm)
Step 7: formÎ {N, . . ., 1} do
Step 8: y˜m ← ym
Step 9: if m = N and type = regression then,
Step 10: eN ← aN+1 − b
Step 111: else if m = N and type = classification then,
Step 12: eN ← σ(aN+1) − b
Step 13: else
Step 14: em ← (Y˜m+1 _| Cm+1)
     ◦   DΨm+1 (Cm+1(Y˜m+1, am+1))
× D∗Φm+1(xm+1) × em+1
Step 15: Inserted D∗fm+1
Step 16: Ñymw (a, b; θ) ← (Cm…am) ∗×DΨm (Cm (ym, am)) ×D∗Φm(xm) ×em
Step 17: Inserted Ñ∗ymfm
Step 18: ym ← ym − ηÑymw (a, b; θ)

Data Augmentations come from simple transformations such as horizontal flipping, color space augmentations, and random cropping. It reduces the data generalization problems comes from ML algorithms. One approach to expand the ML model's speculation abilities is to prepare on additional data. Augmentations artificially inflate the preparation dataset size by either information distorting or oversampling. However, gaining a lot of high-quality training data for preparing data is almost unthinkable to practice, particularly for the medical sectors. The process of augmentation has arisen to expand the preparation data by making more manufactured information to increase it on the preparation set of data. The augmentation of data can be extensively classified into two processes that are: I) the change of unique data and II) the artificial data generation. New data are produced by adding different changes on the first data with the change of unique dataset, which incorporate relative changes where includes turn, expanding images, editing, and interpretations), versatile changes like shape varieties and power varieties (Anthony, L., 2017; Magadza, T., et.al, 2021).

In the following data augmentation algorithm has explained from training the dataset to resizing the image by splitting the dataset, applying validation of dataset and thresholding processes.

The detailed Algorithm of data augmentation is in following:

Step 1: At first Dataset to be Loaded, Ld (m).
Step 2: Then Splitting of Dataset (S$_p$(m)) into three parts
(test (m$_t$),

(m_{tr}) training Dataset

(m_v)), ($S_p(m)$) = $S_p(m_t, m_{tr}, m_v)$]validation of Dataset

Step 3: To Get original image ($S_p m_o$)

To get threshold value ($Sp(m_{oTh})$),

find biggest contour ($S_p [B_c(m_{oTh})]$),

extreme point ($S_p \{E_p [B_c(m_{oTh})]\}$) and

to crop the image ($S_p C_i$)

Step 4: on original image apply $S_p m_o = = >$ threshold

Step 5: then

Step 6: on threshold value apply ($Sp(m_{oTh})$) = = >($S_p [B_c(m_{oTh})]$) to get biggest contour

Step 7: then

Step 8: After getting biggest contour apply ($S_p [B_c(m_{oTh})]$) = = >to get extreme point; ($S_p \{E_p [B_c(m_{oTh})]\}$)

Step 9: then

Step 10: Crop the image by applying ($S_p (E_p [B_c(m_{oTh})])$) = = >($S_p C_i$)

Step 11: Apply step (iii) for all images

Step 12: Then

Step 13: apply loop for all ($S_p C_i$) = $S_p (m_o, m_{o+1}, m_{o++p}$);

Step 14: then resize all the images $S_p(C_m)$ == >$S_z (224,224)$

Step 15: Finally applying augmentation on resized image $S_z (Cm)$ == >$A_g \{S_z (C_m)\}$

RESULTS AND DISCUSSIONS

Two original colored digital medical images have been taken for the experimental purpose having dimensions of a) 509*339 and b) 640*380. In Figure 4 the transformation of first image has been presented where gray scale conversion has applied on original image and then in figure 5 the marker-controlled watershed algorithm has applied to get the final segmented result. The same process has been followed for the second image.

In the following Table 1, the result of the objective analysis of every image had taken on the marker base process by the subjective measurements of images. The objective evaluation of every image are analyzed on PSNR (Peak Signal to Noise Ratio), SNR (Signal to Noise Ratio), MSE (Mean Square Error) and Elapsed Time. Elapsed Time is the duration from when the process was started until the time it terminated. These helped to make changes or evaluate an image for a good quality. This analysis helped in improvement of images and quality assessment with the descriptive information by using XAI. The comparison was done on original, gray scale and marker base for both digital medical images. The more PSNR, SNR value is the more segmented image we will get and the less MSE value we receive we will get good quality of the images is. Also the elapsed time we getting is less when we executing the marker controlled base algorithm rather than original one. The following statistical tables fulfill all the requirements to get more segmented and noise free images.

In the figure 6, the graphical representation of the comparison table has been present to check it in a more informative way. From the presentation we can easily grasp the statistical measurement of every processed image and can understand the differences from each other.

In the following figures the histogram of original image in figure 7 and histogram of marker image in figure 8 has been shown. The histogram actually shows a graphical display of the pixel intensity

Figure 4. First Image after applying Marker-Controlled Algorithm

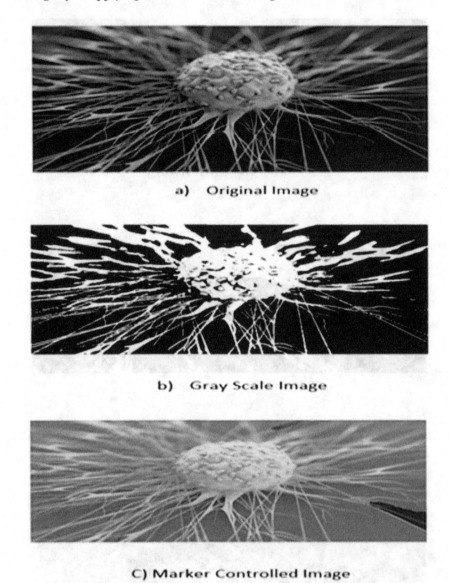

a)   Original Image

b)   Gray Scale Image

C) Marker Controlled Image

distribution for the digital images. In figure 7 we can see both the original images histogram procedure and in figure 8 we can see the marker-controlled watershed segmented images with reduced noise. The result clearly shows the implication of marker-base which helps to reduce the disturbance in images and to segment the images in a proper way.

CONCLUSION

A concise survey of pre-processing procedures in view of morphological operations in medical images has been introduced in this chapter where Pre-processing procedure in light of morphological activi-

Figure 5. Second Image after applying Marker-Controlled Algorithm

a) Original Image

b) Gray Scale Image

c) Marker Controlled Image

ties for two distinct MRI images have been talked about. The machine learning CNN framework with the help of XAI to be adjusted with marker-controlled Watershed Segmentation calculation method after pre-processing MRI images and grouping calculation is suggested for portioning and naturally distinguishing brain growths from MRI images all the more usefully. XAI provided the explanations of image analysis with more credibility and helped to interpret the output. It helps to understand the images behaviors and improve the segmentation performance of image analysis with marker-controlled

Table 1. Comparison Table of Statistical Measurements

Input Images	PSNR	SNR	MSE	Execution Time
Original Image1	17.5670	10.3162	45.8004	6.256501 Seconds
Original Image2	17.9744	13.1198	62.8631	4.855086 Seconds
Grayscale Image1	22.1453	20.4963	116.9568	7.083083 Seconds
Grayscale Image2	21.8828	20.0730	119.6635	5.627679 Seconds
Marker Controlled Image1	19.6706	17.3539	68.7558	4.976834 Seconds
Marker Controlled Image2	19.8422	17.4825	76.1396	3.811646 Seconds

algorithm followed by the gray scale conversion process. CNN model has been proposed to separate both neighborhood and worldwide elements in two distinct ways with various sizes of extraction patches with XAI which helped in explanation process. The statistical measurements helped to get proper mathematical constructions where we easily get the error analysis and noise with proper times of elapsed. As well as the histogram analysis also gave us the pixel intensity performance measurements to improve image graphical representation. This prompt lessening ability to make expectations quick for ordering the clinical image as it eliminates additional noises from the images by utilizing the pre-processing steps and image augmentation algorithms.

Figure 6. Graphical Presentation of Statistical Comparison Table

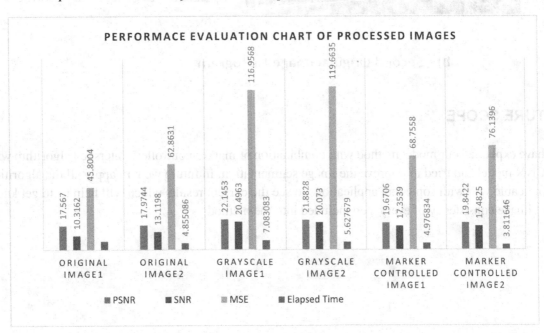

Figure 7. Histogram of Original Images

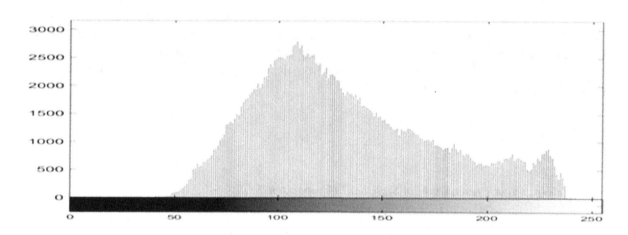

a)   First Original Image Histogram

b)   Second Original Image Histogram

FUTURE SCOPE

We have explained our model method with combination of marker-controlled watershed algorithm with the CNN model and tried to improve the image segmentation. In future we will apply all the algorithm in applicable way with some real applications to see the current results which will help us to get know about image consistency of every step included into the methods.

Figure 8. Histogram of Marker-Controlled Images

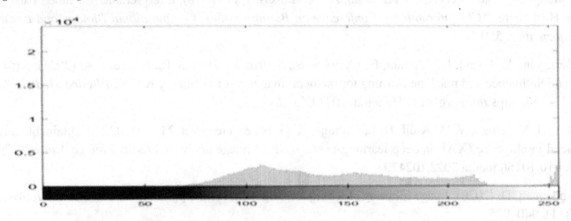

a) First Marker Controlled Segmented Image Histogram

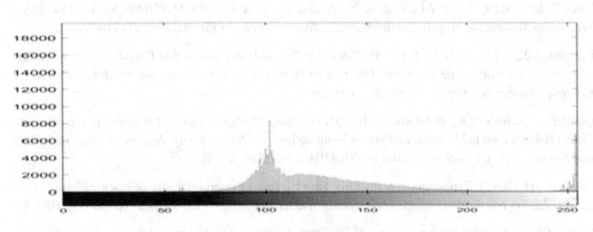

b) Second Marker Controlled Segmented Image Histogram

REFERENCES

Ana, B. M., Javaid, U., Valdés, G., Nguyen, D., Desbordes, P., Macq, B., Willems, S., Vandewinckele, L., Holmström, M., Löfman, F., Michiels, S., Souris, K., Sterpin, E., & Lee, J. A. (2021). Artificial intelligence and machine learning for medical imaging: A technology review. *Physica Medica*, *83*, 242–256. https://doi.org/10.1016/j.ejmp.2021.04.016

Anthony, L. (2017). *A Novel Mathematical Framework for the Analysis of Neural Networks*. http://hdl.handle.net/10012/12173

Anum, K., Irfan, M., Moin, A., Rho, S., & Maqsood, M. (2020). An Efficient Liver Tumor Detection using Machine Learning. *2020 International Conference on Computational Science and Computational Intelligence (CSCI)*. DOI 10.1109/CSCI51800.2020.00130

Aurangzeb, A. M., Eckert, C., Teredesai, A., & McKelvey, G. (2018), Interpretable Machine Learning in Healthcare. *ACM International Conference on Bioinformatics, Computational Biology and Health Informatics*, 559-560.

Barragán, A., Javaid, U., Löfman, F., Michiels, S., Souris, K., Sterpin, E., & Lee, J. A. (2021). Artificial intelligence and machine learning for medical imaging: A technology review. *Physica Medica, 83*, 242–256. https://doi.org/10.1016/j.ejmp.2021.04.016

Bas, H. M., Hugo, V. D., Kuijf, H. J., Gilhuijs, K. G. A., & Viergever, M. A. (2022). Explainable artificial intelligence (XAI) in deep learning-based medical image analysis. *Medical Image Analysis, 79*. doi:10.1016/j.media.2022.102470

Bhishman, D. (2020). Image Filtering -Techniques, Algorithm and Applications. *GIS Science Journal, 7*(11), 940–975.

Erickson, B. J. (2017). Machine learning for medical imaging. *Radiographics, 37*, 505–515.

Essa, Z. M., Zainab, M., & Al-Jamal, A. N., Abood, Z. M., & Essa, D. M. (2020). Marker Controlled Watershed Method for Magnification Materials. *Journal of Green Engineering, 10*(9), 6261–6270.

Ferreira, J. J., & Monteiro, M. S. (2020). *What Are People Doing About XAI User Experience? A Survey on AI Explainability Research and Practice. In Design, User Experience, and Usability. Design for Contemporary Interactive Environments.* Springer.

Ghaderi, S., Ghaderi, K., & Ghaznavi, H. (2021). Using Marker-Controlled Watershed Transform to Detect Baker's Cyst in Magnetic Resonance Imaging Images: A Pilot Study. *Journal of Medical Signals and Sensors, 12*(1), 84–89. https://doi.org/10.4103/jmss.JMSS_49_20

Gilpin, L. H. (2018). Explaining explanations: An overview of interpretability of machine learning. In *2018 IEEE 5th InternationalConference on data science and advanced analytics* (pp. 80–89). DSAA.

Gu, Z., Cheng, J., Fu, H., Zhou, K., Hao, H., & Zhao, Y. (2019). Context encoder network for 2D medical image segmentation. *IEEE Transactions on Medical Imaging, 38*(10), 2281–2292.

Heming, J. (2019). Multilevel Thresholding Segmentation for Color Image UsingModified Moth-Flame Optimization. *IEEE Access: Practical Innovations, Open Solutions, 7*, 44097–44134.

Jin, W., Li, X., & Hamarneh, G. (2022). Evaluating Explainable AI on a Multi-Modal Medical Imaging Task: Can Existing Algorithms Fulfill Clinical Requirements? Association for the Advancement of Artificial Intelligence, 1-9.

Krig, S. (2014). Image Pre-Processing. In Computer Vision Metrics. Apress. https://doi.org/10.1007/978-1-4302-5930-5_2.

Lambin, P., & Leijenaar, R. T. H. (2017). Radiomics: The bridge between medical imaging and personalized medicine. *Nature Reviews. Clinical Oncology, 14*, 749–762.

Lambin, P., & Rios, V. E. (2021). Radiomics: Extracting more information from medical images using advanced feature analysis. *European Journal of Cancer (Oxford, England), 48*, 441–446.

LeCun, Y., & Bengio, Y. (1998). Convolutional networks for images, speech, and time-series. The handbook of brain theory and neural networks, 255–258.

Li, C., Wang, X., Eberl, S., Fulham, M., Yin, Y., Chen, J., & Fang, D. D. (2013). A Likelihood and Local Constraint Level Set Model for Liver Tumor Segmentation from CT Volumes. *IEEE Transactions on Biomedical Engineering*, 60(10), 2967–2977. doi:10.1109/TBME.2013.2267212 PMID:23771304

Liu, X., Deng, Z., & Yang, Y. (2019). Recent progress in semantic image segmentation. *Artificial Intelligence Review*, 52, 1089–1106. https://doi.org/10.1007/s10462-018-9641-3

Magadza, T., & Viriri, S. (2021). Deep Learning for Brain Tumor Segmentation: A Survey of State-of-the-Art. *Journal of Imaging*, 7(19), 1–22. https://doi.org/10.3390/jimaging7020019

Maier, A., Syben, C., Lasser, T., & Riess, C. (2018). A gentle introduction to deep learning in medical image processing. *Zeitschrift fur Medizinische Physik*, 29(2), 86–101. https://doi.org/10.1016/j.zemedi.2018.12.003

Molnar, C. (2020). *Interpretable Machine Learning, A Guide for Making Black Box Models Explainable*. Leanpub.

Morra, L., Delsanto, S., &Correale, L. (2019). *Artificial Intelligence in Medical Imaging.* . doi:10.1201/9780367229184

Nida, M., & Zaitouna, M. J. (2015). Survey on Image Segmentation Techniques. *Procedia Computer Science*, 65, 797–806. doi:10.1016/j.procs.2015.09.027

Pandey,P., Pallavi,S.,&Chandra,S., (2019). Pragmatic Medical Image Analysis and Deep Learning: An Emerging Tren. *Advancement of Machine Intelligence in Interactive Medical Image Analysis*, 1–18. . doi:10.1007/978-981-15-1100-4_1,2019

Priyanka, P., Garg, R., Pathak, P., Trivedi, A., & Raj, A. (2020). Image Processing Using Machine Learning. *International Journal of Scientific Development and Research*, 5(9), 471–477.

Puttagunta, M., & Ravi, S. (2021). Medical image analysis based on deep learning approach. *Multimedia Tools and Applications*, 80, 24365–24398. https://doi.org/10.1007/s11042-021-10707-4

Puttagunta, M., & Ravi, S. (2021). Medical image analysis based on deep learning approach. *Multimed Tools Appl*, 80, 24365–24398. doi:10.1007/s11042-021-10707-4

Ranschaert, E. R., Morozov, S., & Algra, P. R. (2019). *Artificial Intelligence in Medical Imaging: Opportunities, Applications and Risks*. Springer. doi:10.1007/978-3-319-94878-2

Singh, R., Wu, W., Wang, G., & Kalra, M. K. (2020). Artificial intelligence in image reconstruction: The change is here. *Physica Medica*, 79, 113–125. doi:10.1016/j.ejmp.2020.11.012 PMID:33246273

Sivagami, M., & Revathi, T. (2003). Marker Controlled Watershed Segmentation Using Bitplane Slicing. *International Journal of Image Processing and Vision Science*, 1(3), 179–183. doi:10.47893/IJIPVS.2013.1033

Suganyadevi, S., Seethalakshmi, V., & Balasamy, K. (2022). A review on deep learning in medical image analysis. *International Journal of Multimedia Information Retrieval*, *11*, 19–38. https://doi.org/10.1007/s13735-021-00218-1

Thompson, R. F., Valdes, G., Fuller, C. D., Carpenter, C. M., Morin, O., Aneja, S., Lindsay, W. D., Aerts, H. J. W. L., Agrimson, B., Deville, C. Jr, Rosenthal, S. A., Yu, J. B., & Thomas, C. R. Jr. (2018). Artificial intelligence in radiation oncology: A specialty-wide disruptive transformation? *Radiotherapy and Oncology: Journal of the European Society for Therapeutic Radiology and Oncology*, *129*(3), 421–426. doi:10.1016/j.radonc.2018.05.030 PMID:29907338

Wang, C., Zhu, X., Hong, J. C., & Zheng, D. (2019). Artificial Intelligence in Radiotherapy Treatment Planning: Present and Future. *Technology in Cancer Research & Treatment*, *2019*(18). doi:10.1177/1533033819873922 PMID:31495281

Wang, M., Zhang, Q., Lam, S., Cai, J., & Yang, R. (2020). A Review on Application of Deep Learning Algorithms in External Beam Radiotherapy Automated Treatment Planning. *Frontiers in Oncology*, *10*, 580–919. doi:10.3389/fonc.2020.580919 PMID:33194711

Wang, T., Lei, Y., Fu, Y., Wynne, J. F., Curran, W. J., Liu, T., & Yang, X. (2021). A review on medical imaging synthesis using deep learning and its clinical applications. *Journal of Applied Clinical Medical Physics*, *22*(1), 11–36. doi:10.1002/acm2.13121 PMID:33305538

Chapter 4
Cataract Classification and Gradation From Retinal Fundus Image Using Ensemble Learning Algorithm

Moumita Sahoo
Haldia Institute of Technology, India

Somak Karan
Haldia Institute of Technology, India

Soumya Roy
Haldia Institute of Technology, India

ABSTRACT

Visual impairment, such as cataract, if not detected and treated early, might lead to blindness. Cataract detection still takes a long time and is quite subjective, depending on ophthalmologist's preference. To expedite cataract screening procedure, an automated cataract detection system should be developed. Fundus image analysis for automatic categorization and grading of cataracts has the potential to reduce the burden of competent ophthalmologists while also assisting cataract patients in learning about their diseases and getting treatment suggestions. The optic disc and blood vessel data play a significant role in the detection and grading of cataracts. Normal, mild, moderate, and severe cataract stages are differentiated based on texture, colour, size, and contrast. Classification and severity rating are carried out using random forest classifier, an ensemble machine-learning method. The accuracy discovered is equivalent to prior study in the literature. This study is expected to help doctors detect cataracts early and prevent cataract-related suffering.

DOI: 10.4018/978-1-6684-7524-9.ch004

INTRODUCTION

Cataract (Chua, 2017; Allen, 2006) is a highly prevalent disorder that affects the aged. As a result, of the sluggish rate at which cataracts develop, they are not recognised until the patient's eyesight begins to be obstructed. Examination of the ocular fundus pictures is one method for spotting cataract. The detection of anomalies in the ocular fundus and the identification of cataract patients may both be accomplished using machine learning approaches that have been trained on datasets that are readily available. Cataract is a condition where lens of the eye becomes cloudy or opaque, blocking the lens' ability to receive light. It forms in the eye's lens and is a thick, cloudy area. The development of cataract is triggered by protein clusters in the eye's structure, which avert the lens from relaying clear pictures to the eye. Based on where in the retina it occurs, cataract is primarily divided into three types: nuclear, cortical and posterior capsular cataract. Vision is distorted as a result of the nuclear cataract, which develops in the lens's central part and colors it yellow. Cortical Cataract develops at the corner of the lens and is typically encountered in elderly individuals. In contrast, A severe kind of cataract called a posterior capsular cataract can damage the back of the lens. The majority of persons with cataracts are older adults who are over 40, and this ratio rises quickly with age. The World Health Organization is quite concerned about cataract detection and diagnosis at this rising rate (WHO). Since an ophthalmologist is the only person who can now identify cataracts, the decision-making process is quite thorough and takes a lot of time. Early identification and treatment can lessen the pain that cataract sufferers experience and stop vision impairment from becoming incapacitating.

The blood-vessels, macula, and optic disc (OD) make up the majority of a retina. The optic disc, which communicates with brain nerves and is the tallest circular disc in the centre of the retina, reflects the health of the brain as well as the entire body. The macular, which is the optical centre of the eye, has a high lutein content, giving it a yellow appearance. Artery and vein are the two halves of the blood vessel. At the optic disc, all blood arteries converge. Compared to the artery, the vein is larger and darker. The term "large vessel" is used in this work to refer to arteries and veins. Several capillaries connect to the large vessel. They are referred to as small vessels. Segmenting retinal vessels is the only method for identifying retinal disorders, although doing it manually needs retinal specialists. Examining the fundus picture is one technique to find cataracts. This examination can aid in the early finding of cataracts to lessen the risk of blindness.

Generally speaking, fundus scans and the clinical information provided by ophthalmologists may be used to diagnose and detect cataracts. In order to prevent blindness, one of the possible expenses of cataract illness, cataract diagnosis must be made simpler. The effort of ophthalmologists dealing with illnesses and surgeries affecting the visual pathways must be reduced, and automated means of preventing visual problems and spotting cataracts must be developed. The use of fundus pictures in AI-assisted diagnostics has lately caught the interest of scientists in medical image field.

This study employed retinal fundus pictures to classify and grade cataracts using an ensemble learning approach. Compared to cataract pictures, normal images typically show more distinct details, like as blood vessels and optic disc. Four levels of cataract severity are categorised in this study: normal, mild, medium, and severe. If the optic disc, large vessel, and small vessel are all free of obstructions, the retinal picture is said to be normal. A modest cataract is one that just has one tiny vessel that is cloudy. A medium cataract is one in which both the tiny and large blood vessels are cloudy. It is referred as a severe cataract if the optic disc is completely cloudy. To create a feature-based dataset, texture, contrast, form, and size-based characteristics are extracted. Using Random forest, the classification procedure is

Figure 1. Example of various levels of cataract. (a) Without cataract: the blood-vessels and OD are clearly observable. (b) Mild cataract: blurriness increases and loses very thin vessel information. (c) Moderate cataract: only main vessels are visible and losses the optic disc information. (d) Severe cataract: Hardly any anatomical structures of retina is visible.

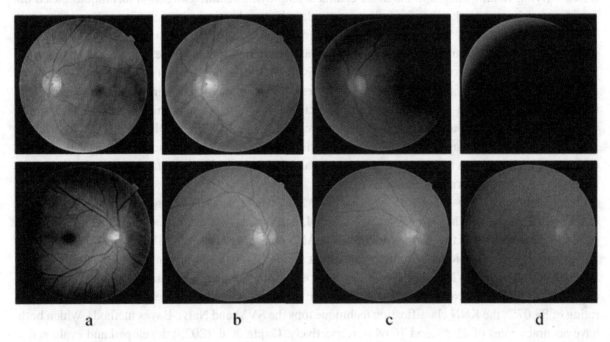

a   b   c   d

carried out following feature extraction. Ophthalmologists should be able to identify cataract patients more precisely and rapidly with the use of automatic cataract detection system. We are aware that ophthalmologists can identify cataracts by evaluating how clear the fundus pictures are. The classification job of fundus image is predicated on the idea that technical issues with picture capture do not lead to image blurring. Actual blurred image due to technical fault is estimated as cataract image by our method. Figure 1 shows fundus images with different severity grading of cataract.

RELATED WORK

Numerous studies on the automated identification and categorization of cataracts from fundus image have been published in the literature. It is generally acknowledged that ensemble learning, which combines different learning models, has a larger potential to produce more truthful categorization than any individual learner model (Polikar, 2006). In order to enhance cataract identification and grading, we have conducted experiments using the ensemble-learning framework (Rokach, 2010), which are presented in this article. Each fundus picture is processed to extract several features, such as texture, colour, intensity-based features, and annular masking features, in order to achieve classifier heterogeneity.

Nuclear (Li, 2008a; Li, 2008b; Li, 2010; Gao; 2012), cortical (Li, 2010b; Li, 2010b), and posterior sub-capsular cataracts (Li, 2008b) are among the particular cataracts that Li et al., 2008a, 2008b, 2010 attempted to automatically identify and diagnose using split pictures and retro-illumination images. To process the ocular picture, the texture and brightness information were recovered as features by Yang et al., (2013) using an enhanced bottom and top hat transformation. A 2-layered back propagation neural-network was then employed to build the classifier. The research in (Guo et al. 2015), offered a mechanism for classifying fundus images to diagnose cataracts employing feature extraction techniques based on wavelet transforms and sketches, as well as multi-class Fisher discriminant analysis.

An ensemble learning-based strategy is suggested in (Yang et al., 2016) in which 3 feature extraction approaches (texture, wavelet and sketch) and two base predicting models are examined. The numerous base classifiers are then combined using two extensively used ensemble techniques, stacking and majority voting. On a private dataset, the algorithm was tested. For autonomous cataract prediction, Fan et al. (2015c) employed sketch-based and wavelet characteristics with classic machine learning approaches, whereas wavelet, colour, and texture features were combined with SVM by Qiao et al. (2017c). Machalwar et al. (2017) used a minimal distance classifier and a histogram of gradient features to identify cataracts. Using decision tree classifiers and mean and standard deviation features, Xiong et al. (2017) assessed 5 classes of blurriness in retinal pictures.

Using coupled 2D log-gabor with ANN and SVM, Tawfik et al. (2018) performed study on the early diagnosis of cataracts. Three grade levels—normal, early-stage, and advanced stage—from a private dataset were employed in this investigation. While ANN's accuracy is 92.3%, SVM's accuracy is 96.8%.

On the basis of android architecture, Agarwal et al. (2019a) focused on the design of cataract diagnosis. With the KNN, SVM, and Naive Bayes approaches, the outcomes of cataract identification were compared in this study. Normal and cataract are the two categories that are defined. With an accuracy rating of 83.07%, the KNN classification technique tops the SVM and Naive Bayes methods, which both have accuracy rates of 75.2% and 76.64%, respectively. Gupta et al. (2023) developed and evaluated a variety of machine learning methods to conduct binary categorisation for cataract diagnosis on pictures of the ocular fundus. Naive bayes(NB), support vector machines(SVM), logistic regression (LR), decision trees(DT), k-nearest neighbours (KNN), XG-Boost, light gradient boosting, random forests, and voting classifiers are among the contemporary methods used. With the use of light gradient boosting, outcomes were improved. A paradigm for collective learning by (Elloumi, 2022), that effectively predicts cataracts by stacking the information from three convolutional deep neural networks. Base classifiers are developed and taught using the well-known Deep Learning architectures. When basic classifier predictions need to be stacked, meta classifier is employed by an Extreme Learning Machine. 590 fundus photos were chosen from two public databases for the evaluation's dataset, which is used. The proposed framework yields accuracy-94.07%, sensitivity-94.37%, specificity-93.62%, precision-95.71%, and F-measure-95.04% for cataract severity gradation. The input eye photos for this investigation (Angeline et al., 2022) are labelled as normal or cataractic. Instead than utilising the traditional fundus pictures, this method uses front-viewed eye photos obtained using a smartphone camera application as the input image, which makes the diagnostic system more accessible and affordable and helps to identify cataracts earlier. In this model, Using the gathered data set as a starting point, a convolutional neural network framework is utilized and the VGG16, a pre-trained model, is used as on it. After modelling the system using the samples that were gathered, the neural network method produced a cataract detection accuracy of 92.1%, and lastly, the system is trained to distinguish between a cataract and a normal eye from an input image of an eye. Heuristic approaches and deep learning methods can be used to categorise investigations of automatic cataract categorization based on retinal fundus pictures. Heuristics employ highly qualified inventive techniques to extract present properties (Xu et al., 2021). The centre of optic disc and dish-disc ratio are divided to estimate the likelihood of a cataract. Predefined feature sets need substantial engineering knowledge and subject-matter expertise even if many of the algorithms have proven useful in computerised cataract detection. It takes time and is laborious to complete this process. Furthermore, when doing manual diagnostic procedures, doctors and experts may be swayed by personal variables and may overlook certain crucial underlying patterns.

Several deep learning approaches are utilised in the current state of art. For automated cataract categorization in (Xiong et al., 2018c), ResNet, a pre-trained residual network, and GLCM, a grey-level co-occurrence matrix, are used, respectively, for extraction of local and global features. DCNN, a deep convolutional neural network(DCNN) technology was used by Zhang et al. (2017c) to classify cataracts into 4 categories. Ran et al. (2018b) suggested a deeper network in addition to DCNN and random forest (RF) for the categorization of cataracts into 6 classes. The diagnosis of cataracts in (Pratap & Kokil, 2019) was carried out utilising transfer learning. Automatic feature extraction is performed using a pre-trained CNN, and 4 class cataract grading is performed using SVM. The tests are carried out on a publicly available dataset, and with the inclusion of an image quality-selecting module, any image may be accepted or rejected depending on the findings of the perceptron image quality evaluator and the naturalness image quality evaluator. The accuracy of the suggested approach was 92.91%.

DCNN based cataract segregation methodology was suggested by (Imran et al., 2019b). To solve the problem of data unbalance, they used unique data augmentation methods such the Gaussian scale-space theory (GST) and universal data augmentation. For automated feature extraction and categorization, they also employed the underlying CNN approach. According to the findings, the suggested approach with an expanded dataset had success rates of 93.79% for cataract grading and 96.91% for cataract diagnosis. Syarifah et al. (2020c) used the Look ahead optimizer and the optimised Convolutional Neural Network to conduct a cataract classification research using fundus pictures. With a classification accuracy of 97.50%, this study employs the AlexNet architecture to distinguish between normal and cataract.

Weni et al. (2021) did research on cataract identification based on image wise features. Convolutional Neural Networks were employed to identify cataracts. With the best accuracy of 88%, this study separates the GoogleNet architecture into two classifications, namely normal and cataract.

An ensemble strategy based on ResNet101V2, VGG-19, and InceptionV3 was presented in Chauhan et al., (2022a) to diagnose cataracts using an eye fundus picture. The final classification was determined via soft voting. On the test dataset, the ensemble system produced an F-1 score of 95.90%.

It was investigated and developed to categorise ocular fundus pictures as normal or cataractous using a mixed CNN-LSTM model (Padalia et al., 2022). The input picture was initially delivered to CNN layers of the proposed system, which then extracted pertinent characteristics from the image. These features were then passed to the Long Short Term Network (LSTM) layers, which functioned as a classifier.

Although DL models have shown to perform the best for diagnosis and classification of cataracts, creating these models from the ground up is a very time-consuming procedure, and their effectiveness is strongly reliant on bigger retinal datasets. In terms of ophthalmology, Deep-learning algorithms (Nuzzi et al., 2021; Khan et al., 2022) are challenging to explain. The "black box" phenomena could eventually make doctors less likely to adopt this technology. While from clinical perspective, image-level evaluation is more realistic, the bulk of research concentrate on the overall performance of the complete dataset.

Table 1. Details of database

Database Name	Total Image	Healthy Image	Images with Cataract			
			Mild	**Moderate**		**Severe**
Kaggle	400	300	22	46	32	
ODIR	6019	5501	518			
Total	**6419**	**5801**	-	-	-	

MATERIALS

A dataset from Kaggle was utilised (available from https://www.kaggle.com/jr2ngb/cataractdataset/version/2) in this study. The collection includes 100 photos of cataracts and 300 images of normal retinas. The pictures have a lot of resolution (2464 X 1632 pixels). All of the photos are graded into four categories with the aid of ophthalmologists: normal, mild, moderate, and severe cataract. The ground truth dataset is then used to assess and validate our cataract detection system.

Another dataset is used in this suggested system includes of 1088 pictures of the fundus. Shanggong Medical Technology Co. Ltd. gathered the images from several hospitals and healthcare centres around China. The ODIR (Ocular Disease Intelligent Recognition) database, a structured ophthalmic database, has data on 5000 people, including their ages, colour fundus pictures of their left and right eyes, and diagnostic keywords are specified by clinicians (Available from https://www.kaggle.com/andrewmvd/ocular-disease-recognition-odir5k). Actually collected patient data make up the dataset. We only used photographs of cataracts for our purposes from the aforementioned databases. In this database, 212 people have cataracts in one or both eyes and 1140 people have normal retina. In Table 1, details of database is shown with the help of expert's opinion and knowledge base.

METHODOLOGY

Cataract diagnosis and severity gradations divided into four sections. Firstly, all the fundus images are pre-processed to remove the noise, to preserve boundary information and to enhance the quality. Secondly, the anatomical structures of retina such as OD, blood vessels are segmented and highlighted in binary form. Thirdly, image wise different relevant, computationally inexpensive features are extracted to make a feature based dataset. Lastly, image level multi class classification is done for determining severity of the cataract disease. Flow diagram of the whole work is depicted in Figure 2

Pre-Processing of Fundus Images

The retinal raw image data collection included pictures of patients with diverse eye pigment colours, from various age groups, and under various lighting circumstances. Pre-processing is done to get rid of certain irregularities, which will help us with the next processing. The following procedures are included in the pre-processing of retinal images and also depicted in Figure 3.

Figure 2. Work flow diagram of cataract detection and gradation system

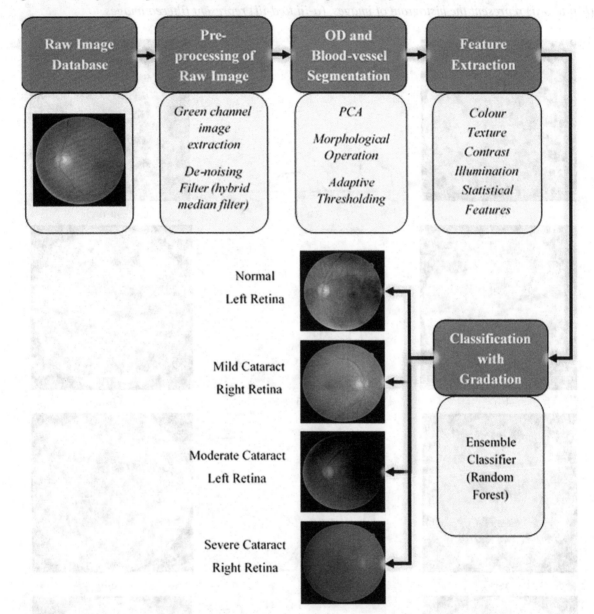

Green Channel Image Extraction

All the anatomical components of the retina, including the blood vessels and optic disc, need to be more clearly visible. As the green channel has the highest intensity of all the colour images, and the most contrast compared to the other colour channels, it is the channel that has been chosen to use because it enables us to further segment the retinal image.

Figure 3. Pre-processed fundus image. (a-i to d-i) represent RGB fundus images with different severity. (b-ii to d-ii) represent the histogram of images. (a-iii to d-iii) represent filtered images.

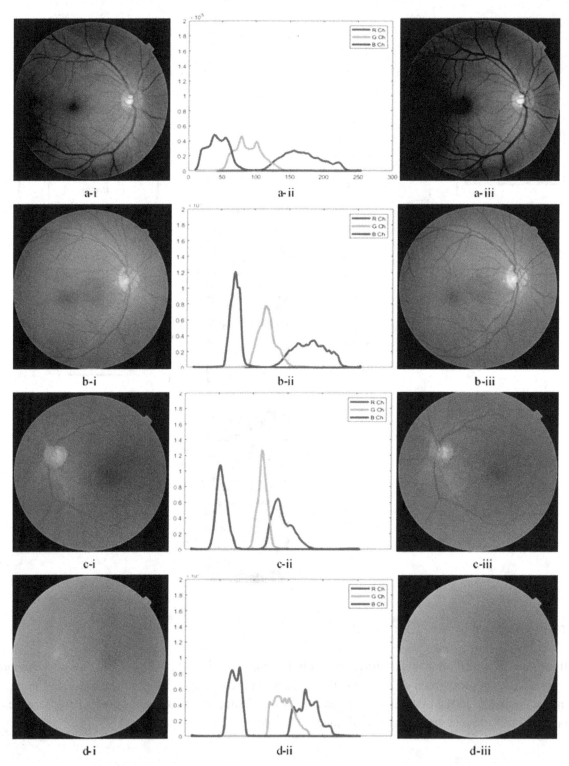

De-Noising Filtering

A diamond mask is often employed in combination with different kinds of median filters since it is well known that the median filter is particularly good at reducing impulsive noise. After that, the hybrid median filter (Seetharaman et al., 2021c) was created to sharpen images while maintaining their edges. Contrary to the traditional method, the hybrid filter generates the group or cluster of diagonal, reverse diagonal, and median values from the filter mask. Following each group's sorting, the median value is calculated for that group. By combining the median values for each group with the mask's median value, the final resulting median value is then determined. In Figure 3, all the pre-processed images are shown along with the histogram of each channel (R, G, B Channel) of colour fundus images.

Segmentation of Optic Disc (OD) and Blood Vessel

The optic disc and blood vessel are the retina's primary anatomical components. Each structure possesses a few distinctive clinical traits. We have employed principal component analysis (PCA), morphological operation and adaptive thresholding for this structure identification. First, we constructed three components of fundus image using PCA transformation and then morphological operations are employed for OD detection and adaptive thresholding is applied to extract the blood-vessel.

Principal Component Analysis (PCA)

According to statistical approaches, PCA is a type of linear transformation. This approach offers a potent tool for pattern identification and data analysis, which is frequently applied to signal and image processing (Abdi & Williams, 2010) as a way for data compression, data dimension reduction, or their decorrelation as well.

The most often used algorithms are the conversion of colour images to grayscale (intensity) images. Usually, it is implemented using the weighted sum of the three colour components R, G, and B in accordance with the relation shown below in Equation 1.

$$Im = w_R R_{im} + w_G G_{im} + w_B B_{im} \tag{1}$$

Image colour components are present in the R, G, and B matrices, and w_i denotes their respective weights. A different approach to this concept is offered by the PCA approach. Equation 2 demonstrates the concept by stating that the matrix A_l only requires l of the biggest eigenvalues, as opposed to n, to build it. Following relation is then used to provide the vector $\widehat{X}$ of the reconstructed variables.

$$\widehat{X} = A_l^T y + m_x \tag{2}$$

where m_x is a vector representing the mean values of each input variable.

True colour photographs of size $M{\times}N$ are often recorded in the three-dimensional matrix I with size $M{\times}N{\times}3$, which indicates that the data on the intensity of the colour components is kept in the three specified planes. The 3-dimensional vector of each colour may be used to generate the vector of input variables X. For easier comprehension and programming, three 1-dimensional vectors of length $M{\times}N$

may be formed from each plane $I(M,N,i)$. According to Equation 2, the 3-dimensionally reconstructed vector $\widehat{X}$ may be referred to as the first, second, and third components of the provided picture once the covariance matrix Cx and associated matrix A have been assessed. These three components of fundus images are shown in Figure 4 & Figure 5. These components are further segmented for OD and blood vessels.

Morphological Operation

Morphological procedures (Shaoo et al., 2018c) need the use of a structuring element, which is applied to the input image to produce an output image with the identical size. Every pixel's value in the generated output picture is determined by comparing it to its surrounding pixels in the input image. Images are dilated, eroded, and closed using three different morphological operators. Image (Im) dilation in Equation 3 with structuring element S is provided by

$$Im(D) = Im \oplus S \tag{3}$$

Picture erosion in Equation 4 with structural component S, which is located at its origin, is

$$Im(E) = Im \ominus S \tag{4}$$

A dilatation and erosion in Equation 5 accompany the image's closure. It's indicated by

$$Im(C) = Im \cdot S = (Im \oplus S) \ominus S \tag{5}$$

The blood-vessels are initially eliminated utilising a morphological operator of a closed picture with the appropriate structural element in order to determine the OD position. The choice of the structural element was made based on how brilliant the coloured fundus pictures were. To convert an RGB image to a binary image, the appropriate threshold value must be chosen since colour fundus images have variable brightness and contrast values. Images that have been distorted and erased are removed to create another image. This picture has now been converted to an intensity picture by the addition of the blue, red, and green channel pictures. This image has been transformed into a binary image after obtaining the intensity image. Hard and soft exudates, haemorrhages, and tiny red spots are all seen in the binary picture. Among all of them, the OD has been successfully identified using the suggested procedure. In this method, each blob's border pixel position values from the binary picture have first been saved. The area, perimeter, and roundness measure of each blob were then calculated. The form of the optic disc is known to be about round, and metrics closer to one suggest that the item is roughly spherical (little elliptical). The next step is to compare the area, perimeter, and roundness metrics for each blob and determine where the right optical disc should be located. In Figure 4 & 5, actual OD boundary marked by the expert and detected OD boundary by the morphological algorithm have shown.

Figure 4. Extraction of blood vessel and OD.(i to vi) Healthy image with PCA components (ii-PCA1, iii-PCA2, iv-PCA3), extracted blood-vessel, marked OD by expert in green and extracted OD in blue. (vii-xii) Mild cataract image with PCA components (viii-PCA1, ix-PCA2, x-PCA3), extracted blood-vessel, OD.

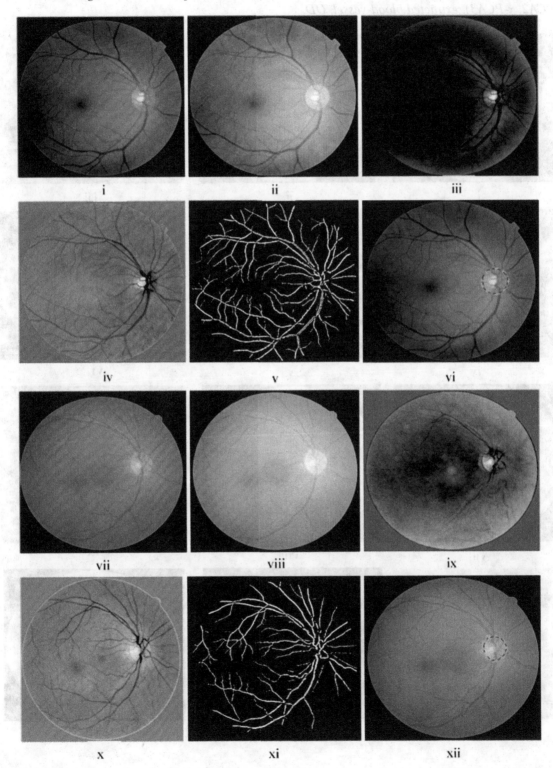

Figure 5. Extraction of blood vessel and OD for moderate and severe cataract.(i to vi) Moderate cataract image with PCA components (ii-PCA1, iii-PCA2, iv-PCA3), extracted blood-vessel, marked OD by expert in green and extracted OD in blue. (vii-xii) Severe cataract image with PCA components (viii-PCA1, ix-PCA2, x-PCA3), extracted blood-vessel, OD.

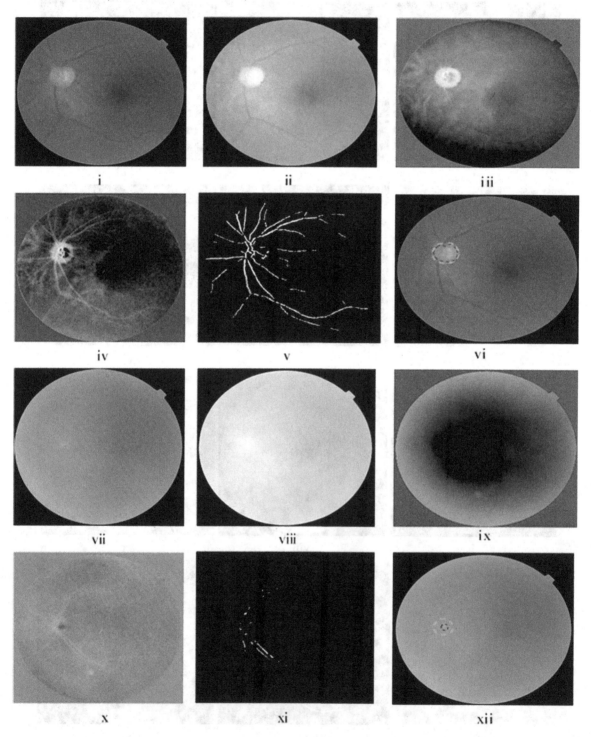

Adaptive Thresholding

An adaptive thresholding algorithm (Sahoo et al., 2018) is employed to extract the blood vessels. Extracted blood-vessel for different stage of cataract is shown in Figure 4 & 5. This method distinguishes between the foreground and background depending on the non-uniform lighting. In adaptive threshold, the threshold value at each pixel position is estimated by the intensities of the nearby pixels. The following is a description of the suggested adaptive thresholding algorithm:

Step 1: The pixel position (x,y) is surrounded by a user-defined $W{\times}W$ window.
Step 2: Make a calculation to determine the mean or average of each pixel point inside the $W{\times}W$ frame.
Step 3: Determine the weighted value of each pixel, represented by $A\left(x`,y`\right)$.
Step 4: The following expression in Equation 6, is then applied to calculate the threshold value $Th\left(x`,y`\right)$
at pixel location $\left(x`,y`\right)$:

$$Th\left(x`,y`\right) = A\left(x`,y`\right) - const \tag{6}$$

where *const* denotes the value stated as a fixed value in relation to the local average or median grey value, below which the local threshold is established.

Step 5: Dark patches on a white backdrop have been thresholded using positive values.
Step 6: All the pixel values inside the selected window are replaced by the calculated threshold value.
Step 7: Next window is selected of same size $W{\times}W$ and repeat the above steps until whole image is thresholded.

Image Level Feature Extraction

In order to segregate cataract images into different severity stages, classification plays a vital role and classifier depends on informative feature set extracted from the image.

Extracted Feature Based Dataset

Images with a cataract and those without one differ in colour, texture, intensity, contrast, shape, and size. In order to design an automated system that can evaluate the seriousness of an older person's cataract, a feature set is built for each picture. Table 2 provides a portrayal of the features set which is employed in the suggested scheme. In a classification model, different features play distinct roles. The annular mask feature of binary image with blood-vessel is an important feature for cataract detection. In various directions, the blood-vessels are dispersed. To exhibit the texture feature completely, the detail component from one direction is inadequate. As shown in Figure 6, feature extraction is carried out using annular masks (Yang et al., 2016) of various radii. We have drawn total 10 concentric circles on the basic region of interest. Distance between each circle is same. Hence, there are total 10 masks of same width each mask's pixel count is recorded. In this article. This annular mask wise pixel count is considered as fea-

Table 2. Features description for cataract detection at image level

Features types	Descriptions
Colour	Hue, saturation from HSV colour space. Mean, standard deviation and variance are determined from three component of RGB image using PCA.
Intensity	Contrast, correlation, global threshold of each gray image of retina.
Shape & Size	Area, perimeter of OD and blood-vessel, aspect ratio between actual OD and detected OD of each image
Texture	Homogeneity, energy, entropy, variance, correlation of gray scale image and annular mask feature of binary image.

tures. Less count of pixel results less details of blood-vessel. Information of blood-vessel helps to grade the severity of cataract image.

Classification and Severity Gradation

In order to categorise and rank the retinal fundus pictures into four distinct severity levels based on the retrieved characteristics, we used an ensemble classifier. Meta estimators include random forests that averages the results of many decision tree classifier fits to different subsamples of the dataset in order to increase predicted accuracy and reduce overfitting. A popular algorithm for classifying and predicting data is supervised machine learning, or Random forest (Gomes et al., 2017). It creates decision trees (DTs) on several samples and uses their average in the case of regression and majority vote for classification. An ensemble model, such as the random forest, simply combines different models. In order to create predictions, a set of models rather than just one is needed. As a sizable group of de-correlated DTs, the Random Forest algorithm functions. This method is often referred to as bagging. Bagging is

Figure 6. Annular mask on detected blood vessel to count the pixel number at each mask. (a) Annular mask on healthy image which provides more number of pixel count. (b) Annular mask on image with moderate cataract, which provides less number of pixel count.

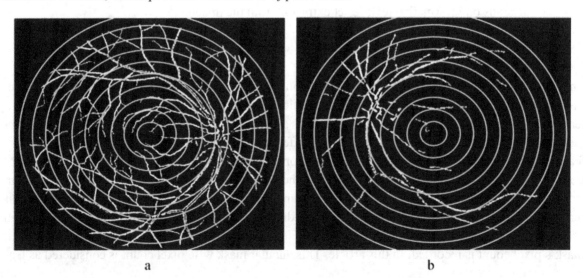

a   b

Figure 7. Working diagram of random forest classifier.

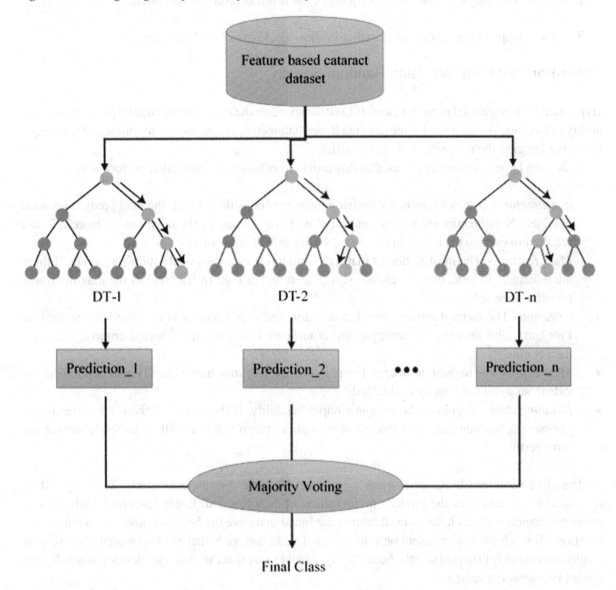

a form of ensemble learning that is based on the idea that by combining noisy and unbiased models, a low variance model may be produced.

The following describes the steps in the random forest algorithm:

The Random Forest Algorithm (Akar & Güngör, 2012) operates in a very simple manner. It is accomplished in two stages: the first involves constructing a random forest from N decision trees, and the second involves making predictions for each tree that was built during the first stage.

Step 1: Randomly select N data samples from the practise set.
Step 2: Each sample's DT is built separately.
Step 3: An output will be produced by each DT.

Step 4: Based on a majority vote for classification, the result is taken into account.

The above steps of random forest classifier is shown in Figure 7 as flow diagram.

Hyper-Parameter Tuning Using Random Search

Hyper-parameters are used in random forests to either speed up the model or enhance its performance and ability to forecast. We have used some selected hyper-parameters to tune using random search technique to further increase the assessment of the classifier.

Following hyper-parameters are used in this article to enhance the prediction performance.

- *n_estimators*– It shows how many decision trees were constructed until the final predictions were obtained. N estimators are mostly connected with the amount of the data; hence, more DTs are required to capture the trends in the data than the default value of 100.
- *Max_features*– The most attributes that a random forest evaluates while splitting a node. If there are n features in total, one can choose sqrt (n features) or log2 (n features) as the maximum features for node splitting.
- *Criterion*- The method through which a decision tree's split quality is evaluated (Classification Problem). Gini impurity or entropy-based criteria are examples of supported criteria. The standard is gini.
- *Max_depth*- The highest number of layers a decision tree may have. The DT will continue to divide if set to nil until purity is obtained.
- *Random_state*– Regulates the sample's unpredictability. If the model is given the same hyper-parameters, training data, and random state with a known value, it will consistently deliver the same results.

The aforementioned hyper-parameters were tweaked using the random search (Zabinsky, 2009) approach, which evaluates the model's performance while trying a different random combination of hyper-parameters with each iteration. It returns the blend that gave the best outcome after a number of iterations. It is a basic improvement on grid search. The advantage is that random search often returns results more quickly than grid search. Additionally, it makes sure that the model we develop is not skewed toward user-selected value sets.

RESULT AND DISCUSSION

Our algorithm is tested on two publicly available datasets namely Kaggle and ODIR dataset. The assessment is done at image level. From all the images, relevant features are extracted and make a feature based dataset. From this dataset, 70% data samples are considered as training set and 30% data samples are considered as testing set. We have trained the ensemble based random forest classifier with hyper-parameter tuning and this classification task is carried out into four-class two-class classification. For Kaggle dataset, 4 class and for ODIR dataset two-class classification are performed. The values of several performance metrics, including as accuracy (Equation 7), specificity (Equation 9), sensitivity (Equation 8), recall, precision (Equation 10), kappa-score, F-score (Equation 11), and confusion matrix, are

Table 3. Cataract gradation confusion matrices at the picture level

	True class	Predicted class			
		C_0	C_1	C_2	C_3
Kaggle Dataset	C_0	84	2	1	0
	C_1	1	7	0	0
	C_2	0	0	15	0
	C_3	0	0	1	10
		N		C	
ODIR Dataset	N#	1635		10	
	C$	4		156	

 # Healthy image. $ Cataract image

calculated during performance analysis. The correctly categorised samples are displayed by accuracy. The accurately categorised true positives and true negatives are sensitivity and specificity, respectively. Precision tells us how many of the projected good results are actually positive. The recall (sensitivity) and accuracy weighted average is known as the F1-score. A quality measure that links observed accuracy (A_0) and random accuracy (A_r) is the Kappa statistic (K-score). The following formula, shown in Equation 12, can be used to compute it. The confusion matrices show how many photos are correctly and wrongly categorised into the different grade groupings. Table 3 describe the confusion matrices, where C_0, C_1, C_2 and C_3 are represented as healthy retina, mild, moderate and severe cataract respectively. These metrics have the following mathematical expressions:

$$Accuracy\,(Acc) = \frac{TP+TN}{TP+FP+TN+FN} \tag{7}$$

$$Sensitivity\,(Spc) = \frac{TP}{TP+FN} \tag{8}$$

$$Specificity\,(Sen) = \frac{TN}{TN+FP} \tag{9}$$

$$Precision\,(Prc) = \frac{TP}{TP+FP} \tag{10}$$

Table 4. Evaluation of the suggested Cataract grading technique on a quantitative class-level basis

	Acc %	Sen	Spc	Prc	f-score	K-score
Kaggle Dataset	0.9667	96.55	96.97	98.82	-	-
	0.9748	87.50	98.20	77.78	-	-
	0.9831	100	98.06	88.24	-	-
	0.9915	90.91	100	100	-	-
Overall	97.93	95.87	98.62	95.87	95.87	0.911

$$F_1 - score = \frac{2TP}{2TP + FP + FN} \tag{11}$$

$$Kappa - score = \frac{A_0 - A_r}{1 - A_r} \tag{12}$$

The samples are split into four categories: true positive(TP), true negative(TN), false positive(FP), and false negative(FN) based on the original value and forecasted value (FN). Table 4 indicates the quantitative evolution of projected method.

Comparison with Previous Approaches

Comparing the proposed system to methods that have already been published at the picture level are used to quantitatively validate the system, as shown in Table 5. This table compares the widely used methods of cataract grading with our suggested method. Here, we have reported four class classification. We have achieved comparable performance analysis with respect to other methods in the literature. Achieved performance metrics for cataract detection include *Sen, Spc, Acc* for each class, and total *Acc*. The results shown are based on the test data set.

Table 5. Results of comparisons for cataract categorization

Methods	No of Classes	Sen%	Spec%	Acc%
Sirajudeen & Karthikeyan, 2021	2 –Class (N, C)	100	95	98.75
Imran et al., 2019c	2 –Class (N, C)	89.25	91.08	91.7
Pratap & Kokil, 2019	2 –Class (N, C)	92.92	93.09	92.91
Imran et al., 2019b	2 –Class (N, C)	95.4	93.7	93.79
Imran et al., 2020	4 class (C_0, C_1, C_2 & C_3)	95.64	96.01	95.65
Proposed Method	4-Class (C_0, C_1, C_2 & C_3)	95.87	98.62	**97.93**
	2 –Class (N, C)	99.76	93.98	**99.22**

CONCLUSION

This work presents a computer-aided supplementary diagnostic approach for categorising and evaluating cataracts using fundus images. It is useful for enhancing the cataract screening test in impoverished regions with insufficient medical resources such that patients of cataract in these places may quickly learn about their cataract diseases and receive treatment recommendations from physicians. Since false positives and false negatives have a substantial impact on medical views, we focus image-level evaluation while lowering both. The confusion matrices show how many photos are correctly and wrongly categorised into the various grade categories. Using the publicly accessible database, the suggested grading system produced good overall accuracy.

By employing some more trustworthy characteristics to differentiate between different levels of cataract severity, we hope to increase the system's efficacy in the future. Deep learning methods might be used to boost diagnostic accuracy. Performance assessments of the suggested technology, however, have shown that a system like this may be employed for a preliminary screening of cataract patients. This grading system aids in determining if a patient need more care.

REFERENCES

Abdi, H., & Williams, L. J. (2010). Principal component analysis. *Wiley Interdisciplinary Reviews: Computational Statistics*, *2*(4), 433–459. doi:10.1002/wics.101

Agarwal, V., Gupta, V., Vashisht, V. M., Sharma, K., & Sharma, N. (2019a). Mobile application based cataract detection system. In *2019 3rd International Conference on Trends in Electronics and Informatics (ICOEI)* (pp. 780-787). IEEE. 10.1109/ICOEI.2019.8862774

Akar, Ö., & Güngör, O. (2012). Classification of multispectral images using Random Forest algorithm. *Journal of Geodesy and Geoinformation*, *1*(2), 105–112. doi:10.9733/jgg.241212.1

Allen, D., & Vasavada, A. (2006). Cataract and surgery for cataract. *BMJ (Clinical Research Ed.)*, *333*(7559), 128–132. doi:10.1136/bmj.333.7559.128 PMID:16840470

Angeline, R., Vani, R., Jeshron Sonali, A., & Rao, D. A. (2022). Automated Detection of Cataract Using a Deep Learning Technique. In *Computational Intelligence in Machine Learning: Select Proceedings of ICCIML 2021* (pp. 399-408). Singapore: Springer Nature Singapore. 10.1007/978-981-16-8484-5_38

Chauhan, K., Dagar, K., & Yadav, R. K. (2022a). Cataract detection from eye fundus image using an ensemble of transfer learning models. In *2022 2nd International Conference on Advance Computing and Innovative Technologies in Engineering (ICACITE)* (pp. 2194-2198). IEEE. 10.1109/ICACITE53722.2022.9823638

Chua, J., Lim, B., Fenwick, E. K., Gan, A. T. L., Tan, A. G., Lamoureux, E., Mitchell, P., Wang, J. J., Wong, T. Y., & Cheng, C. Y. (2017). Prevalence, risk factors, and impact of undiagnosed visually significant cataract: The singapore epidemiology of eye diseases study. *PLoS One*, *12*(1), e0170804. doi:10.1371/journal.pone.0170804 PMID:28129358

Elloumi, Y. (2022). Cataract grading method based on deep convolutional neural networks and stacking ensemble learning. *International Journal of Imaging Systems and Technology, 32*(3), 798–814. doi:10.1002/ima.22722

Fan, W., Shen, R., Zhang, Q., Yang, J. J., & Li, J. (2015c). Principal component analysis based cataract grading and classification. In *2015 17th International Conference on E-health Networking, Application & Services (HealthCom)* (pp. 459-462). IEEE.

Gao, X., Wong, D. W. K., Ng, T. T., Cheung, C. Y. L., Cheng, C. Y., & Wong, T. Y. (2012, November). Automatic grading of cortical and PSC cataracts using retroillumination lens images. In *Asian Conference on Computer Vision* (pp. 256-267). Springer.

Gomes, H. M., Barddal, J. P., Enembreck, F., & Bifet, A. (2017). A survey on ensemble learning for data stream classification. *ACM Computing Surveys, 50*(2), 1–36. doi:10.1145/3054925

Guo, L., Yang, J. J., Peng, L., Li, J., & Liang, Q. (2015). A computer-aided healthcare system for cataract classification and grading based on fundus image analysis. *Computers in Industry, 69*, 72–80. doi:10.1016/j.compind.2014.09.005

Gupta, V., Jaiswal, A., Choudhury, T., & Sachdeva, N. (2023). Cataract Detection on Ocular Fundus Images Using Machine Learning. In P. Dutta, S. Chakrabarti, A. Bhattacharya, S. Dutta, & C. Shahnaz (Eds.), *Emerging Technologies in Data Mining and Information Security. Lecture Notes in Networks and Systems* (Vol. 490). Springer. doi:10.1007/978-981-19-4052-1_20

Imran, A., Li, J., Pei, Y., Akhtar, F., Yang, J. J., & Dang, Y. (2020). Automated identification of cataract severity using retinal fundus images. *Computer Methods in Biomechanics and Biomedical Engineering. Imaging & Visualization, 8*(6), 691–698. doi:10.1080/21681163.2020.1806733

Imran, A., Li, J., Pei, Y., Akhtar, F., Yang, J. J., & Wang, Q. (2019c). Cataract detection and grading with retinal images using SOM-RBF neural network. In *2019 IEEE Symposium Series on Computational Intelligence (SSCI)* (pp. 2626-2632). IEEE. 10.1109/SSCI44817.2019.9002864

Imran, A., Li, J., Pei, Y., Mokbal, F. M., Yang, J. J., & Wang, Q. (2019b). Enhanced intelligence using collective data augmentation for CNN based cataract detection. In *International Conference on Frontier Computing* (pp. 148-160). Springer.

Kaggle Cataract Dataset. (n.d.). https://www.kaggle.com/jr2ngb/cataractdataset/version/2

Khan, M. S., Tafshir, N., Alam, K. N., Dhruba, A. R., Khan, M. M., Albraikan, A. A., & Almalki, F. A. (2022). Deep Learning for Ocular Disease Recognition: An Inner-Class Balance. *Computational Intelligence and Neuroscience, 2022*, 2022. doi:10.1155/2022/5007111 PMID:35528343

Li, H., Ko, L., Lim, J. H., Liu, J., Wong, D. W. K., & Wong, T. Y. (2008b). Image based diagnosis of cortical cataract. In *2008 30th Annual International Conference of the IEEE Engineering in Medicine and Biology Society* (pp. 3904-3907). IEEE.

Li, H., Lim, J. H., Liu, J., Mitchell, P., Tan, A. G., Wang, J. J., & Wong, T. Y. (2010). A computer-aided diagnosis system of nuclear cataract. *IEEE Transactions on Biomedical Engineering, 57*(7), 1690–1698. doi:10.1109/TBME.2010.2041454 PMID:20172776

Li, H., Lim, J. H., Liu, J., Wong, D. W. K., Foo, Y., Sun, Y., & Wong, T. Y. (2010b). Automatic detection of posterior subcapsular cataract opacity for cataract screening. In *2010 Annual International Conference of the IEEE Engineering in Medicine and Biology* (pp. 5359-5362). IEEE.

Li, H., Lim, J. H., Liu, J., Wong, T. Y., Tan, A., Wang, J. J., & Mitchell, P. (2008a). Image based grading of nuclear cataract by SVM regression. In Medical Imaging 2008: Computer-Aided Diagnosis (Vol. 6915, pp. 985-992). SPIE. doi:10.1117/12.769975

Manchalwar, M., & Warhade, K. (2017). Detection of cataract and conjunctivitis disease using histogram of oriented gradient. *Int. J. Eng. Technol.*.

Nuzzi, R., Boscia, G., Marolo, P., & Ricardi, F. (2021). The Impact of Artificial Intelligence and Deep Learning in Eye Diseases: A Review. *Frontiers in Medicine, 8.*

Ocular Disease Recognition Dataset. (n.d.). https://www.kaggle.com/andrewmvd/ocular-disease-recognition-odir5k

Padalia, D., Mazumdar, A., & Singh, B. (2022). *A CNN-LSTM Combination Network for Cataract Detection using Eye Fundus Images.* arXiv preprint arXiv:2210.16093.

Polikar, R. (2006). Ensemble based systems in decision making. *IEEE Circuits and Systems Magazine, 6*(3), 21–45. doi:10.1109/MCAS.2006.1688199

Pratap, T., & Kokil, P. (2019). Computer-aided diagnosis of cataract using deep transfer learning. *Biomedical Signal Processing and Control, 53*, 101533. doi:10.1016/j.bspc.2019.04.010

Qiao, Z., Zhang, Q., Dong, Y., & Yang, J. J. (2017c). Application of SVM based on genetic algorithm in classification of cataract fundus images. In *2017 IEEE International Conference on Imaging Systems and Techniques (IST)* (pp. 1-5). IEEE. 10.1109/IST.2017.8261541

Ran, J., Niu, K., He, Z., Zhang, H., & Song, H. (2018b). Cataract detection and grading based on combination of deep convolutional neural network and random forests. In 2018 international conference on network infrastructure and digital content (IC-NIDC) (pp. 155-159). IEEE. doi:10.1109/ICNIDC.2018.8525852

Rokach, L. (2010). Ensemble-based classifiers. *Artificial Intelligence Review, 33*(1), 1–39. doi:10.100710462-009-9124-7

Sahoo, M., Pal, S., & Mitra, M. (2018c). A Novel Optic Disc and Blood Vessel Detection Algorithm. In 2018 IEEE Applied Signal Processing Conference (ASPCON) (pp. 74-78). IEEE. doi:10.1109/ASPCON.2018.8748519

Seetharaman, R., Tharun, M., & Anandan, K. (2021c). A novel approach in hybrid median filtering for denoising medical images. *IOP Conference Series. Materials Science and Engineering, 1187*(1), 012028. doi:10.1088/1757-899X/1187/1/012028

Sirajudeen, A., & Karthikeyan, S. (2021). *Detection of cataract through feature extraction by the novel angular binary pattern (NABP) and classification by kernel based convolutional neural networks.* Academic Press.

Syarifah, M. A., Bustamam, A., & Tampubolon, P. P. (2020c). Cataract classification based on fundus image using an optimized convolution neural network with lookahead optimizer. In AIP Conference Proceedings: Vol. 2296. *No. 1* (p. 020034). AIP Publishing LLC. doi:10.1063/5.0030744

Tawfik, H. R., Birry, R. A., & Saad, A. A. (2018). Early recognition and grading of cataract using a combined log Gabor/discrete wavelet transform with ANN and SVM. *International Journal of Computer and Information Engineering*, *12*(12), 1038–1043.

Weni, I., Utomo, P. E. P., Hutabarat, B. F., & Alfalah, M. (2021). Detection of Cataract Based on Image Features Using Convolutional Neural Networks. *Indonesian Journal of Computing and Cybernetics Systems*, *15*(1), 75–86. doi:10.22146/ijccs.61882

Xiong, L., Li, H., & Xu, L. (2017). An approach to evaluate blurriness in retinal images with vitreous opacity for cataract diagnosis. *Journal of Healthcare Engineering*, *2017*, 2017. doi:10.1155/2017/5645498 PMID:29065620

Xiong, Y., He, Z., Niu, K., Zhang, H., & Song, H. (2018c). Automatic cataract classification based on multi-feature fusion and SVM. In *2018 IEEE 4th International Conference on Computer and Communications (ICCC)* (pp. 1557-1561). IEEE. 10.1109/CompComm.2018.8780617

Xu, X., Guan, Y., Li, J., Ma, Z., Zhang, L., & Li, L. (2021). Automatic glaucoma detection based on transfer induced attention network. *Biomedical Engineering Online*, *20*(1), 1–19. doi:10.118612938-021-00877-5 PMID:33892734

Yang, J. J., Li, J., Shen, R., Zeng, Y., He, J., Bi, J., Li, Y., Zhang, Q., Peng, L., & Wang, Q. (2016). Exploiting ensemble learning for automatic cataract detection and grading. *Computer Methods and Programs in Biomedicine*, *124*, 45–57. doi:10.1016/j.cmpb.2015.10.007 PMID:26563686

Yang, M., Yang, J. J., Zhang, Q., Niu, Y., & Li, J. (2013c). Classification of retinal image for automatic cataract detection. In *2013 IEEE 15th International Conference on e-Health Networking, Applications and Services (Healthcom 2013)* (pp. 674-679). IEEE.

Zabinsky, Z. B. (2009). *Random search algorithms*. Department of Industrial and Systems Engineering, University of Washington.

Zhang, L., Li, J., Han, H., Liu, B., Yang, J., & Wang, Q. (2017b). Automatic cataract detection and grading using deep convolutional neural network. In *2017 IEEE 14th international conference on networking, sensing and control (ICNSC)* (pp. 60-65). IEEE.

Chapter 5
Study of the Image Segmentation Process Using the Optimized U-Net Model for Drone-Captured Images

Gunjan Mukherjee

(iD) https://orcid.org/0000-0002-3959-3718

Brainware University, India

Arpitam Chatterjee

Jadavpur University, India

Bipan Tudu

Jadavpur University, India

Sourav Paul

Ramakrishna Mission Vidyamandira, India & Swami Vivekananda Research Centre, India

ABSTRACT

Aerial views of the scenes captured by UAV or drone have become very familiar as they easily cover the wide view of the scene with different terrain types and landscapes. The detection of the scene images captured by drone and their subparts have been done on the basis of simple image processing approach involving the pixel intensity information. Many computer vision-based algorithms have successfully performed the tasks of segmentation. The manual approach of such segmentation has become time consuming, resource intensive, and laborious. Moreover, the perfection of segmentation on the irregular and noisy images captured by the drones have been lowered to greater extents with application of machine learning algorithms. The machine learning-based UNet model has successfully performed the task of segmentation, and the performance has been enhanced due to optimization. This chapter highlights the different variations of the model and its optimization towards the betterment of accuracy.

DOI: 10.4018/978-1-6684-7524-9.ch005

INTRODUCTION

The image processing operations have successfully been done by computer vision process. It encompasses image acquisition, processing and finally analysis by means of different computer vision oriented algorithms (Liu et al., 2012). For capturing and analysing images of different scenes like the images of landforms, land types, agricultural crops types etc., the Unmanned Aerial Vehicle (UAV) or the drone (Noor et al.,2018) has been engaged as it can capture images over the large surface area of regular or irregular landforms efficiently. Drones commonly known as Remotely Piloted Aircrafts (RPA)appears in different types like multirotor, fixed wings hybrid, etc. according to their scopes and principles of works. Highly resolved imageries and coverage of wide geographical area for the detailed and meticulous analysis of different scenes on the surface of earth helps in formation of robust database of various different but coherent images.

Several factors like less operational costs, less atmospheric inferences and the capability of flying with low altitudes has made the UAV much effective mean in commercial and scientific exploration of data from varieties of landforms on the surface of earth. The main challenge lies in accurate identification of landforms and proper segmentation of different regions with loss of minimum information in identification of any objects, crop lands. The timely identification process with rapid and accurate information of different objects has become possible by advent of deep learning approach.

The drones have been successfully used to capture images of moving traffics, green crops fields, dense forests, busy road ways, individual cars parked at different traffic spots, traffic moving on the flyovers, people flocking over the zones, farm terrain topography, congested trafficking, images of surveillance etc. The imageries captured by the UAV contain many types of noises as well as mutual overlapping and hence requires proper segmentation in order to be identified accurately. The application of deep learning approach has made the process of segmentation much smooth, easy and less time taking. Initially the segmentation of area of interest zones of any image has been performed on the basis of pixel intensity where basic concepts of image processing have been utilized. The subpart of the image has been extracted on the basis of colour and other image features. The colour feature (Ahmed & Wesam, 2012) based extraction of the image part was not always accurate so much as it appeared to be in the image. The rapid and abrupt variation of local patch of colour intensity made the overall process fail. Moreover the image of irregular terrains captured by the drones might not be discernable to the highest and utmost accuracy level. The typical landforms along with the undefined irregularity of captured scene sometimes falls beyond the proper identification of the segmented image by means of mere computer vision approach. The machine learning approach has been a boon as it overcomes many aspects of difficulties involved in the manual approach and sometimes skip hazards of long feature engineering steps. The shortcomings like the labour-intensive manual approach in separation process of image segmentation, time constraints for segmentation of subsection of the mages, maintaining proper accuracies in properly identifying image parts. All these concerned problems could be tackled by using the machine learning approach. The U-Net model (Huimin et al., 2020) has been based on the machine learning principles and consists of many layers of convolution filters. The typical structure of the U-Net based on both the expansive and contracting paths has made the architecture a good fit for segmentation of image properly. Later on the model U-Net has undergone many changes and proposed modifications as per different multiple problem situation. The optimisation of the model has also helped in overcoming time lags in operation and execution of the model. The Binary Particle Swarm Optimisation (BPSO) (Pegado et al., 2019) and Grey Wolf Optimisation (GWO) (Wang & Lil, 2019) technique-based optimisation has been addressed in this paper. The detailed discussions regarding model architecture and other variations have been dealt in details in the following sections.

The brief discussion over many eminent research papers has provided a fruitful discussion and the result analysis of the optimisers applied on U-Net model has provided the good research direction. Some of the previous works involving the U-Net model and its variation has been recorded with analysis of concerned methodologies in Table 1. The result accuracy analysis of the works confirms the further application of the model in more complex situations.

Review of Different Image Segmentation Methodologies

The deep convolution network has been proved to have outperformed other machine learning models in case of visual perception. The Convolution neural network (CNN) (Shin et al.,2016) and its different variants have been utilized to perform the classification tasks of different objects based on feature engineering. The wide variety of concerned and the discriminatory features help in more efficient classification of the objects. In spite of such efficient accuracy in classification process, it still suffers from the drawback related to the size of the training datasets and the network sizes. For large datasets with the millions of parameters, the model urgently requires more efficient, larger and deeper network structure.

In case of traditional convolution network appointed in visual perception of single class label, the output can be efficient classifier but in many visual tasks like the biomedical image classification or the drone captured image classification, the model fails as the localisation of pixels have been provided much priority with attachment of class labels to each pixels and continued for the large sized image having millions of pixels as content.

The newly formed model shows much creditworthiness due to its capacity of proper localization and handling of large set of training data with relatively larger size in the patch formed. It also suffers from two distinct shortcomings like slowness in execution as the number of patches are concerned even with the overlapping and secondly the requirement of more number of max pooling layers act in reducing overall accuracy while the smaller patches with reduced accuracies. Many different models have been proposed in this direction in order to perform the image segmentation with the utmost accuracy (Shi & Malik, 2000). proposed an algorithm N-cut to enhance the criterion of cutting the segments of images. Boycov et al. (2006) reported a graph cut algorithm to extend the traditional graph based cutting to the image domain. Huang et al. (2011) proposed a fuzzy based algorithm amalgamated with the watershed algorithm towards better accuracy in implementation of Fuzzy C Means (FCM) in image segmentation. Dhanachandra et al. (2015) reported an K Means base subtractive algorithm which has been further extended to deep learning domain to extract the image segments with high value of accuracy. Trusculescu et al. (2020) proposed an deep learning based conventional networks in order to smoothly and accurately extract the image contours from the input image. Noh et al. (2017) extended the convolution neural network architecture to more robust deep convolution by including VGG16 layers. Gu et al. (2018) proposed an unique model based on the combination of convolution neural net along with the probability map model resulting into the more accurate and precise image segmentation. Marmanis et al. (2015) showed an deep learning model based on the combination of carpooling and down sampled in Deep Convolution Neural Networks (DCNN) towards achieving the invariance. Zhao et al. (2019) proposed a combinational model with the responses in the final layer attached to the fully connected conditional random field. Hamdi et al. (2022) designed the adversarial network with Multi-scale SegAN. Çiçek et al. (2016) proposed much updated and robust model U-Net resulting into relatively greater accuracy in segmenting the bio

Table 1. Related works with methodologies

Research	Methodologies Used	Result Accuracy
(Zongwei et al., 2018)	U-Net++ model has been used for medical segmentation. The use of the skip pathways reduces semantic gap between the encoder and decoder. The residual block along with the attention mechanism has been introduced in to the encoding and decoding phase of the U-Net in order to improve the model to get more better accuracy	The Intersection over Union (IOU) gain of 3.9 and 3.4 have been reported over the U-Net and wide U-Net architecture.
(Deng et al., 2020)	The USM-U-Net algorithm has been used to overcome the colour deviation and contrast shift problems reserving the image information intact.	The SSM value has been computed at 75% and with PSNR value at 17.64%.
(Zhang et al., 2021)	CrackU-Net model has been designed to overcome the problems of detection of cracks in low pixel precision environment of the deep learning model	The precision value achieved in the work has been estimated up to 91% in test datasets and up to 99% in the Crack Forest dataset.
(Bhatnagar et al., 2020)	The CNN based transfer learning algorithm has been utilised. The combination of the ResNet50 and Segnet has been used for semantic segmentation of the drone captured images.	The accuracy value of the segmentation has been estimated at 90%.
(Feng et al., 2020)	The end-to-end U-Net with the residual blocks have been designed to tackle the inverse problem in photoacoustic imaging.	The performance accuracy obtained in the reconstructed images has been estimated at 95% using Pearson correlation. It shows the improvement in performance over in PSNR in the simulation environment by nearly 18%.
(Du et al., 2021)	The attention mechanism-based U-Net model has been proposed with the PSP-Net pyramid pooling model. The global information has been collected on the basis of context information with inclusion of Attention Net.	The accuracy obtained in this procedure has been estimated up to 98%.
(Ulmas et al., 2020)	The U-Net model has been developed to automatically perform the land cover mapping and to cope up with the changes in the landcover with the classification ad semantic segmentation. The research work was based on the dataset CORINE land cover map of Estonia.	The F1 score estimated in this project is at 75% in the multiclass classification with 43 possible image labels.
(Li et al., 2021)	The U-Net model developed in this work is concerned to the data augmentation, normalization, defining h image size and loss functions with high performance accuracy result.	The mean IOU of 70% has been achieved on the drone deployed dataset.
(Xiangyi et al., 2021)	The concept of the Axial Fusion Transformer U-Net based on the dual features of convolutional layer's capability of extracting the detailed features and transformer's capability of representing the long sequence modelling.	The ablation study has been estimated at 97.8% approximately.
(Wang et al., 2022)	The proposed working is based on the atrous convolution and multi kernel pooling in order to get more contextual information.	The accuracy value of 97% has been achieved in this work.
(Boycov et al., 2006)	This paper introduced the concept of Fuzzy c means algorithm by using the auto adjustment of the kernel weight.	The reported NMI value of 92% has been achieved
(Huang et al., 2011)	In this work the global perspective has been represented in the hierarchical way. The groping problems has been solved in terms of graph to get the normalised and unbiased measure.	High relative ratio of the histogram bins.
(Day et al., 2001)	The proposed work referred to the extension of the UNet architecture from the two dimension to the three dimensional operational form by using the elastic deformation for efficient data augmentation.	The reported IOU of 98.3% has been achieved.
(Li et al., 2021)	This research directed a path for the segmentation of any image extraction of the spatial and context information. This also combined the higher semantic information from the decoder to the lower semantic information of the encoder.	The achieved result of 94% has been reported.
(Wu et al., 2018)	The proposed method is performing the multi constraint approach to the building of high resolution aerial imageries	The coefficient of Kappa measured for this research work at 98.7%
(Khelifi et al., 2017)	Multi objective optimisation based fusion model has been proposed in order to overcome the shortcomings of single criterion for region-based variation of information.	The reported estimation of the scores over the others have been found above 90% approx.

medical images. Day et al. (2001)designed V-Net performing on the three-dimensional image data with outstanding result of accuracy. Cakir et al. (2019) proposed another improved type of segmenting model named Unaccustomed to the unsupervised image segmentation. Canziani et al. (2016) proposed anther more efficient and faster model ENet due to the presence of a smaller number of flops.

UNET MODEL

Two-Dimensional U-Net Model Architecture

The newly proposed fully convolutional network is the modification which works with comparatively smaller dataset with precise segmentation accuracy. The entire network has been formed out of the contracting networks with the pooling operators being replaced by up-sampling layers. The high-resolution image features are being combined together with up sampled outputs. This architectural pattern is followed in the convolution network to make assembly of information to maintain the precision in production of outputs. The presence of large number of feature channels in the up-sampling path helps in learning the context information towards path of higher resolution. The contracting paths are similarly being shaped in expanding form making the model looking like an 'U' shaped one. The absence of the fully connected layers in the model provides exposure to all the pixels and the contexts of the image at large. The seamless segmentation strategies for any arbitrarily oriented images can be interpreted well by managing the missed out pixels by means of extrapolation.

The network model architecture of 2-dimensional U-Net(Li et al.,2021) in shown in Figure 1 consists of two distinct paths namely contracting path appearing on the left side and expanding path appearing on right side of the structure. The contracting path comprises of the sudden course of repetition of two 3X3 convolution networks with each followed by a rectified linear unit (ReLU) and a 2X2 max pooling operation with stride size 2. The contracting path is responsible for down sampling operation. The expansive path appearing on the right side of the structure consists of the up sampling of the feature map. Each step of operations on the expansive path consists of the up-sampling operation of feature map followed by the 2X2 by convolution followed by the two 3X3 convolutions with each followed by the rectified linear unit (ReLU). The 2X2 convolutions makes the feature channels halved. The concatenation of the cropped feature maps coming from the contracting path takes place with the feature maps available in expansive path. In order to compensate the loss of border pixels, the cropping has been pursued. Finally, a 1X1 convolution has been used in order to do the mapping of 64 component features to the number of classes desired. The network altogether manipulates 2 convolution layers.

Multi Constraint Fully Convolution Networks

Building detection by segregating the building from surrounding is the challenging task which involves UAV. Many numbers of algorithms have been proposed to track this problem and the major disciplines of categorisation of such detection process are of the categories like threshold based, edge based, region based and classification based. The abrupt changes in illuminance and texture prevent the edge and region-based thresholding and cannot provide any stable results. Thresholding technique cannot segment different regions having the similar grey scale values. The multi scale features led to the imposition of multicentricity on the variables concerned to the model (Wu et al., 2018).

Figure 1. 1D U-Net model architecture

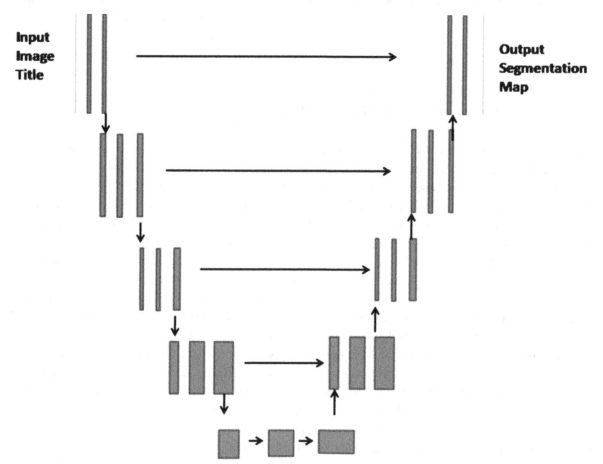

Multi Criterion-Based U-Net

Classification based method is efficient enough to segregate the pixels by putting them into respective categories. The machine learning algorithm can easily perform the task in two step processes first step involves extraction of features from the image and the second one involves classification task. The entire procedure involves the convolution filters combined with fully connected layers in sequential way. Feature extraction is concerned to the data and with the better generalization capability. The CNN works depends on the patches formed. Memory cost of covering the entire image increases with patch-based approach. The lowering of computing efficiency becomes the major factor in this method.

The replacement of fully connected layers with up-sampling operation improves the computing performance part to some extent. Some encoder decoder convolution models like Segment and DeconvNet use the part of network and thus reduces lower edge accuracy. As a remedial panacea to such problem the U-Net model with the bottom up or Top down architecture design has been introduced with skip connection. The performance has been enhanced further by combining the lower and upper layers.

Instead of good relative efficiency with respect to the U-Net architecture also suffers from some drawbacks (i) The typical shape of the U-Net prompts updating its parameters in the fringe layers with higher priority compared to the intermediate layer during the back propagation iteration recursively (Khelifi et al., 2017). As a consequence, the intermediate layers are affected and get ignored in the semantic contribution towards segmentation process. (ii)The multistage representation is capable of generalizing the features of the model and so has been preferred more. (iii) The application of explicit constraints is significant in order to enhance the loose constraints to be applied to the intermediate layers. The continuous and repeated updation of parameters helps in keeping the parameters at abeyance from being biased with any single constraint.

Three-Dimensional U-Net Architecture

3D U-Net architecture (Cicek et al., 2016) shown in Figure 2 is the variation of 2D U-Net model which works on the volumetric segmentation in 3D space. The model structure consists of contracting and expansive path. The core structure consists of the 3D convolution, followed by the max pooling and up convolution of 3 dimensions. The 3-dimensionalimages show better merits over the 2D images as 3D images consist of number of repeating structures which result into redundant information. This sort of data makes overall training process of the model a lot easier as relatively smaller number of annotated examples have been sufficiently used for training of the model. Some medical applications of U-Net 3D model can be stated as liver tumour segmentation, lung node segmentation, brain tumour segmentation etc. The 3D U-Net model has sought application in the Aerial images captured by the drones due to its semi automatic and fully automated segmentation and his network was used also for the multilevel abstraction of different sort of images.

Attention U-Net

This network has been developed based on the abstraction of information from the object of interest. The object of importance has been focused ignoring rest of the images. The principles of such Network is to scrap the irrelevant information in order to focus on the object of interest only with help of Attention gate (Fiebelkorn et al., 2020). The redundant features have been trimmed off on use of such unit. The task of transmission of the features takes place from contracting layers to the expansive layers before being mixed with the unsampled features in the expansive path. The performance of model has been enhanced due to repeated use of the Gate resulting into drastic fall of complexities of the layered architecture. As opposed to the global classification, the local classification has been given priority in such Network as per the tuning with particular objects specified inside the image which can better be controlled with the local classification process rather than the global approach of classification.

Reviews of U-Net Model

The aerial images captured by drones contain mixed type components against the complex background. The objects can easily be segmented by using such Attention Net. Moreover, during the hovering of drone over the certain routes, the captured aerial image may be treated as localized with respect to entire scene captured by the device. Out of the different attention gates, the additive attention gate has been proved to be efficient in the segmentation aspect. Some of the contribution in attention-based U-Net model have been stated (Elsayed et al., 2019) referred to the hard attention-based model utilising the reinforcement learning for parameter updates. The work was equally visible on the recursive and extraction approach.

Figure 2. Three-dimensional U-Net model architecture

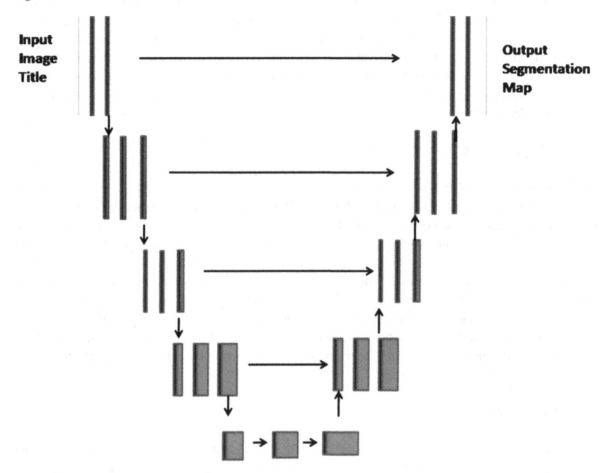

Ypsilantis et al. (2017) proposed an advanced hard Attention based U-Net model to detect anomalies in the chest Xray scans. Hu et al. (2017) implemented channel wise attention based model to highlight the prime features dimension and scored accolades in the ILSVRC2017. Jetley et al. (2018) and Wang et al. (2017) proposed an attention framework independent of the Gating information using the nonlocal approach. Jetley et al. (2018) and Wang et al. (2017) have performed the class specific pooling resulting into robust image classification performance.

Tracking Irregular Segmentation Using Shaped Network

Crop disease detection is of paramount interests in order to prevent huge economic losses due to damaging of large number of crops in the field of agriculture. The crops can get affected by different types of fungal or bacterial infections. Such infections can easily be prevented if the early detection of the scenario is tracked. The crops may get recovered also from such bacterial infection depending on the degree of infection of plants. Firstly, the regular calendar-based pesticide application cannot be always proved as effective means to get rid of such menace. Secondly in the vast stretch of land, it becomes very difficult to track all portion of the fields for diseased plants. Moreover, the entire process cost us huge and takes a lot of time as well. One important solution towards that problem is to capture images through satellites or UAV. Different research works have been carried out by means of some efficient and high resolution cameras such as the UAV with RGB camera at an altitude of 100 meters has been used to capture the images of the crops field. In case of detection of disease like yellow rusts, it has been proved that multispectral imagery of crops has been proved to be much more efficient in tracking the disease type easily. It has been also reported that the UAV with five-band multispectral camera showed extra information towards detection process. With the advancement of deep learning technology, the CNN model has been successfully used to track such disease infection both in two and the three-dimensional fields.

In addition to the presence of such improved arrangements and the technological progress, still some problems get prominent in getting the exact and accurate image. The yellow rust image appears to be irregular especially to the boundary patch of image captured by the camera. At the same time the middle portion of the patch image may be represented as very serious and can be tracked as having the high and regular intensity value which gradually decreases towards boundary of patch and fails to provide with enough information in extracting the image part of infected zones. The irregular boundary problem could be handled with many approaches with high accuracy in extracting the sharp boundary of urban landscape but fails to provide the exactness in extracting the crop disease detection.

OPTIMISATION IN UNET ARCHITECTURE

The U-Net architecture consists of number of convolution layers, pooling layers and dense layers. The variables under the convolution layers are image size, kernel size and stride size. Variables under the pooling layers are kernel size, stride size and the dense layer consists of number of nodes. The model can be optimised by subjecting it to either the Binary Particle Swarm Optimisation (BPSO) or Grey Wolf Optimisation (GWO) techniques. Each of the optimising methodologies has been discussed in the sections 4.1 and 4.2 respectively.

Binary Particle Swarm Optimisation (BPSO)

Binary Particle Swarm Optimisation (BPSO) is the evolutionary optimization algorithm based on the swarms. The social behaviours of the animals or birds flocking in search of foods are used to study these special algorithms. The particles in swarm always keep on updating their position and velocities according to the change in situation. In order to meet the real need of proximity and quality with continuous change of two attributes, the searching continues in optimal search space. The particles in the swarm track position and velocities of individuals and the swarm as well. The search process for the particles is confined to the multidimensional search space and the position and velocity value of the concerned particle is computed on the basis of combined effect of position and velocity of other particles. The overall process consists of swarm optimization followed by the particle fitness evaluation, calculation of individual particle wise optimal position and swarm optimal position. The velocity of individual particle and the swarm has been calculated as per the equation. The particles in the swarm keep track with personal best or the pbest and global best gbest. The particle velocity gets updated following the Eq. 1.

$$V_i^d\left(t+1\right)=WV_i^d\left(t\right)+c_1r_1\left(P_{b_1}^d\left(t\right)-P_i^d\left(t\right)\right)+c_2r_2\left(g_b^d\left(t\right)-P_i^d\left(t\right)\right) \tag{1}$$

Where d implies the dimension of the particle, t implies the iteration, $r1$ and $r2$ are the random numbers in the interval $(0,1)$. The positive acceleration constants are denoted by $c1$ and $c2$ respectively. $P_{b_1}^d$ implies the personal best and g_b^d implies the global best in the swarm. W stands for the positive inertia weight.

The position of the particle gets updated as per the Eq. (2)

$$x_i^d(t+1) = x_i^d(t) - V_i^d(t+1) \tag{2}$$

The convergence characteristic curve for the BPSO model has been shown in the Fig 1.2 for optimisation of the U-Net model.

Grey Wolf Optimisation (GWO)

Grey Wolf Optimisation (GWO) is the meta heuristic and bio-inspired based algorithm which emulates the wolf behaviour where the wolves inside the pack are running after the target prey. This algorithm narrates the social behaviours of the wolves in a pack while facing any prey in front of them. The entire wolf community has been divided into four categories with each one having been ranked by their activeness like alpha(α), beta(β), delta(δ) and omega(ω) wolves. Grey wolves start attacking the prey after encircling it once the search for the same is over. The position update for α, β, δ and ω happens following the Eq. (3) and (4).

$$\bar{D} = |\bar{C} \cdot \bar{X}_p(t) - \bar{X}(t)| \tag{3}$$

$$\bar{X}(t+1) = |\bar{X}_p - \bar{A} \cdot \bar{D}(t)| \tag{4}$$

where, $\vec{A}, \vec{C}$, and $\vec{D}$ are the respective random vectors representing encircling behaviours of the wolves. t denotes the current iteration, $\bar{A} = 2a \cdot \vec{r}_1 a$ and $\vec{C} = 2 \cdot \vec{r}_2 a$ implies the control parameter expressed as in Eq. (5).

$$a = 2\left(1 - \frac{it}{N}\right) \tag{5}$$

Where, N implies the maximum number of iterations, $\bar{r}_1$ and $\bar{r}_2$ denote the random numbers in $(0,1)$. The vectors $\vec{X}$ and $\vec{X}_p$ are used to denote the location of the grey wolf and the prey, respectively. The variable a is used in iteration and changes from 2 to 0 linearly. The relative updates are mathematically presented as Eqs (6) -(8).

$$\vec{D}_\alpha = |C_1 \cdot \vec{X}_\alpha - \vec{X}| \tag{6}$$

$$\vec{D}_\beta = |\,C_2 \cdot \vec{X}_\beta - \vec{X}\,| \tag{7}$$

$$\vec{D}_\delta = |\,C_3 \cdot \vec{X}_\delta - \vec{X}\,| \tag{8}$$

X_α, $X\beta$ and $X\delta$ denote the position of α, β and δ. C1, C2, and C3 implies the set of random vectors in (0, 1). $\vec{X}$ represents the current solution position. The step size of the ϖ wolf is represented in terms of the Eqs (9) - (12).

$$\vec{X}_1 = \vec{X}_\alpha - \vec{A}_1 \cdot \vec{D}_\alpha \tag{9}$$

$$\vec{X}_2 = \vec{X}_\beta - \vec{A}_2 \cdot \vec{D}_\beta \tag{10}$$

$$\vec{X}_3 = \vec{X}_\delta - \vec{A}_3 \cdot \vec{D}_\delta \tag{11}$$

$$\vec{X}(t+1) = \frac{\vec{X}_1 + \vec{X}_2 + \vec{X}_3}{3} \tag{12}$$

X_1, X_2, and X_3 are the final and updated position vectors of the α, β, and δ wolves, respectively. $\vec{A}_1, \vec{A}_2$, and $\vec{A}_3$ vectors represent the random vectors in (0, 1). The vectors $\vec{A}_1$ and $\vec{C}$ are effective in exploration and exploitation for the GWO algorithm. The exploration phase for the wolves occurs when $|\bar{A}| < -1$ and $|\bar{A}| > 1$. The exploitation of wolf occurs when $|\vec{C}| > 1$. The controlling parameter a has impact on the vector $\vec{A}$. It is also responsible for change in behaviour of the ϖ wolves with respect to the prey. $|\bar{A}| > 1$, implies that the grey wolf run away from the prey resulting in the larger search domain mapped out as the global search space in optimisation. On other hand, the $|\bar{A}| < 1$, implies that the ϖ wolves approach the dominant resulting in the shrinking of the search space termed as the local search.

The average of all the updated positions of the corresponding wolves determines the solution position in the standard GWO. This implies that each of the wolves approaches or run away from the prey with the average weight of the respective wolves. α, β, and δ wolves are dynamic in nature. At the beginning, the position of the α wolf is near most to the prey and in the due course of time, the position gets shifted away. On the other hand the position of β and δ wolves can vary keeping the position of β wolves less than or equal to that of α wolves and position of δ wolves less than or equal to that of the β wolves with respect to the dominant wolf or prey. The prior scenario describes the fact that the α wolves are not always dominant and its weight can decrease at the cost of increase in the weight values of the β and δ wolves.

In order to achieve optimised approach of attack to the prey, the algorithm can further be altered. Many research works are being carried out for the intended results.

Review of Binary Particle Swarm Optimisation (BPSO)

Optimisation of the hyper parameters concerned to the U-Net model can be done using BPSO algorithm. In this regard, some of the works have been cited (Lee et al., 2008) reported the modified BPSO algorithm adopting the genotype- phenotype representation and the mutation operators. (Young & Mohamed., 2014) Referred to the application of BPSO algorithm on the localization of the distributed nodes cluster. The case of localisation has been extended to the unknown nodes. (Ding 2017) informed about the multi objective particle swarm optimisation based on the improved culture with highly improved convergence values. (Tuyen 2021) has reported about the PSO U-Net model with best number of layers and parameters of layers in the U-Net based architecture in order to improve the flash flood segmentation on satellite captured images.

Reviews of Grey Wolf Optimisation (GWO)

Some of the works based on GWO algorithm are (Hou et al., 2022) has reported about the improved GWO algorithm towards the global search optimisation using the nonlinear convergence factor based on the Gaussian distribution. (Hassan et al., 2017) proposed the optimised 5 BUS and Western System Coordinating Council (WSCC 9) BUS test systems in gaining the shorter CPU time and minimized cost (Mustaffa et al., 2016) has described about the hybridisation of the GWO with Least square support vector machine (LSSVM) for the prediction of water level with high score of comparisons over the other existing algorithm. Negi et al. (2021) presented different development in the GWO and its multiple applications towards more complex real-world problem domains. Gao and Zhao (2019) proposed the variable weight based GWO algorithm with possible reduction solution in the probability of being trapped in local maxima resulting into the better accuracy in the high dimensional problems. Mirjalili et al. (2014) described the GWO algorithm benchmarked on the 29 well known test functions with the comparative studies of PSO, GSA, DE, EP, ES, etc. with the better results of accuracy. Mukherjee et al. (2022) proposed the modified Grey wolf optimised mobile net classier in order to classify the different tomato fruit diseases with accuracy result of nearly 98%.

Convergence of the Curves

The convergence curves for the optimiser Binary Particle Swarm Optimisation (BPSO) and Gray Wolf Optimisation (GWO) have been shown in the Figure 3 and Figure 4. In both the figures, the accuracy values have been plotted against the number of iterations. Figure 3 shows the classification of drone captured image datasets by the UNet model optimised by the BPSO optimiser. The accuracy value shows a steep rise with the iteration which further gets converged slowly with increase in iteration and finally has reached an accuracy value of 99% approximately. On the other hand for figure 4, the convergence curve has been plotted for the UNet model optimised by the GWO optimiser. The convergence curve has attained 98% accuracy over 100 iterations.

Both the curves in Figures 3 and Figures 4 have vouched for good and consistent convergence for optimisers BPSO and GWO applied on the proposed Net model. The nature of convergence for both

Figure 3. The convergence curves for BPSO

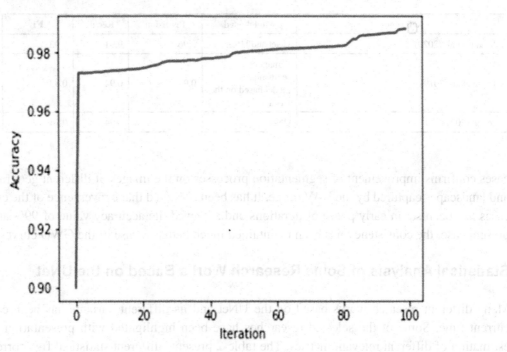

Figure 4. The convergence curves for GWO curves

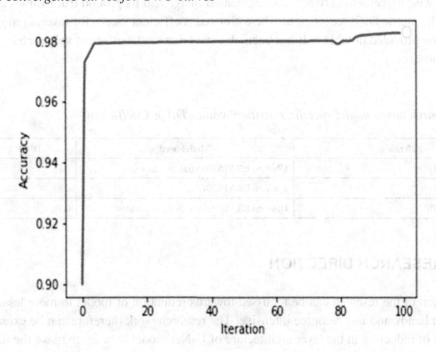

Table 2. Research based model specific statistical values for metrics

Reference	Model used	Precision	Recall	F1	Accuracy
Alexakis et al. (2020)	UNet and UNet++	0.96	0.91	0.93	0.99
Girisha et al. (2019)	Semantic segmentation model based on the UNet	0.94	0.94	0.93	0.97
Li et al. (2021)	UNet	0.94	0.94	0.94	0.98

cases confirms improvement of segmentation processes on the images of different geographic terrains and landscapes captured by the UAV drone. It has been observed that convergence of the curves in both cases has been set in early phase of iterations and achieved the accuracy value of 99% around. In the present case, the consistency has been maintained much better in case of the GWO curves.

Statistical Analysis of Some Research Works Based on the UNet

Many different research works based on the UNet and its different variants has been carried out in current time. Some of the selected researches have been highlighted with presentation of statistical estimation of different relevant metrics. The table-2 presents different statistical figs corresponding to different research works. The metric F1 score is a measure of accuracy of two classification problems. It has been observed that the F1 score or the UNet based segmentation as reported in (Li et al., 2021) has been higher compared to the others.

The pixel wise agreement between any segmented image and its ground truth values are compared by means of the metric DICE coefficient. The estimated coefficient values for several reported research works has been provided in table 3. It has been observed that the Coefficient values change with training dataset chosen.

Table 3. Research based model specific statistical values DICE Coefficient

Reference	Model used	DICE Coefficient
Dong et al. (2017)	UNet on BRATS2015 training data sets	0.86
Le et al. (2018)	UNet on BRATS2013	0.85
Kapdi et al. (2020)	UNet on BRATS2019 with 75%quantiles	0.96

FUTURE RESEARCH DIRECTION

Future direction of the research can be focussed towards reduction of model to more lesser size in order to make it handy and less resource intensive. The research work therefore can be extended to have higher degree of reduction in the layer architecture of U-Net model in order to make the model lighter, less resource centric and highly capable for precision performance. Further the model can further be optimised to make it implemented on the hand-held device like mobile phone to make it reachable to bigger section of public domain for analysis of captured images by drone.

CONCLUSION

This paper reviews on drawbacks faced in traditional approach of segmentation of the images captured by Drones and improvement of the same in successive deep learning-based approach on introduction of U-Net. The variation of U-Net model for many different application areas followed by optimisation of the model by two eminent algorithms BPSO and GWO have been discussed at length in this paper. Analysis of images of different scenes like geographic landforms, vast stretch of irregular landscapes, distribution of the stretch of forest, range of mountains or images concerned to medical domains like carcinogenic tumours etc. are of utmost importance. The segmentation process is vastly applied in order to extract relevant information from scenes in local domain. The architecture of U-Net has been discussed highlighting the convenience of image segmentation. The accuracy value of segmentation has been improved by using deep learning concept based on U-Net architecture. This paper covers U-Net architecture and performance upgradation of the segmentation task and its improvement with the help of optimisation using BPSO and GWO optimisers. The accuracy of images captured can be enhanced further and the process can be pursued by applying optimisation principles to the model. This paper depicts the application scenario where the modified optimisation algorithm has produced considerably higher response towards accuracy of segmentation.

REFERENCES

Ahmed, J. A., & Wesam, M. A. (2012). Image Retrieval Based on Content Using Color Feature. *International Scholarly Research Notices, 2012*, 1–11.

Alexakis, E. B., & Armenakis, C. (2020). Evaluation of unet and unet++ architectures in high resolution image change detection applications. *ISPRS – International Archives of the Photogrammetry, Remote Sensing and Spatial Information Sciences*. . doi:10.5194/isprs-archives-XLIII-B3-2020-1507-2020

Bhatnagar, S., Gill, L., & Ghosh, B. (2020). Drone Image Segmentation Using Machine and Deep Learning for Mapping RaisedBog Vegetation Communities. *Remote Sensing, 12*, 2602. doi:10.3390/rs12162602

Boycov, Y., & Funka-Lea, G. (2006, November). Graph cuts and efficient ND image segmentation. *International Journal of Computer Vision, 70*(2), 109–131.

Cakir, F., He, K., Xia, X., Kulis, B., & Sclaroff, S. (2019). Deep metric learning to rank. In Proceedings of the IEEE/CVF conference on computer vision and pattern recognition (pp. 1861-1870). IEEE.

Canziani, A., Paszke, A., & Culurciello, E. (2016). *An analysis of deep neural network models for practical applications*. arXivpreprint arXiv:1605.07678.

Çiçek, Ö., Abdulkadir, A., Lienkamp, S., & Brox, T. (2016). 3D U-Net: Learning Dense Volumetric Segmentationfrom parse Annotation. In S. Ourselin, L. Joskowicz, M. Sabuncu, G. Unal, & W. Wells (Eds.), Medical Image Computing and Computer-Assisted Intervention: Vol. 9901. MICCAI 2016. MIC-CAI 2016. Lecture Notes in Computer Science. Springer. https://doi.org/10.1007/978-3-319-46723-8_49.

Çiçek, Ö., Abdulkadir, A., Lienkamp, S. S., Brox, T., & Ronneberger, O. (2016). 3D U-Net: learning dense volumetric segmentation from sparse annotation. In *International conference on medical image computing and computer assisted intervention 2016 Oct 17* (pp. 424-432). Springer.

Day, A. L., & Livingstone, H. A. (2001, October). Chronic and acute stressors among military personnel: Do coping styles buffer their negative impact on health? *Journal of Occupational Health Psychology*, *6*(4), 348.

Deng, J., Feng, J., Li, Z., Sun, Z., & Jia, K. (2020). Unet-based for Photoacoustic Imaging Artifact Removal. In *Imaging and Applied Optics Congress.* Optica Publishing Group.

Dhanachandra, N., Manglem, K., & Chanu, Y. J. (2015, January 1). Image segmentation using K-means clustering algorithm and subtractive clustering algorithm. *Procedia Computer Science*, *54*, 764–771.

Ding, Z. (2017). Research of improved particle swarm optimization algorithm. *AIP Conference Proceedings, 1839*, 020148. doi:10.1063/1.4982513

Dong, H., Yang, G., Liu, F., Mo, Y., & Guo, Y. (2017). Automatic brain tumor detection and segmentation using U-Net based fully convolutional networks. In *Annual conference on medical image understanding and analysis* (pp. 506-517). Springer.

Du, X.F., Wang, J.S., & Sun, W.Z. (2021). UNet retinal blood vessel segmentation algorithm based on improved pyramidpooling method and attention mechanism. *Phys Med Biol.*, *66*(17). doi:10.1088/1361-6560/ac1c4c

Elsayed, G., Kornblith, S., & Le, Q. V. (2019). Saccader: Improving accuracy of hard attention models for vision. *Advances in Neural Information Processing Systems, 2019*, 32.

Feng, J., Deng, J., Li, Z., Sun, Z., Dou, H., & Jia, K. (2020). End-to-end Res-Unet based reconstruction algorithm forphotoacoustic imaging. *Biomedical Optics Express*, *11*, 5321–5340.

Fiebelkorn, I.C., Saalmann, Y.B., & Kastner, S. (2020). Functional specialization in the attention network. *Annual Review of Psychology, 71*(221).

Gao, Z. M., & Zhao, J. (2019). An Improved Grey Wolf Optimization Algorithm with Variable Weights. *Computational Intelligence and Neuroscience*. doi:10.1155/2019/2981282

Girisha, S., Pai, M. M. M., & Pai, R. (2019). Performance Analysis of Semantic Segmentation Algorithms for Finely Annotated New UAV Aerial Video Dataset (ManipalUAVid). *IEEE Access: Practical Innovations, Open Solutions*, *7*, 136239–136253. doi:10.1109/ACCESS.2019.2941026

Gu, J., Wang, Z., Kuen, J., Ma, L., Shahroudy, A., Shuai, B., Liu, T., Wang, X., Wang, G., Cai, J., & Chen, T. (2018, May 1). Recent advances in convolutional neural networks. *Pattern Recognition*, *77*, 354–377.

Hamdi, A., Shaban, K., Erradi, A., Mohamed, A., Rumi, S.K., & Salim, F.D. (2022). Generative adversarial networks for spatio-temporal data: A survey. *ACM Transactions on Intelligent Systems and Technology, 13*(2), 1-25.

Hassan, H. A., & Zellagui, M. (2017). Application of Grey Wolf Optimizer Algorithm for Optimal PowerFlow of Two-Terminal HVDC Transmission System. *Advances in Electrical and Electronic Engineering., 15*(5), 701–712.

Hou, Y., Gao, H., Wang, Z., & Du, C. (2022, May 17). Improved Grey Wolf Optimization Algorithm and Application. *Sensors (Basel), 22*(10), 3810. doi:10.339022103810

Hu, J., Shen, Li., Albanie, S., Sun, G., & Wu, E. (2017). *Squeeze-and-excitation networks.* arXiv:1709.01507

Huang, H. C., Chuang, Y. Y., & Chen, C. S. (2011, September 29). Multiple kernel fuzzy clustering. *IEEE Transactions on Fuzzy Systems, 20*(1), 120–134.

Huimin, H., Lin, L., Tong, R., Hu, H., Zhang, Q., Iwamoto, Y., Han, X., Chen, Y., & Wu, J. (2020). UNet3+: A Full-Scale Connected UNet for Medical Image Segmentation.. *ICASSP 2020 - 2020 IEEE International Conference on Acoustics, Speech and Signal Processing (ICASSP)*: 1055-1059.

Jetley, S., Lord, N. A., Lee, N., & Torr, P. H. S. (2018). Learn to pay attention. *International Conference on Learning Representations.* https://openreview.net/forum?id=HyzbhfWRW

Kapdi, R., & Raval, M. (2020). Brain Tumor Segmentation and Survival Prediction. *Lecture Notes in Computer Science, 11992*, 338–348. doi:10.1007/978-3-030-46640-4_32

Khelifi, L., & Mignotte, M. (2017, November 1). EFA-BMFM: A multi-criteria framework for the fusion of colour image segmentation. *Information Fusion, 38*, 104–121.

Le, H. T., & Hien, P. (2018). Brain tumour segmentation using U-Net based fully convolutional networks and extremely randomized trees. *Vietnam Journal of Science, Technology and Engineering, 60*, 19–25. doi:10.31276/VJSTE.60(3).19

Lee, S., Soak, S., Oh, S., Pedrycz, W., & Jeo, M. (2008). Modified binary particle swarm optimization. *Progress in Natural Science, 18*(9), 1161-1166. doi:10.1016/j.pnsc.2008.03.018

Li, X., Wenhua, Q., Xu, D., & Liu, C. (2021). Image Segmentation Based on Improved Unet. *Journal of Physics: Conference Series, 1815*, 012018. doi:10.1088/1742-6596/1815/1/012018

Liu, D., Soran, B., Petrie, G., & Shapiro, L. (2012). *A Review of Computer Vision Segmentation Algorithms.* Academic Press.

Marmanis, D., Datcu, M., Esch, T., & Stilla, U. (2015, December 1). Deep learning earth observation classification using ImageNet pretrained networks. *IEEE Geoscience and Remote Sensing Letters, 13*(1), 105–109.

Mirjalili, S., Mirjalili, S.M., & Lewis, A. (2014). Grey Wolf Optimizer. *Advances in Engineering Software, 69*, 46-61. https://www.sciencedirect.com/science/article/pii/S0965997813001853

Mukherjee, G., Chatterjee, A., & Tudu, B. (2022). Identification of the types of disease for tomato plants using a modified gray wolf optimization optimized MobileNetV2 convolutional neural network architecture driven computer vision framework. *Concurrency and Computation: Practice and Experience, 34.*

Mustaffa, Z., Sulaiman, H. M., Yusob, B., & Ernawan, F. (2016). Integration of GWO-LSSVM for time series predictive analysis. *4th IET Clean Energy and Technology Conference (CEAT 2016),* 1-5. doi: 10.1049/cp.2016.1360

Negi, G., Kumar, A., Pant, S., & Ram, M. (2021). GWO: A review and applications. *Int J Syst Assur Eng Manag, 12,* 1–8. doi:10.1007/s13198-020-00995-8

Noh, H., You, T., Mun, J., & Han, B. (2017). Regularizing deep neural networks by noise: Its interpretation and optimization. *Advances in Neural Information Processing Systems, 2017,* 30.

Noor, N. M. (2018). *IOP Conference Series. Earth and Environmental Science,* 169.

Pegado, R., Ñaupari, Z., Molina, Y., & Castillo, C. (2019). Radial distribution network reconfiguration for power losses reduction based on improved selective BPSO. *Electric Power Systems Research, 169,* 206-213. doi:10.1016/j.epsr.2018.12.030

Shi, J., & Malik, J. (2000, August). Normalized cuts and image segmentation. *IEEE Transactions on Pattern Analysis and Machine Intelligence, 22*(8), 888–905. doi:10.1109/34.868688

Shin, H. C., Roth, H., Gao, M., Lu, L., Xu, Z., Nogues, I., Yao, J., Mollura, D., & Summers, R. (2016). Deep convolutional neural networks for computer-aided detection: CNN architectures, dataset characteristics and transfer learning. *IEEE Transactions on Medical Imaging, 35*(5).

Trusculescu, A. A., Manolescu, D., Tudorache, E., & Oancea, C. (2020, November). Deep learning in interstitial lung disease—How long until daily practice. *European Radiology, 30*(11), 6285–6292.

Tuyen, D. N., Tuan, T. M., Son, L. H., Ngan, T. T., Giang, N. L., Hieu, V. V., Gerogiannis, V. C., Tzimos, D., & Kanavos, A. (2021). A Novel Approach Combining Particle Swarm Optimization And Deep Learning for Flash Flood Detection from Satellite Images. *Mathematics, 9,* 2846. doi:10.3390/math9222846

Ulmas, P., & Liiv, I. (2020). *Segmentation of Satellite Imagery using U-Net Models for Land Cover Classification. ArXiv* abs/2003.02899.

Wang, F., Jiang, M., Qian, C., Yang, S., Cheng, L., Zhang, H., Wang, X., & Tang, X. (2017). Residual attention network for image classification. IEEE CVPR, 3156–3164.

Wang, J. S., & Li, S. X. (2019). An Improved Grey Wolf Optimizer Based on Differential Evolution and Elimination Mechanism. *Scientific Reports, 9*(1), 7181. doi:10.103841598-019-43546-3 PMID:31073211

Wang, X., Girshick, R., Gupta, A., & He, K. (2017). *Non-local neural networks.* arXivpreprintarXiv:1711.07971

Wang, Z., Yin, Y., & Yin, R. (2022) Multi-tasking atrous convolutional neural network for machinery fault identification. *Int J Adv Manuf Technol.* doi:10.1007/s00170-022-09367-x

Wu, G., Shao, X., Guo, Z., Chen, Q., Yuan, W., Shi, X., Xu, Y., & Shibasaki, R. (2018). Automatic Building Segmentation of Aerial imagery Using Multi-Constraint Fully Convolutional Networks. *Remote Sensing, 10*(3), 407. https://doi.org/10.3390/rs10030407

Xiangyi, Y., Tang, H., Sun, S., Ma, H., Kong, D., & Xie, X. (2021). AFTer-UNet: Axial Fusion Transformer UNet for Medical Image Segmentation. *2022 IEEE/CVF Winter Conference on Applications of Computer Vision (WACV)*, 3270- 3280.

Young, S. S., & Mohamed, Z.I.F. (2014). *Binary Particle Swarm Optimization (BPSO) Algorithm for Distributed Node Localization.* Trans Tech Publications Ltd. www.scientific.net/AMM.556-562.3666

Ypsilantis, P. P., & Montana, G. (2017). *Learning what to look in chest X-rays with a recurrent visual attention model.* arXivpreprint arXiv:1701.06452.

Zhang, L., Shen, J., & Zhu, B. (2021). View A research on an improved Unet-based concrete crack etectionalgorithm. *Structural Health Monitoring, 20*(4), 1864–1879. doi:10.1177/1475921720940068

Zhao, R., Yan, R., Chen, Z., Mao, K., Wang, P., & Gao, R.X. (2019). Deep learning and its applications to machine health monitoring. *Mechanical Systems and Signal Processing, 115*, 213-37.

Zongwei, Z., Siddiquee, M. M. R., Tajbakhsh, N., & Liang, J. (2018). UNet++: A Nested U-Net Architecture for Medical Image Segmentation. *Deep Learning in Medical Image Analysis and Multimodal Learning for Clinical Decision Support: 4th International Workshop, DLMIA, and 8th International Workshop, ML-CDS, held in conjunction with MICCAI 2018*, 3-11.

Chapter 6
Distributed Technologies and Consensus Algorithms for Blockchain

Cynthia Jayapal

ⓘ https://orcid.org/0000-0002-9318-7948

Kumaraguru College of Technology, India

Clement Sudhahar

Karunya Institute of Technology and Sciences (Deemed), India

ABSTRACT

Centralized and decentralized systems are prone to security breaches while storing private data. It is challenging to establish trust when an administrator is not known. Blockchain-based technologies use distributed ledgers that can be trusted, audited, validated, and verified by network nodes. The assets stored in a blockchain are immutable, timestamped, and cannot be tampered because of the integrated cryptographic mechanisms. Consensus algorithms are used to validate the transactions and blocks stored in a blockchain. Multiple research reviews focus either on various application domains of blockchain or comparative study of consensus algorithms or security aspects. This chapter aims at providing a comprehensive review on blockchain technologies, performance metrics, and guidelines for choosing a blockchain technology and consensus algorithm based on an organization's requirements and protocols. This chapter also captures concepts on blockchain types, consensus algorithms, and typical applications of blockchain with its features.

INTRODUCTION

Centralized systems have a single point of control. They work based on the client-server paradigm. Issues in centralized systems are single-point failure, less fault tolerance, easy to hack, and lack of trust. It has less maintenance cost. Decentralized systems have multiple authoritative nodes that coordinate the system. In decentralized systems, there is no single-point failure, it is difficult to hack, trust is higher

DOI: 10.4018/978-1-6684-7524-9.ch006

and is more reliable. Nodes of distributed systems are located in a distributed fashion; they have equal authority and act as peer nodes. They prevent single-point failure and are more robust because of data replication. It has high throughput and is more reliable.

A database is a centralized ledger that stores data in a structured fashion. It is maintained by an administrator and is designed for Create, Read, Update and Delete (CRUD) operations. It works based on client-server architecture. It is recommended to store confidential relational data that need not be verified. A blockchain is decentralized and works based on distributed ledger architecture. It has READ and APPEND operations. It has complex algorithms for maintaining the blockchain. It is recommended where sharing, validation, and verification are required. Blockchain is a decentralized distributed ledger that stores information as a trusted entity by avoiding any middlemen. Various implementations of distributed ledger technologies are discussed by El Ioini and Pahl (2019).

A Group of transactions is held in a block, and the blocks are linked as a chain by storing the next block's hash in the previous block. A blockchain is recommended if redundant copies are to be maintained in distributed nodes if participating entities are not known to each other and are from different organizations; if a trusted 3rd party is required and if state information is to be stored.

Monrat et al. (2019) have curated blockchain architecture, structure, consensus algorithms, challenges, and typical use cases. Albayati et al. (2020), recommends regulatory support from the government, and enhanced user support has a major impact on building trust amongst users to adopt blockchain. Rizal Batubara et al. (2019) have also stressed the need for transparency and accountability for the widespread usage of blockchain. Al-Jaroodi and Mohamed (2019) have identified the requirements and benefits of blockchain implementation for healthcare, finance, logistics, manufacturing, energy, agriculture, robotics, and entertainment applications. Zheng et al. (2018) and Risius and Spohrer (2017) have reviewed the research perspective of blockchain framework.

This chapter gives an overview of blockchain properties, components, types, structure, operations, technologies, and consensus algorithms. Blockchain technologies focus on different technologies available to build a blockchain-based application and underlying framework. Each of these technologies provides additional support for authentication, transaction verification, consensus algorithm, identification, access control, and rewarding mechanism. Consensus algorithms are those used by peer nodes present in a distributed blockchain network to arrive at a consensus to decide on the next block that must be added to the blockchain. The nodes that run these algorithms are rewarded in public networks and are designated in the case of a private network.

PROPERTIES OF BLOCKCHAIN

Following are the properties of blockchain that aid in building trust amongst unknown peers and various entities that use the information stored in a blockchain.

1. Decentralization – Information stored in a blockchain is stored in different peer nodes of the network instead of storing in a central system, and there is no single governing authority
2. Distributed ledger Technology – A ledger holding details of a group of transactions are time stamped and are stored in an immutable, distributed manner amongst peer nodes and can be viewed by anyone

3. Immutable – Any transaction or asset information stored in a blockchain cannot be altered later as they are linked using hashing technique.
4. Tamperproof – Any change to a transaction stored in a block alters the hash of the remaining block in the chain and results in the removal of the block. Hence it's tamperproof
5. Transparent – The transaction history is evident at any given time and is available for audit.
6. Less Expensive – Blockchain is less expensive as any middlemen are avoided.

Blockchain Components

The five main components of blockchain, as illustrated in Figure 1, are,

1. Distributed Ledger – A distributed shared ledger stores the blocks of the blockchain. The transactions are cryptographically verified, timestamped, and recorded in the ledger.
2. Peer to Peer network – Participant nodes in the blockchain are peer-to-peer and operate in a decentralized manner. They have equal authority and participate in each step of the blockchain process.
3. Virtual Machine – It is used to execute blockchain smart contracts and decentralized apps for different platforms.
4. Cryptography – Cryptographic principles are embedded in every step of blockchain implementation using asymmetric and symmetric keys, encryption, digital signatures, and secured wallets.
5. Consensus Mechanism – The participating nodes execute the consensus algorithm to approve the current state of the blockchain operation and ensures authentication even when the peers are not known to each other, protects from the invalid transaction such as double spending, and prevents hackers from altering the transactions.

TYPES OF BLOCKCHAIN NETWORKS

There are various types of blockchains based on the purpose of a blockchain. If blockchain is used to record transactions in distributed ledgers for a smaller organization, public blockchain may be used. If the blockchain is used to record a transaction in distributed ledger but also involves privacy and authorization according to the protocols and hierarchy defined by a bigger organization, then private blockchain is preferred. If a group of similar organizations prefers to use a typical blockchain exclusively built to target their business motives but also would like privacy and authorization, tailor-made for their organization, hybrid or consortium blockchain may be used.

Public Blockchain

A public blockchain is an extensive distribution network. Anyone can participate and view the transactions. No third party is involved. Security is ensured using a consensus algorithm. A transaction fee is required. Applications can be deployed and removed without seeking any ones permission. In a permissioned network, nodes are invited to join and are approved, and network nodes can join, contribute and leave without anyone's permission at their own will. E.g., Bitcoin, Ethereum.

Figure 1. Blockchain components

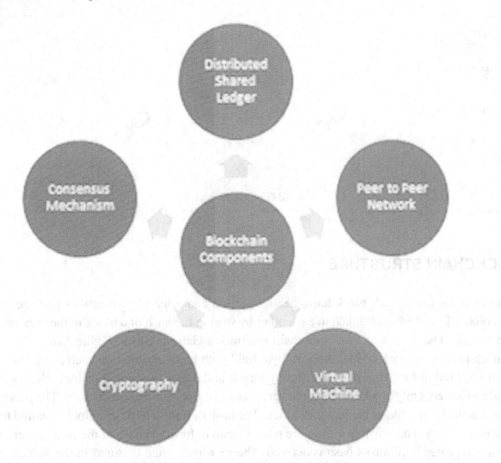

Private Blockchain

Membership in a private blockchain is limited to authorized people. The validators and authorization policy are decided during the development phase. An administrator can control access and maintain privacy because of limited read access. Applications joining the network need to be invited and can be removed. E.g., Ripple

Hybrid Blockchain

Hybrid blockchain combines properties of public and private blockchain. It allows individuals to add their preferences and still utilize the decentralized features of a blockchain.

Consortium Blockchain

In a consortium blockchain, not all entities are known to all participants. Multiple parties can be participants in the network, and access to the network is restricted. The authorization policy and administrator nodes are also decided during the development phase. E.g., CORDA, Hyperledger.

Figure 2. Blockchain structure

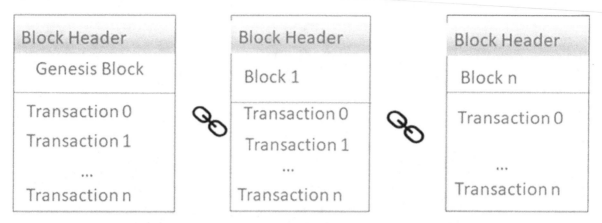

BLOCKCHAIN STRUCTURE

As shown in Figure 2, each block has a header portion and a list of transactions that are grouped to form a block. The blocks are linked to each other by storing the hash of a block in the previous block to create a chain. The first block of a blockchain is termed a Genesis Block. Figure 3 illustrates the fields of a block header. A block header is an 80-byte field with meta information such as version, Previous block hash, Merkle root, timestamp, difficulty target, and nonce. Version indicates which set of block rules are followed. Only blocks of the same version can be a part of that blockchain. The previous block hash stores the hash value of the previous block. The hash of transactions in a block is paired together to form a parent hash. These parent hashes are paired again to form the hash of the next higher level. This process is repeated until a root hash is derived. The root hash value is stored in the Merkle root field. Timestamp stores the time at which a block has been mined, ensuring the validity of a transaction and allowing the transactions to be audited at any time. The target difficulty is a difficulty level set to make finding a hash more difficult. The value is changed every few blocks. A nonce is a set of strings with a certain number of leading zeros. A miner tries to alter the block header hash to find a hash value that is lesser than the value specified in the difficulty target.

Integration of Cryptography Principles in Blockchain implementation

Public key cryptography, hashing, block, and transaction integrity are ensured using blockchain principles. In the public blockchain, the credentials of participants cannot be checked as in other physical systems since they are anonymous. Yet they have to be brought into a trusted environment of the blockchain. Feng et al (2019) have analyzed various privacy threats in blockchain and the associated cryptographic defense mechanisms and privacy-preserving mechanisms. Both privacy of a transaction's content and the identity of the entities associated with the transaction are important.

The transaction or asset of Alice is encrypted using Alice's private key and Bob's public key. Hence Bob can decrypt the transaction using his private key. Ethereum and bitcoin use Elliptic Key Cryptography for generating key pairs. The security of the asset relies on the protection of the private key used. Hence, a private key, usually a passphrase in the blockchain, needs to be secured as a password. Using a

Figure 3. Blockchain header

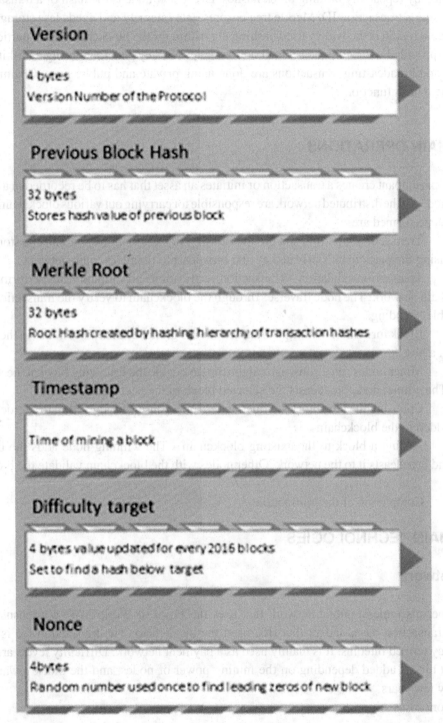

hash function ensures consistency and verification of the transaction. The transaction's hash is generated and authorized by the sender's digital signature. This makes the transaction non-repudiable. Anyone can verify the transaction by applying the public key of the sender. Merkle tree hash is a binary hash tree constructed by repeatedly hashing block hashes. Every leaf node is the hash of a transaction and is represented using a transaction ID. Merkle tree ensures data integrity and needs less storage space as a data structure. SHA256 is the widely used hashing algorithm for the blockchain. Each participant in the blockchain is provided with a unique account address, a public key generated using a hashing function.

Initiation and broadcasting transactions are done using private and public keys. Chaining of block happens using a hash function.

BLOCKCHAIN OPERATIONS

A blockchain participant creates a transaction or initiates an asset that has to be recorded in a blockchain.

The peer nodes of the distributed network are responsible for carrying out various blockchain operations. Operations performed are

Step 1: Transaction Initiation and broadcasting – Any transactions that must be stored are digitally signed using the participant's private key and broadcast to the blockchain network.

Step 2: Transaction validation – Transaction verification and validation are performed by nodes in the blockchain network. The node traverses through the blockchain to verify the transaction. This also prevents double-spending.

Step 3: Block formation – Multiple transactions are grouped, and miner nodes in the blockchain network form a block.

Step 4: Miner nodes run a consensus algorithm to decide the following block to be added to the blockchain. The winner node broadcasts the selected block to the peer nodes.

Step 5: Choosing the next block – Miner nodes run a consensus algorithm to decide on the next block to be added to the blockchain

Step 6: Adding a block to the existing blockchain - The winning node adds the block to the blockchain and broadcasts it to the network. Other nodes with the blockchain validate the block and add it to its chain.

Step 7: Completion of the transaction

BLOCKCHAIN TECHNOLOGIES

Bitcoin Network

Bitcoin is a permissionless, public network that uses the Proof of Work(PoW) consensus algorithm. Bitcoin is a transaction-based ledger that first used the blockchain. The transaction fee is paid using cryptocurrency termed bitcoins. It is mainly used as a payment network. Difficulty levels are revamped for every few blocks added depending on the mining power of nodes, and the block reward also gets reduced every few years.

Bitcoin Consensus Algorithm:

Step 1: A new transaction created is broadcasted in a bitcoin network.

Step 2: The miners verify and group the transactions to form a block.

Step 3: A fixed difficulty level defines the number of leading zeros in a block hash. The more the number of leading zeros, the more difficult it is. The miners perform high computations to find a random

Figure 4. Ethereum stack

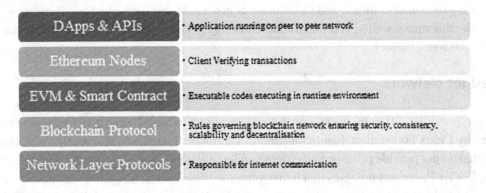

nonce used to find a hash of a block that is less than the difficulty level. Successful miners receive a reward for adding a block to the blockchain.

Step 4: The miner who found a nonce solution broadcasts the block to the nodes of the bitcoin network

Step 5: Other nodes verify the block; subsequently, the block is added to the longest chain, and any fork in the chain is discarded using the longest chain rule. The block reward for creating a new block and transaction fee for validating a transaction is paid to the public address of a miner.

Ethereum Network

Ethereum is a permissionless public or private blockchain that uses Proof of Stake (PoS). The cryptocurrency used in ethereum is Ether(ETH). Ethereum smart contracts are programmable using languages such as solidity or Vyper. Any decentralized application can be built using the ethereum platform. It helps in avoiding any middlemen and works based on mutual agreement, termed a smart contract. Smart contracts are executable code triggered automatically by a transaction without any intervention. Ethereum Virtual machine (EVM) is the run time environment for executing a smart contract. The miner provides the transaction cost after the execution of a smart contract. Each operation in the agreement has a cost termed 'gas' and every transaction sets a gas limit for its implementation. Laurent et al(2022), have discussed models to optimize transaction fees in ethereum networks. Metamask is the ethereum wallet that interacts with DApp and smart contracts. Figure 4 illustrates the Ethereum stack.

Below are the steps to deploy Ethereum in a test network like Robsten. The same steps can be done using actual ethers in a real ethereum network. Verify and execute the smart contract in Etherscan. Ganache is used to develop a private ethereum blockchain for testing. It can be downloaded from https://www.trufflesuite.com/ganache. After deploying the smart contract, several default accounts are provided to test the transactions. Web3.js can be used to interact with ethereum nodes. It is used to retrieve data from the blockchain. Truffle can be used to write and test smart contracts. Truffle provides a framework for designing DApp applications.

Steps to deploy Ethereum

Step 1: Add metamask as a browser extension and create a wallet.

Step 2: Select a test network from the list

Step 3: Add Ethers to the wallet from the test faucet

Step 4: Use Remix IDE to write a smart contract and save it. sol extension

Step 5: Deploy the smart contract, and the address is generated

Step 6: In the metamask wallet, add tokens and enter any smart contract address to check the balance after each transaction.

Hyperledger Network

Hyperledger provides different open-source tools required to build enterprise applications and is maintained by Linux Foundation. Identity attributes cannot be trusted and are mostly correlated across platforms that do not provide privacy. Self-Sovereign Identity (SSI) and Decentralised Identifiers (DID) Trust over IP (ToIP) are technologies that help overcome these issues. SSI allows users to control their verified credentials and present their claims on portable identity without involving any centralized authority using cryptographic and blockchain principles. DIDs are identifiers that resemble a URL and can be created at any time by anyone. It is globally unique and can be cryptographically verified. A DID is resolved to a DIDDoc that holds the public key and endpoint that controls the DID. Any messages sent are decrypted by the private key available on the other end and serve as a verifiable credential. ToIP is a set of protocols that enable trust on the internet

The roles for operation are divided amongst various nodes. Channels provide a communication path amongst participants to perform private transactions with confidentiality. A few nodes are assigned as endorsing peers to approve the transaction and committing peers to commit a block to a blockchain. Chaincode is the smart contract equivalent. Orderers are nodes that group transactions to form a block and send them to committing peers. Golang can be used for coding. Hyperledger Fabric is used to create blockchain applications. Hyperledger Sawtooth uses Proof of Elapsed Time(PoET) as a consensus mechanism. Hyperledger Ursa provides cryptographic packages that can generate cryptographic keys, digital signing, encryption and decryption, zero-knowledge proof creation and verification, and hash generation and verification. Hyperledger Indy provides support to build distributed ledgers and applications that interact with the ledger

Multichain

Multichain allows communication across different blockchains. It has Secure Multiparty Computation nodes independent of the blockchain but collectively signs the transactions using their part of the private key. These nodes are provided incentives for the service provided. They maintain a Decentralised Management Account. Multichain nodes can be either member nodes or admin nodes. Transactions are validated, sent and received by member nodes. In addition the admin nodes may add new nodes to the multichain and can create and approve filters(Mayle et al. 2020). Some of the services are bridge, router, and cross chain across blockchains. Bridge service can operate only between two blockchains, like an asset present in the smart contract of one blockchain is released using an asset present in another blockchain. Router service allows asset transfer between any blockchain by interacting with different native or bridged assets. To swap assets with multichain routers, connect with a wallet, set up the network, get the approval of the contract for a given token, and exchange the assets at very high speed. An usecase for secured voting system using multichain technology is discussed by Jayapal et al. (2020).

Steps involved in Multichain:

Step 1:

Handshaking- Nodes of blockchain connect with each other using unique address and list of permissions. The node that is requested will verify the address of the requesting node by sending a challenge message to nodes in the network; for which the nodes replies ensuring the authenticity of the requestor. Every node in multichain can send message to other nodes and may abort the P2P connection if there is no satisfying outcome.

Step2:

Mining- Identifiable entities are designated as miners. The miners create validated blocks using PoW consensus algorithm in a round robin fashion in order to add to the blockchain. There is no mining reward or transaction fee as in other technologies.

CORDA

CORDA is a consortium-based permissioned open source, highly scalable, and more secure platform. It allows organizations with similar business problems to come to an agreement written into a smart contract and interact within a very safe environment. It shares data only between parties involved in a transaction and is hidden from all other counterparts. Smart contracts are written using any JVM-compatible language. It's compatible with existing and emerging standards. Consensus is based on the validation and uniqueness of the assets. Transactions need not be sequential. Participants associated with legal entities are only given access. It provides functionalities for maintaining a ledger, membership management, secure communication, and accounts. A participant in CORDA network has to submit a request to identity manager. The manager checks if participant meets all requirements of the network and then issues a participant certificate. This certificate is produced to network map which in turn sends it to all network nodes. A notary validates the transactions, digitally signs the transaction and provides consensus based on validation and uniqueness. Transactions in CORDA need not be sequential. The network participants can enter into legal agreement for accepting the signed transaction by confirming the same. The transaction data is shared only between the counterparts that have confirmed the transaction. The communication protocol is invisible to other participants of the network.

Quorum

Quorum is also a consortium-based permissioned platform primarily used for banking and financial enterprises and is also open source. It can be used for solving any financial query. Security and privacy are constrained. It allows only permissioned nodes to participate. It uses 'Quorum-chain,' a voting-based consensus algorithm. Transaction privacy, participant authentication, and transaction history are maintained. It provides services such as member and node identification, authentication, and setting up permissions. The network operates at a very high speed. Quorum uses RAFT or Istanbul BFT consensus algorithm for transaction validation in which selected nodes are allowed to vote and majority voting is considered for arriving at consensus. It provides multiple pluggable consensus required for multiple enterprises. It provides enterprise wide access control and performance. Smart contracts are coded using solidity as in ethereum and the contract can be wither public or private but cannot be changed later. A quorum node is an ethereum client that allows connection only among permissioned nodes. Private transactions are also validated. In order to preserve private data, the encrypted data is also accepted as transaction data. Gas fee is not there. A constellation node ensures security by maintaining the transaction manager and enclave. Transaction manager is responsible for encrypting the transaction and assuring its privacy. It allows access and exchange of private data. It is capable of maintaining multiple public private key pairs. Enclave ensures scalability, optimal performance, participant authentication and maintains transaction history. It controls access to public and private keys and handles identity of participant nodes. It encrypts and decrypts transactions.

Stellar

Stellar is another public distributed blockchain ledger platform built to connect multiple financial organizations to operate on a single platform. It allows transactions to be performed using any currency. It reduces the time and cost involved in trans-border transactions as the entire transaction happens as a single atomic operation[https://stellar.org/learn/the-power-of-stellar]. It has got no central authority. Proof of Agreement (PoA) is achieved between peers using the Stellar Consensus Protocol. The stellar network chooses trustworthy nodes for approving the transactions. The stellar ledger maintains details of a user's account balance and the operation he performs. After a consensus is attained on a transaction, it is published on the public ledger. The transactions are updated every few seconds with all nodes of the network. Stellar allows using a tradable entity called tokens such as stellar lumens or XLM, which can also be tied to real currencies. It allows fast transactions as the transactions are validated by quorum slices. It is possible to exchange or redeem tokens as a tradable entity. The stellar core maintains a copy of the ledger that is used for synchronization amongst multiple servers. Unique feature of stellar is the distributed exchange that is used to trade currencies and virtual assets. These exchanges deal with different types of transactions such as peer-to-peer, indirect and indirect chain transactions. Peer-peer-transactions involve multiple exchanges for completing a transaction. An indirect transaction uses Stellar tokens in exchange for a currency. Indirect chain transactions convert one currency into other before converting into any desired currency.

HEDERA

Hedera is a permissioned distributed ledger similar to blockchain that uses a hashgraph as a consensus mechanism. Hedera network has graph like structure where every node can communicate to other nodes in the graph. It provides smart contract, token, and consensus services. Smart contracts can be used to develop decentralized applications to include a layer of trust. Hedera consensus services can be utilized to timestamp and order transactions. Token services can be utilized to have micro-level control over Fungible and Nonfungible tokens. Tokens are used in blockchain to validate the ownership of a holder as an asset. Fungible tokens like cryptocurrencies, ERC 20 have a value attached to them and can be used for exchanging an asset for that value. Nonfungible tokens like ERC 721 do not have any value attached to them and are not interchangeable. The authenticity of the asset is publicly verifiable and auditable (Leemon Baird et al, 2020). It uses Gossip about Gossip and virtual voting to arrive at consensus in the network. In Gossip about Gossip a node communicate with another random node to convey synchronization information. This ensures virtual voting where a node can know what other nodes have voted without even participating in the voting process. The consensus services creates ordered assets and verifiable time-stamps. It is preferred for applications that need real time auditing, custom specified privacy control and automatic transaction ordering. The consensus state of a transaction is confirmed using Response – Receipt mechanism. Before adding a transaction to the nodes of the network, a node validates the consensus state with the client that has submitted the transaction. Only after confirmation the transaction is submitted to the peer nodes for consensus. The client node can request for a receipt from the network nodes to confirm the consensus state and object identifier. The unique feature of Hedera smart contract is that the developers may choose to have mutability to the contract in future. It also has facility to deploy the contract using public key of arbitrators which allows them to edit, add features, reverse desired transactions and fix bugs if any in future.

CONSENSUS ALGORITHMS

The consensus algorithm is an agreement used to verify if a block added to a blockchain is the only version agreed upon by various peer nodes. A consensus mechanism ensures agreement, collaboration, cooperation, and active participation amongst various peers in the blockchain network. This helps in establishing trust among unknown peers in a blockchain. A consensus algorithm acts as a leader election algorithm to select a miner to validate a block. A consensus algorithm can be chosen based on factors required for application, such as incentivizing, energy requirement, security, and scalability.

A distributed consensus algorithm in a blockchain is an agreement between the pees of a blockchain network about the current state of the distributed ledger before adding a block to the blockchain. This algorithm ensures trust between unknown peers in a distributed environment and maintains a single valid copy in the entire network. Every node running a consensus algorithm must cooperate, collaborate, participate, and be equally active. Some objectives of consensus algorithms are fault tolerance, liveness, synchronicity, safety, security, node permissioning, and less energy consumption.

Challenges of distributed environment for executing consensus algorithm are having global Knowledge and maintaining state information of the entire system, detecting inconsistency, maintaining timestamp of events, identifying delayed and duplicate messages, handling concurrent operations such as double spending, ensuring security, and handling failure of nodes in the network. State change is replicated in each of the distributed nodes and is resilient. Given a state for a specific input, the new state is consistent at any given instance at any node.

Consensus algorithms aim to prevent specific attacks such as 51%, double spending, Sybil attack, and many more. A double-spending attack is when an attacker tries to spend the same money twice. An attacker performs a transaction that is stored in a block, does a conflicting transaction, then tries to include the conflicting transaction in a block of a forked chain, and then may even try to make this fork chain the main chain. Such double spending is feasible with the help of a 51% attack wherein a miner or group of miners takes control of more than 50% of the blockchain network to inappropriately arrive at a consensus to approve an invalid transaction or add an invalid block to the blockchain. Sybil attack is possible in a peer-to-peer network, wherein a single node tries to create multiple identities or accounts and impersonates to perform transactions simultaneously.

The consensus algorithms in a blockchain can be classified based on the proof of activity, a voting scheme used, or fault-tolerant capacity (Nguyen and Kim 2018), (Yao and Wang 2021). It can operate over private or public blockchains and be permissionless or permissioned. Bamakan (2020) gives an overview of consensus algorithm and the effect of various performance metrics on choosing the algorithm.

Fu et al. (2021), have evaluated the performance of consensus algorithms based on accountant selection, block selection, and transaction confirmation. Yao et al. (2021) have discussed the working of various consortium based consensus algorithms such as Paxos, Raft, PBFT, Stellar, and RPCA.

Some of the permissionless consensus algorithms are Proof of Work (PoW), Proof of State(PoS), Delegated Pos(DPoS), Proof of Burn(PoB), Proof of Activity(PoA), Proof of Elapsed Time(PoET) and permissioned consensus algorithms are Practical Byzantine Fault Tolerant(PBFT), RBFT, FBFT, TBFT.

The consensus protocols can be compared based on their type, fault-tolerant percentage, power consumption, scalability, and application. The performance of the algorithms can be evaluated based on criteria such as algorithm throughput, communication model, mining profitability, degree of decentralization, securities, and vulnerabilities. Performance metrics to evaluate the consensus algorithms are the following,

1. Cost: A node must invest in specialized hardware or cryptocurrency to be spent on emerging as a winner. The cost also includes the mining reward, transaction fee, and power consumed
2. Efficiency: Amount of valuable time spent or bandwidth used in participating in executing the consensus algorithm
3. Throughput: Number of transactions that can be handled per second. It depends on block size and the time to create and verify a block.
4. Fairness: It is the fairness in the selection of a validating node or fairness in timing within which a transaction submitted by a node is added to the block
5. Fault Tolerance: Ensure integrity and availability on the failure of nodes
   Consistency: Ensure data is the same in all nodes in the network, and any change is reflected immediately in all copies.
6. Security: Resilience of a consensus algorithm to double spending attack, Sybil attack, 51% attack, and other vulnerabilities.
7. Block Verification Time: Once a transaction is created it has to be verified by a miner node before including it in a block and the block must be included in the longest chain.

Proof of Work Algorithm

In the PoW algorithm, a mathematical puzzle for which it is hard to find a solution is generated, and the miners compete amongst themselves to solve it by finding an acceptable hash and broadcasting the solution to all other nodes for verification. The difficulty level of solving the puzzle and mining rewards are periodically altered. After verification, the block is added to the blockchain, and the miner is rewarded. It is used in Bitcoin, Zcash, and Litecoin. PoW can be Computation – bound, Memory-bound, or chained depending on whether they profusely need a large computation requirement of CPU or more memory read-write operations or need to solve a chain of hash functions.

Algorithm Proof of Work

Propose_Block():

```
While true do
    Nonce n = random_value ()
```

```
Create block b by choosing verified transactions
Solve_puzzle(n,b):
    If hash(b,n) < difficulty then
        Broadcast(b)
```

Advantage:

It has a high degree of decentralization

Easy to implement

It has increased security and trust

Disadvantage:

It demands enormous computation power and energy requirement

It may lead to a network monopoly by nodes with high computation power.

Block validation time is increased.

The network can be compromised by a 51% attack, wherein 51% of miner nodes can group to alter the transactions in a blockchain.

Proof of Stake Algorithm

In the PoS algorithm, the validators must possess a certain amount of stake or cryptocurrency in the wallet to act as a participating node and have to stake some amount to validate the block. After the block is added to the blockchain, the validator is rewarded based on their stake amount. The algorithm is more energy efficient and secure as the attacker would have to stake their money. It is used in Ethereum. It may result in blockchain forks, and eventually, consensus may not be reached.

Algorithm Proof of Stake

Propose_Block():

```
While true do
    Create block b by choosing verified transactions
    Stake coins to become validator
        If chosen as validator by peer nodes then
            Receive reward according to staked amount
    Else
            Loose stake
```

Advantage:

It uses less computing power and energy when compared to PoW.

Block validation time is reduced.

Disadvantage:

Less secure when compared to PoW.

Delegated Proof of Stake(DPoS)

In DPoS, the witness nodes are delegated by a voting system. They are rewarded with transaction fees instead of mining rewards for verifying and signing the transactions and creating a block. The number of votes a delegate node receives depends on the stake possessed by the nodes participating in the voting process, as in PoS. The participating nodes stake their assets in a centralized pool and link them to the delegate node they elect. Few nodes are elected as delegate nodes. Delegate nodes do not participate in transaction verification. Still, they can participate in governing the blockchain by proposing changes in reward allocation or changes in the size of the block, and the change proposed is accepted or denied by the rest of the nodes by voting mechanism. Some block validators validate the blocks created by witness nodes and verify the network. Validator nodes are not incentivized. The algorithm is much faster and collaborative but can be biased. DPoS is decentralized but is more scalable.

Algorithm Delegated Proof of Stake

Propose_Block():

```
While true do
    Stake coins to become witness
    If chosen as Witness node then
        Verify transactions and group them to create block
            Receive transaction fees if approved by block validators
            Else
                Loose stake
```

Advantage

It provides more decentralization as more participants are involved in the voting process, and more witness nodes can participate

It needs less computing power or energy requirement

Prevents double spending as the delegator nodes are different from the node that delegates

Disadvantage

It takes some time to identify hones witness nodes

In the Proof of Burn(PoB) algorithm, Validators burn some coin to claim their chance of validating a block. Instead of spending time or resource certain amount of coins are transferred to an account that is not returned but burnt. Based on the number of coins burned, the validator is selected randomly. Burning more coins is required to increase the likelihood of getting selected.

Proof of Activity (PoA)

PoA is a combination of PoW and PoS. The miners solve the puzzle as PoW and broadcast the block for validation. The validators stake their amount to validate the block as in PoS before adding the block to the blockchain. This algorithm is resilient to 51%attack.

Algorithm Proof of Activity

Vaidate_Block():

```
While true do
    Stake coins to become validator
    Miner_Solve_puzzle:
        Create Empty block with block header
        Broacast_block
    Validate_Header:
        Validates block header
        Receive reward on successful addition of block
```

Proof of Elapsed Time(PoET)

In PoET, the participating nodes are assigned a random waiting time, and the node with less elapsed time emerges as a winner to form the block. The block is validated and attached to the blockchain by validators.

Algorithm Proof of Elapsed Time

Propose_Block():

```
While true do
    If elapsed time allocated by a central controller < Other miners elapsed
time then
        Create block b by choosing verified transactions
        Attach block to block cahin
        Receive reward
```

Practical Byzantine Fault Tolerant(PBFT)

BFT algorithms can handle Byzantine Fault, despite specific nodes exhibiting malicious behavior. PBFT operates even when malicious nodes are operating in the system. One node becomes a primary node, while all others continue to be secondary nodes. All honest nodes, including primary and secondary nodes, help arrive at a consensus by responding to the requestor. If m+1 nodes do validation, then it can tolerate m faulty nodes. It is used in HyperLedger.

Algorithm Practical Byzantine Fault Tolerant

Propose_Block():

```
While true do
        Client sends request to Primary node
        Primary node validates request and broadcasts to secondary nodes
        Primary and secondary nodes replies to client
        Client accepts after receiving m+1l identical replies
```

Advantage:
It has more speed and throughput. More trust is required for each node.
Disadvantage:
Scalability is limited in PBFT as it needs to communicate with all nodes during every step.

PAXOS

PAXOS is a fault-tolerant distributed consensus algorithm that assigns different roles for a node. A proposer node can submit a proposal, acceptor nodes can approve the proposal, and a learner node learns about the proposal. The proposer node submits a proposal with a unique ID to more than half of the acceptors in the network. The acceptor nodes approve the proposal if the proposal number received is greater than the largest one received previously and send it as a response to the proposer.

Algorithm PAXOS

Propose_Transaction():

```
While true do
        Prepare Phase:
                Proposes a transaction
                Request acceptors permission
        Accept phase:
                Sends the transaction to acceptors that have agreed
                Acceptors validates the transaction
        Commit Phase:
                Proposer commits the transaction
```

RAFT

RAFT is similar to Paxos but aims to reduce the number of states to be considered. It has different phases: electing a powerful leader, consistent log replication, safety, and maintaining cluster membership. It begins with certain states and goes through certain operations to arrive at a consistent state[Yao, W., Ye, J., Murimi, R., & Wang, G. (2021). Initially, all servers act as passive followers. The candidate nodes run the election algorithm to choose a leader node for each cluster. The elected leader node in a cluster receives client requests and forwards them to the followers. It also responds to log replication requests from the leader by replicating its log.

Algorithm RAFT

Propose_Transaction():

```
While true do
        Leader Election:
                Majority of nodes elects a leader
                The leader confirms its state to all nodes
        Log Replication:
                Leader logs the transaction received from a client
                The transaction is replicated in follower nodes
                Ensures safety by allocating one index per transaction
```

Advantage:
Any candidate node can become a leader; hence there is fairness.
It is resilient to server failures
Disadvantage:
It operates with a single leader that might become overloaded
Directed Acyclic Graph uses a different approach of consensus algorithm, wherein they add blocks in parallel instead of one by one. They are highly scalable. It is used IOTA, NANO…Byteball.

Hashgraph

Hashgraph is a novel approach for distributed consensus. Its represented in a tree-like structure and requires frequent pruning to prevent the blockchain from growing out of control. Instead of pruning the forks of blockchain as in other blockchain approaches, the new chain is woven into the body of the ledger. It offers robust validation but does not guarantee fairness in the order of adding a transaction. Consensus on a transaction is achieved using gossip protocol to achieve synchronization between nodes called 'Gossip Synch.' The resultant event is stored in memory along with a timestamp, parent hashes, cryptographic signature, and transactions. The relation between such events is called 'Gossip about Gossip.' The cost of a hashgraph is inexpensive. No Pow or computation overhead is involved. It's highly efficient, and a block never becomes stale. Bandwidth requirements and overhead are also minimal. It has a very high throughput to handle any number of transactions if a fast internet speed is available.

Unlike other consensus algorithms, once a transaction occurs, history verification is unnecessary. The current transaction can be stored with the assurance that every other node has updated state information. It uses Asynchronous Byzantine Fault Tolerance. It is possible to achieve consensus even in the presence of malicious nodes and is resilient to attacks such as DDoS. ACID property adheres in hashgraph. It exhibits fairness in achieving consensus in deciding on the timestamp, the order in which the transactions are stored based on their timestamps, and accepting a transaction without hindrance from a malicious node.

Figure 5. Blockchain Supply chain

BLOCKCHAIN USE CASE REQUIREMENT

A blockchain is a technology that is suitable for use cases that need a shared database, where multiple untrusted parties are involved, the rules governing the participants are uniform, and there is a need for an immutable log. The transaction registry can be either static or dynamic.

1. Static registry – Applications like patents, land titles, and insurance claims where the information stored is not likely to change and has identity information attached.
2. Dynamic registry – Applications like supply chain with some tradable information attached. The assets are exchanged in digital platform amongst unknown authorized peers

Figure 5 illustrates a supply chain use case where blockchain is used to store and track the transfer of goods from supplier to distributor to a vendor to customer. The information can be audited at any time to trace back any faulty goods or security breaches. Gonczol et al. (2020) and Min (2019) have studied the effects and challenges of using blockchain for supply chain.

Typical blockchain use cases are in finance, healthcare, supply chain, asset management, identity management, digital payments, and many more. Figure 6 summarizes typical blockchain use cases along with their features that require the usage of blockchain technology. Deepa et al. (2022) and Gao et al. (2018) have explored the scope of blockchain in applications about big data, IoT, SDN, Industry 5.0, and federated learning. Maesa and Mori (2020) have discussed elaborately the use of blockchain technology for certain applications based on access control, identity management, and decentralized notary.

CONCLUSION

This chapter summarizes the salient features of blockchain technology, their types, and structure and consensus algorithm. Blockchain provides trust amongst unknown peers and avoids middlemen thereby reducing the cost of execution. It gives insight for an organization trying to use blockchain technology for their use cases; to choose appropriate technology and define their access control, privacy, and authentication features. It also guides an application developer to choose the appropriate technology, platform, consensus algorithm, and tools to code the smart contract. A public blockchain provides transparency and trust but lacks scalability and performance. A private, hybrid, or consortium blockchain provides access control, scalability, and performance but has less transparency. Distributed consensus algorithms, aid in arriving at a common state that is stored in various distributed nodes of a blockchain. This ensures

Figure 6. Blockchain Usecases

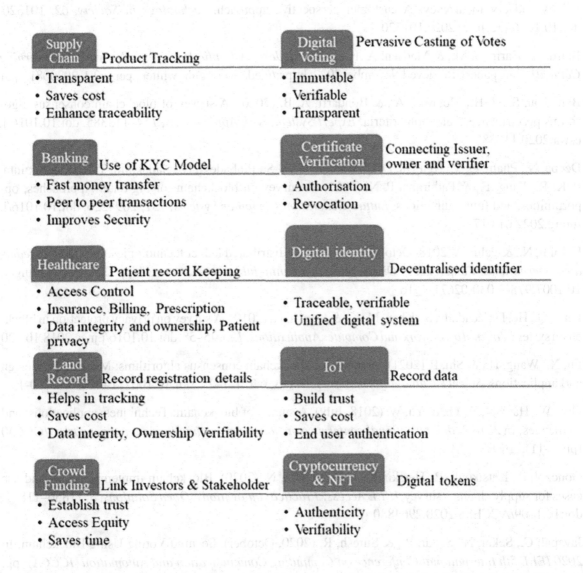

termination, integrity, and agreement. The future of blockchain applications is not limited to those discussed in this chapter but will penetrate every government department, every organization that demands transparency in financial handling, every application that demands trust amongst unknown peers, and every application that currently stores its digital data in the cloud.

REFERENCES

Al-Jaroodi, J., & Mohamed, N. (2019). Blockchain in industries: A survey. *IEEE Access: Practical Innovations, Open Solutions, 7,* 36500–36515. doi:10.1109/ACCESS.2019.2903554

Albayati, H., Kim, S. K., & Rho, J. J. (2020). Accepting financial transactions using blockchain technology and cryptocurrency: A customer perspective approach. *Technology in Society*, *62*, 101320. doi:10.1016/j.techsoc.2020.101320

Baird, L., Harmon, M., & Madsen, A. P. (2020). *Hedera: A Public Hashgraph Network & Governing Council* [white paper]. Retrieved November 2022: https://hedera.com/hh_whitepaper_v2.1-20200815.pdf

Bamakan, S. M. H., Motavali, A., & Bondarti, A. B. (2020). A survey of blockchain consensus algorithms performance evaluation criteria. *Expert Systems with Applications*, *154*, 113385. doi:10.1016/j.eswa.2020.113385

Deepa, N., Pham, Q. V., Nguyen, D. C., Bhattacharya, S., Prabadevi, B., Gadekallu, T. R., Maddikunta, P. K. R., Fang, F., & Pathirana, P. N. (2022). A survey on blockchain for big data: Approaches, opportunities, and future directions. *Future Generation Computer Systems*, *131*, 209–226. doi:10.1016/j.future.2022.01.017

El Ioini, N., & Pahl, C. (2018, October). A review of distributed ledger technologies. In *OTM Confederated International Conferences "On the Move to Meaningful Internet Systems"* (pp. 277-288). Springer. 10.1007/978-3-030-02671-4_16

Feng, Q., He, D., Zeadally, S., Khan, M. K., & Kumar, N. (2019). A survey on privacy protection in blockchain system. *Journal of Network and Computer Applications*, *126*, 45–58. doi:10.1016/j.jnca.2018.10.020

Fu, X., Wang, H., & Shi, P. (2021). A survey of Blockchain consensus algorithms: Mechanism, design and applications. *Science China. Information Sciences*, *64*(2), 1–15. doi:10.100711432-019-2790-1

Gao, W., Hatcher, W. G., & Yu, W. (2018, July). A survey of blockchain: Techniques, applications, and challenges. In *2018 27th international conference on computer communication and networks (ICCCN)* (pp. 1-11). IEEE.

Gonczol, P., Katsikouli, P., Herskind, L., & Dragoni, N. (2020). Blockchain implementations and use cases for supply chains-a survey. *IEEE Access: Practical Innovations, Open Solutions*, *8*, 11856–11871. doi:10.1109/ACCESS.2020.2964880

Jayapal, C., Sekar, N., Sekar, R., & Suresh, R. (2020, October). Secured Voting Using Blockchain. In *2020 IEEE 5th International Conference on Computing Communication and Automation (ICCCA)* (pp. 177-184). IEEE. 10.1109/ICCCA49541.2020.9250859

Laurent, A., Brotcorne, L., & Fortz, B. (2022). Transactions fees optimization in the Ethereum blockchain. *Blockchain: Research and Applications*, 100074.

Maesa, D. D. F., & Mori, P. (2020). Blockchain 3.0 applications survey. *Journal of Parallel and Distributed Computing*, *138*, 99–114. doi:10.1016/j.jpdc.2019.12.019

Mayle, n. 2020. Blockchain based Communication Architectures with Applications to Private Security Networks (No. Sand-2020-12719r). Univ. of New Mexico.

Min, H. (2019). Blockchain technology for enhancing supply chain resilience. *Business Horizons*, *62*(1), 35–45. doi:10.1016/j.bushor.2018.08.012

Monrat, A. A., Schelén, O., & Andersson, K. (2019). A survey of blockchain from the perspectives of applications, challenges, and opportunities. *IEEE Access: Practical Innovations, Open Solutions, 7*, 117134–117151. doi:10.1109/ACCESS.2019.2936094

Nguyen, G. T., & Kim, K. (2018). A survey about consensus algorithms used in blockchain. *Journal of Information Processing Systems, 14*(1), 101-128.

Risius, M., & Spohrer, K. (2017). A blockchain research framework. *Business & Information Systems Engineering, 59*(6), 385–409. doi:10.100712599-017-0506-0

Rizal Batubara, F., Ubacht, J., & Janssen, M. (2019, June). Unraveling transparency and accountability in blockchain. In *Proceedings of the 20th annual international conference on digital government research* (pp. 204-213). 10.1145/3325112.3325262

Yao, W., Ye, J., Murimi, R., & Wang, G. (2021). *A survey on consortium blockchain consensus mechanisms.* arXiv preprint arXiv:2102.12058.

Zheng, Z., Xie, S., Dai, H. N., Chen, X., & Wang, H. (2018). Blockchain challenges and opportunities: A survey. *International Journal of Web and Grid Services, 14*(4), 352–375. doi:10.1504/IJWGS.2018.095647

ADDITIONAL READING

Antonopoulos, A. M., & Wood, G. (2018). *Mastering ethereum: building smart contracts and dapps.* O'Reilly Media.

Mazieres, D. (2015). The stellar consensus protocol: A federated model for internet-level consensus. *Stellar Development Foundation, 32*, 1–45.

Ramamurthy, B. (2018). Blockchain basics. Coursera platform Offered by University at Buffalo, The State University of New York.

Ramamurthy, B. (2020). *Blockchain in action.* Manning Publications.

KEY TERMS AND DEFINITIONS

Consortium Blockchain: Distributed network in which multiple parties with similar business goals and agreed upon common authorization and access control policies participate in operations of a blockchain.

Distributed Consensus Algorithm: Algorithm that is used by peer nodes present in a distributed blockchain network to arrive at a consensus, to decide on the next block that must be added to the blockchain.

Distributed Ledger: An e-ledger that is stored in a distributed fashion at peer nodes of a blockchain. It holds details of assets or transactions that are time stamped, stored in an immutable fashion, and are updated whenever there is state change.

Merkle Tree: Binary hash tree constructed by repeatedly hashing pairs of child node hash values in order to ensure data integrity.

Miner: A node in a blockchain network that runs a consensus algorithm to decide on the next block to be added to the blockchain.

Permissioned Blockchain: Public or private blockchain network in which participants must be given permission to view or write a transaction.

Permissionless Blockchain: Public or private blockchain network in which participants require no permission to view or write a transaction.

Private Blockchain: Distributed blockchain network in which members are authorized to participate in operations of a blockchain with predefined roles and access control.

Public Blockchain: Distributed blockchain network in which anyone can participate, view transaction and leave the network without anyone else's permission.

Smart Contract: Agreement stored as an executable code and is triggered automatically on execution of a transaction without any intervention.

Chapter 7
A Novel Steganography Approach Using S–CycleGAN With an Improvement of Loss Function

Minakshi Sarkar
Haldia Institute of Technology, India

Indrajit Banerjee
Indian Institute of Engineering Science and Technology, Shibpur, India

Tarun Kumar Ghosh

ⓘ https://orcid.org/0000-0003-4685-5381
Haldia Institute of Technology, India

Anirban Samanta
Haldia Institute of Technology, India

Anirban Sarkar
Guru Nanak Institute of technology, India

ABSTRACT

Technologies related to the internet of things (IoT) have been extensively employed in business operations, military research, networking technologies, etc. With the proliferation of the IoT, data theft and leakage have gradually increased because the data communication system is public. Various novel steganography algorithms have been proposed for data hiding. But in this process, the quality of the hidden image decreases badly. We want to give an accurate color to the image instead of severe color changes. To change it, we have to perform a colorization process by mapping the original image to the stego image. It gains more characteristics according to the actual embodiment. Here, the objective is to improve the appearance by calculating the loss function. The stego image can withstand steganalysis by using the authors' proposed scheme by maintaining its integrity while to some extent improving the quality of the image. The experimental results confirmed the proposed method outperforms the existing methods (SGAN and CycleGAN) for information hiding with enhanced image transmission quality.

DOI: 10.4018/978-1-6684-7524-9.ch007

1. INTRODUCTION

The wide use of personal computers and the availability of multimedia content on the web provided the ideal conditions for the exposing of private information since information might contain valuable, personal, medical information (Hore et al. 2016; Chakraborty et al. 2017) or even confidential information (Roy et al. 2019; Seal et al. 2017). Furthermore, there are certain major risks to the leaked information, including unauthorized manipulation, copying, and transmission. Image steganography has evolved as a crucial matter in the prospect of secret communication and copyright infringement. Since steganography involves complex computations to embed secret information in cover images, implementing it for technology speeds up the process and increases its acceptability (Shet et al. 2019; Roy et al. 2020; Chakraborty & Mali, 2021a, 2021b; Singh et al. 2020). However, the cover image will still show the changes brought about by the embedding, allowing it to apply processes more effectively called steganalysis, a technique for finding secret data. The exchange of information between the mobile unit and the server creates the interface between the items and the network, which sends information to the mobile terminal over the network (Qiu et al. 2018; Chakraborty et al. 2016; Mali et al. 2021). Public service computing in this context is typically provided by high-performance servers (Qiu et al. 2018). The emergency packets are now being used and upgraded to effectively handle the network congestion issue in the Internet of Things, we propose a novel steganography method based on generative adversarial networks (GAN). If the cover data are available to the public, a third party can easily decode the secret message by comparing the cover data to the message being hidden. We require a distinct cover data for each piece of secret communication in order to prevent this problem. In this study, we rely on images as the cover data. We can employ GAN to create a great deal of unique and authentic-looking photos. In reality, GAN training leads to the creation of the generator and discriminator neural networks. The discriminator evaluates the virtual pictures' naturalness once the generator generates them. The generator and discriminator are both used in the proposed methods to secure the sender side cover information is authentic and to remove stego data provided by unreliable third parties. In this work, before considering the viability of using the discriminator we need to test naturalness of images, we first established that the generator can produce an infinite amount of cover data. We hope that the proposed method can provide a more effective way of information concealment.

In this study, we describe a technique that can be applied to achieve the same goal with unique attributes of one image collection and evaluate how these attributes may be applied to the second image collection—all without any paired training sets. A more general definition for this issue is described in image-to-image translation (Wang et al. 2013). It involves altering an image to show a scene from one representation, x, to another, y, for as from gray scale to color, from an image to semantic labels, or from an edge-map to a photograph. Since the expected result is pretty complex and generally needs artistic composition, finding input-output combinations for graphic operations like artistic stylization could be more complicated. The expected result isn't even clear for many tasks, including object transformation (like zebra-to-horse). In order to avoid paired input-output instances, we want an algorithm that can translate between different domains. We assume that there is a fundamental relationship between the domains; for example, that they are two different perceptions of the same fundamental environment, and we seek to identify that relationship. Even though we aren't given paired examples of supervision, we are therefore given one set of image collections in domain A and another set in domain B, allowing us to take advantage of supervision at the level of sets. A mapping relationship between two domains is established. In this case, G converts an image from domain A to domain B. Such a translation does not yet guarantee the meaningful matching of the individual inputs and outputs are a and b. However, we have observed difficulties when trying to optimize the adversarial goal in practice: common practices normally take place in the well-known issue of mode collapse, when optimization fails and all input images map to the same output image (Shrivastava et al. 2017). We must add extra strategy to our goal in order to address these issues. As a result, we take advantage of the fact that translation should be "cycle consistent" which states that the original statement should arise from, for example, translating a sentence from English to French and then back from French to English (Taigman et al. 2016).

Here, we have a translator G: A→ B and another translator F: B→A. Both mappings should be bijections, and G and F should be the integrals of one another. By simultaneously training the mapping G and F and introducing a cycle consistency loss, that argues F(G(a)) » a and G(F(b)) » b. Combining this loss with adversarial losses on domains A and B allows us to achieve our entire goal for image-to-image translation. Using our method, we may transfer styles, change objects, transfer attributes, and improve images, among many other activities. Moreover, we show how our approach outperforms past approaches that either rely on manually generated factorizations of style and content or on common embedding functions.

The remaining sections of the work are structured as follows. The concepts, technologies, and quality of the research in relation to the suggested technique are discussed in Section 2. Section 3 presents the fundamental concept of the proposed approach. To show the usefulness of the approach described in the study, different experiments are carried out using the comparison results in Section 4. In Section 5, conclusions are given.

2. RELATED WORKS

Steganography is a technique for hiding the presence of secret data from digital media. Traditional steganography, however, becomes insecure if the cover data are made available to the public since a third party might be able to extract hidden information by contrasting the original digital content with the embedded one (e.g., available in the internet). In order to use steganography safely, each piece of secret communication must have a unique cover datum. We concentrate on photos as the cover image, Li et al. (2018) have developed a steganography approach for the Internet of Things. This method concentrates on selecting an excellent cover image, which is the ideal image to implant hidden messages through preprocessing. Furthermore, Chen et al. (2005) used a mobile platform information masking technique. They designed a more effective image steganography technique for transmitting data securely from a computer to a mobile device. With their technique, users could use a password to encrypt communications in computer-generated images that could be downloaded to mobile devices. The decryption program will use Java applications on the phone to retrieve concealed data. Shirali-Shahreza (2007) later developed secret information sharing using classified short messages and text and image-based MMS steganography to realize concealed communication. Cui et al.(2019) offered a technique for creating foreground objects by employing GAN and edge computing on the Internet of Things.

A feed-forward convolutional neural network can be trained to perform image transformation tasks, and the difference between the output and reference images can be calculated by using a per-pixel loss function. For instance, Dong et al. (2016) employed this approach for super-resolution, Cheng et al. (2015) used it for colorization, Long et al. (2015) used it for segmentation and Eigen et al. (2014) used it for depth estimation and surface normal prediction. Such techniques are efficient during testing since they only require one forward transit over the training set. The per-pixel losses used by these methods. However, do not take into consideration perceptual differences between the output and actual images by texture synthesis and style transfer (Gatys et al. 2015), these methods create high-quality images but take a long time since prediction necessitates resolving an optimization issue.

In the proposed scheme we are using the S-CycleGAN to hide information for secure communication. In order to accomplish good quality image and the embedded images ability to withstand steganalysis at the same time, we are carrying out information hiding in accordance with CycleGAN while converting the image from the A-domain into the style image of the B-domain. The strategy that contains three stages. Generator G, converts the A-domain image into a B-domain style image at the first step, that is b'. D_B is used to make a differentiate between the produced image b' and the original image $b(b \in B)$. If the difference can be found, the generator will change how the image is distributed until it can deceive the D_B. In the second stage of covert communications, the stego image is named as b'' by applying the LSB matching steganography technique to implant the hidden messages into the produced image b'. The stego images as fake images and the generated images as actual images are going to steganalysis module S as input. Increasing the difference between the generated image and the stego image is the aim of steganalysis S. The generator will change the distribution of b' after S is able to recognize the dissimilarity between a stego image and a produced image. This will continue until S can be fooled once the secret messages have been revealed. As a result, a good-quality stego image that can withstand steganalysis is produced. The third stage enables the generator F to reconstruct the stego image from the generator $G's$ input image a, producing $\bar{a}$ and actual image at which are as similar as possible.

Other information-hiding algorithms, such as HUGO (Pevný et al. 2010), WOW (Holub & Fridrich, 2012), UNIWARD (Holub et al. 2014), and others, have been developed based on the essential concepts of the LSB algorithm. The concealed approach in DWT (discrete wavelet transform), DFT (discrete Fourier transform), DCT (discrete cosine transform), and IWT (integer wavelet transform) domains are only a few of the transform domain steganography techniques that have been presented. Recently, other steganography algorithms with stronger security have been developed based on them, the most current IWT steganography has a high level of security that is based on a 3D sine chaotic map. Chaos theory has an widespread application in image encryption and steganography (Cao et al. 2018; Chakraborty et al., 2021a, 2021b).The most recent IWT steganography based on a 3D sine chaotic map, which has good security and tolerable robustness, was developed using the steganography algorithms that have enhanced security in recent years (Valandar et al. 2018). Security can be further enhanced by combining it with hardware, particularly FPGAs (field programmable gate arrays) (Liang et al. 2015). However, it is not hard to find out that traditional image steganography modifies the image's information to some extent, making it challenging to avoid being detected by image steganalysis tools. Classification, object and face recognition, forensics, etc. all usually employed deep learning extensively (Chakraborty, 2020; Chakraborty et al. 2017; C. Li et al. 2018; Nogueira et al. 2016). The progress of deep learning has led to the development of numerous CNN-based algorithms(Chakraborty et al. 2020; Mali et al. 2018, 2020). DNA based approaches are also used in securing digital data (Chakraborty et al. 2019, 2020).

2.1 Generative Adversarial Network

In 2020, the GAN model proposed by Goodfellow et al. (2020) that replicates the distribution from reasonably realistic computer image production to natural images. It contains two fundamental substructures: generators and discriminators. Using a convolution process and noise from random input, a generator produces an image. The produced image and the original image are then transmitted to the classifier, which then classifies them in order to find out if the distribution of the produced image and the original image satisfies the lowest value of the maximal difference of her KL divergence, the discriminator employs supervised learning to learn the features that were taken from the real image and the produced image. The generator modifies the produced image to the discriminator's ideal orientation up until the point at which the discriminator fails to recognise the produced image effectively at a certain point.

The stability between the generator and discriminator, as well as the stability between the variety and quality of created instances, were all successfully controlled in the recommended version. According to (Ma et al. 2018), DA-GAN may be employed to produce instance images by converting a textual description into an image (Chakraborty et al. 2018, 2021).

The concept of an adversarial loss, which drives the generated images to be, in theory, indistinguishable from real images, is essential for the success of GANs. As this is basically the aim of computer graphics which tries to improve, that will be effective for jobs that involve image generation. By using adversarial loss function, we can learn the mapping in a way that the translated image cannot be discriminated from images in the target domain. Higher-order cycle consistency has been applied more recently in depth estimation (Sangkloy et al. 2017), structure from motion (Sangkloy et al. 2017), co-segmentation (Isola et al. 2017), and dense semantic alignment. Of these, Aytar et al. (2018) and Godard et al. (2017) are most relevant to our work since they employ transitivity to supervise CNN training by using a cycle consistency loss. In order to compel G and F to be identical with one another, we are implementing an equivalent loss in this work.

2.2 Image-To-Image Translation

Hertzmann et al. (2001) suggested that non-parametric texture version for translating one image to another using the approach of picture analogies. GAN is perfectly suited to generate natural images because of its adversarial properties. By altering conditional adversarial networks, Isola et al.(2017)developed the "pix2pix" framework. The approach provides a U-Net architecture to the generator. Additionally, *L1* loss was implemented on the basis of adversarial loss to evaluate the difference between the input image and the output image, making it suited for image translation and allowing the output image to be formed from the input image for the matching domain. On the basis of pix2pix, Wang et al. (2018) achieved the production of high-resolution images. Multiple GAN served as the foundation for the Single GAN presented by (Yu et al. 2019). To produce a multi-domain picture, it just used one generator for translating the images. Anoosheh et al. (2019) suggested RoDayGAN where the night driving picture was transformed into a more useful day driving image using an altered image translation model and the nearest day image's known 6-DOF location.

2.3 Unpaired Image-to-Image Translation

In unpaired scenario, different approaches are used to connect the two information domains, A and B, is likewise addressed by a variety of different techniques. Rosales et al. (2003) create a Bayesian framework with a prior based on a patch-based Markov random field produced from a source image and a probability term derived from several style images. CoupledGANs (Aytar et al. 2018) and cross-modal scene networks (Liu et al. 2017) have more recently employed a weight-sharing strategy to build a shared model across domains. In parallel with our approach, Liu et al. (2017) expands this approach using generative adversarial networks and variational autoencoders (Kingma & Welling, 2013). Although the input and output may differ in "style," in another line of parallel work (Bousmalis, Shrivastava et al. 2017; Taigman et al. 2016) which emphasizes the sharing of certain "content" features. Additionally, they employ adversarial networks with extra terms, such as class label space (Bousmalis et al. 2017), image pixel space (Shrivastava et al. 2017), and image feature space (Taigman et al. 2016), to force the output to be similar to the input in a present metric space. Unlike the existing techniques, our approach does not require that the input and output must be located in the same low-dimensional embedding space, nor does it rely on any task-specific, predetermined similarity function between the two. Our approach is now a direct answer to a variety of vision and graphics problems.

2.3 Steganography

To conceal personal data, it is difficult for a viewer to identify, image steganography methods make use of redundant information in the cover image. It is accomplished by transmitting confidential information through the stego image's public transmission. The least significant bit (LSB) substitution was initially used. Secret information is placing into the pixel's least significant bit, for concealing the information. Although the LSB technique is simple to extract and use and has a huge concealing capacity, its stability and anti-detectability are poor. Sajedi & Jamzad (2010) developed the boosted steganography system (BSS) to increase the resilience of stego images. Before using steganography techniques, it is having a preprocessing step where a cover image could be chosen from a large database. Additionally, the experimental findings demonstrated that the approach might significantly increase steganography security. Content adaptive algorithms like S-UNIWARD (Holub et al. 2014), WOW (Holub & Fridrich, 2012), HUGO (Pevný et al. 2010) and others are constructed using the idea of reducing distortion. By creating a distortion cost function, this type of algorithm determines the image distortion that results from the embedding of secret messages and provides the optimal value at which each unit should be implanted. The hidden message is covered by the embeddable unit before the stego image is produced. GAN's image was more adapted for steganography because of the conflict between its generator and GNCNN. Although, the unpaired image-to-image translation problems had been resolved at the time CycleGAN was introduced, there were still some issues.

3. THE PROPOSED STEGANOGRAPHIC SCHEME

In this scheme, we developed a new hybrid steganography algorithm known as S-CycleGAN. An example of embedded communication between terminals in the Internet of Things using a public channel is shown in Fig.1. The IoT terminals in this example are *X1, X2, X3,* and *X4*. On *X1* and *X2*, there is embedded transmission. In this proposed approach the terminal*X1*is used to conceal the hidden information in a cover image, and *X2* receives the stego image with the private message encoded in it. The extraction algorithm is used by *X2* to extract the message. CycleGAN was modified by our work to be more sophisticated by including steganography and steganalysis modules.

Our main target is to develop a mapping function between two domains A and B, training samples are given $\{a_i\}_{i=1}^{N} \in A$ and $\{b_j\}_{j=1}^{M} \in B$. As shown in Fig. 2(A), This model has two cycles embedded in it:(G: A→ B) →b̆, F: b̆ → A and Embedding: (F: B → A) →ă, G: ă→ B. Here A and B represents the

Figure 1. The process of embedded communication between terminals and the IoT

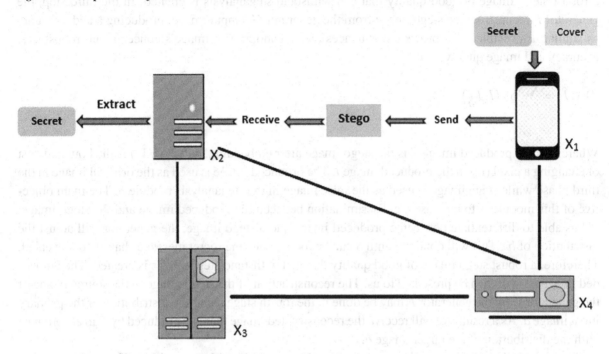

two domains. There are total three discriminators D_A, D_B and S where the function of D_A and D_B are same as D_A and D_B of CycleGAN. The produced image is discriminated from the target domain image by D_A and D_B. The enhanced steganalysis module S, is utilized to make a discrimination between the stego image and original domain's produced images. In order to match the distribution of generated images to the given data in the target domain, our target is to use of adversarial losses (Chen et al., 2005) and a cycle consistency loss to prevent the obtained mappings A and B from contradicting one another.

We are recommending S-CycleGAN for our suggested strategy. We employ the concept of CycleGAN, which is used to hide information when we convert an image from the A-domain into a style image of the B-domain, to reach optimal quality image alteration and the stego image's ability to withstand steganalysis at the same time. D_B distinguishes between the produced image b' and the original image $b(b \in B)$. If we can determine the difference, the generator will modify the obtained image's distribution untilit can deceive D_B. If the difference can be identified, the generator will revise the distribution of the produced image until it can fool the D_B. In the second stage of covert communication steganography has started. LSB matching steganography algorithm is used to implant the hidden messages into the produced image b' and after embedding the image is formed as b'. The main objective of this steganography approach is to pad the binary representation of a secret message before storing it in a stego-container by overwriting the LSB of each byte. By randomly adding or removing 1 from a pixel's color channel so that the final bit matches it, each bit of the message is concealed. Here, the embedding positions are selected to reduce the distortion function and each pixel is provided an embedding cost. The produced images as authentic images and the stego images as false images serve as the inputs to steganalysis S. This model is employed here to increase the difference between the produced image and the stego image. If S is able to differentiate between a produced image and a stego image, the generator will revise the distribution of b'. This will continue until S can be fooled once the secret messages have been revealed. Therefore, a robust stego image of good quality that can withstand steganalysis is created. In the third step, the generator F reconstruct the stego image from the generator G's input image, producing $\bar{a}$ and a that are as similar as possible. This procedure enhances the steganographic image's concealment, robustness, accuracy and image quality.

$$D(I, \hat{I}) = \sum_{i,j} \rho_{i,j}(I, \hat{I}_{i,j})$$

Where, I is the produced image, $\hat{I}$ is the stego image after embedding, and $\rho_{i,j}(I, \hat{I}_{i,j})$ is the bounded cost of changing a pixel (i,j) in the produced image I. The produced image is used as the original image in the third phase while stego image is used as the false image in the steganalysis module S. The main objective of this module is to increase the discrimination between the produced image and the stego image. If S is able to differentiate between a produced image and a stego image, the generator will adjust the distribution of b'. This will continue until S can be fooled once the secret messages have been revealed. Therefore, a robust stego image of good quality that can withstand steganalysis is created. The embedded image b'' will then be presented to us. The reconstruction of the stego image to the source image of the generator G by the generator F may be done in the fourth stage using the distribution of the primary input image a. As a result, we will receive the reconstructed image that is $\bar{a}$ produced by F in accordance with the distribution of the target image a.

Thus, we will obtain an excellent stego image that can withstand steganalysis. The conversion and steganography process from B-domain to A-domain is similar to the conversion and steganography process from A-domain to B-domain which is shown in Figure 2(B).

3.1 Embedding Algorithm

Algorithm 1: Algorithm of Embedding applied in the proposed S-CycleGAN

Input: The Image of domain A and the hidden message M_{secret}
Output: The stego image b'' of domain B, transforming by the trained Model: $a \rightarrow b'$
Embedding the M_{secret} into produced image b':

```
1       for j ← 1 to length (M_secret)  do
2             if LSB(b'(j)) == LSB(M_secret(j)) then
3                   pass
4             else if b'(j) == 0 then
5                   b'(j) + = 1
6             else if b'(j) == 255  then
7                   b'(j) - = 1
8       else
9                   b'(j) + = randomInt (0, 1)
10
11    return b' as b "
```

Figure 2. The full processes of S-CycleGAN, (A) conversion from A domain to B domain (B) conversion from B domain to A Domain

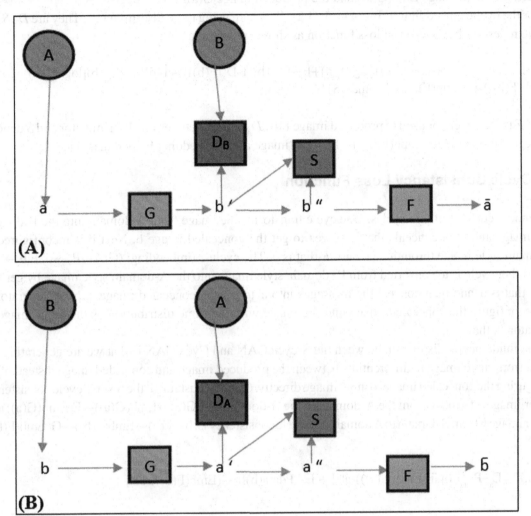

3.2 Adversarial Loss Function

Regarding the cyclic embedding (G:A→B)→ƀ, F:ƀ→A, we are using here three discriminators. They are D_A, D_B, and S. We calculate adversarial loss function as shown in formula (1).

$$L_{GAN}((G,S D_B,A,B)=\delta((E_b \sim P_{data}(b)[\log D_B(b)+E_a \sim P_{data}(a)[1-D_B(G(A))])+(1-\delta)E_a \sim P_{data}(a)[\log S(G(a))+\log(1-S(Emb(G(a))))]\rightarrow \min(G)\max(D_B)\max(S) \qquad (1)$$

Here, $P_{data}(a)$ and $P_{data}(b)$ denotes the distribution of real image from A domain and B domain. D_B, D_A and S are respectively two discriminator and steganalysis module. Emb(G(a)) is the setgo image after concealing the secret information into the produced image. Function of generator G is used to produce image G(a). The purpose of the discriminator D_B is to distinguish the difference between the generated image G(b) and the real image b. The purpose of the discriminator D_B is to distinguish the difference between the stego image Emb(G(a)) and the produced image G(a).

For the cyclic embedding (F:B→A)→ã, G:ã→B, we are using three discriminants. They are D_A, S and D_B. We redesign the adverserial loss function as shown in formula (2).

$$L_{GAN}((F,S D_A,A,B)=\delta((E_a \sim P_{data}(a)[\log D_A(a)+E_b \sim P_{data}(b)[1-D_A(F(b))]+(1-\delta)E_b \sim P_{data}(b)[\log S(F(b))+\log(1-S(Emb(F(b))))] \rightarrow \min(F)\max(D_A)\max(S) \tag{2}$$

where F is the generator used to produced image F(b). D_A and D_B denotes the discriminator and S denotes the steganalysis module. Emb(F(b)) is the stego image after embedding hidden message.

3.3. Cycle Consistency Loss Function

This model consists of two cycles. One cycle transforms the image from A-domain into the B-domain style image and then conceals the messages to get the concealed image ƀ, Next ƀ is reconfigured to A-domain style image through generator F that is a. The cycles: Embedding: (G:A→B)→ƀ, F:ƀ →A.

Another cycle is to converted from B- domain style image into the A-domain style image by generator F, that is a' and then conceal the messages into a' to get the concealed image ã. Next generator G will reconfigure the concealed image into the image with the same distribution as the input image of generator F, that is a.

The fundamental distinction between the S-cycleGAN and CycleGAN is that we are generating the output from stego image to differentiate between the produced image and concealed image instead of re-configuring the concealed image to input image directly. G and F must fulfill the reverse cycle consistency.

For image a to move from the A-domain to the B-domain: a→G(a)→Emb(G(a))→F(Emb(G(a)))≈a.

For image b from B domain to A domain, the cycle consistency is: b→F(b)→Emb(F(b))→G(Emb(F(b))) ≈ b

$$L_{cyc}(G,F)=E_a \sim P_{data}(a)[\|F(Emb(G(a)))-a\|] + E_b \sim P_{data}(b)[\| G(Emb(F(b)))-b\|] \tag{3}$$

3.4. Full Objective Function

The full objective function is given in formula (3). Ithas two cycles they are adversarial losses $L_{GAN}(G,S,D_B,A,B)$ and $L_{GAN}(F,S,D_A,A,B)$ and a cycle consistency loss that is

$$L_{cyc}(G,F). L(G,F,S,D_A,D_B)=L_{GAN}(G,F,S,D_B,A,B)+ L_{GAN}(F,S,D_A,A,B) + \lambda L_{cyc}(G,F) \tag{4}$$

4. EXPERIMENTAL OUTCOMES

We carried out the following studies to determine how well the suggested S-CycleGAN scheme works.

1.   Adding a steganography and steganalysis module to CycleGAN, that is our approach.

2. Measuring the image quality of two sets of stego images produced by two steganographic algorithms using the Fréchet Inception Distance (FID) and Inception score (IS) (Dhawan & Gupta, 2021).

3. To evaluate the level of concealment of the three groups of stego images produced by the steganographic algorithms SGAN, S-CycleGAN, and CycleGAN with S-UNIWARD, steganalysis methods SPA and SRM are employed to analyse the stego images.

4. We calculate PSNR and MSE to make a differentiation in between the real image and stego images.

The proposed steganographic approach is applied to various standard test images. The suggested technique is validated with the help of both qualitative and quantitative analysis. The proposed approach is evaluated on 107 test images and quantified using various standard evaluation matrices. Some sample qualitative outcomes are reported in Figures 3 and 4.

In our approach at training process, the learning rate is by default fixed to 0.0001 with update parameters $\beta_1 = 0.5$ and $\beta_2 = 0.999$. Adam is the optimization function we use here, with a momentum of 0.5. In this approach, the weight of the regulatory term is set to 12. According to CycleGAN's architecture, the generative network has 10 residual blocks with instance adjustment(Pradhan et al., 2018) for data processing during style shifting. In the first layer of the discriminant networks and steganalysis networks, Instance Normalization is not configured, and leaky Relu with a value of 0.2 is added in the following three levels. After feeding the inputs, a high pass convolutional kernel is applied to extract poor embedded attributes. The extracted attributes are then applied for steganalysis. We will mimic confidential material as random binary codes with the same size as the pixels in the input image throughout the training process. Then we get output stego images of size 256 x 256 from the generated images. Consequently, the payload is 1 and the embedded binary code length is 256 x 256 x 3. Table 3 presents some experimental results. Stego images were produced using the steganography algorithms S-CycleGAN and SGAN using the datasets for cameraman, mandril and jet plane respectively in Figures 3 and 4. We can clearly see that stego images generated by S-CycleGAN have significantly better image quality than those generated by SGAN through the comparison and presenting of various experimental outcomes.

From Table 3, we can say that the IS value of the stego image created by S-CycleGAN is higher than that of the stego image produced by SGAN, with the exception of the Pepper data set. In the comparison using the Cameraman data set, the IS value of the image generated by S-CycleGAN is in particular 2.7 times greater than that of the image generated by SGAN. It indicates that the diversity impact of S-CycleGAN is higher and that the image distribution produced by the method of SGAN.

FID is calculated here as another evaluation metric to overcome the drawback of IS in the evaluation of image quality. Using Inception-v3 metric, FID evaluates the Wasserstein-2 distance between the generated and real image. The better the image quality, the closer the distance between the two distributions is shown by a lower FID value. Compared to IS, FID is more noise-resistant. Furthermore, FID presents a more accurate approximation of the human visual system. We therefore conclude that FID more accurately conveys the quality of generated images. The comparative results of FID and IS are given in Table 3. From the FID evaluation, all images produced by S-CycleGAN outperform those produced by SGAN. In comparison to the FID value of the stego image created by SGAN, the maximum FID value of the stego image produced by S-CycleGAN can be nearly 7 times higher. Here, FID values further establishes that our proposed approach produces generated stego images of higher quality than SGAN.

The proposed approach is evaluated using some standard metrices like mean squared error (MSE), peak signal-to-noise ratio (PSNR), structural similarity index measure (SSIM), and image fidelity (IF), Inception score (IS) and Fréchet inception distance (FID) of the generated stego images by S-CycleGAN

Figure 3. Obtained outcomes after applying the proposed approach

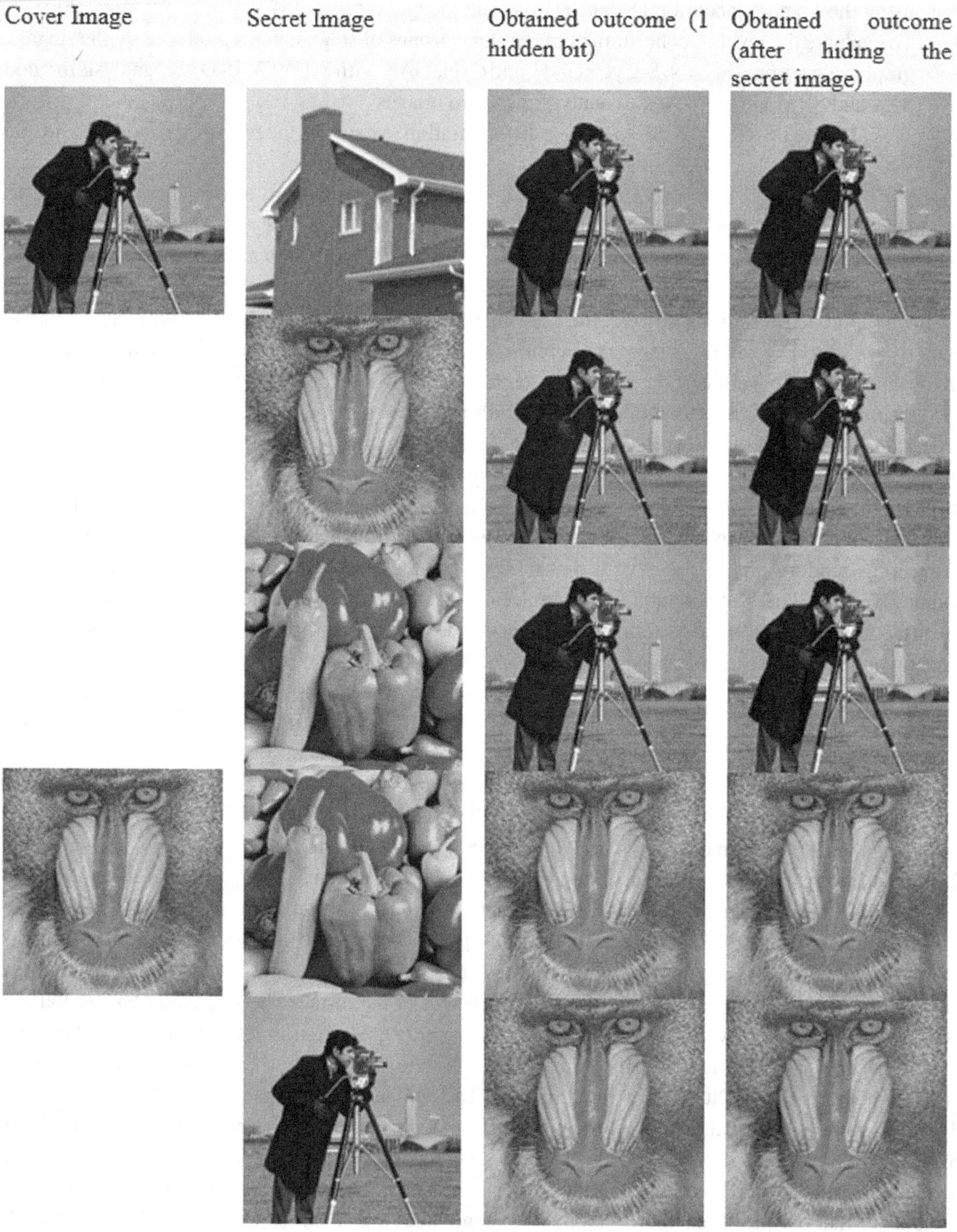

Figure 4. Obtained outcomes after applying the proposed approach

and SGAN. Equations 5 to 9 are used to define these parameters respectively. Quantitative outcomes are reported in tables 1,2 and 3 respectively(Mali et al. 2015).

$$MSE = \frac{1}{r \times c} \sum_{i=1}^{r} \sum_{j=1}^{c} \left(C(i,j) - S(i,j) \right)^2 \tag{5}$$

here, C and S denote the cover image and secret image respectively. r and c denotes the row and column dimension of an image respectively.

$$PSNR = 10 \cdot \log_{10}\left(\frac{255^2}{MSE}\right) \tag{6}$$

$$SSIM\left(\omega_1, \omega_2\right) = \frac{\left(2 \cdot \mu_{\omega_1} \cdot \mu_{\omega_2} + \alpha_1\right) \cdot \left(2 \cdot \sigma_{\omega_1 \omega_2} + \alpha_2\right)}{\left(\mu_{\omega_1}^2 + \mu_{\omega_2}^2 + \alpha_1\right) \cdot \left(\sigma_{\omega_1}^2 + \sigma_{\omega_2}^2 + \alpha_2\right)} \tag{7}$$

In equation 7, $\omega 1$, $\omega 2$ denotes two windows that are extracted from the cover image and hidden image respectively. μ and σ represents the average and variance respectively and two constants are $\alpha 1$ and $\alpha 2$.

$$IF = 1 - \frac{\sum_{i=1}^{r}\sum_{j=1}^{c}\left(C(i,j) - S(i,j)\right)^2}{\sum_{i=1}^{r}\sum_{j=1}^{c}\left(C(i,j) \times S(i,j)\right)} \tag{8}$$

Table 1. Comparison of MSE and PSNR

Cover image	Secret image	Dhawan et. al. (Dhawan & Gupta, 2021)		Pradhan et.al. (Pradhan et al., 2018)		Proposed	
		MSE	PSNR	MSE	PSNR	MSE	PSNR
Cameraman	House	1.2206	47.26506995	1.03369	47.98690046	0.4406	51.69035868
	Mandril	2.5908	43.99646472	0.88639	48.65455513	0.6605	49.93207539
	Peppers	0.9968	48.14472332	0.5966	50.37397112	0.8051	49.07230534
Mandril	Peppers	1.2996	46.99270658	0.7783	49.2193333	0.7066	49.63906728
	Cameraman	0.8869	48.65205706	0.9972	48.14298091	0.9036	48.57104139
	Livingroom	4.5086	41.59038654	1.5966	46.09884236	0.7109	49.61271847
Jetplane	Pirate	4.6603	41.44666486	1.3664	46.77502508	0.9994	48.13341016
	Woman darkhair	3.5506	42.62778612	2.0889	44.93162711	0.9716	48.25592855
	Livingroom	2.9906	43.37322032	0.8896	48.63885587	0.9933	48.15999925

The following equation is used to determine the FID score, where C 1 and C 2 are the covariance matrices for the real and produced feature vectors, respectively. The sum squared difference between the two mean vectors is denoted by the term ||b – G(b)||2. ^{T}r denotes trace linear algebra operation. Here, b is real image and G(b) is produced image. The score is denoted as d2, indicating that the produced and real images are separated by a Wasserstein-2 distance.

d2 = ||b – G(b)||2 + Tr(C1 + C2 – 2*sqrt(C1*C2)) (9)

Table 2. Comparison of SSIM and IF

Cover image	Secret image	Dhawan et. al. (Dhawan & Gupta, 2021)		Pradhan et.al. (Pradhan et al., 2018)		Proposed	
		IF	SSIM	IF	SSIM	IF	SSIM
Cameraman	House	0.789210	0.925387	0.930860	0.9800879	0.9540460	0.92751816
	Mandril	0.8062822	0.9973540	0.9371532	0.9105776	0.9800198	0.95544474
	Peppers	0.8110723	0.9719873	0.8988819	0.9988598	0.9492847	0.98343733
Mandril	Peppers	0.8163892	0.9686750	0.9230296	0.9705966	0.9050239	0.99603508
	Cameraman	0.8466197	0.9476650	0.9053847	0.9247648	0.9763741	0.95492981
	Livingroom	0.8186557	0.9426407	0.9473074	0.9190674	0.9334662	0.98353311
Jetplane	Pirate	0.7954019	0.9813576	0.9351899	0.9097745	0.9967096	0.9970169
	Woman darkhair	0.8531001	0.9695801	0.9301590	0.94534823	0.9898401	0.9756969
	Livingroom	0.7879290	0.9740423	0.9533363	0.9734556	0.9052368	0.9911214

Table 3. Inception score and Fréchet inception distance of the generated stego images by S-CycleGAN and SGAN

Cover image	Secret image	S-CycleGAN(Proposed)		SGAN	
		FID	IS	FID	IS
Cameraman	House	113.75	5.26	268.38	3.87
	Mandril	136.31	4.65	314.67	4.55
	Peppers	54.57	3.67	113.42	4.43
Mandril	Peppers	46.32	1.56	309.17	1.49
	Cameraman	55.63	5.66	205.38	2.13
	Livingroom	51.03	3.78	62.73	3.08
Jetplane	Pirate	59.78	2.49	132.84	2.06
	Woman darkhair	72.03	2.54	159.43	2.03
	Livingroom	78.65	3.77	195.23	2.93

5. CONCLUSION

Image steganography is an essential and almost inevitable part of the secured data communications. In this work, an approach towards securing digital images by hiding it inside another image is made. The experimental outcomes shows that the proposed approach is effective enough to successfully hide digital images. Both qualitative and quantitative outcomes are encouraging and establishes the real-life applicability of the proposed approach in various domains. This approach can be further extended by modifying the basic architecture of the proposed framework. Moreover, this approach can also be applied on various type of datasets.

REFERENCES

Anoosheh, A., Sattler, T., Timofte, R., Pollefeys, M., & Van Gool, L. (2019). Night-to-day image translation for retrieval-based localization. *2019 International Conference on Robotics and Automation (ICRA)*, 5958-5964. 10.1109/ICRA.2019.8794387

Aytar, Y., Castrejon, L., Vondrick, C., Pirsiavash, H., & Torralba, A. (2017). Cross-modal scene networks. *IEEE Transactions on Pattern Analysis and Machine Intelligence*, *40*(10), 2303–2314. doi:10.1109/TPAMI.2017.2753232 PMID:28922114

Bousmalis, K., Silberman, N., Dohan, D., Erhan, D., & Krishnan, D. (2017). Unsupervised pixel-level domain adaptation with generative adversarial networks. *Proceedings of the IEEE conference on computer vision and pattern recognition*, 3722-3731. 10.1109/CVPR.2017.18

Cao, C., Sun, K., & Liu, W. (2018). A novel bit-level image encryption algorithm based on 2D-LICM hyperchaotic map. *Signal Processing*, *143*, 122–133. doi:10.1016/j.sigpro.2017.08.020

Chakraborty, S. (2020). An advanced approach to detect edges of digital images for image segmentation. Applications of Advanced Machine Intelligence in Computer Vision and Object Recognition: Emerging Research and Opportunities, 90-118. doi:10.4018/978-1-7998-2736-8.ch004

Chakraborty, S., Mali, K., Banerjee, A., & Bhattacharjee, M. (2021). A Biomedical Image Segmentation Approach Using Fractional Order Darwinian Particle Swarm Optimization and Thresholding. Springer. doi:10.1007/978-981-15-9433-5_29

Chakraborty, S., Chatterjee, S., Ashour, A. S., Mali, K., & Dey, N. (2018). Intelligent computing in medical imaging: A study. *Advancements in applied metaheuristic computing*, 143-163. global.doi.org/10.4018/978-1-7998-8048-6.ch030

Chakraborty, S., Chatterjee, S., Dey, N., Ashour, A. S., Ashour, A. S., Shi, F., & Mali, K. (2017). Modified cuckoo search algorithm in microscopic image segmentation of hippocampus. *Microscopy Research and Technique*, *80*(10), 1051–1072. doi:10.1002/jemt.22900 PMID:28557041

Chakraborty, S., Chatterjee, S., Dey, N., Ashour, A. S., & Shi, F. (2017). Gradient approximation in retinal blood vessel segmentation. *2017 4th IEEE Uttar Pradesh Section International Conference on Electrical, Computer and Electronics (UPCON)*, 618-623. 10.1109/UPCON.2017.8251120

Chakraborty, S., & Mali, K. (2018). Application of multiobjective optimization techniques in biomedical image segmentation—a study. *Multi-Objective Optimization: Evolutionary to Hybrid Framework*. doi.org/10.1007/978-981-13-1471-1_8

Chakraborty, S., & Mali, K. (2023). An overview of biomedical image analysis from the deep learning perspective. *Research Anthology on Improving Medical Imaging Techniques for Analysis and Intervention*, 43-59.

Chakraborty, S., Mali, K., Chatterjee, S., Banerjee, S., Roy, K., Dutta, N., & Mazumdar, S. (2017). Dermatological effect of UV rays owing to ozone layer depletion. *2017 4th International Conference on Opto-Electronics and Applied Optics (Optronix)*. 10.1109/OPTRONIX.2017.8349975

Chakraborty, S., Seal, A., Roy, M., & Mali, K. (2016). A novel lossless image encryption method using DNA substitution and chaotic logistic map. *International Journal of Security and Its Applications, 10*(2), 205–216. doi:10.14257/ijsia.2016.10.2.19

Cheng, Z., Yang, Q., & Sheng, B. (2015). Deep colorization. *Proceedings of the IEEE International Conference on Computer Vision,* 415-423.

Cui, Q., Zhou, Z., Fu, Z., Meng, R., Sun, X., & Wu, Q. J. (2019). Image steganography based on foreground object generation by generative adversarial networks in mobile edge computing with Internet of Things. *IEEE Access: Practical Innovations, Open Solutions, 7,* 90815–90824. doi:10.1109/AC-CESS.2019.2913895

Dhawan, S., & Gupta, R. (2021). High quality steganography scheme using hybrid edge detector and Vernam algorithm based on hybrid fuzzy neural network. *Concurrency and Computation, 33*(24), e6448. doi:10.1002/cpe.6448

Dong, C., Loy, C. C., He, K., & Tang, X. (2016). Image Super-Resolution Using Deep Convolutional Networks. *IEEE Transactions on Pattern Analysis and Machine Intelligence, 38*(02), 295–307. doi:10.1109/TPAMI.2015.2439281 PMID:26761735

Eigen, D., Puhrsch, C., & Fergus, R. (2014). Depth map prediction from a single image using a multi-scale deep network. *Advances in Neural Information Processing Systems, 27.*

Gannouni, A., Ouraghi, M., Boughdiri, S., Bessrour, R., Benaboura, A., & Tangour, B. (2012). C6H2@ single walled carbon nanotube first principle theoretical study: Equivalent temperature confinement effect of carbon nanotubes. *Journal of Computational and Theoretical Nanoscience, 9*(3), 379–383. doi:10.1166/jctn.2012.2034

Gatys, L., Ecker, A. S., & Bethge, M. (2015). Texture synthesis using convolutional neural networks. *Advances in Neural Information Processing Systems, 28.*

Godard, C., Mac Aodha, O., & Brostow, G. J. (2017). Unsupervised monocular depth estimation with left-right consistency. *Proceedings of the IEEE Conference on Computer Vision and Pattern Recognition,* 270-279. 10.1109/CVPR.2017.699

Goodfellow, I., Pouget-Abadie, J., Mirza, M., Xu, B., Warde-Farley, D., Ozair, S., & Bengio, Y. (2014). Advances in neural information processing systems. Curran Associates, Inc.

Hertzmann, A., Jacobs, C. E., Oliver, N., Curless, B., & Salesin, D. H. (2001). *Proceedings of the 28th Annual Conference on Computer Graphics and Interactive Techniques.* Academic Press.

Holub, V., & Fridrich, J. (2012). Designing steganographic distortion using directional filters. In *2012 IEEE International workshop on information forensics and security (WIFS)* (pp. 234-239). IEEE. 10.1109/WIFS.2012.6412655

Holub, V., Fridrich, J., & Denemark, T. (2014). Universal distortion function for steganography in an arbitrary domain. *EURASIP Journal on Information Security, 2014*(1), 1–13. doi:10.1186/1687-417X-2014-1

Hore, S., Chakraborty, S., Chatterjee, S., Dey, N., Ashour, A. S., Van Chung, L., & Le, D. N. (2016). An integrated interactive technique for image segmentation using stack based seeded region growing and thresholding. *Iranian Journal of Electrical and Computer Engineering, 6*(6), 2088–8708.

Isola, P., Zhu, J. Y., Zhou, T., & Efros, A. A. (2017). Image-to-image translation with conditional adversarial networks. *Proceedings of the IEEE Conference on Computer Vision and Pattern Recognition,* 1125-1134.

Kingma, D. P., & Welling, M. (2013). *Auto-encoding variational bayes.* arXiv preprint arXiv:1312.6114.

Leng, S., Gao, X., Pei, T., Zhang, G., Chen, L., Chen, X., ... Wan, Y. (2017). Spatial analysis and simulation. *The Geographical Sciences During 1986—2015: From the Classics To the Frontiers,* 339-366.

Li, C., Jiang, Y., & Cheslyar, M. (2018). Embedding image through generated intermediate medium using deep convolutional generative adversarial network. *Computers, Materials & Continua, 56*(2), 313-324. doi.org/10.3970/CMC.2018.03950

Li, H., Hu, L., Chu, J., Chi, L., & Li, H. (2018). The maximum matching degree sifting algorithm for steganography pretreatment applied to IoT. *Multimedia Tools and Applications, 77*(14), 18203–18221. doi:10.100711042-017-5075-1

Liu, M. Y., Breuel, T., & Kautz, J. (2017). Unsupervised image-to-image translation networks. *Advances in Neural Information Processing Systems,* 30.

Long, J., Shelhamer, E., & Darrell, T. (2015). Fully convolutional networks for semantic segmentation. *Proceedings of the IEEE Conference on Computer Vision and Pattern Recognition,* 3431-3440.

Ma, S., Fu, J., Chen, C. W., & Mei, T. (2018). Da-gan: Instance-level image translation by deep attention generative adversarial networks. *Proceedings of the IEEE Conference on Computer Vision and Pattern Recognition,* 5657-5666. 10.1109/CVPR.2018.00593

Mali, K., Chakraborty, S., & Roy, M. (2015). A study on statistical analysis and security evaluation parameters in image encryption. *Entropy, 34,* 36.

Nogueira, R. F., de Alencar Lotufo, R., & Machado, R. C. (2016). Fingerprint liveness detection using convolutional neural networks. *IEEE Transactions on Information Forensics and Security, 11*(6), 1206–1213. doi:10.1109/TIFS.2016.2520880

Pevný, T., Filler, T., & Bas, P. (2010). Using high-dimensional image models to perform highly undetectable steganography. In *Information Hiding: 12th International Conference, IH 2010, Calgary, AB, Canada, June 28-30, 2010, Revised Selected Papers 12* (pp. 161-177). Springer. 10.1007/978-3-642-16435-4_13

Pradhan, A., Sekhar, K. R., & Swain, G. (2018). Digital Image Steganography Using LSB Substitution, PVD, and EMD. *Mathematical Problems in Engineering, 2018,* 1–11. doi:10.1155/2018/1804953

Qiu, T., Qiao, R., & Wu, D. O. (2017). EABS: An event-aware backpressure scheduling scheme for emergency Internet of Things. *IEEE Transactions on Mobile Computing, 17*(1), 72–84. doi:10.1109/TMC.2017.2702670

Rosales, R., Achan, K., & Frey, B. J. (2003, October). Unsupervised image translation. *ICCV*. doi. org/10.1109/ICCV.2003.1238384

Roy, M., Chakraborty, S., & Mali, K. (2020). A robust image encryption method using chaotic skew-tent map. In *Applications of advanced machine intelligence in computer vision and object recognition: emerging research and opportunities* (pp. 1–29). IGI Global. doi:10.4018/978-1-7998-2736-8.ch001

Roy, M., Chakraborty, S., & Mali, K. (2021a). The MSK: A simple and robust image encryption method. *Multimedia Tools and Applications*, *80*(14), 21261–21291. doi:10.100711042-021-10761-y

Roy, M., Chakraborty, S., & Mali, K. (2021b). A chaotic framework and its application in image encryption. *Multimedia Tools and Applications*, *80*(16), 24069–24110. doi:10.100711042-021-10839-7

Roy, M., Chakraborty, S., Mali, K., Banerjee, A., Ghosh, K., & Chatterjee, S. (2020). Biomedical Image Security Using Matrix Manipulation and DNA Encryption. *Advances in Intelligent Systems and Computing*, *1065*, 49–60. doi:10.1007/978-981-15-0361-0_4

Roy, M., Chakraborty, S., Mali, K., Mitra, S., Mondal, I., Dawn, R., ... Chatterjee, S. (2019). A dual layer image encryption using polymerase chain reaction amplification and dna encryption. *2019 International Conference on Opto-Electronics and Applied Optics (Optronix)*, 1-4. IEEE.doi.org/10.1109/OPTRONIX.2019.8862350

Roy, M., Chakraborty, S., Mali, K., & Roy, D. (2021). Utilization of Hyperchaotic Environment and DNA Sequences for Digital Image Security. In *Advances in Smart Communication Technology and Information Processing: OPTRONIX 2020*. Springer. doi:10.1007/978-981-15-9433-5_28

Roy, M., Chakraborty, S., Mali, K., Roy, D., & Chatterjee, S. (2021). An Image Security Method Based on Low Dimensional Chaotic Environment and DNA Encoding. In *Advances in Smart Communication Technology and Information Processing: OPTRONIX 2020*. Springer. doi:10.1007/978-981-15-9433-5_26

Roy, M., Chakraborty, S., Mali, K., Roy, D., & Chatterjee, S. (2021). A robust image encryption framework based on DNA computing and chaotic environment. *Microsystem Technologies*, *27*(10), 3617–3627. doi:10.100700542-020-05120-0

Roy, M., Mali, K., Chatterjee, S., Chakraborty, S., Debnath, R., & Sen, S. (2019). A study on the applications of the biomedical image encryption methods for secured computer aided diagnostics. In *2019 Amity International Conference on Artificial Intelligence (AICAI)* (pp. 881-886). IEEE. 10.1109/AICAI.2019.8701382

Sajedi, H., & Jamzad, M. (2010). BSS: Boosted steganography scheme with cover image preprocessing. *Expert Systems with Applications*, *37*(12), 7703–7710. doi:10.1016/j.eswa.2010.04.071

Sangkloy, P., Lu, J., Fang, C., Yu, F., & Hays, J. (2017). Scribbler: Controlling deep image synthesis with sketch and color. *Proceedings of the IEEE conference on computer vision and pattern recognition*, 5400-5409. 10.1109/CVPR.2017.723

Seal, A., Chakraborty, S., & Mali, K. (2017). A new and resilient image encryption technique based on pixel manipulation, value transformation and visual transformation utilizing single–level haar wavelet transform. In *Proceedings of the First International Conference on Intelligent Computing and Communication* (pp. 603-611). Springer Singapore. 10.1007/978-981-10-2035-3_61

Shet, K. S., Aswath, A. R., Hanumantharaju, M. C., & Gao, X. Z. (2019). Novel high-speed reconfigurable FPGA architectures for EMD-based image steganography. *Multimedia Tools and Applications*, *78*(13), 18309–18338. doi:10.100711042-019-7187-2

Shirali-Shahreza, M. (2007). Steganography in MMS. *2007 IEEE International Multitopic Conference*, 1-4. IEEE.doi.org/10.1109/INMIC.2007.4557698

Shrivastava, A., Pfister, T., Tuzel, O., Susskind, J., Wang, W., & Webb, R. (2017). Learning from simulated and unsupervised images through adversarial training. *Proceedings of the IEEE Conference on Computer Vision and Pattern Recognition*, 2107-2116. 10.1109/CVPR.2017.241

Singh, L., Singh, A. K., & Singh, P. K. (2020). Secure data hiding techniques: A survey. *Multimedia Tools and Applications*, *79*(23-24), 15901–15921. doi:10.100711042-018-6407-5

Taigman, Y., Polyak, A., & Wolf, L. (2016). *Unsupervised cross-domain image generation*. arXiv preprint arXiv:1611.02200.

Valandar, M. Y., Barani, M. J., Ayubi, P., & Aghazadeh, M. (2019). An integer wavelet transform image steganography method based on 3D sine chaotic map. *Multimedia Tools and Applications*, *78*(8), 9971–9989. doi:10.100711042-018-6584-2

Wang, F., Huang, Q., & Guibas, L. J. (2013). Image co-segmentation via consistent functional maps. *Proceedings of the IEEE International Conference on Computer Vision*. doi.org/10.1109/ICCV.2013.110

Wang, T. C., Liu, M. Y., Zhu, J. Y., Tao, A., Kautz, J., & Catanzaro, B. (2018). High-resolution image synthesis and semantic manipulation with conditional gans. *Proceedings of the IEEE Conference on Computer Vision and Pattern Recognition*, 8798-8807. 10.1109/CVPR.2018.00917

Yu, X., Cai, X., Ying, Z., Li, T., & Li, G. (2019). Singlegan: Image-to-image translation by a single-generator network using multiple generative adversarial learning. In *Computer Vision–ACCV 2018: 14th Asian Conference on Computer Vision, Perth, Australia*, December 2–6, 2018, *Revised Selected Papers, Part V 14* (pp. 341-356). Springer. doi.org/10.1007/978-3-030-20873-8_22/COVER

Chapter 8
AI–Based DBMS Controlled Speech Recognition Model for Some Common Computing Commands

Mrinmoy Sen
Haldia Institute of Technology, India

Sunanda Jana
Haldia Institute of Technology, India

Swarnajit Bhattacharya
Haldia Institute of Technology, India

Gitika Maity
Dr. Meghnad Saha Institute of Technology, India

ABSTRACT

Speech recognition has become an important part of the AI model. It plays a vital role in the correct function of different AI enabled devices that we see today. Many automobile industries use this voice recognition technology in their AI to develop modern voice enabled cars. To that end we have implemented a deep learning-based voice recognition model in the MySQL database to execute various DBMS command automatically through speech recognition by using intelligent Google Speech API and match-LSTM model. Our proposed model accept speech as input and by using intelligent Google Speech API service we construct MySQL database and perform training using match-LSTM. The latency rate and data transfer speed of this model is very fast because of its prior training approach. This type of methodical approach can be made in any DBMS systems to make it more convenient, smart and easy to use for normal user.

DOI: 10.4018/978-1-6684-7524-9.ch008

1. INTRODUCTION

Speech signals are one dimensional and can change with time. Because of different speaking style, speaking rate, emotional status and stress given, speech recognition becomes difficult. Style of speaking may be or may not be clear, the rate of speaking can be slower or faster and emotion may be happy or sad or may be filled with any other kind of human feelings. Because of presence of background noise in the voice, a major problem arises. There can be many types of unwanted sound that may be recorded via microphone during the speech. So, it is an important task to first separate unwanted background noise and make the audio clear. To that end we need to set a particular decibel (db) of voice pitch that will be considered during the filtration process. Mathematical expression for speech recognition is difficult because of its structure. Audio data is fed as input to the voice recognition system and then pre-processing of the data is done. Feature extraction and classification are done in next phase and finally, output is displayed in the form of text. Accepted input format can be either .wav or .mp3 file format. Pitch, duration, SNR etc. are considered as extracted features from the segmented frames. The output Model is trained first, and then we get the output from the Speech Recognition module as a string. We are feeding this string to different query continuously to check that it matches with which particular keyword in the IF-Else clauses.

Now a days, different voice enabled user interfaces are being used to solve real life problems and can be applied in Healthcare, Internet of Things, and Telecommunication etc. This voice enabled user interfaces are being applied in educational aids also to help learners to learn SQL. Techniques provided here are used to teach the learners in an intuitive, hands-free and interactive manner. To perform speech synthesis, Google API is used. This technology may assist visually impaired learners and will provide them with the opportunity to learn SQL. Speed up in data querying is possible even by a non-technical person as such system is hands-free and only rely upon voice input to interact with a database. Our paper mainly highlights on how using intelligent voice-based system can construct database and using match-LSTM model how we can extract response for given query. LSTM stands for Long Short Term Memory Networks which is an advanced RNN (Recurrent Neural Network). It solves the problem of vanishing gradient and allows information to persist.

This paper is arranged as follows. Section 2 contains a literature review of speech recognition in general. Information about the proposed model, feature extraction techniques and classifier used can be found in Sections 4. Section 5 shows the experimental result analysis. Finally, section 6 concludes the paper.

2. LITERATURE REVIEW

SQL is a very powerful skill and this skill is necessary to master over database handling. In learning SQL, there may be difficulties like deceptive and counter, learning SQL with procedural language together, learning and visualizing database schema, tables and attribute names etc. Even a non-technical user in industry will be able to understand electronic aid-based SQL. For a non-technical person, it is desired to learn SQL in a free form expressed in natural language like English, without need of any prior technical knowledge. In Natural Language Interface into Database (NLIDBs) system, such a free form approach can be found.

Voice recognition technology has made revolution as because computer can understand human voice and as well as human languages (Himanshu, 2014). Different voice recognition systems are there like isolated word voice recognition systems (Fu, 2020; Slívová et al., 2020) that require speaker to be paused briefly between the words while continuous voice recognized system required spontaneous speech otherwise it is difficult to recognize the speech (Lee et al., 1996; Levinson et al., 1983). Some voice recognition system first capture and digitized the sound waves, then contextually analyse the words to ensure the right spelling of words whose sound is same (Ghaidan & Issa, 2015). There are several models exists for speech recognition. Recently various deep neural networks-based speech recognition model has been developed. Yuki Saito et al. (2018) proposed an approach to for high-quality parametric speech synthesis based on the DNN (deep neural network) and using the ATR3 data which consists of two neural networks. In another work, Lilia et al. (2017) proposed a hybrid type of stochastic/connectionist model where it uses FCM14 / GA15 clustering by considering French and Arabic.

Another Voice control system developed in 2012 for serving the purpose of robotized manufacturing cells and also for creating tools for providing its simple mixing in manufacturing (Rogowski, 2012) work. For semantic analysis, using specific features of voice commands one algorithm is developed (Ayres & Nolan, 2006) whose main aim is to serve controlling industrial devices and machines. It is mainly incorporated into the system itself. It is a Lego Mindstorm robot which uses speech activated command as well as control framework for controlling remote devices in a ubiquitous computing environment. Samiya Silarbi et al. (2014) proposed adaptive network fuzzy inference system (ANFIS) for speech recognition.

In 2015, M. Thangamani et al. (2015) implemented a voice command recognition system. As we know that voice output is not always available, but voice control is a unique challenge till now. This system can overcome the voice variance problem between different human voices.

3. OVERVIEW OF THE SPEECH RECOGNITION SYSTEM

3.1 Speech Recognition Approaches

There are mainly three types of speech recognition approaches (Kherdekar & Naik, 2019) as shown in Figure 1 and they are as follows:

i)   An acoustic phonetic approach:

This approach mainly considers sound waves of human vocal organ during interaction and observe that there is a finite distinctive phonetic unit in the speech. The properties of speech signal are used to classify these phonetics units.

ii)   Speech pattern recognition approach:

In this approach, speech patterns are used directly. There are two steps, training of speech pattern is the first step to be followed in this approach and second one is recognizing the pattern. The most common pattern recognition approach is Hidden Markov Model (HMM).

iii)   Artificial intelligence approach:

Figure 1. Approaches of speech recognition (Kherdekar & Naik, 2019)

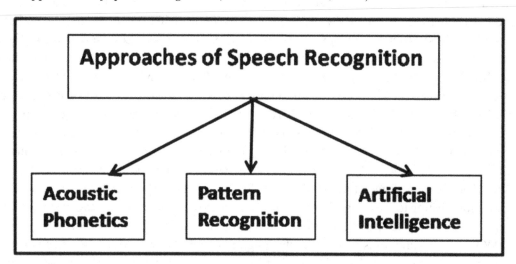

Speech recognition software is defined as a technology that can process speech uttered in a natural language and convert it into readable text with a high degree of accuracy, using Artificial Intelligence (AI), Machine Learning (ML), as well as Natural Language Processing (NLP) techniques.

There are three types of speakers based on speaker-Mode. Speaker dependent system is the first type of speaker, who are trained by the individual user. These speakers are capable of achieving a high command count and more than 95% accuracy for word recognition. Speaker independent system is second type of speaker and is trained to respond to a word regardless of speaker. It can respond to a huge variety of voice patterns, inflections and enunciation of the target word. Third type of speaker is an adaptive speaker which has the capacity of changing characteristics of a new speaker and gradually improves the accuracy of the system.

3.2 Speech Recognition and its Classification

Speech recognition systems are categorized based on their utterances, mode of speaker and size of vocabulary. Types are as follows and, also shown in figure 2;

- isolated word
- connected word
- continuous speech
- spontaneous speech.

The isolated word works for the alphabet when each utterance has single pronunciation at a time. At a time, single word is recognized in this mode. If there is a connected word, there will be a small pause between the separate utterances (Darabkh et al., 2013; Radha, 2012). The word is accepted in a minimum interval of time. Ex – "a...Good...one". In case of Continuous speech, the technique works on sentences. Ex –"Have a good day". On the other hand, Spontaneous speech works for speech that is not prepared. Ex –"hmm, ahh". There are three types of Speaker Mode and they are as follows-

Figure 2. Classification of speech recognition based on utterance (Kherdekar & Naik, 2019)

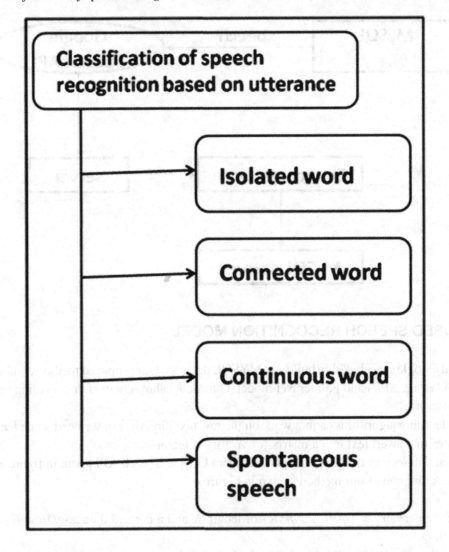

a) The speaker is dependent - It is easy to develop and can work with more accuracy.
b) The speaker is an independent - For any kind of speaker it can perform.
c) Adaptive speaker mode - It can change characteristics of a new speaker and accuracy improves gradually.

The speech recognition system can be differentiated from one another by the vocabulary size. The vocabulary size is divided into small, medium, large, very large, and not present in a dictionary.

Figure 3. Dataset construction using Google speech API

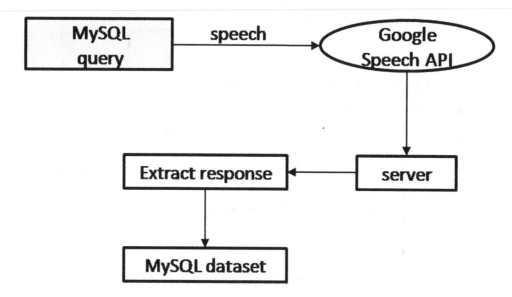

4. PROPOSED SPEECH RECOGNITION MODEL

We have used Google speech API to build our MYSQL datasets. Our proposed method combined match-LSTM (Nahid et al., 2017) and Pointer Net model. Our model shows how after providing certain query we can get response.

Machine learning algorithms cannot work on the raw text directly. So, we need some feature extraction techniques to convert text into a matrix (or vector) of features.

The formal dataset construction through intelligent Google Speech API given in figure 3, as well as the basic block diagram of our method shown in Figure 4.

- Inputs: A query qry = {$qry1$, ..., $qryK$} of length K and a context databaseDB = {$db1$, ...,dbQ } of length Q.
- Output: Response {rB, rE} where rB is the index of the first answer token in DB, rE isthe index of the last answer token in DB, $0 \leq \{rB, rE\} \geq m$, and $rB \leq rE$. Word representation of our model is considered as d-dimensional embeddings from the dataset DB, which was trained on a limited dataset which was built by the help of Intelligent Google Speech API. We use these to represent our query-response dataset DB. We have applied three-layer machine learning model to predict rB, rE. Here forward-LSTM model performs pre-processing of dataset DB and qry to create contextual encodings of each H_{DB} and H_{qry}, respectively. After thar bidirectional match-LSTM will map queries and database encoding and finally a Pointer-Net used to predict the beginning and ending queries and its response from DB location.

Feature Extraction

In this work we have performed feature extraction technique using Machine Learning algorithm LSTM which can learn from a pre-defined set of features by performing training and then we will do testing

Figure 4. Basic block diagram of proposed model

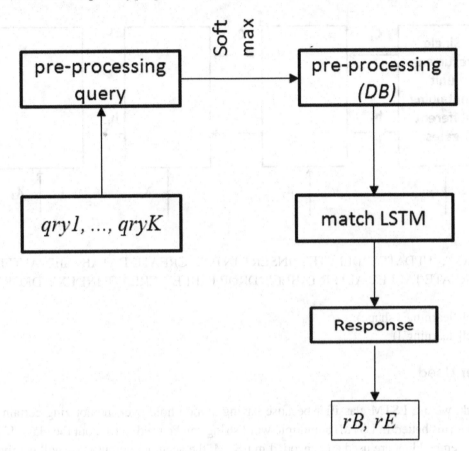

to produce output. In learning phase, feature extraction technique has been included to convert text into a vector of features. In our method Word2Vec, Word Embedding process is used that converts a given word into a vector as a collection of numbers. Here self-trained model is used for this purpose. We are sending MySQL data and then applying word2vec model which generates dense vector. The self trained model used, is as follows.

Self-Trained Model

sent=['SELECT', 'UPDATE', 'DELETE', 'INSERT INTO', 'CREATE DATABASE', 'ALTER DATA-BASE', 'CREATE TABLE', 'ALTER TABLE', 'DROP TABLE', 'CREATE INDEX', 'DROP INDEX']

model=Word2Vec(sent, min_count=1, size=100)
print(model)
Word2Vec(vocab=12, size=100, alpha=0.025)
words=list(model.wv.vocab)
print(words)

Figure 5. LSTM classifier used for the proposed model

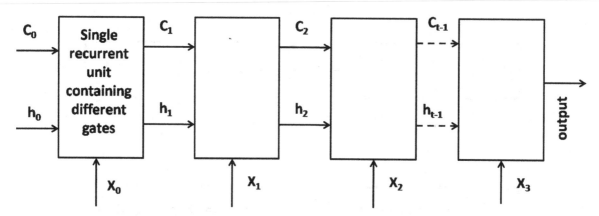

['SELECT', 'UPDATE', 'DELETE', 'INSERT INTO', 'CREATE DATABASE', 'ALTER DATA-BASE', 'CREATE TABLE', 'ALTER TABLE', 'DROP TABLE', 'CREATE INDEX', 'DROP INDEX']

print(model['learning'].shape)
print(model['learning'])

Classifier Used

In this work, we use LSTM classifier because having a good hold over memorizing certain patterns, LSTMs performs better. In LSTM, a multiple word string can be used to find out the class. If appropriate layers of embedding are used and encoded in LSTM, the accurate output class will be given by the model after finding actual meaning in input string. In figure 5, the working principle of LSTM classifier is explained with a block diagram. In the diagram, C_1, C_2 and C_{t-1} are the cell states; h_0, h_1, h_2 and h_{t-1} are the previous hidden states; and X_0, X_1, X_3 and X_4 are inputs to the cell states.

5. RESULT ANALYSIS

We initialize the model using our own created *DB* word embeddings using intelligent Google Speech API. Our model considers 100-dimensional embeddings. If a word embedding was not in the *DB*, then it was initialized as a zero vector. We have considered query length at 20 and context paragraph length at 50. For tanning purpose, we have used 97% of the dataset, while keeping padding to a minimum. We have taken different weights for both cases of the forward and backward calculation of the match-LSTM. We use a hidden layer of dimension $d = 150$. We used TensorFlow and AdamOptimizer with learning rate .001 and minibatches of size 100. Depending on word embedding size, our model had 1,000 - 2,000 parameters. Here dropout has not been incorporated.

MySQL Database

In MySQL database, a Query question is a request. We can query a database and get a recorded dataset back as response. For example, a following part from the code has been shown -
    elif 'connect to mysql database' in query or 'connect to my sql database' in query:

```
speak('please enter host name')
d4=input("Enter HOST name:")
speak('please enter user name')
d5=input("Enter USER name:")
speak('please enter password')
d6=input("Enter Password:")
speak('connecting to mysql database')
print('trying to connect to database......')
try:
connection = mysql. connector. connect (host= d4, user= d5, password= d6)
```

In the above code we are trying to connect to MySQL database through query, which we are proving through speech or voice in mic.
    elif 'show tables in the database' in query:

```
try:
cursor. execute ("show tables;")
speak('showing all tables present in the database')
print(cursor.fetchall())
```

In this paper we are construction and also performing tanning considering some basic query in the MySQL database through Google speech API and match-LSTM model.

Query Fetching in MySQL Database

```
try:

cursor.execute("SET AUTOCOMMIT=OFF")
speak('auto commit turned off')
```

The overall accuracy of the proposed system is 90.05% using python and AI. We have compared the performance of our proposed system by considering similar parameters, the system yielded optimal results. Table 1 shows comparisons among different techniques with the proposed design using AI. Most important thing of our method is that we are mainly concentrating DBMS query writing. Our proposed method makes it easy to control DBMS with optimized accuracy. A comparative study of the works mentioned in Table 1 and our proposed work, has been shown in figure 6.

Table 1. Comparison of different techniques with proposed technique

SI. No.	SI. No. Author(s)	Title of Paper/Thesis	Model/Technique Used	Accuracy Level
1.	Radha (2012)	Speaker Independent Isolated Speech Recognition System for Tamil Language using HMM	HMM	88%
2.	Darabkh (2013)	DTW-based Automatic Speech Recognition	DTW	87.8%
3.	Dua (2022)	Convolutional Neural Network and Python for developing Speech Recognition System for Recognizing Speech Signals with different tones	CNN & Python	89.15%
4.	Proposed System	AI Based DBMS Controlled Speech Recognition Model for Some Common Computing Commands	Match LSTM	90.05%

Figure 6. Model/Technique vs. accuracy (speech recognition) graph

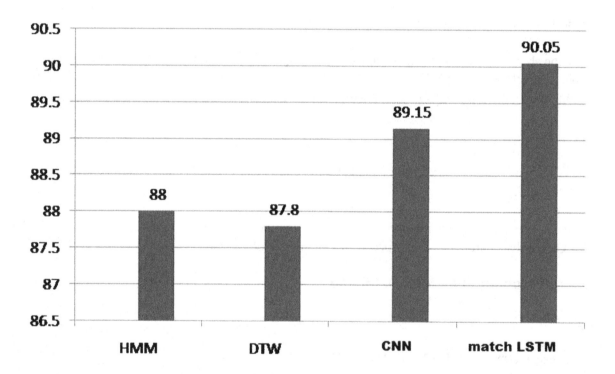

6. CONCLUSION

This paper reflects how intelligent Google API and deep learning-based match-LSTM can perform speech recognition considering MySQL Database to make the DBMS system more convenient to use in our daily lives. For manually typing the query and entering data into this database takes a long time, so an easier and more convenient way of doing the same is via speech and voice input. We have shown how our model is working on some basic MySQL commands with good accuracy. Our model compared to some model also produces superior results. In future we will try to solve more complex real-world problem by developing more perfect model of speech recognition. Our Speech recognition model is mainly applicable in case of basic Database query and response. In future ,there is a huge scope to work with speech recognition to handle more amount of vocabulary at the same time.

REFERENCES

Ayres, T., & Nolan, B. (2006). *Voice activated command and control with speech recognition over WiFi, science of Computer Programming* (Vol. 59). Elsevier.

Darabkh, Khalifeh, Bathech, & Sabah. (2013). Efficient DTW-Based Speech Recognition System for Isolated Words of Arabic Language. *World Acad. Sci. Eng. Technol. Int. J. Comput. Electr. Autom. Control. Inf. Eng.*, 586–593.

Fu, W. (2020). Application of an Isolated Word Speech Recognition System in the Field of Mental Health Consultation: Development and Usability Study. *JMIR Medical Informatics*, 8(6), e18677. doi:10.2196/18677 PMID:32384054

Ghaidan, K. A., & Issa, H. A. (2015). Artificial Intelligence for Speech Recognition Based on Neural Networks. *Journal of Signal and Information Processing*, 6, 61–72.

Himanshu, S. K. (2014). *Literature Survey on Automatic Speech Recognition System.* Academic Press.

Kherdekar & Naik. (2019). Speech Recognition System Approaches, Techniques and Tools For Mathematical Expressions: A Review. *International Journal of Scientific & Technology Research*, 8(8).

Lee, C. H., Soong, F. K., & Paliwal, K. K. (1996). Automatic Speech and Speaker Recognition: Advanced Topics. Kluwer.

Levinson, S. E., Rabiner, L. R., & Sondhi, M. M. (1983). An Introduction to the Application of the Theory of Probabilistic Functions of a Markov Process to Automatic Speech Recognition. *Bell Syst. Tech.*, 62(4), 1035–1074. doi:10.1002/j.1538-7305.1983.tb03114.x

Lilia, L., Mohamed, T. L., & Rachid, B. (2017). Discriminant Learning for Hybrid HMM/MLP Speech Recognition System using a Fuzzy Genetic Clustering. *Intelligent Systems Conference*, 7-8.

Nahid, Purkaystha, & Islam. (2017). Bengali Speech Recognition: A Double Layered LSTM-RNN Approach. *International Conference of Computer and Information Technology (ICCIT)*.

Radha, V. (2012). Speaker independent isolated speech recognition system for Tamil language using HMM. *Procedia Engineering*, 30, 1097–1102. doi:10.1016/j.proeng.2012.01.968

Rogowski, A. (2012). Industrially oriented voice control system. *Robotics and Computer-Integrated Manufacturing, Elsevier*, 28(3), 303–315. doi:10.1016/j.rcim.2011.09.010

Silarbi, S., Abderrahmane, B., & Benyettou, A. (2014, November). Adaptive Network Based Fuzzy Inference System For Speech Recognition Through Subtractive Clustering. *International Journal of Artificial Intelligence & Applications*, 5(6), 43–51. doi:10.5121/ijaia.2014.5604

Slívová, M., Partila, P., Továrek, J., & Vozňák, M. (2020). Isolated Word Automatic Speech Recognition System. In Multimedia Communications, Services and Security, Communications in Computer and Information Science (vol. 1284). Springer.

Thangamani, M. (2015). Automatic Speech Recognition through Artificial Intelligence. *International Journal of Advanced Trends in Computer Applications*, *1*(5), 82–85.

Yuki, S., & Shinnosuke, T. (2018). Statistical Parametric Speech Synthesis Incorporating Generative Adversarial Networks. *IEEE/ACM Transactions on Audio, Speech, and Language Processing*, *26*(1).

Chapter 9
MEDA–Based Biochips:
Proposed New Structural Testing Techniques for Fault Detection

Priyatosh Jana

Haldia Institute of Technology, India

Pranab Roy

Institute of Engineering and Technology, J. K. Laxmipat University, Jaipur, India

Sarit Chakraborty

Government College of Engineering and Leather Technology, India

Tanmoy Biswas

Shyamaprasad College, India

Soumen Ghosh

Haldia Institute of Technology, India

ABSTRACT

Digital microfluidic biochips (DMFB), a newly developed lab-on-chip device, has evolved in recent years as a significant miniaturized platform for applications in the area of point-of-care investigations, DNA sequencing, and further biomedical detection and analysis. By means of rapid escalation in scalability, complexity, and requirements of more accurate control and accuracy, a novel DMFB-based architecture known as microelectrode dot array (MEDA) has been introduced. Due to its higher complexity and parallel execution of multiple bioassays, conventional testing methods used for DMFBs may not be adequate for fault diagnosis and detection in such devices. In this chapter, the authors proposed new techniques compatible with higher complexity and applicable for structural testing of MEDA-based biochips. The proposed testing methods provide detection of faults or failure (if any) within a given layout using minimal resources with minimal test completion time. The testing simulations are carried out with specified layout dimensions and variable droplet size.

DOI: 10.4018/978-1-6684-7524-9.ch009

I. INTRODUCTION

Lab-on-chip devices have been principally developed with an attention in the direction of automation of typical operations in laboratory within a miniaturized platform as alternative. These types of lab on chip devices are quite capable to handle the operation on microfluidic by making use of fluids like micro level volumes or nanolitre level volumes. The LoC devices for typical applications actually consist of DNA sequencing, immunoassays, sample preparation, point-of-care investigates, drug detection, and many more (Jebrail et al., 2012). The classification of microfluidic platforms has been made by the norm of droplet actuation or liquid propulsion for fluidic action, surface acoustics (Alistar et al., 2016) or electro kinetic, pressure driven and specifically capillary.

Continuous flow microfluidic biochips termed as the former generation of LoC devices. Which are consisting of pumps, micro fabricated channels, valves and actuators? Within a silicon or glass substrate these components are permanently etched. These devices are highly controlled in their functionality. Intended for a restricted class of applications they are employed. Designed for re-configurability in addition to higher scalability matters such type of lab devices may not found to be appropriate intended for complicated applications.

In comparison to continuous flow microfluidic biochips design, There is digital microfluidic biochip (DMFB) also considered to be as second cohort of LoC device. Which offers many advantages like reagent isolation, individual sample addressing and compatible with the array-based approaches for biochemical applications (Pollack et al., 2000)? Fluids are operated in the form of discrete droplets within a 2 dimensional array of electrodes in digital microfluidic biochips. For originating specified droplet actions the clock regulated electrical actuation systems are used. The specified droplet actions namely like transportation, mixing, merging, splitting, detection and dispensing. The inflection of interfacial tension amid an electrode and a conductive sample by applying electric field among them for carrying out droplet movements. For actuating the electrodes through the control sequences can be reconfigured within the same biochip concurrently for different bioassays. Electro wetting on Dielectrics (EWOD) for droplet actuation is considered to be one of the encouraging approaches. An imbalance of the Electro wetting on dielectric actuation force is developed on the droplet through application of electric field of the droplet to one side only. As a result it creates an interfacial tension incline. This interfacial tension is robust enough to move the droplet (Wang et al., 2014). Digital microfluidic biochip is typically built up with a 2-dimensional electrode array. For electrode actuation this 2-dimentional electrode array are fixed with peripheral devices specifically optical detector circuits, dispensing ports connected to required control pins and integrated logic.

Two dimensional microfluidic arrays comprise a set of basic cells containing of two parallel glass plates (Figure 1). Independently controllable electrodes in patterned array are used at the bottom plate. The top plate is coated with a continuous ground electrode. Silicon oil is used as the filler medium composed with the droplet under control which is sandwiched between the plates. Droplets could be stimulated along the predetermined path by independently adjusting the voltages on respective electrode inside the electrode array using the standard of electro wetting-on-dielectric has been mentioned earlier. The droplet shipping arrangement together by means of other microfluidic actions which are pre-programmed into a microcontroller. According to the actuation sequence of the corresponding electrodes the microcontroller drives the control pins.

Though, as quantity of bioassays is executed simultaneously is predictable to intensification significantly within a given 2 dimensional array on a Digital Microfluidic Biochip, higher level of control for

Figure 1. Schematic cross sectional view of DMFB

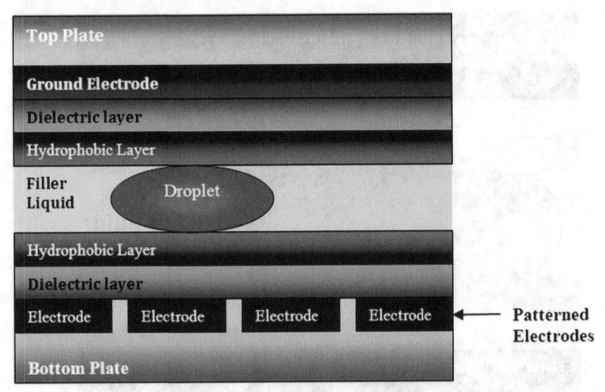

resource organization, system incorporation and design complexity becomes important. Henceforth to afford the comparable CAD provision like the semiconductor strategy a top down plan methodology is needed. Aimed at the categorized design procedure of digital microfluidics (Wang & Teng, 2011) necessary requirements are configurability, portability and scalability of fundamental block elements. Hence a new architecture for DMFB has been suggested to reach higher re-configurability and scalability. This architecture termed as micro electrode dot array (MEDA) built design is based on the concept of micro-electrode dot arrays where an array of smaller controllable electrodes constitute a unit cell within a DMFB. Each identical component of the dot array is termed as individual microfluidic cell. Common CMOS technology has been used to realize this architecture. A micro-electrode cell comprised of a single dot electrode is considered as a CMOS standard cell that combines a group of CMOS transistors, interconnections and a physical micro-electrode. Droplets on the MEDA based architecture is controlled through actuation of a cluster of microelectrodes (Figure 2), having size 10 times lesser than the orthodox electrodes (Chen et al., 2011). The microelectrodes are clustered on the fly to form droplets of sizes customized on demand and can be actuated simultaneously for parallel bioassay execution.

As the level of scalability in MEDA based biochips are increasing considerably with higher levels of integration and design complexity requirements –dependability and reliability become a major issue for microfluidic operations in these devices. The underlying multiple energy domains as well as the microfabrication technology used for manufacturing may lead to potential faults resulted during production and on field application (Shukla & Noohul, 2016). Hence effective testing techniques become

Figure 2. Cross sectional Schematic for a MEDA Based Biochip

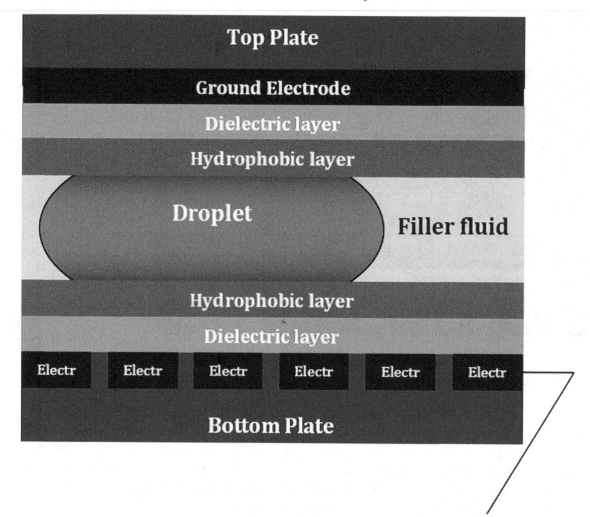

Micro Electrode Dot Array

necessary for MEDA based biochips for ensuring reliability necessary towards their applicability for safety critical applications.

The minute size of the micro-electrodes may lead to significant loss of droplet volumes as any of the defective micro-electrode may leave several stuck up parts on the substrate of the MEDA built digital microfluidics biochip (Wang et al., 2014). These may lead to erroneous results as well as degradation in performance of the device. i) Reduction in liquid volume can impede droplet movement resulting in wrong detection results. ii) The composition and dynamics of large volume droplets may differ if the remaining volume is compositionally dissimilar causing unwanted contamination. iii) It may lead to the depletion of numerous molecules like nucleic acids or protein leading to the poor influence on final output (Lai et al., 2013). As the electrodes are considerably smaller the conventional testing techniques applicable for general DMFBs may not be sufficient enough for testing of MEDA based biochips.

In this paper we have considered a set of fault models for MEDA based biochips as proposed in (Shukla & Noohul, 2016) and proposed structural testing techniques for detection of such faults. The objective is to detect faults in MEDA based biochips with minimal number of test droplet usage and lesser test completion time. We have utilized the flexibility of droplet movement in all possible nine directions in MEDA based design for intelligent exploration of test paths with variable sizes of test droplets.

The rest of the paper is arranged as follows. Section II briefs the details of important contemporary contribution on testing of conventional as well as the MEDA based biochips. Section III states the types of faults and the causes being considered for testing together with the basic testing methodology using RC oscillator. Section IV briefs the basics of test droplet routing followed by elaboration of proposed testing techniques for structural testing of MEDA based DMFBs. Section V illustrates the experimental results with conclusion and future scopes for improvement are being stated in section VI.

II. RELATED WORKS

Numerous works related to fault modeling and fault detection in direct addressing types of DMFB has been contributed in recent years. However only a few works have been so far reported on testing of MEDA based biochips. Initial works on testing of DMFBs primarily focused on fault classification and modelling. Faults were classified as manufacturing and operational, and different test methods were developed for detection of such faults (Kerkhoff, 2007; Su, 2003). A unified test methodology for digital microfluidic biochips is presented, where faults were detected through controlling and tracking droplet motion electrically in (Su et al., 2005). Test droplets comprising of a conductive fluid (e.g., KCL solution) are dispensed from the source reservoir and using a prescheduled test plan they are guided through the unit cells towards a specified location or destination termed as the droplet sink. The sink uses an integrated capacitive detection circuit to signal the scheduled arrival of the test droplet (Xu & Chakrabarty, 2007). In addition to this - numerous approaches were suggested for detection of faults in two-dimensional (2-D) regular microfluidic arrays (Datta et al., 2009; Davids, 2008; Gayem et al., 2009; Mitra, 2008). (Su et al., 2006) presented a concurrent testing technique for detecting catastrophic faults and investigation of the related issues regarding test scheduling as well as resource optimization. In a more recent work of (Li et al., 2014) a new pipelined scan-like testing method was proposed. In the work of (Li et al., 2014) each unit cell of the DMFB is mapped to a lumped RC circuit model. This model was then used to analyze the influence of actuation voltage and clock frequency on dielectric degradation, which followed in developing an evaluation method for designing the test.

However scopes for testing of MEDA based Biochips were first introduced in the works of (Shukla et al., 2013). The work specifically mentioned the challenges involved in testing of MEDA based biochips. A defect diagnosis methodology for conventional digital microfluidics based on the diagonal movement of MEDA based biochips has been introduced in the works of (Shukla & Noohul, 2014). Here the parallel scan testing method was incorporated using diagonal movement for MEDA based biochips. The works of (Shukla & Noohul, 2016) provided a major contribution through presentation of the fault models associated with the MEDA architecture for one as well as multiple microelectrodes. The work further proposed an oscillation based testing model to measure the droplet frequency in cases of faulty operations in terms of capacitance variation, found to be related directly to the droplet volume.

III. FAULTS MODELS AND TESTING PROCEDURE

While implementation of Bioassay in MEDA based biochips – it is imperative to ensure the reliability and accuracy of the results through detection of faulty cells within the 2D layouts. Such cells are to be identified through prior testing as they are highly likely to perform erroneously during actual bioassay execution.

Faults in MEDA based biochips are classified into two types.

i) Catastrophic faults – These types of faults may lead to complete failure of the DMFB device. Following defects are identified as catastrophic faults in MEDA based design.

   a) *Microelectrode Short* – Caused by connecting two or more adjacent microelctrodes due to particle contamination while manufacturing. This may result in droplet covering 1x1 microelectrode may get stuck among two or more microelectrodes. For droplets covering $n \times n$ microelectrodes - unwanted shape and unpredictive motion of the droplet may occur.

   b) *Droplet Electrode Short* – Caused by dielectric breakdown resulting from very high voltage actuation at the microelectrodes.This may result in droplet electrolysis in case of droplets covering 1x1 microlectrodes. Unwanted droplet drift along specific direction due to viscous drag for droplets covering $n \times n$ microelectrodes.

   c) *Resistive open between Microelectrodes and control source* – Caused by protein adsorption during bioassay resulting in failure in microelectrode actuation. The effect is disruption or complete seizure in droplet motion.

   d) *Misalignment of parallel plates* – Caused by excessive application of mechanical force to MEDA based biochip resulting in resultant static pressure in single direction. The effect is unpredictable droplet motion without actuation of microelectrodes.

   e) *Non uniform diectric layers* – Caused by coating failure while manufacturing resulting formation of dielectric clusters. The effect is the unprecedented change in droplet shapes and restrained or complete stopage of droplet motion.

   f) *Continuous activation of microelectrodes* – Caused by microelectrode activation for a long duration resulting in irreversible concentration of charges on microelectrodes (Shukla & Noohul, 2016). The effect is unintentional droplet motion or complete stuck up of droplets.

ii) Parametric faults – These may result in moderate or major deviation from the normal performance of the DMFBs.

   a) *Change of droplet viscosity and that of filler medium* – Caused by physical variation of the droplet environment namely temperature (Shukla et al., 2013). The effect is variation in droplet motion due to change in viscosity.

   b) *Deviation in geometrical parameters* – Any variation in component parameters that may affect the overall performance. The variation in insulator thickness or microelectrode length or area may result in faulty system operations.

The general testing procedure for MEDA based biochip involves a source and a sink electrode. We follow the Oscillation based testing model (OBT) as mentioned in (Shukla & Noohul, 2016). A RC relaxation oscillator arrangement is formed with the droplet micro electrode cell. At the output of the oscillator a capacitance value of C and an oscillation frequency of f are measured. At the sink electrode the capacitance changes with presence or absence of droplets. As the oscillation frequency is inversely proportional to the capacitance – this also changes accordingly. The test procedure is as follows:

At the source electrode a test droplet of pre specified volume covering specific set of microelectrodes (n *x* n where n = 2, 3, 4 etc.)is dispensed. The droplet is transported along a pre-defined path (using specific routing algorithm) to cover all the microelectrodes within the 2D array. The test droplet covers all the microelectrodes and reaches the sink. The arrival of the droplet at the sink results in change in capacitance due to its volume. The oscillation module linked with the sink electrode measures the frequency variation caused by the alteration in capacitance. For a droplet covering a single microelectrode (1 x 1) presence or absence of droplet at the sink electrode is measured to determine existence of faults in microelectrodes covered through test droplet transportation. With larger size of test droplets (*n x n*), where n >1, defect in any microelectrode within the droplet path may result in variation in droplet size. Thereby the droplet volume as well as the capacitance and hence the measured frequency will vary. Hence any variation in oscillator frequency provides a clear indication of the existence of faults within the 2D layout. A classical relaxation oscillator comprising of a RC network together with a Schmitt trigger circuit has been used for testing (Shukla & Noohul, 2016).

Figure 3. MEDA based biochip testing schematic using RC Oscillator (Shukla & Noohul, 2016)

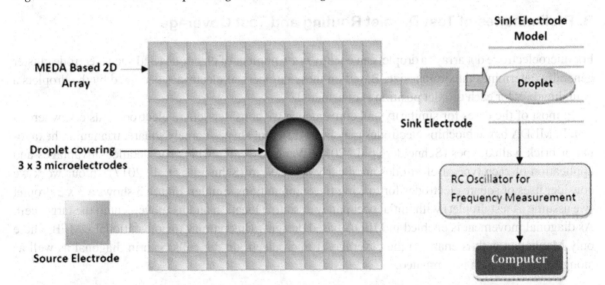

Here we have shown droplets covering *n x n* (where *n = 3*) microelectrodes. In later sections we have also used droplets covering *n x n* microelectrodes where *n = 2m+1 (m = 1, 2, 3...)*. The motivation for using *n* as an odd number is that in such cases the centre of the microelectrode cluster is clearly visible (using the bounding box) and identification of the covered and uncovered cells within the cluster becomes comparatively easier.

Figure 4. Movement of test droplets and the dot electrode coverage

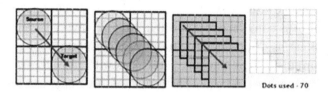

a) Diagonal movement of droplets from source to target and number of microelectrodes covered.

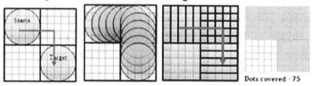

b) Droplet movement along Manhattan path and the number of micro electrodes covered

IV. PROPOSED STRUCTURAL TESTING TECHNIQUES

B. Prelimineries of Test Droplet Routing and Test Coverage

For microelectrode dot arrays a droplet can occupy $m \times n$ number of electrodes and such electrode cluster generally determines the droplet size. Based on these numbers of electrodes occupied by the droplets a bounding box for each droplet position is considered.

In most of the cases for similarity and convenience we consider square electrode clusters, where $m = n$. In MEDA based biochips electrodes may be of different shapes namely square, triangular, hexagonal or brick walled types (Schneider et al., 2017; Wang & Teng, 2011). The detailed advantages and application of each type of electrodes are clearly depicted in (Schneider et al., 2017). In our work we consider uses of square electrodes for making the computations simpler. Figure 3 shows a 3 x 3 droplet (we assume as test droplet) with initial occupancy at source location and its movement to the target cell. As diagonal movement is enabled in MEDA based design – (in contrary to conventional DMFB where only Manhattan path is enabled) the coverage of microelectrode dot cells both in diagonal as well as along Manhattan path is computed.

a)   Diagonal movement of droplets from source to target and number of microelectrodes covered.
b)   Droplet movement along Manhattan path and the number of micro electrodes covered,

It has been found that diagonal movement of test droplets has microelectrodes coverage = 70 with number of actuations sequences of CMEs = 6. Whereas Manhattan movement of test droplets has microelectrodes coverage = 75 with number of actuations sequences of CMEs = 10. Hence coverage/ actuation is found to be higher for diagonal movement which is computed as 11.66 as compared with that for movement along Manhattan path = 7.5. Another calculation regarding additional cell coverage for each consecutive diagonal transition is computed from a given specific case as shown in figure 6.

Figure 5. Droplet occupancy of microelectrodes with CMAs of size w1 x h1

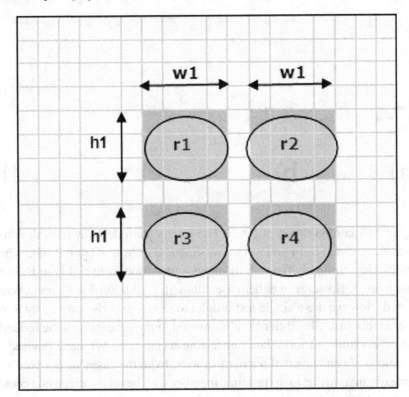

The configured microelectrodes occupied by a given droplet are computed as the square or rectangular boundary of the covered dot array and is computed as of size w x h - shown in figure 5.

We start with a 2D MEDA layout with a case of adjacent diagonal cell transition of a droplet of size 3 x 3. The sequential diagonal transitions with covered microelectrodes are shown in figure 6. It has been observed that for a diagonal transition of 3 x 3 droplets to diagonally adjacent cell additional electrode coverage is 6. Similarly in figure 7 a, b and c for m x m sized droplet with m = 2, 5 and 6 the number of additional electrodes covered are 2, 20 and 30 respectively. The additional cell coverage is indicated using grey colours. The respective source and target locations are labeled with S and T respectively.

It has been observed that diagonal transition to adjacent cell for any *n x n* droplet the additional cells being computed as

$$2 \ x[(n\text{-}1)+(n\text{-}2)+...+1] = 2 \ x \ n \ x \ (n\text{-}1)/2 = n(n\text{-}1). \ .... \tag{1}$$

So if we involve diagonal transition for MEDA based structural testing – more electrode coverage can be accomplished with lesser number of actuation (as was already observed in our earlier computation for coverage/actuation for diagonal movement).

Based on these observations we propose three deployed test droplet movement to measure coverage as well as diagnosis and detection of probable fault locations.

As we have seen earlier (Fig. 6 and Fig.7) the angular or diagonal transition covers additional microelectrode dot arrays In Fig 8 we consider MEDA architecture being comprised of a 2 x 2 cell array with

Figure 6. A sequential transition of a 3 x 3 droplet to diagonally adjacent cell

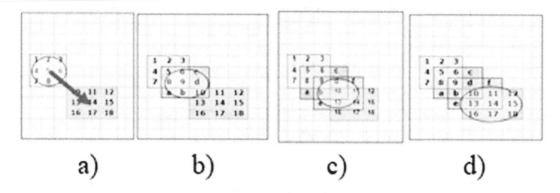

each cell having a CMA configuration of 3 x 3. The microelectrode array is of dimension 6 x 6. The cells are marked as A, B, C and D. Figure 8a) shows diagonal transition from A to C with additional dot coverage denoted by grey. Similarly figure 8 b) shows a transition from cell D to B. In each case no of actuation sequences are 3. However in either case although 6 additional dots are covered – another 18 remained uncovered. Now we use a single test droplet to move in a criss-cross way to cover all 4 cells (fig.8 c). However in this case all additional cells covered in the process become redundant.

We use these observations to formulate our testing techniques. We have devised two techniques namely closed diamond, up and inverted pitcher methods. In all the cases we adopted angular coverage to for faster coverage/actuation that saves test time together with better coverage on account of additional dots being covered in the process.

Method 1: Closed Diamond Technique

Here we used the coverage technique adopted in fig.8 c). But we extended it for larger dimension arrays. We again used each cell with CMA configuration of 3 x 3 dot microelectrodes.

In figure 9 a) a 2 column array is used to display criss-cross traversal of test droplet (as proposed earlier in fig.8.c).A single test droplet with single source and sink has been used. If we use larger array it is partitioned into separate two column partitions and the same procedure is followed as shown in

Figure 7. Sequential transition to diagonally adjacent cells of different sized droplets and additional cell coverage

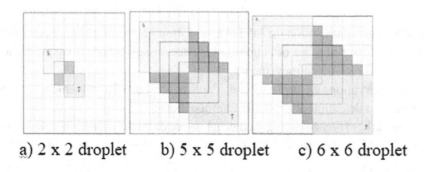

a) 2 x 2 droplet   b) 5 x 5 droplet   c) 6 x 6 droplet

Figure 8. a) Single transition from cell A to C b) Single transition from cell D to B c) Criss-cross coverage with angular transition of a single droplet

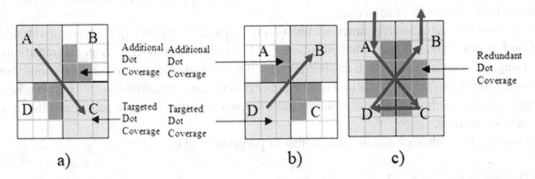

figure 9.b. in each case the tour starts from the top left corner of the array and finishes at the top right corner. However, with more droplets (say two for two separate columned partitions) – same process is followed. Accordingly two source and sinks are used. As droplet dispenser and detectors are to be limited for cost optimization thereby number of test droplets is maintained to be minimum. Figure 10 shows the process with more than one droplet. The process is termed as closed diamond technique as the overall path resembles a set of diamond boxes.

Figure 9. a) Closed diamond traversal of test droplet in 3 x 2 array; b) Closed diamond traversal in 3 x 4 array (partitioned in two parts)

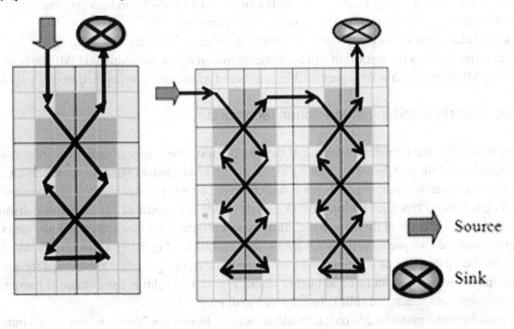

A more generalized computation shows that for adjacent diagonal transition of one $m \times m$ droplet involves m number of actuations. For horizontal or vertical transition of adjacent cells a droplet of $m \times m$ size also performs m no of actuations.

We assume each actuation consumes one unit of time. So for 2×2 layout (fig 8c) criss-cross transition involves 2 diagonal and one horizontal transition. For a 3×2 layout number of diagonal transitions is 4 with a single horizontal transition. It has been observed that for an array with $n \times 2$ dimensions number of diagonal transitions will be $= 2 \times (n-1)$ and number of horizontal transitions is $=1$. However, in order to implement this method number of columns must be even – so that it can be partitioned into a set of two column partitions.

So for an array with $n \times k$ dimensions number of partitions will be

$p = k/2$, where k is $= 2,4,6 \ldots 2q$ (an even number).

In such cases number of diagonal transitions $= p \times 2 \times (n-1)$ and number of horizontal transitions $= p+(p-1)$.

This is due to the fact that each partition involves one horizontal transition and changeover between two partitions involves one more horizontal transition.

Total number of transitions $t = p \times 2 \times (n-1) + p+(p-1) = 2pn - 1$.
Hence number of actuations $= m \times (2pn - 1)$.
So total test time $= m \times (2pn - 1)$.
Microelectrode dot coverage $= m^2 \times n \times k$.

With multiple droplets (one for each partition) partition change over is not required. Total number of transitions $= p \times 2 \times (n-1) + p = 2pn - p$. Total test time $= m \times (2pn - p)$ and coverage being the same. However number of droplets required $= p$ (one for each partition).

Proposed algorithm for single test droplet routing is given as follows:

For multiple droplets the algorithm will continue up to step 4. For conventional DMFB where movement along Manhattan path is only permissible, number of transitions is computed as $= n \times k +k-1$.

Method 2: Upright and Inverted Pitcher Technique

In order to improve the overall transition and thereby the test time – a new method termed as up and inverted pitcher is followed. However, although in down traversal a number of cells remained uncovered and in upward traversal remaining cells are being covered. However in this method also number of redundant cells is being traversed multiple times. But there was improvement in number of transitions as well as test time. However in this case we require two test droplets and two source and two sinks. Here like earlier methods we partition the array into 4 column blocks. Figure 11 a) and b) shows separate movement of each droplet one starting downward resembling an upright pitcher shape and the other one starting upward resembling an inverted pitcher shape. Figure 11 c) shows the combined movement of the test droplets with redundant cells being denoted with grey.

For each 4 column partition diagonal transitions for each droplet is $=2(n-1)$ and horizontal transitions $=1$. For two droplets total no of transitions $= 4(n-1)+2$.

Figure 10. Closed diamond test droplet traversal with multiple droplets

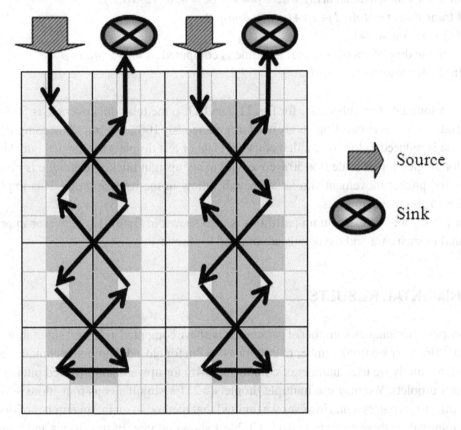

Figure 11. a) Upright pitcher traversal b) inverted pitcher traversal c) Combined traversal of test droplets in MEDA based architecture

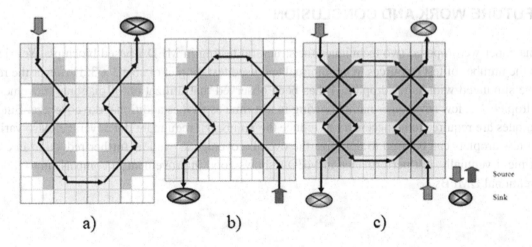

We consider a n x k dimensional array where $p = k/4$ (k = 4, 8, 12. 16...)

Total no of transitions $t = 4p(n-1)+2p +(p-1)= 4pn-p-1$.

In terms of k; $t = k$ x $n -(k/4)-1$

Thereby for m x m droplet transition total test time is computed as $= m$ x $(4pn -p -1)$.

Microelectrode dot coverage $= m^2$ x n x k.

It has been found that in either case for fig. 11.a and 11. b the total dot coverage is 50% of the total microelectrodes. Whenever two droplets are used simultaneously 100% coverage is accomplished, and the coverage time is reduced to ½ - as simultaneous traversal of test droplets are carried out. The proposed algorithm for single droplet route (for 50% coverage) using upright pitcher technique is given below:

For inverted pitcher movement similar steps will follow in the reverse order. This implies that we start with i = m and move upwards.

Another procedure using 3 column partitions is also shown in figure 12. However improvement is only marginal in such case and the details are omitted for brevity.

V. EXPERIMENTAL RESULTS

Using the proposed techniques a number of parameters we have computed using test simulation on different sized layouts. However we used number of columns k = 2m for closed diamond techniques using single test droplets. Similarly we used number of columns k = 4m for upward and inverted pitcher techniques using two test droplets. We may use multiple droplets(>2) for simultaneous transitions – which might reduce test time to certain extent. However we omitted that method to maintain number of dispenser and sinks to be minimal (in these cases to be 1or 2).Table 1 shows number of transitions and transitions, test time and comparison with those of conventional DMFBs for single droplet closed diamond technique. Similar test results for upright and inverted pitcher technique is displayed in table 2. A horizontal bar graph comparison for test completion time is displayed in figure 13.

VI. FUTURE WORK AND CONCLUSION

In this paper we proposed two techniques for structural testing in MEDA based biochips. We tried to keep the number of test resources to be minimal and used test droplet of size 3 x 3. However the result can be simulated with larger droplets. It has been observed that utilization of diagonal movement of test droplets has few advantages namely saving in test time as well as additional dot coverage. But new techniques are required to be necessary to reduce the number of redundant dot coverage. Also variable sized test droplets can be used to optimize the overall coverage as well as further reduction in coverage time. Eventually, test performance in MEDA shows good improvement in comparison to those in conventional DMFBs.

Figure 12. A closed diamond single droplet coverage using 3 partitions

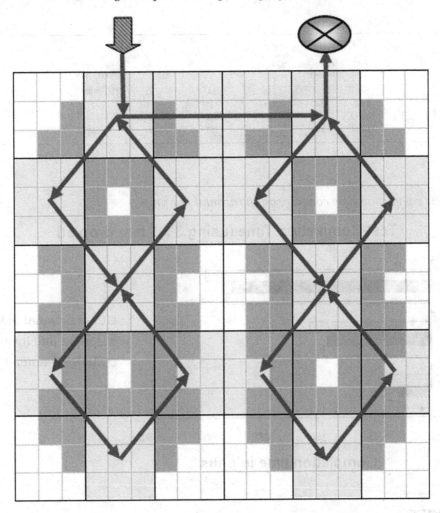

Table 1. Test results using closed diamond technique and comparison with conventional DMFBs

Size of array (M•N)	Cell coverage Using Test droplets Size (3 x3)	No. of Transitions in MEDA	Test Coverage Time in MEDA	No. of Transitions in conventional DMFB	Test Coverage Time in Conventional DMFB
5×4	20	19	57	23	69
6x6	36	35	105	41	123
8x8	64	63	189	71	213
10x10	100	99	297	109	327
10 x 12	120	119	357	131	393

Table 2. Test results using upright and inverted pitcher technique and comparison with conventional DMFBs

Size of array (M×N)	Cell coverage Using Test droplets Size (3 x3)	No. of Transitions in MEDA	Test Coverage Time in MEDA	No. of Transitions in conventional DMFB	Test Coverage Time in Conventional DMFB
5×4	20	18	54	23	69
8 x 8	64	61	183	71	213
10 x 12	120	116	348	131	393
16 x 16	256	251	753	271	813

Figure 13. Test completion time comparison (horizontal bar graph)

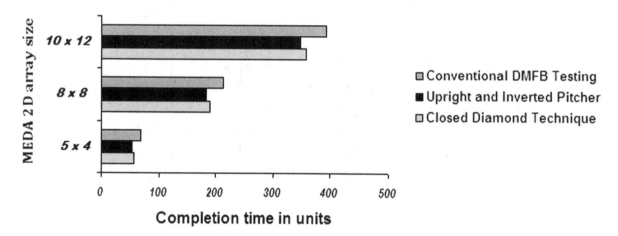

REFERENCES

Alistar, M., Pop, P., & Madsen, J. (2016, May). Synthesis of Application-Specific Fault-Tolerant Digital Microfluidic Biochip Architectures. *IEEE Transactions on Computer-Aided Design of Integrated Circuits and Systems, 35*(5), 764–777. doi:10.1109/TCAD.2016.2528498

Chen, Z., Teng, D. H.-Y., Wang, G. C.-J., & Fan, S.-K. (2011). Droplet routing in high-level synthesis of configurable digital microfluidic biochips based on microelectrode dot array architecture. *Journal of BioChips, 5*(4), 343–352. doi:10.100713206-011-5408-5

Datta, S., Joshi, B., Ravindran, A., & Mukherjee, A. (2009). Efficient parallel testing and diagnosis of digital microfluidic biochips. *ACM Journal on Emerging Technologies in Computing Systems, 5*(2), 10. doi:10.1145/1543438.1543443

Davids, D. (2008). A fault detection and diagnosis technique for digital Microfluidic biochips. *IEEE International Mixed- Signal, Sensor and Systems Test Workshop.* 10.1109/IMS3TW.2008.4581597

Gayem, Q., Liu, H., Richardson, A., & Burd, N. (2009). Builtin test solutions for the electrode structures in bio-fluidic microsystems. *Proc. ETS*, 73-78.

Jebrail, M. J., Bartsch, M. S., & Patel, K. D. (2012, July). Digital microfluidics: A versatile tool for applications in chemistry, biology, and medicine. *Lab on a Chip, 12*(14), 5452–2463. doi:10.1039/c2lc40318h PMID:22699371

Kerkhoff, H. G. (2007). Testing of microelectronic-biofluidic systems. *IEEE Design & Test of Computers, 24*(1), 72–82. doi:10.1109/MDT.2007.28

Lai, K. Y.-T., Yang, Y.-T., Wang, G., Lu, Y.-W., & Lee, C.-Y. (2013). A digital microfluidic processor for biomedical applications. *Signal Processing Systems (SiPS)*, 54-58. 10.1109/SiPS.2013.6674480

Li, Z., Dinh, T. A., Ho, T.-Y., & Chakrabarty, K. (2014). Reliability-Driven Pipelined Scan-Like Testing of Digital Microfluidic Biochips. *Proc. of IEEE 23rd Asian Test Symposium*, 57-62. 10.1109/ATS.2014.22

Mitra, D. (2008). Accelerated functional testing of digital microfluidic biochips. *IEEE Asian Test Symposium*, 295-300.

Pollack, M. G., Fair, R. B., & Shenderov, A. D. (2000). Electrowetting-based actuation of liquid droplets for microfluidic applications. *Applied Physics Letters, 77*(11), 1725–1726. doi:10.1063/1.1308534

Schneider, Keszocze, Stoppe, & Drechsler. (2017). Effects of Cell Shapes on the Routability of Digital Microfluidic Biochips. *Design Automation and Test in Europe Conference*, 1627-1630.

Shukla, V., & Noohul, B. B. (2014). Diagonal Testing in Digital Microfluidics Biochips Using MEDA Based Approach. *Proc. of 5th IEEE International Conference of Intelligent and Advanced Systems*, 469-474.

Shukla, V., & Noohul, B. B. (2016). Fault Modeling and Simulation of MEDA based Digital Microfluidics Biochips. *Proc. of 29th IEEE International Conference on VLSI Design*.

Shukla, V., Noohul, B. Z. A., Hussin, F. A., & Zwolinski, M. (2013). On Testing of MEDA Based Digital Microfluidics Biochips. *5th IEEE Asia Symposium on Quality Electronic Design*, 60-65. 10.1109/ASQED.2013.6643565

Su, Ozev, & Chakrabarty. (2006). Concurrent testing of digital microfluidic based biochips. *ACM TODAES, 11*(2).

Su, F. (2003). Testing of droplet-based microelectrofluidic systems. *Proc. IEEE Int. Test Conf.*, 1192-1200.

Su, F., Ozev, S., & Chakrabarty, K. (2005). Ensuring the operational Health of droplet-based microelectrofluidic biosensor systems. *IEEE Sensors Journal, 5*(4), 763–773. doi:10.1109/JSEN.2005.848127

Wang, G., & Teng, D. (2011). Digital Microfluidic Operations on Microfluidic Dot Array Architecture. *IET Nanobiotechnology, 5*(4), 152–160. doi:10.1049/iet-nbt.2011.0018 PMID:22149873

Wang, G., Teng, D., Lai, Y.-T., Lu, Y.-W., Ho, Y., & Lee, C.-Y. (2014). Field-programmable lab-on-a-chip based on microelectrode dot array architecture. *IET Nanobiotechnology / IET, 8*(3), 163–171. doi:10.1049/iet-nbt.2012.0043

Xu, T., & Chakrabarty, K. (2007). Parallel scan-like test and multiple-Defect diagnosis for digital micro-fluidic biochips. IEEE Trans. Biomed.Circuits Syst., 1(2), 148–158. doi:10.1109/TBCAS.2007.909025

Chapter 10
A Radical Image Steganography Method Predicated on Intensity and Edge Detection

Abhijit Sarkar
Haldia Institute of Technology, India

Sabyasachi Samanta
Haldia Institute of Technology, India

ABSTRACT

The internet has grown to be widely used by billions of individuals in our digital age. The internet is required for a variety of platforms, online apps, and standalone applications. Numerous methods, including cryptography, encryption/decryption, and data concealment algorithms, are developed for this goal. However, the employment of these methods was not very secure, making it simple for hackers to get the secret message. A new method called "steganography" was developed to offer the highest level of protection for sensitive data. Steganography's primary goal is to conceal the presence of concealed messages. Additionally, it seeks out concealed messages using factors like the kind of embedding method, the message's length, its content, or the carrier's secret key. At this point in the chapter, a single bit of data has been embedded into edge-based pixel positions with arbitrary bit positions. The authors have compared their method to three standard edge detection algorithms for a more comprehensive assessment. Different statistical measures also have been made for the uniqueness of the technique.

INTRODUCTION

Information security is regarded as one of the utmost crucial components of technology based on the exchange of information and messages due to the expansion of the Internet and computer technology in recent decades. Information security refers to the processes put in place by corporations to keep sensitive data secure. This entails installing safeguards to prevent unauthorized individuals. Information security encompasses a wide range of subjects, including but not limited to networking and security architecture,

DOI: 10.4018/978-1-6684-7524-9.ch010

monitoring, and accounting. Information security safeguards vital records from being illegally accessed, modified, recorded, interrupted, or destroyed. Cryptography and steganography are one of the most crucial methods for protecting sensitive data (Safarpour et al.,2016). The intention of cryptography is to ensure that only the intended recipients of a message or transmission can decipher and utilize the data contained inside it (Kaur et al., 2010). This ensures that sensitive data remains secure from prying eyes. Steganography is the study of concealing information in unremarkable items such that an opponent cannot detect its presence (Dadgostar et al., 2016). To evade discovery, data may be steganographed by being buried inside an otherwise benign file or message. Confidential material may be recovered from a conventionally sent file or message after it has delivered at its recipient. In addition to encryption, steganography may be used to covertly hide or secure sensitive information. This technique involves concealing data or a hidden message inside another digital media file, such as a picture, song, or video (Pal et al., 2013). Its origins lie in the Greek words for "to write" (graph) and "covered" (steganos). As a result, we refer to it as "secret writing."

There are typically five distinct approaches in the steganography process namely audio steganography, text steganography, video steganography, image steganography and network/protocol steganography. Data concealment in text steganography is accomplished by encoding it into the alphabetic sequence of words. Steganography with images involves hiding information inside a picture of something else. Steganography in audio is the practice of concealing information using sound. The term "video steganography" refers to the practice of discreetly concealing data or other files inside a video file on a computer. Steganography on the network refers to the process of concealing data within another network protocol, such as TCP, UDP, ICMP, IP, etc.

One of the most effective methods of adding information to a picture while maintaining its visual quality is called Image steganography. Image steganography denotes to the practice of walloping information (such as text, an image, or a video) within a seemingly unrelated background image. The classified information is concealed so that human eyes cannot see it. Even though achieving effective protection is a wonderful state of affairs, communication security is the essential demand in current society. Steganography is focused on preserving the message hidden, whereas cryptography is indeed concerned with protecting the substance of the communication. The terms that are crucial in image steganography are the image's quality just after classified information has been embedded and its capacity to retain as much private information as feasible. There are several algorithms and techniques that may be used for image steganography. In contrast to the primary image, these methods offer excellent incorporation capabilities and little warping. Steganography payload placement is the term used to describe the method used to locate the stego locations. In the world of steganography, payload is a key component that improves carrier quality. When using the steganography method, picture pixel positions and intensity might be seen as an important consideration. Due to flaws in the Human Visual System and the decreased cost of storing and sending the picture, the practice of concealing a hidden message in an image has been extensively adopted (Dadgostar et al., 2016). In order to enable safe communication, this paper provides a steganographic method of obscuring the sensitive information. Images are utilized as covers in this paper because they often have a high level of redundancy, which makes them excellent for including information without diminishing their aesthetic appeal. The value of each pixel in a picture with 8 bits of greyscale may be any number between 0 and 255. At each given place, the intensity of the light photons that are hitting at that point corresponds to the value of the pixel at that point. Every pixel stores a value that is proportionate to the amount of light that was there at that specific spot. Using edge recognition and picture intensity, this research presents a new-fangled method for image steganography. The processing detects edges of image for embedding purpose of the secret message. Every pixel may be associated with a single value. By row-wise processing of the detected edge, the initial pixel location of the carrier image is chosen for embedding purpose in a non-linear way. The suggested approaches have been compared using several statistical quality measures and metric with encouraging results.

ASPECTS OF STEGANOGRAPHY

The practise of veiled or concealed writing is known as steganography. Steganography is used in encrypting to prevent a third party from discovering the presence of a message. People in the military, law enforcement, and intelligence sectors place an increasing value on knowing steganography. By simply hiding a message inside another file, picture, or video, we might use the steganography method to cast doubt on its existence. Robustness, Imperceptibility, capacity are the three hallmarks of steganography (Bassil et al., 2012). It is shown in Figure 1.

Figure 1. Steganography characteristics triangle

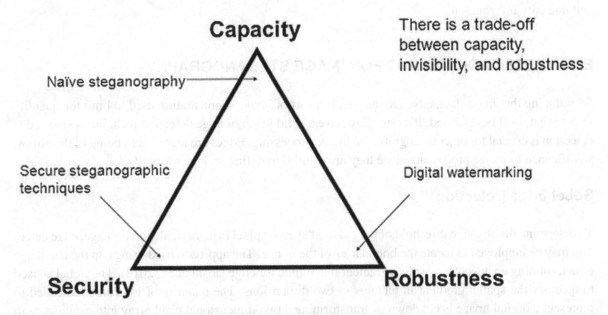

Capacity is set by the quantity of clandestine bits entrenched in apiece cover pixel. With more space, the cover image might conceal even more sensitive information. Imperceptibility is typically measured as the peak signal-to-noise ratio (PSNR). The greater the PSNR, the better is the steganographic image. Protection against unauthorized access to or use of private data is synonymous with robustness. There is a fundamental trade-off in a steganographic system between storage capacity, robustness, and stealth. The most common cover media is particularly image. As its name indicates, "Image Steganography" refers to the practise of concealing information within an input image. Cover image refers to the picture that is employed for this purposes, while stego image refers to the final product of steganography. A memory representation of an image is a N*M (for greyscale pictures) or N*M*3 (for colour images) matrices, where each entry corresponds to the intensity value of a pixel. Using altering the values of a few pixels selected by an encryption algorithm, picture steganography embeds a message into an image. Steganography offers security by obscurity when employed alone, although doing so increases the risk of the hidden message being discovered. The best technique to conceal a message from enemies while yet safeguarding it if it is found is to use steganography and cryptography together. The choice of pixels used for embedding in the carrier determines how secure a steganography approach is. Because they are challenging for any model, texture and noise-related pixels are a preferable alternative for integration. Because of sudden fluctuations in the gradient of the coefficient, pixels near the edge are referred to as noisy pixels because their intensity is either lower or greater than that of their neighbours. Edges are more challenging to predict than finer area pixels due to these sudden changes in statistical and picture attributes. Everybody agrees that any steganographic technology needs two key components: excellent stego fidelity and enough data capacity. The challenge of simultaneously optimising all the characteristics is exceedingly difficult. The cover or carrier refers to the form of media used to transmit the covert message. The finished artefact is known as the stego when the hidden message has been inserted into the cover. The major aim of image steganography is to minimize the contrast seen between stego as well as cover images. Secret information can be hidden in a distributed manner using image position and intensity information.

EDGE DETECTION METHOD FOR IMAGE STEGANOGRAPHY

By reducing the image data, edge recognition is a sort of image segmentation used to limit the quantity of data that must be analysed. It's crucial to have a solid grasp of edge detection techniques since edge detection is crucial for object recognition in image processing. Edges are regarded as being of the utmost significance in image processing since they are utilised to define an image's borders.

Sobel Edge Detection

To determine the absolute threshold of the gradient at every pixel in a grayscale input image, edge detection may be employed to locate the boundaries of the image. The approach used brings up the challenge of determining an adequate absolute gradient magnitude for edge (Joshi et al., 2014). The Sobel is used to quantify the spatial gradient in pictures in two dimensions. The quantity of information needed to represent a digital image is cut down by transforming a two-dimensional pixel array into a dataset with no statistical correlation. This edge detector employs a pair of paired 3x3 convolution masks, one for estimating x-direction gradients and a second for y-direction gradients. The Sobel detector effectively exposes noise in images as edges because to its great sensitivity to it. Therefore, in conversations involving large amounts of data that are identified during data transmission, this operator is advised. Figure 2 provides a description of Sobel masks.

Every single one of those masks is entwined with the picture. There are two numbers, S1 and S2, located at each and every pixel position. Those certain values represent the mask's results for every row and column. Those certain numbers are used in Equation 1 and Equation 2 to determine the border amplitude and direction matrices, respectively.

Figure 2. 3x3 Sobel edge detection masks

-1	-2	-1
0	0	0
1	2	1

G_x

-1	0	1
-2	0	2
-1	0	1

G_y

Edge Scale: $\sqrt{S1^2 + S1^2}$ (1)

Edge Track: $\tan^{-1} \dfrac{S1}{S2}$ (2)

Prewitt Edge Detection

The mask coefficients are dissimilar, but otherwise this operator seems to be quite comparable to the Sobel operator. The following characteristics need to be included in the derivatives (Ahmed et al., 2018):

- The mask should have contrasting signals on it.
- The sum of the mask must be equal to zero at all times.
- Greater edge detection as a result of the increased weight.

The masks are constructed in the same manner as shown in Figure 3.

Figure 3. Prewitt edge detection masks

1	1	1
0	0	0
-1	-1	-1

G_x

-1	0	1
-1	0	1
-1	0	1

G_y

All of these masks have been seamlessly integrated into the final product. The row and column masks' outputs are represented by two numbers at each pixel point. P1 and P2 are the symbols used to signify these numbers. The next equations (Equation 3 and Equation 4) detail how this information is used to determine the edge magnitude and edge orientation.

Edge Magnitude: $\sqrt{P1^2 + P1^2}$ (3)

Edge Direction: $\tan^{-1} \dfrac{P1}{P2}$ (4)

Canny Edge Detection

There are a number of edge detection algorithms available, but the Canny edge detection methodology is unique in terms of precision and reliability. Due to its simplicity of implementation and ability to satisfactorily meet all three of the aforementioned edge detection criteria, it has quickly become a popular choice. Canny's strategy is built on three fundamental goals. Canny set out to identify the best edge detection method. An "optimal" edge detector in this case means: As many genuine edges in the picture as is practical should be marked by the algorithm for good detection. Edges indicated should be as near as feasible to the edge of the actual picture for good localisation. The specified edge should only be marked once in the picture, and noise should not be allowed to produce any false edges, if at all feasible.

LITERATURE REVIEW

We have reviewed some of the similar approaches of edge based steganography method done in the recent past for understanding the open research areas. A contemporary method for steganography in grayscale images has been suggested (Islam et al., 2014). Data is concealed in the cover image's margins, which are selected periodically dependent on the size of the text. Compared to the current edge-based strategies, the suggested method can withstand visual, structural, and non-structural assaults better. Research findings show that the proposed technique outperforms or is competitive with state-of-the-art steganography methods while providing a higher hiding capacity. Given that there may be more information hidden in the edge areas compared to the smoother sections, a scheme that accounts for this possibility was recommended (Dadgostar et al., 2016). This strategy employs a revised LSB substitution process and an interval-valued intuitionistic fuzzy border detection methodology, both of which improve image both quality and capacity. In addition to enhancing picture quality, the usage of intuitionistic fuzzy sets increases the accuracy of identifying edges and smooth regions. A variety of standard photos containing hidden messages of varied lengths are used to trial the recommended procedure. An original strategy was suggested that uses the Canny edge detector in conjunction with 2k correction (Sun et al, 2016). Comprehensible bit span and Huffman encoding are two more technologies used into the innovative method. The border of the cover picture is first detected by a Canny edge detector, and just the pixels along the detected edge are selected to shelter the payload. To improve security, the edge pixels are randomly generated using a sorting process. After that, a Huffman table is built. The confidential information is encoded using Huffman encoding, which is based on the Huffman table. Additionally, the Huffman table should be sent as a secret key to the recipient. Eventually, the 2k correction method is employed to further increase the stealth of stego images. A new steganography method based on the exclusive disjunction (XOR) property and local reference edge detection approach has been put forward (Gaurav et al., 2018). The suggested approach effectively increases embedding capacity while maintaining a desirable level of resilience and imperceptibility. Simulated results, evaluated using a comprehensive image quality assessment strategy, demonstrate improved embedding capacity (BPP) over state-of-the-art steganography techniques without sacrificing PSNR or structural similarity (SSIM). An innovative steganographic method was offered that may conceal messages in grayscale photographs (KICH et al., 2018). It is an adaptive edge approach that conceals the sensitive data in the pixels along the edge. The over segmentation that was performed using modified simple linear iterative clustering served as the foundation for the selection of the edge pixels (M-SLIC). The findings of the experiment shown that the suggested method improves the performance of the stego picture in comparison to more contemporary steganographic approaches in terms of capacity, imperceptibility, and resilience. A novel picture steganography method that facilitates embedding and extraction methods has been suggested later (Mukherjee et al., 2018). The cutoff is manually tweaked for every input feature test instance in the tried-and-true edge detection approach. Each edge picture is produced using the threshold generation process according to a unique key threshold value. The insertion and extraction techniques are then guided by this. With several evaluation criteria as Payload, Mean Squared Error, Peak Signal to Noise Ratio, Kullback-Leibler Divergence etc., this method helps provide top-notch results. Its power to embed is quite remarkable. Furthermore, measurements of the Peak Signal to Noise Ratio and the Structural Similarity Index demonstrate that the stego-indiscernibility image is in excellent condition. In an enhanced image steganography approach, embedding of data was suggested in the carrier image's edge pixels (Ayub et al., 2020). Security is enhanced by edge pixels, which are less likely to be suspiciously eyed by attackers. The proposed approach takes use of various existing image steganography techniques that use edge-based data concealment in the DCT domain, including Prewitt, Sobel, Canny. And the proposed method performs well, with a PSNR and SNR of 99% and 96%, correspondingly. To improve the stego quality, a unique concealment approach was presented that maintains the overall structure of the inconsequential DCT coefficients (Rabie et al., 2021). Nonlinear surface-fitting of the irrelevant DCT coefficients is used in a model-based technique to create a stego image in which the undisclosed data is layered on top of the coefficients while still maintaining the inclusive edifice of the initial concealment image. Investigational findings showing enhancements in the proposed steganography technique's stego quality and security levels compared to cutting-edge techniques are given. To improve picture embedding, a novel approach is suggested that makes use of the edge area. The novel method utilises the binary OR operation to integrate the edge detection methods of Canny and Prewitt. The Least Significant Bit (LSB) technique is used to obfuscate the secret message. The results indicated that the suggested technique had a larger embedding capacity without significantly altering the PSNR, SSIM, and MSE values, indicating that the stego image's invisibility was maintained. A radical approach was advocated which uses expanded synthetic edge detection on the 3 key bits (MSB) pixels of cover images to augment the border size and the capability for embedding process in image steganography (Setiadi et al., 2022). With this method, extraction may be done without using the original cover picture for edge detection. Results showed that the proposed steganography approach improved stealthiness by roughly 1–2 dB likened to the preceding method. A comparative analysis of all the reviewed work has been shown in Table 1.

Table 1. Comparative analysis of the reviewed work

Proposed By	Mechanism	Benefits/ Features
Islam et al., 2014	The secret information in the cover picture is selected periodically dependent on the content of the message.	Method can withstand graphical, organisational, and non-structural assaults better.
Dadgostar et al., 2016	The offered method employs a revised LSB substitution technique and an interval-valued intuitionistic edge detection technique.	Method increases the accuracy of identifying edges and smooth regions.
Sun et al, 2016	The Canny edge detector and the 2k adjustment form the basis of the proposed technique. It also employs Huffman encoding and a consistent bit length.	Experiments show that the suggested method improves upon the state of the art in terms of capacity, Q, and PSNR.
Gaurav et al., 2018	Proposed technique is based on the exclusive disjunction (XOR) property and local reference edge detection approach.	Proposed method effectively increases embedding capacity while maintaining a desirable level of resilience and imperceptibility.
KICH et al., 2018	In order to protect sensitive information, the proposed technique employs an adaptive edge strategy to mask it in neighbouring pixels along the edge, and it also layers an adaptable segmentation on top of a revised basic linear recurrent clustering.	The proposed approach boosts the stego picture's efficiency, stealth, and durability.
Mukherjee et al., 2018	The cutoff value is determined based on the properties of the picture, which is the basis of the suggested technique.	Proposed method shows a very high embedding capacity along with well maintenance of stego-imperceptibility of image.
Ayub et al., 2020	The proposed strategy takes use of the several existing image steganography methods that use edge-based data walloping in the DCT province.	PSNR and SNR of the suggested technique's performance are good.
Rabie et al., 2021	The proposed approach is a model-based technique that makes use of polynomial surface-fitting of the inconsequential DCT factors in order to conceal sensitive information by superimposing it on the coefficients.	Experimental findings shows enhancements in the proposed steganography technique's stego quality and security levels.
Mohsin et al., 2021	To improve picture embedding, the novel approach makes use of the edge area. The novel method utilises the binary OR operation to integrate the edge detection methods of Canny and Prewitt. The Least Significant Bit (LSB) technique is used to obfuscate the secret message.	The results indicated that the suggested technique had a larger embedding capacity without significantly altering the PSNR, SSIM, and MSE values, indicating that the stego image's invisibility was maintained.
Setiadi et al., 2022	The proposed technique makes advantage of the three most significant bits (MSB) of the pixel data in cover pictures to perform dilated hybrid edge detection.	Suggested steganography methodology was successful in enhancing imperceptibility.

PROPOSED WORK

In our proposed method, we have embedded secret message in standard images i.e. Lena, Pepper, Building etc. using edge pixel location in a non-linear positions. Our algorithm have been tested also with various standard edge detection algorithm for comparative analysis with existing work. Statistical measures like PSNR, SSIM have been calculated for various images and various edge detection algorithm. First Grey scale image goes pass through edge detection algorithm. Then detected edge location intensity value is used to embed clandestine message characters in a non-linear way. Last 4 position of edge pixel intensity values have been used for embedding the payload arbitrarily. Different edge detection algorithms have shown different results. Workflow diagram of the overall process have been shown in Figure 4.

Figure 4. Work Flow diagram of the proposed scheme

Embedding/Encoding Process

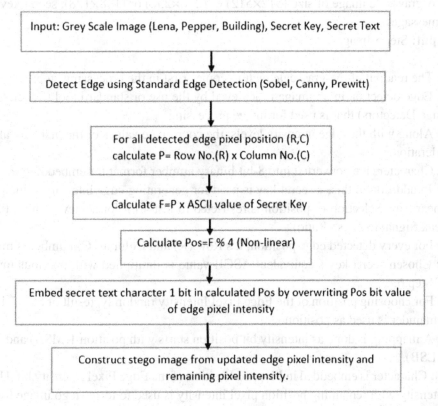

Extraction Process

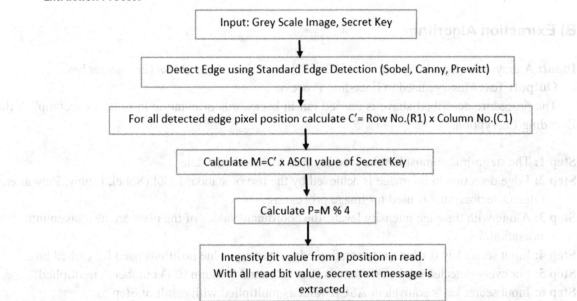

A) Embedding Algorithm (Encoding)

Input: A grayscale image of size (512×512) or (256×256) or (128×128), secret key and different size of text messages.
   Output: Stego-Image

Step 1: The readout of the grayscale picture comes first in the processing step.
Step 2: Edge detection in an image is achieved by the use of standard tool (Sobel, Canny, Prewitt etc. Edge Detectors) that is used for image processing.
Step 3: Along with the edge intensity levels, the coordinate values of the pixel are also taken into consideration.
Step 4: Characters are converted into 8-bit binary number format for embedding in edge intensity.
Step 5: In addition to this, a secret key is used for generating edge intensity value positions in a non-linear way. Selection of position is restricted to last 4 bit for achieving high PSNR value. (High Peak Signal to Noise Ratio)
Step 6: For every detected edge position, it's Row (R) and Column (C) number is multiplied.
Step 7: Chosen secret key's equivalent ASCII value is multiplied with previous multiplication result of Step 6.
Step 8: For choosing position of the Edge Pixel Intensity randomly, result of Step 7 is divided by 4 and remainder is used as position.
Step 9: A mapping is done as intensity bit position starts with position 1(MSB) and ends with position 8(LSB).
Step 10: Character is embedded in Mapped Position of the Edge Pixel Intensity bit. Updated Edge Pixel intensity with remaining position pixel intensity is used to form stego image for transmission.
Step 11: Stop

B) Extraction Algorithm

Input: A grayscale stego-image of size (512×512) or (256×256) or (128×128), secret key.
   Output: Text Message used in Encoding Process.
   The procedure described above is carried out in backwards orientation in order to accomplish the Encoding/Encryption.

Step 1: The stego-image must first be read in order to decode the data.
Step 2: Edge detection in an image is achieved by the use of standard tool (Sobel, Canny, Prewitt etc. Edge Detectors) that is used for image processing.
Step 3: Along with the edge intensity levels, the coordinate values of the pixel are also taken into consideration.
Step 4: Input secret key is used for generating edge intensity value positions used for embedding.
Step 5: For every detected edge position, it's Row (R1) and Column (C1) number is multiplied.
Step 6: Input secret key's equivalent ASCII value is multiplied with result of Step 5.
Step 7: For getting position of the Edge Pixel Intensity, result of Step 6 is divided by 4 and remainder is used as position.

Step 8: A mapping is done as intensity bit position starts with position 1(MSB) and ends with position 8(LSB).

Step 9: Bit value from mapped position of respective Edge Pixel Intensity is read and stored accordingly in an array A. Once all edge pixel is read, A is converted to character array and thus output Text Message is extracted.

Step 10: Stop

PERFORMANCE ANALYSIS

We completed the experiment in this part to show the effectiveness of the suggested steganography technique. We have calculated the embedded capacity using the maximum allowed number of embedded data as bits per pixel (BPP). The following is the definition

$$bpp = \frac{\textbf{maximumembeddingbits}}{\textbf{row} \times \textbf{col}} \tag{5}$$

Where the row and col values represent the elevation and thickness of the original cover picture, correspondingly.

The quality of a steganographic picture has been evaluated from two vantage points, namely: The first measurement is called the peak signal-to-noise ratio (PSNR), and second is structural similarity index measure (SSIM). PSNR is used to figure out how much of a discrepancy there is between the label and the steganographic picture. The formula for PSNR may be defined as follows:

$$PSNR = \frac{10.log_{10}(255 \times 255)}{MSE} db \tag{6}$$

$$MSE = \frac{1}{MN}\sum_{i=1}^{M}\sum_{j=1}^{N}\left(img_{i,j} - C_{i,j}\right)^2 \tag{7}$$

A greater PSNR value indicates that the suggested algorithm has the highest quality, and an MSE value that is as low as possible implies that the method has a low error rate. In MSE, the steganographic picture is denoted by C(i, j), whereas the original image is denoted by img(i, j).

Pictures and other digital images and videos may have their perceived quality predicted using a technique called the structural similarity index measure (SSIM). If you want to see how similar two photographs are to one another, utilise the Similarity Coefficient between Images (SSIM). Since the SSIM index uses an uncompressed or distortion-free baseline picture in its evaluations and forecasts, it is a comprehensive reference metric.

Multiple windows of an image are used to determine the SSIM index. Given two windows x and y of identical size N x N, SSIM is:

$$SSIM(x, y) = \frac{(2\mu_x\mu_y + c_1)(2\sigma_{xy} + c_2)}{(\mu_x^2 + \mu_y^2 + c_1)(\sigma_x^2 + \sigma_y^2 + c_2)} \tag{8}$$

It takes pixel sample mean, variance, covariance of two windows x and y as input.

Grayscale pictures with corresponding dimensions of 512 by 512, 256 by 256, and 128 by 128 were employed for our experiment using the standard image of Lena, Pepper, Building. Detected edges along with achieved stego images has been shown in Table 2.

Table 2. Comparison of Lena, Building, Pepper Stego Images of dimension 512x512 with different edge detectors

Figure 5. PSNR Comparison for Image Lena of input size (a) 512x512 (b) 256x256 (c) 128x128

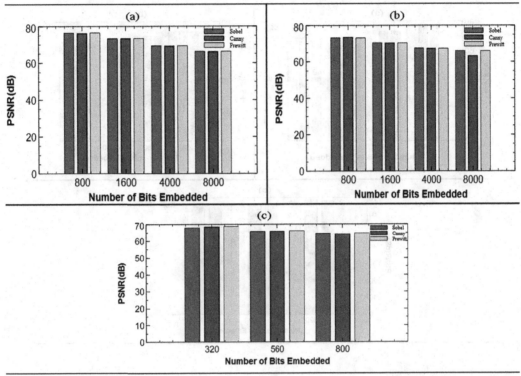

Figure 6. PSNR Comparison for Image Pepper of input size (a) 512x512 (b) 256x256 (c) 128x128

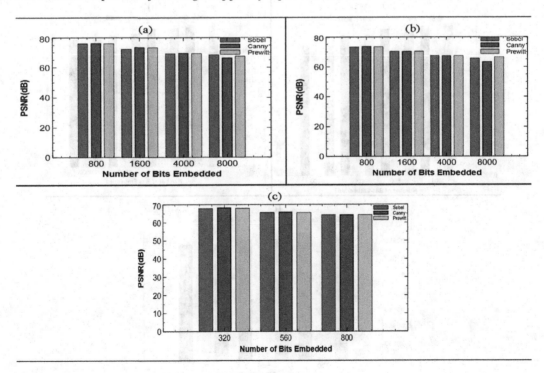

Figure 7. PSNR Comparison for Image Building of input size (a) 512x512 (b) 256x256 (c) 128x128

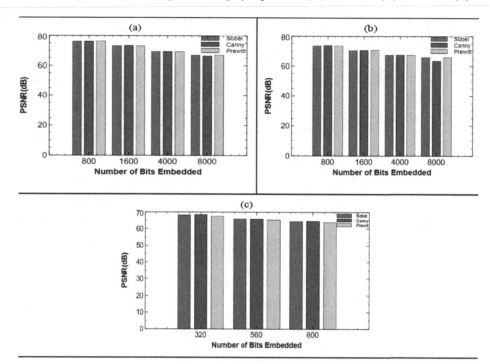

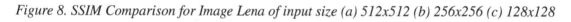

Figure 8. SSIM Comparison for Image Lena of input size (a) 512x512 (b) 256x256 (c) 128x128

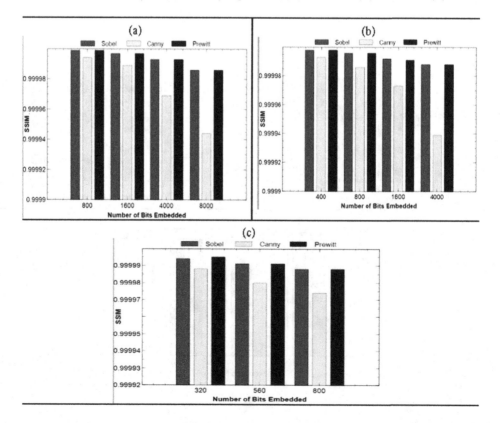

Figure 9. SSIM Comparison for Image Pepper of input size (a) 512x512 (b) 256x256 (c) 128x128

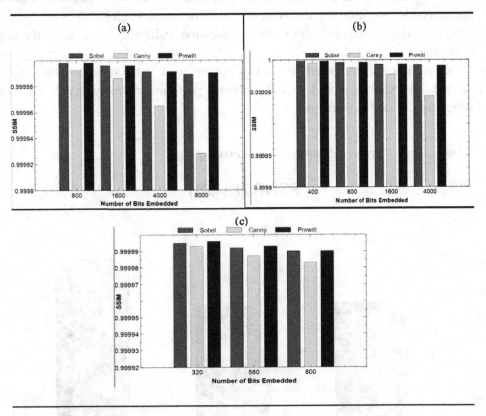

Figure 10. SSIM Comparison for Image Building of input size (a) 512x512 (b) 256x256 (c) 128x128

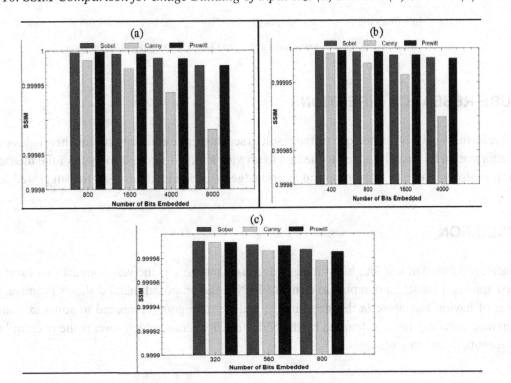

PSNR and SSIM value for the 3 standard image has been shown below in Figures 5 through 10. 3 standard edge detection algorithm has also been used and compared. High PSNR is achieved in our experiment along with SSIM value close to 1 in most of the times indicating less noise in the stego-image and close to the cover image quality.

Our proposed work is also compared against two existing work in the same domain as mentioned in Figure 11. In terms of PSNR, proposed work shows better performance implying that it accommodates less noise which results hard in detection.

Figure 11. Comparison of proposed approach with existing work

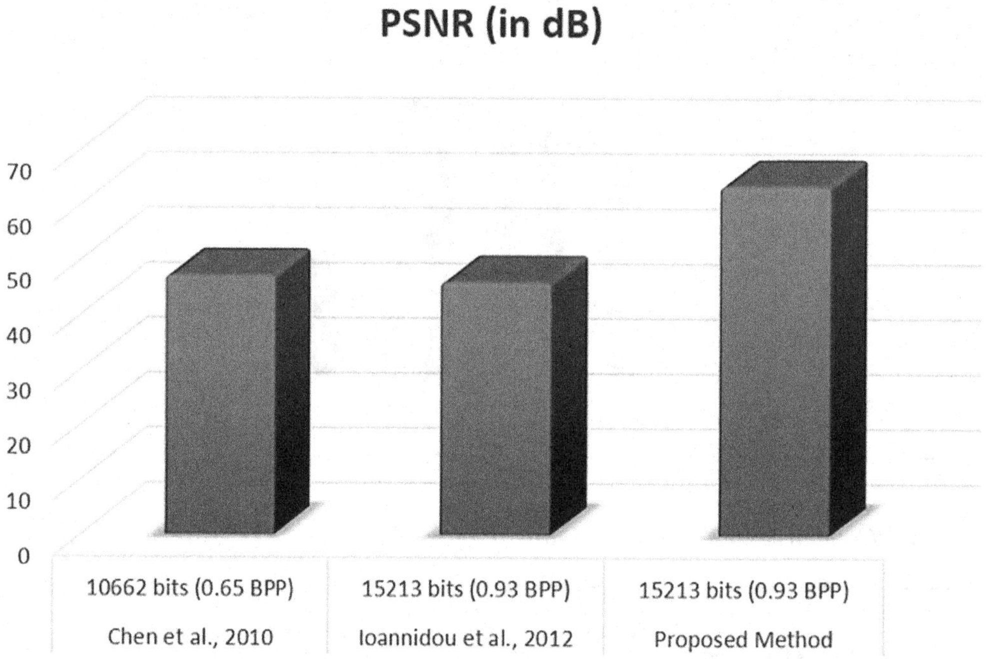

PSNR (in dB)

	10662 bits (0.65 BPP)	15213 bits (0.93 BPP)	15213 bits (0.93 BPP)
	Chen et al., 2010	Ioannidou et al., 2012	Proposed Method

FUTURE RESEARCH DIRECTIONS

In future, further analysis can be done on the result to see the prime elucidation using heuristic approach. More information bits may be added to the mix to provide a more thorough analysis of the metric's evolution. It is also possible to include several hybrid edge detection methods with the suggested strategy.

CONCLUSION

Nonlinear generation of last four bit of image edge pixel intensity is the very foundation of our recommended approach for steganography. In terms of PSNR, the proposed method shows promising result in terms of having less noise in the stego-image and it's also good compared to some existing work done in this domain. This is supported by the SSIM quality score, which reveals the overlap between the concealment and stego-images.

REFERENCES

Ahmed, A. S. (2018). Comparative study among Sobel, Prewitt and Canny edge detection operators used in image processing. *Journal of Theoretical and Applied Information Technology, 96*(19), 6517–6525.

Ayub, N., & Selwal, A. (2020). An improved image steganography technique using edge based data hiding in DCT domain. *Journal of Interdisciplinary Mathematics, 23*(2), 357–366. doi:10.1080/09720 502.2020.1731949

Bassil, Y. (2012). *Image Steganography based on a Parameterized Canny Edge Detection Algorithm* (Version 1). arXiv.

Chen, W.-J., Chang, C.-C., & Le, T. H. N. (2010). High payload steganography mechanism using hybrid edge detector. *Expert Systems with Applications, 37*(4), 3292–3301. doi:10.1016/j.eswa.2009.09.050

Dadgostar, H., & Afsari, F. (2016). Image steganography based on interval-valued intuitionistic fuzzy edge detection and modified LSB. In *Journal of Information Security and Applications* (Vol. 30, pp. 94–104). Elsevier BV. doi:10.1016/j.jisa.2016.07.001

Gaurav, K., & Ghanekar, U. (2018). Image steganography based on Canny edge detection, dilation operator and hybrid coding. In *Journal of Information Security and Applications* (Vol. 41, pp. 41–51). Elsevier BV. doi:10.1016/j.jisa.2018.05.001

Ioannidou, A., Halkidis, S. T., & Stephanides, G. (2012). A novel technique for image steganography based on a high payload method and edge detection. *Expert Systems with Applications, 39*(14), 11517–11524. doi:10.1016/j.eswa.2012.02.106

Islam, S., Modi, M. R., & Gupta, P. (2014). Edge-based image steganography. In EURASIP Journal on Information Security (Vol. 2014, Issue 1). Springer Science and Business Media LLC. doi:10.1186/1687-417X-2014-8

Joshi, M., & Vyas, A. (2014). Comparison of Canny edge detector with Sobel and Prewitt edge detector using different image formats. *International Journal of Engineering Research & Technology, 2*(3).

Kaur, A., Dhir, R., & Sikka, G. (2010). *A New Image Steganography Based On First Component Alteration Technique.* arXiv.

Kich, I., Ameur, E. B., & Taouil, Y. (2018). Image Steganography Based on Edge Detection Algorithm. *2018 International Conference on Electronics, Control, Optimization and Computer Science (ICECOCS).*

Mohsin, N. A., & Alameen, H. A. (2021). A Hybrid Method for Payload Enhancement in Image Steganography Based on Edge Area Detection. In Cybernetics and Information Technologies (Vol. 21, Issue 3, pp. 97–107). Walter de Gruyter GmbH. doi:10.2478/cait-2021-0032

Mukherjee, S., & Sanyal, G. (2018). Edge based image steganography with variable threshold. *Multimedia Tools and Applications, 78*(12), 16363–16388. doi:10.100711042-018-6975-4

Pal, A. K., & Pramanik, T. (2013). Design of an Edge Detection Based Image Steganography with High Embedding Capacity. In Lecture Notes of the Institute for Computer Sciences, Social Informatics and Telecommunications Engineering (pp. 794–800). Springer Berlin Heidelberg. doi:10.1007/978-3-642-37949-9_69

Rabie, T., Baziyad, M., & Kamel, I. (2021). Secure high payload steganography: A model-based approach. In *Journal of Information Security and Applications* (Vol. 63, p. 103043). Elsevier BV. doi:10.1016/j.jisa.2021.103043

Safarpour, M., & Charmi, M. (2016). *Capacity Enlargement of the PVD Steganography Method Using the GLM Technique* (Version 1). arXiv.

Setiadi, D. R. I. M. (2022). Improved payload capacity in LSB image steganography uses dilated hybrid edge detection. In Journal of King Saud University - Computer and Information Sciences (Vol. 34, Issue 2, pp. 104–114). Elsevier BV. doi:10.1016/j.jksuci.2019.12.007

Sun, S. (2016). A novel edge based image steganography with 2 k correction and Huffman encoding. *Information Processing Letters*, *116*(2), 93–99. doi:10.1016/j.ipl.2015.09.016

Chapter 11
Secure Cryptography Using Chaotic Algorithm

Uday Kumar Banerjee
Dr. B.C. Roy Engineering College, Durgapur, India

Anup Kumar Das
Dr. B.C. Roy Engineering College, Durgapur, India

Rajdeep Ray
Dr. B.C. Roy Engineering College, Durgapur, India

Chandan Koner
Dr. B.C. Roy Engineering College, Durgapur, India

ABSTRACT

A chaotic cryptographic method and bit shuffle methodology for image encryption and decoding have both been suggested. In order to evaluate the encryption's effectiveness and determine whether it met the desired standard, a number of performance analysis tools were also used. These included the number of pixel change rate (NPCR), the unified average changing intensity (UACI), the entropy analysis, which is a component of an encryption scheme that shows how random the image is, and the correlation coefficient. These results reveal the safety of the suggested cryptographic technique.

INTRODUCTION

Secure Cryptography: An Overview

Security is not only a word; it is a very important aspect in today's world especially for communication and data or information transmission. As the increase of online transmission not for only simple information but for economic data, the protection of this information becomes very crucial. To do so security techniques like cryptography becomes more and more important as well before. Information security has emerged as the most fascinating and interesting technological sector in the modern world in the informa-

DOI: 10.4018/978-1-6684-7524-9.ch011

tion age as a result of widespread computerization and their interaction via networks. Confidentiality, authentication, integrity, non-repudiation, access control, and availability are the guiding principles of every security mechanism. A crucial component of secure communications is cryptography, which was designed with the intention of providing secret communication since it shields information transmission from the impact of adversaries. The concept of security and its characteristics have come to the forefront due to the overabundance of digital content and the ossification of internet technology. For instance, telemedicine provides interactive healthcare in far-off places while transmitting patient health information and imaging data over an insecure connection. Second, the satellite image provides time-specific data that is useful for a variety of purposes, including environmental protection, meteorology, defence and remote sensing. The government, private detectives and criminal organizations may now closely monitor people and public behavior online thanks to the development of surveillance technology. The security of picture data during transmission and storage is a key factor in determining the quality of the service in the aforementioned applications. The word, cryptography came from ancient Greek which contains two words: "kryptos" means "hidden" or "vault" and "graphy" means "writing" or "study". Cryptography is the study of secure communication between the sender and the receiver and it allow viewing the message to intended recipient without intervention of the adversary element.

The history of cryptography is really old. At the time of ancient Egyptian civilization around 2000 B.C. the hieroglyphic language makes complex by using cryptography picture and only the elite community knew the meaning then. At the time of Julius Caesar at 100 B.C. to 44 B.C. the modern-day cipher concept was found. Julius Caesar did not want that the message should read by the messenger or anyone so he changes the original letter by its next third letter and make a coded form of message which can only be understood by those who knew the decoding process. The modern day's techniques come along lot of paths and it becomes a strong mechanism to protect information. Nowadays the different mathematical concepts with the help of different rule base calculation are used which are called cryptographic algorithm. By applying these algorithms different text, image, audio, video or other type of files can be encoded such a way that the original meaning of this file is hidden in a masking and cannot be understood easily.

The conversion of plain text to a cipher text is called encryption process. The reverse process to convert the cipher text to original message is called decryption process. The persons who deal with cryptography are called cryptographers. The algorithms are used mainly for cryptographic key generation, to protect the email documents, digital signing, verification to protect data authenticity and privacy, secure web browsing through internet and confidential communications such as debit and credit card transactions.

The modern cryptography has four objectives, confidentiality, integrity, non-repudiation and authenticity. Confidentiality means only the intended recipient will understand the meaning of the information, no one else. The integrity means any alteration or eavesdropping cannot be possible without knowing the sender and receiver. In non-repudiation features the receiver or sender can't deny the involvement for information creation or transmission in future. When sender and the receiver of the transmitted information can confirm each and every ones identity as well as the origin and destination of the information, the deciphering can be done.

The four different subcategories of cryptography are Modern cryptography, Chaos based cryptography, DNA based cryptography and quantum cryptography. There are mainly two types of cryptographic techniques used, single key or symmetric key encryption and public key or asymmetric key encryption. In single key encryption system, the same key is used to encrypt the data as well as decrypt it. This is also called private key encryption. The Advanced Encryption System (AES), Data Encryption System

(DES) are different types of symmetric key encryption. There are two keys used in public key encryption, one key is used to encrypt the data and another key is used to decrypt it. RSA (Rivest–Shamir–Adleman), Elliptic Curve Digital Signature Algorithm (ECDSA), Digital Signature Algorithm (DSA), Diffie-Hellman key exchange are some algorithms of public key infrastructure. Due to their exceptional speed and low complexity, symmetric encryption methods are typically used to encrypt private data. In contrast, asymmetric encryption imposes a heavy computational cost, tends to be much slower, and is frequently employed for digital signature and key distribution. Traditional cryptography, on the other hand, is not suited for quick encryption of a huge volume of data (for instance, colour photos and video) in real time. Traditional picture encryption schemes are more difficult to accomplish when realised by software due to the significant correlation between image pixels. As a result, there is still more effort to be done in the creation of novel encryption techniques.

Chaotic Algorithms: A Brief Discussion

The study of non-linear dynamical systems that show sensitivity to initial conditions is the focus of the mathematical field known as chaos theory. Nature contains chaotic situations. The weather is a good and typical illustration of this. Since its introduction, chaos theory has found extensive use in a variety of fields, including computer science, ethnography, economics, and meteorology. Sensitivity to beginning conditions, periodic orbit density, and topological mixing are characteristics of chaotic systems. Chaotic systems are appealing for cryptography because of their qualities like determinism and sensitivity (Alvarez et. al. 2006).

Chaotic Systems' Characteristics

Chaotic systems have the following features.

Sensitivity Toward Initial Conditions

This implies that even a small alteration to the starting circumstances can result in unanticipated behaviour. The butterfly effect, a crucial characteristic in producing chaotic cryptographic algorithms and hash functions analogous to the diffusion property, is the most typical analogy used to convey this concept (Bai et. al. 2005).

Periodic Orbit Density

Any chaotic point in the trajectory can approach other locations due to the odd attractor phenomena because of periodic orbit density. This property contributes to the development of affine transformations, which are quite beneficial in cryptography (Behnia et. al., 2008).

Mixing Topologically

Topological mixing, which is similar to the uniform distribution property in cryptography, meaning that the chaotic trajectory formed from a random portion of the phase space can cover the rest of the phase space as the trajectory advances (Benrhouma et. al., 2013).

Determinism

Determinism can be seen as extending the features of sensitivity to initial conditions. The chaotic path taken will always be the same as long as the original circumstances stay the same. This characteristic is comparable to the cryptography techniques' deterministic pseudo-randomness quality (Fu et. al., 2013).

The study of unexpected, the nonlinear, and the unpredictable is known as chaos theory. It teaches us to be ready for the unforeseen. Chaos Theory deals with nonlinear phenomena that are practically hard to anticipate or control, such as turbulence, weather, the stock market, human mental states, and so on, while most traditional science works with seemingly predictable phenomena like gravity, electricity, or chemical reactions. Fractal mathematics, which captures the infinite complexity of nature, is frequently used to explain these phenomena. Landscapes, clouds, trees, organs, rivers, and many other natural objects, as well as many of the systems exhibit fractal qualities. Understanding the fractal, chaotic aspect of our reality can help us gain fresh knowledge, strength, and wisdom (Guan et. al., 2005).

THE PRINCIPLES OF CHAOS

The butterfly effect: A butterfly flapping its wings in New Mexico has the capacity to start a hurricane in China. Even though it could take a very long time, the relationship is genuine. The hurricane would not have occurred if the butterfly's wings had not fluttered at precisely the proper moment in space and time. Small modifications to the underlying circumstances have a significant impact on the outcomes, to put it more precisely. This idea is continually demonstrated in our daily lives. Who knows what the long-term repercussions of introducing chaos and fractals to millions of children will be? (Houcemeddine et. al., 2013).

Unpredictability: Because we can never fully understand all of a complex system's initial conditions, we are unable to forecast the system's eventual outcome. Any prediction will be meaningless due to the tremendous amplifying effect of even small measurement inaccuracies. Accurate long-range weather prediction will always be impossible since it is impossible to quantify the effects of all the butterflies (and other species) in the world (Li et. al., 2010).

Order and disarray: Chaos is more than just disarray. Chaos examines these shifts, which frequently take place in unexpected ways between order and disorder.

Mixing: After some time has passed, turbulence guarantees that two nearby points in a complicated system will eventually end up in significantly different places (Maniccam et. al., 2001). Examples: Two nearby water molecules may wind up in various ocean regions or even in various oceans. Together launched helium balloons will eventually settle in wildly dissimilar locations. Because turbulence occurs at all scales, mixing is comprehensive. Fluids cannot be unmixed since it is nonlinear.

Feedback: When there is feedback, systems frequently degenerate into chaos. The actions of the stock market serve as a good illustration. People are more likely to acquire or sell a stock if its value increases or decreases. This further impacts the stock price, driving it up or down (Norouzi et. al., 2012).

Fractals: A fractal is a pattern that never ends. Fractals are infinitely intricate patterns that resemble one another at all scales. They are made by repeatedly performing a straightforward technique in a never-ending feedback loop (Stinson, 2009). Fractals, which are driven by recursion, are representations of chaotic dynamical systems. They lie between the recognizable dimensions of our world in terms of geometry. Since fractals occur frequently in nature, fractal patterns are quite well known. Consider the following examples: trees, rivers, beaches, mountains, clouds, seashells, etc. (Tang et. al., 2003).

The Greek word "Khaos," which means "gaping nothingness," is where the name "Chaos" originates. Chaos, according to mathematicians, is difficult to define but simple to "recognize when you see it." Chaos, then, is a state of complete ambiguity or predictability in a complex natural system's behaviour. According to chaos theory (Devaney, 1989), a little adjustment now might have a significant impact tomorrow. It is a branch of mathematics that has applications in physics, engineering, economics, biology, and philosophy (Morse, 1967). Its main thesis is that small variations in initial conditions, such as those caused by rounding errors in numerical computation, can result in chaotic systems with wildly diverging outcomes, making long-term prediction impossible in general.

With the conceptualization of the "Butterfly Effect" in 1972, Edward Lorenz introduced the concept of chaos theory to the modern world. Having knowledge of this theory will aid in enhancing predictability in a complicated system. As a result, you should be aware of all the inputs when dealing with a system and maintain control over them. Since numerous mathematicians and scientists contributed to the development of chaos theory, it has applications in a wide range of scientific disciplines. A mathematical model of the movement of air in the atmosphere was created by meteorologist Lorenz. It significantly altered how the model performed. This led him to uncover the Sensitive Dependence on Initial Conditions (SDIC) principle, which is widely recognized as a crucial element in any chaotic system. With the development of computers in the 1970s, a multidisciplinary interest in chaos, complexity, and self-organizing systems emerged. Benoît Mandlebrot discovered the component of the chaos puzzle that connected everything. Similar to Turing's earlier work, Mandelbrot published a book titled The Fractal Geometry of Nature (Devaney and Keen 1989) that explored the mathematical underpinnings of how patterns appear in nature. His fractals, which represent the geometry of fractional dimensions, served to illustrate or characterize chaos rather than to explain it. Now, the workings of chaos were apparent. May was developing a model in the early 1970s that examined how insect birthrate fluctuated with food supplies. He discovered that his equation required twice as much time to return to its previous condition at some crucial values, with the period having doubled in size after a number. His model became unpredictable after period-doubling cycles, just way insect populations typically are. Mathematicians have discovered that this period-doubling is a natural path to chaos for many different systems since May's finding with insects.

Since chaotic systems frequently react in important ways rather than resisting outside shocks, they are unstable. In other words, they don't only ignore outside influences; they also use them to their advantage. Due to their small number of straightforward differential equations and lack of references to any implied chance mechanisms, these systems are deterministic. A system is said to be deterministic if there is no role for chance in how its future states will emerge. When the evolution of something relies on the starting conditions, it is said to be chaotic. According to this property, two trajectories must have two distinct but nearby initial circumstances. However, experimental observations didn't make that observation until the last thirty years of the twentieth century. Chaotic systems are actually rather widespread in nature. It is also possible to describe many natural events as chaotic. The heart and brain of biological things, the solar system, meteorology, and other fields all contain them. Chaotic systems have the following traits:

1. No cyclical behaviour.
2. Sensitivity to the starting circumstances.
3. It is difficult or impossible to predict chaotic motion.
4. The movement appears haphazard.
5. Non-linear

CRYPTOGRAPHY-CHAOS PRIMITIVES

Cryptography must be among the fields where chaos has generated the most interest because of its possible uses. The unique characteristics of chaos, such as sensitivity to initial conditions and system parameters, pseudo-randomness, ergodicity, stretching and folding of the phase space, have made chaotic dynamics a promising replacement for traditional cryptographic algorithms because its innate properties directly relate to the confusion and diffusion characteristics of cryptography that are described in Shannon's works. Chaotic cryptography is the application of chaos theory to various cryptographic operations within a cryptographic system. This emergence of chaotic cryptography is marked by Matews and Pecora, two works. The first suggests using a signal produced by a chaotic system to disguise the clear information in a digital stream encryption. The second suggests using synchronization techniques at the receiver to filter the chaotic signal in order to mask the clear message with a chaotic signal at the physical level of the communication channel. These two publications also introduce two distinct perspectives on the use of chaos in cryptography, later referred to as analogue chaotic synchronization or digital chaotic ciphers.

Numerous chaotic cryptosystems have since been presented. Chaos-based cryptography relies on the intricate dynamics of nonlinear systems or maps that are deterministic but simple, in contrast to standard cryptographic algorithms that are mostly focused on number theoretic or algebraic ideas. As a result, it offers hope for data security. You can find some older reviews in. Numerous chaotic systems, including the Lorenz system, logistic maps, tent maps, piecewise linear chaotic maps, and others, are frequently employed in cryptography. Either continuous or discrete time scales can be used to define them. While discrete maps are described as recursive functions, continuous maps are a collection of differential equations. While continuous systems can only be chaotic with three or more dimensions, chaotic maps can have any number of dimensions. As has already been shown, there is a basic connection between chaos and cryptography. Chaotic systems are logically intriguing for use in cryptography because of their primary properties. More information about this connection is examined here. We will look at how the fundamental qualities of chaos directly relate to the confusion and diffusion properties of cryptography. It is obvious that topological mixing, auto-similarity, and ergodicity all have a direct impact on confusion.

On the other hand, the sensitivity of chaotic systems to their initial settings and control parameters is intimately related to diffusion. The avalanche effect is a result of diffusion, where even a small change in the input to the cryptosystem results in an entirely different output. TABLE 1, which outlines the relationship, is taken from Alvarez (Alvarez et. al., 2006).

In nature, chaotic systems emerge on their own and can be immediately used to security procedures. Compared to traditional cryptography, chaos-based traditional ones (Pisarchik et. al. 2010): (1) It offers a wide range of chaotic functions and parameters that can be applied, allowing for a greater variety of message encoding techniques; also enlarging the key size Traditional cryptosystems, on the other hand, use algorithms where diffusion and the number of iterations and key lengths both have linear relationships with confusion. (2) As mentioned in numerous articles, chaotic mapping functions resemble random

Table 1. Comparisons of chaos and cryptography

Cryptographic characteristic	Chaotic property	Illustration
Confusion	Ergodicity Topological mixing	Any input can produce a similar result from the system.
Diffusion	Sensitivity to initial conditions and control parameters	A minor change in the input results in a significantly different output.
Deterministic pseudorandomness	Deterministic	Pseudorandomness is produced via a predictable process.
Algorithmic complexity	Complexity	A straightforward algorithm yields a highly complex result.

distributions while retaining their deterministic characteristics, preventing any statistical investigation from exposing the spectral qualities of an encrypted signal. (3) Unlike in the past, chaotic analogue cryptography can be implemented directly in hardware without the need for digital-to-analog conversion. The incorporation of a continuous chaotic function is necessary since every conversion result in a loss of precision and slows down the encryption process. (4) The ability to design chaotic systems with straightforward computable deterministic methods is a benefit. As a result, chaos offers a substitute for the traditional cryptosystem that can provide information security on an open network.

Chaotic cryptography is a very active area of research, and there are far too many and a wide variety of chaotic cryptosystems to cover. There are many worthwhile investigations in (Kocarev et. al., 2011). There are two basic methods for applying chaotic systems to cryptography: analogue and digital methods. The analogue based cryptosystems are based on the synchronization technique (Pecora et. al., 1990) (Kocarev et. al., 1992) and use continuous-time systems to generate signals for secure communication over a noisy channel. Numerous strategies have been devised that enable the information signal to be transformed into a chaotic waveform on the transmitter side and to be separated from the broadcast waveform on the receiver side. Chaotic masking, chaotic shift keying, and chaotic modulation are the three that are most significant. Digital based cryptosystems use one or more chaotic maps to encrypt digital data instead of relying on synchronization techniques.

The chaotic cryptosystem can be designed in a number of ways. Ten general guidelines for creating a successful chaos-based cryptosystem have been outlined by Kelber and Schwarz (Kelber et. al., 2005) based on the advantages and disadvantages of existing algorithms.

The many categories will be provided separately and each classification will be introduced as explicitly as feasible in order to create an overall overview of developments in chaos-based cryptosystem. In general chaos-based cryptosystems may be classified in the following categories:

1. Public key cryptosystem
2. Symmetric cryptosystem
3. Pseudorandom Number Generator (PRNG)
4. Hash function.

The field of public key cryptosystem research was introduced in 1976 with the release of Diffie and Hellman's paper, "New directions in cryptography" (Diffie et. al., 1976). Since then, a number of public-key algorithms have been put forth, with the most popular ones being RSA, Elliptic Curve Cryptography,

Elgamal, and so on. In this section, we'll concentrate on a survey of public key cryptosystems based on chaos theory. The first chaotic public key cryptosystem based on inhomogeneous cellular automata was proposed by Puhua Guan in 1987(Guan, 1987). A cellular automaton (CA) is a discrete system model that simulates a parallel computer. But due to several restrictions, it is not feasible. Fengi Hwu (Fengi, 1993) proposed the unsafe chaotic-map public-key cryptosystem and interpolating random spline in 1993.

A new technique for asymmetric encryption using characteristics of nonlinear dynamical systems was developed by Roy Tenny et al. (Tenny et. al., 2003) (Tenny et. al., 2005). There is a distributed unified high-dimensional dissipative nonlinear dynamical system between the transmitter and receiver. By modulating the transmitter's parameters, a message is encoded, and this causes the attractor of the entire system to alter. Unauthorized receivers are unable to interpret messages because they are unaware of the receiver's hidden dynamics. They adopted synchronization of chaos, but they were unable to provide a concrete example. A public key encryption technique based on Chebyshev maps was then proposed by Kocarev et al. (Kocarev et. al., 2003). It was quickly cryptanalyzed, albeit (Bergamo et. al., 2005) (Chong et. al., 2007). Kocarev introduced a modified cryptosystem (Kocarev et. al., 2005) to increase security, extending the definition of Chebyshev polynomials from the real field to the finite field. According to Lima et al (Lima et. al., 2008)'s proof, solving a discrete logarithm issue is comparable to breaking the cryptosystem using triangle substitution in a finite field.

Its effectiveness is still inferior to RSA, though. A method of building public key cryptosystems based on "Merkle's puzzles" by generalized synchronization of coupled map lattices was proposed by Xinggang Wang et al. in 2005(Wang et. al., 2005), however it is still not feasible. For key exchange, Bose (Bose, 2005)

used a number of chaotic systems as well as a collection of linear maps. A novel public key cryptosystem created using the traditional one-way chaotic beta-transformation mapping was described by M.R.K. Ariffin in 2009(Ariffin et. al., 2009). They demonstrated that the hard math issue for this system is probably going to be more difficult than the traditional Discrete Log Problem (DLP). Asymmetric approach based on the Chinese Remainder Theorem and double sequence was developed by Zhang Yunpeng et al. (Zhang et. al., 2011). to interfere the backpack sequence using a sequence of random numbers produced by the interference of the Logistic and Chebychev chaotic mapping. Asymmetric cryptography system suggested by Santo Banerjee (Banerjee et. al., 2012) uses the factorization problem of two huge primes and can only be implemented by using the multiplication operation for both encryption and decryption. Some of the public key schemes that have been presented have been shown to be insecure and to be inefficient. The development of safe and effective algorithms still requires a lot of work, and chaos-based public key cryptography research is far from finished.

Block cipher and stream cipher make up the symmetric cryptosystem. While block cypher encrypts a specific block each time, stream cipher encrypts the plaintext bit by bit or byte by byte. The section will introduce the creation of a block cipher and a stream cipher based on chaos, respectively. Numerous chaos-based stream cyphers have been proposed. A good chaotic stream cypher typically depends on the chaotic map it uses and the generating method it uses. Matthews (Mattews, 2010). made the initial attempt to employ a chaotic dynamical system as a key stream generator. Iterative logistic mapping and a 256-bit external secret key were used in Hassam et alefficient.'s chaos-based feedback stream cypher (ECBFSC) for picture cryptosystems that was developed in 2007. A linked map lattice (CML)-based stream cypher was attacked via linear analysis in 2009, demonstrating that this well-designed chaos-based stream cypher is nevertheless vulnerable to attack. Li et al. (Li et. al., 2010) presented a novel chaotic stream cipher based on a linked nonlinear dynamic filter (NDF) and used it to secure palm print templates. In 2011, Kanso (Kanso, 2011). introduced chaotic systems to the self-shrinking method utilised in conventional cryptography to create chaotic key stream generators that can create key streams with high levels of security and excellent statistical features. A lightweight chaotic stream cipher used for coloured picture encryption that satisfies high throughput, reliable encryption, and minimal hardware area was first realised on hardware by Barakat et al. (Barakat et. al., 2014). Block cyphers use a secret key to change a relatively short string (usually 64 or 128 bits) into a string of the same length. Block cyphers have the benefit of being able to be utilised to create other primitives. The first block cypher to be created using an invertible iterative chaotic system was by Habutsu (Habutu et. al., 1990). Modified chaotic maps are the key component of the concept behind chaotic block cyphers. It must somehow prevent the eigen-modes of the mapping from having negative expansion exponents in order to derive a one-to-one cryptographically mapping from a usually many-to-one chaotic map. If not, the developed encryption is susceptible to straightforward cryptanalysis.

Chaotic block ciphers were created by Masuda et al. (Masuda et. al., 2006) using the structures of contemporary block ciphers. A compression and encryption method using a changeable and unexpected statistical model for arithmetic coding that is generated using a pseudo-random bit stream produced by a few chaotic systems was proposed by Bose et al. (Bose et. al., 2006). Arnold chaotic maps were used by Hamdi et al. (Hamdi et. al., 2008) to develop a four-dimensional chaotic encryption for secure picture transmission. A fast chaotic block cypher for picture encryption was recently proposed by Fouda et al. (Fouda et. al., 2014) based on the sorting of the solutions of the Linear Diophantine Equation (LDE), whose coefficients are integers and dynamically produced from any type of chaotic systems.

Despite these efforts, chaotic or dynamical systems are not connected to commercially or theoretically accepted cyphers. Modern chaos-based symmetric key cryptosystems' main issue is that they don't have comprehensive and verifiable security features and accepted practices.

There are many uses for pseudorandom bit sequences in the fields of communications and cryptography. A pseudo-random number generator is a deterministic technique that generates a bigger set of "random-looking" numbers known as pseudorandom numbers from a smaller group of "random" values known as the seed. The benefit of offering qualitatively simple procedures to produce deterministic pseudorandom numbers is a feature of chaotic dynamical systems. The original concept for creating a pseudorandom number generator using chaotic first-order nonlinear difference equations was put forth in 1982 by Oishi and Inoue (Oishi et. al., 1982). Since then, numerous researchers have taken part in this investigation. In order to create truly random numbers, Gonzalez and Pino (Gonzalez et. al., 1999) generalised the logistic map and created a truly unpredictable random function in 1999. A few chaotic systems-based pseudorandom bit generators (CCS-PRBG) with high security were proposed by Li Shujun et al. in 2001(Shujun et. al., 2001). The use of a piecewise linear, one-dimensional chaotic map as a random number generator was examined by Kocarev and Stojanovski et al. (Stojanovski et. al., 2001) (Stojanovski et. al., 2001). Pseudorandom numbers were produced in 2004 by Huaping et al. using a one-way linked chaotic map lattice (Huaping et. al., 2004). The piecewise linear map and noninvertible nonlinearity transform were used to develop a PRNG in (Wang et. al., 2009), and the multi-value correspondence of asymptotic deterministic randomness was investigated. 2011 saw Liu conduct a separate analysis of the statistics and complexity of two different types of chaotic pseudorandom sequences produced by Chebyshev maps and Lorenz systems (Liu, 2011). A new approach is developed in 2013's Hu et al.'s (Hu et. al., 2013) pseudorandom sequence generator, which is based on Chen chaotic system, to address the issue of non-uniform distribution of the sequence generated. A pseudorandom number generator based on a quantum chaotic map was very recently developed by Akhshani et al. (Akhshani et. al., 2014), whose output is solely dependent on the equations utilised in the quantum chaotic map. Simple chaotic maps are the most common chaotic systems used to produce pseudorandom sequences, and they can be addressed using the nonlinear prediction method based on phase-space reconstruction. Therefore, employing high-dimensional complex chaotic systems to generate pseudorandom sequences is more appropriate.

A fundamental information security technique is the hash function, which is typically used for digital signatures, message authentication, and data integrity protection. A novel approach that has spurred significant research in this area is the chaos-based hash function. Wong created a system that combines encryption and hashing based on Baptista's encryption technique (Wong, 2003). It is the first time that chaos' suitability for hash function construction has been shown. Although it can encrypt messages and provide the associated hash value at the same time, this technique still needs to be more efficient and secure. Since then, other hash algorithms based on chaos have been released. While some of the suggested hash functions are currently being investigated, others still require more study to confirm their efficacy and security. A hash function based on a tent map and message modulation into iterations numbers was suggested by Admin et al. in 2009 (Amin et. al., 2009). However, the plan is quickly examined by Xiao et al. (Xiao et. al., 2010) since it is unable to escape collision attacks. Xiao et al. (Xiao et. al., 2010) developed an approach with both modification detection and localizations, whose structure allows the parallel processing mode, using the piecewise linear chaotic map. A parallel keyed hash function based on a chaotic neural network was created by Di Xiao et al. (Xiao et. al., 2009). Huang (Huang, 2011) used this forgery attack to study the hash algorithm and developed an improved approach based on the analysis.

However, it has been shown that the enhanced algorithm is still insecure. Time series can be anticipated for straightforward chaotic maps. H. Ren et al. (Ren et. al., 2009) created a key hash function based on a complex spatiotemporal chaotic system to prevent this. This system ensures complicated dynamical behaviour to increase security.

Li et al. (Li et. al., 2011) recently suggested a parallel hash function based on an asymmetric tent map and a piecewise linear map with movable parameters. The main drawbacks of this technique, according to Long et al. (Long et. al., 2013), are the incorrect floor, round, and exclusive OR operations, which can result in a collision attack. A quick and effective keyed hash function is proposed by Kanso et al. in (Kanso et. al., 2013). and is based on a single, chaotic, four-dimensional cat map whose erratic outputs are used to calculate a hash value. A novel high-speed, topologically simple keyed hash function was introduced by Jiteurtragool et al. (Jiteurtragool et. al., 2013) based on a sinusoidal map, which delivers a high degree of chaos over most parameter space areas, and a circular network topology with eight sinusoidal maps. Wei et al.'s (Wei et. al., 2014) unique keyed hash function, which uses the chaotic S-box replacement to boost efficiency, combines the traditional iteration structure of hash functions with dynamic S-boxes. There are tons of built-in hash functions that won't be listed here. Perhaps instead of creating various sorts of algorithms, the current research on generating chaos-based hash functions should concentrate on fundamental laws to ensure security and effectiveness. Security entails that the hash function should meet the fundamental requirements to fend off preimage, second-preimage, collision, and other attacks. It is advised to use parallel processing mode rather than sequential realization method to increase efficiency.

CHALLENGES IN CHAOTIC CRYPTOGRAPHY AND FUTURE SCOPE

The unique characteristics of chaotic systems appear to offer significant possibilities for developing reliable and effective cryptosystems. However, it has faced numerous challenges along the way, much like other interdisciplinary study topics. Conventional cryptographers have criticized chaotic cryptographers for their lack of in-depth understanding of the field. A few problems with chaotic cryptosystems are

1. Lack of verifiable security requirements
2. Chaotic system deficiencies
3. computational cost
4. Finite precision representation

Even though chaotic cryptosystems have been studied for many years, there is still a long way to go before they can be successfully used in real-world and business applications. Currently, chaotic cryptography may be viewed as incidental when compared to traditional cryptography. Chaotic cryptography must be implemented and subjected to cryptanalysis in order to become a viable alternative.

Despite the substantial progress previously made, there are still too many issues in the sector that need to be resolved. The study of chaos-based cryptography has only just begun. Although chaotic systems appear to be the best candidates for cryptographic primitives on a theoretical level, chaotic cyphers are nevertheless less effective than the corresponding conventional ones in real-world applications. As a result, chaotic cryptography has been a busy area of research with little influence on traditional cryptography. Therefore, additional research is necessary to assess the effective algorithms for practical applications. Future research should focus on a number of areas to help chaos-based cryptography become mature and perfect: (1) Gain a deeper comprehension of potential connections between chaos and cryptography to offer theoretical backing for the creation of chaotic cryptosystems. (2) Create broad guidelines for designing safe and effective chaotic systems to prevent the current chaotic state. (3) Because one cannot apply the analytical techniques of conventional cryptography, which are based on number theoretic principles or the difficulty of discrete logarithmic problems, the security proof of a cryptosystem based on chaos is also an open issue.

CRYPTOGRAPHY USING CHAOTIC ALGORITHM: A CASE STUDY

In this section, a chaotic cryptographic method (Lujie Wang et.al.,2022) and bit shuffle methodology for image encryption and decoding have both been suggested. In order to evaluate the encryption's effectiveness and determine whether it met the desired standard, a number of performance analysis tools were also used. These included the number of pixel change rate (NPCR), the unified average changing intensity (UACI), the entropy analysis, which is a component of an encryption scheme (Zhang, C et.al., 2022) that shows how random the image is, and the correlation coefficient. These results reveal the safety of the suggested cryptographic technique.

Proposed Scheme

Today's internet-based image transfers are not secure. As a result, it is required to communicate an image using specific secure methods (Lawnik et.al., 2022). To protect transmitted images, a variety of techniques can be utilized. Here, a 128 by 128 color image has initially been captured, and using MATLAB software, the image has been transformed into a 128 x 128 matrix of RGB values. The remaining R matrix is then divided into 4 blocks, each of which is 64 x 64. Then, an XOR operation was performed within those blocks to produce those four blocks with a new bit value and a new matrix with a R component of size 128 x 128. Then, using the magic key generation method, create a 16X16-bit key. Following the generation of the 16 x 16-bit matrix and the transposition of the 16 x 16-bit key, a 64 x 64-bit key was created for use in the encryption and decryption processes. Then, this 64 X 64 bit key was XORed with four blocks of the R colour component to create a new matrix with a different value, The one dimensional chaotic sequence from the logistic map generates the 128 x 128 matrix values and the XOR logical operation has been performed with these.

The one dimensional logistic chaotic equation is given by,

$$x_{n+1} = x_n * r * \left(1 - x_n\right)$$

Where r is the parameter value.

Here the initial value x_n and r has been taken as 0.5 and 3.90 respectively.

Where x_n represents the chaotic sequence whiclies between zero and one as shown in the Figure 1. The initial condition of the map is $x_0 = x_{n=0} \in [0,1]$. The parameter r is a positive number in the range 0 to 4. Depending on the value of r the above equation has different properties. The chaotic regime of r is in between 3 to 3.99.

Figure 1. Variation of x_n with iteration numbers of logistic map in chaotic region

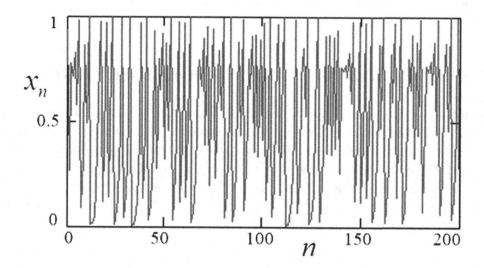

Bifurcation: The logistic map shows different type of behavior as well as transitions between regular to chaotic behaviors as the parameter value *r* is charged as shown in Figure 2. These qualitative transition from regular to chaotic behavior in dynamical system is known as Bifurcation. In cryptographic applications the choice of control parameter value determines the unpredictability of the system. If the parameter is used as the key, then the whole space of possible keys must generate the chaotic behavior of the system.

Figure 2. Bifurcation diagram of the logistic map

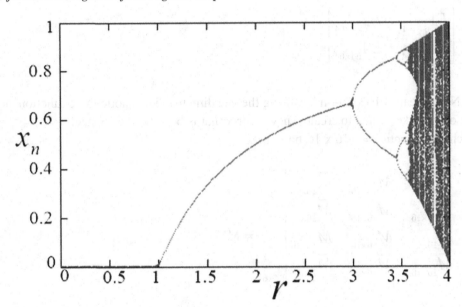

In the similar pattern the G and B colour components will be included in this process as well. The three-color R, G, and B components were then merged with the new value to create an image. This will produce an encrypting image that acts as a masking image and makes it impossible to tell what the original image is (Chaofeng Zhao et.al., 2023) The encrypted image will be decrypted and the original image will be returned via the reverse process. In order to protect the image from malicious hacker intentions, it can transfer encrypted images over the internet. Since attackers concentrate on the key to obtain the original image, our main goal will be to make it stronger. As a result, this process comprises two steps. The first stage involves encryption, and the second stage involves decryption. The image is sent via the encryption process first, and then the ciphered image is sent to the recipient for decryption. MATLAB Software carried out the entire process. The method can be used to regular images.

A. Algorithm (Encryption)

Step 1. Start

Step 2. Data from a 128x128 colour image was collected, and an image graphics object was created by placing each component in a matrix.

Step 3. Assign the components red, green, and blue the letters "r," "g," and "b," accordingly.

Step 4. The r-channel should be divided into four 64 x 64-bit matrices called A, B, C, and D.

$$\text{R matrix} = \begin{bmatrix} A_{64\times64} & B_{64\times64} \\ C_{\ldots} & D_{\ldots} \end{bmatrix}$$

Step 5. To create new blocks of R, combine the blocks of A, B, C, and D using the XOR function. as E1=A $\oplus$ B, E2=A $\oplus$ C, E3=A $\oplus$ D and E4=C $\oplus$ D.

$$\text{R matrix} = \begin{bmatrix} E1_{64\times64} & E2_{64\times64} \\ E3_{64\times64} & E4_{64\times64} \end{bmatrix}_{128\times128}$$

Step 6. Next, create a 16 x 16-bit key using the one dimensional chaotic logic function, and then bit-shuffle the original key value to create a new matrix that is 64 × 64 bits in size.

Key = chaotic function =>16 x 16-bit matrix

$$\begin{bmatrix} M_{16\times16} & \bar{M}_{16\times16} & M_{16\times16} & \bar{M}_{16\times16} \\ M_{16\times16} & \bar{M}_{16\times16} & M_{16\times16} & \bar{M}_{16\times16} \\ M_{16\times16} & \bar{M}_{16\times16} & M_{16\times16} & \bar{M}_{16\times16} \\ M_{16\times16} & \bar{M}_{16\times16} & M_{16\times16} & \bar{M}_{16\times16} \end{bmatrix}_{64\times64} = \text{MM}$$

Step 7: Do the XOR operation with each block of R at this point and MM i.e., E11= E1 $\oplus$ MM, E12= E2 $\oplus$ MM, E13= E3 $\oplus$ MM and E14= E4 $\oplus$ MM

Step 8: The new red component termed E-R, also known as encrypted R, was obtained by combining the four blocks E11, E12, E13, and E14 and the logical XOR operation with chaotic sequence.

$$\text{E-R} = \begin{bmatrix} E11_{64\times64} & E12_{64\times64} \\ E13_{64\times64} & E14_{64\times64} \end{bmatrix}_{128\times128} \quad \text{XOR Chaotic Sequence.}$$

Step 9: To obtain new components for E-G and E-B as encrypted G and encrypted B, respectively, repeat Steps 5, 6, 7, 8, and 9 for G and B components.

Step 10: combined "E-R," "E-G," and "E-B" to create a new encrypted image.

B. Algorithm (Decryption)

Step 1: Start

Step 2: Create data from an encrypted image, then create a graphical object for the image by charting each component of a matrix.

Step 3: Excerpt the components of red, green, and blue as "r," "g," and "b," respectively.

Step 4: Four 64 X 64 blocks should be created from the r component matrix: r1, r2, r3, and r4.

Step 5: We do an XOR operation on each block of r using a key of 64 x 64 bits to produce new blocks labelled r11, r21, r31, and r41.

Step 6: In order to obtain the R colour component of the original image, perform the XOR operation as follows: a= r11 $\oplus$ r21, b= r11 $\oplus$ r31, c= r11 $\oplus$ r41, and d= r31 $\oplus$ r41.

Step 7: For the 'g' matrix to obtain the G colour components and the 'b' matrix to obtain the B colour components of the original image, repeat Steps 4, 5, and 6.

Step 8: To obtain the decrypted or original image, combine "R" "G" and "B" and turn the resulting matrix into an image.

The detail flow diagram of the encryption and decryption are given below:

Figure 3. Flow chart

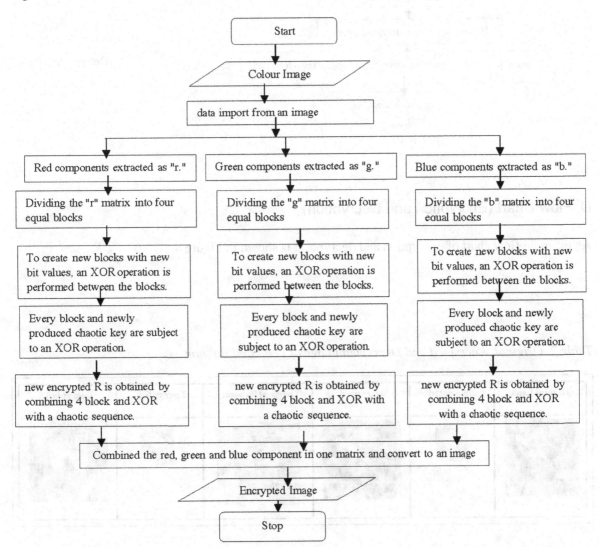

C. Flow Chart (Encryption)

An example encryption flow chart is shown in Figure 3.

Figure 4. Flow chart

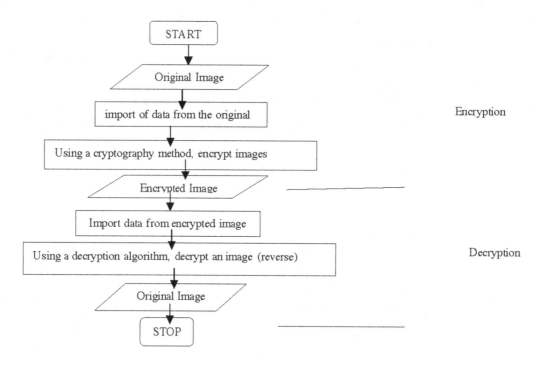

D. Flow Chart (Encryption and Decryption)

An example flow chart of encryption and decryption is shown in Figure 4.

Table 2. Original, Encrypted and Decrypted image of Lena and Baboon

Original Lena	Encrypted	Decrypted	Original Baboon	Encrypted	Decrypted

RESULT AND DISCUSSION

As a result of providing secure encryption and decryption of the image, the outcome we obtained using this approach is adequately acceptable. The image can't be seen or altered by a hacker or attacker, so it gets to its destination more securely. This section presents the findings of the experiment we conducted using the suggested algorithm. We also offer the experiment's performance analysis for the suggested method. We capture various test photos with colour values of 128 X 128 bits. We conduct several experiments and analyses the findings in order to demonstrate the performance of the current image encryption architecture. The encrypted version of the original Lena image is displayed in the table below, where it is clear that the original image cannot be distinguished. We also demonstrate how, with minimal data loss, the original image may be restored once the decryption technique has been applied to the encrypted image.

A. Histogram Analysis

A histogram is a visual representation of how the pixels in an image are distributed. Histogram study supports the correctness of the suggested method for any picture encryption and decryption operation. For a decent encryption and decryption process, the histogram of the encrypted image and the original image must be completely different and uniform. In order to strengthen the security of our technique, we give the histogram analysis here. For an image with 128 X 128-bit colour values, the histogram's formula is:

Figure 5. Histogram analysis of Lena: 1ˢᵗ row and 2ⁿᵈ row shows the R, G and B components of plain and encrypted images

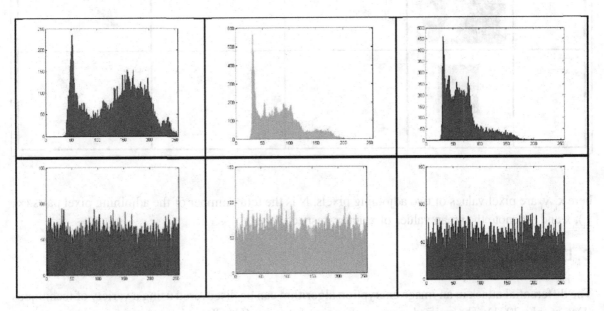

$$x^2 = \sum\nolimits_{i=0}^{127} \frac{(N_i - \overline{N})}{\overline{N}} \qquad (1)$$

where Ni is the frequency of gray level i, N = (W × H)/128.Assuming the significant level of 0.05, the corresponding χ2(0.05,127) is 293.25.

B. Correlation Analysis

A strong and efficient technique is needed to remove the elevated correlation that exists between nearby pixels in a typical image. The correlations between two adjacent pixels in the horizontal, vertical, and diagonal directions are compared in both the unencrypted and encrypted images. The correlations between the plain and encrypted versions of Lena's image are displayed in the table below using 1000 pairs of neighboring pixels in three directions. Utilizing a formula, the correlation coefficients are quantified.

$$r_{xy} = \sum_{i=1}^{N} \frac{\left(x_i - \bar{x}\right)\left(y_i - \bar{y}\right)}{\sqrt{\sum_{i=1}^{N}\left(x_i - \bar{x}\right)} * \sqrt{\sum_{i=1}^{N}\left(y_i - \bar{y}\right)}} \tag{2}$$

Table 3. Correlation graphs of blue component of plain and cipher colour LENA image

Image Name	Image	Correlations		
		R-Horizontal	G-Vertical	B-Diagonal
Lena original				
Lena encrypted				

here x_i, y_i are pixel values of two adjoining pixels, N is the total number of the adjoining pixel pairs (x_i, y_i), x and y denote the mean values of x and y, respectively.

C. Differential Attack

The differential attack in an image encryption algorithm can be discovered using a variety of techniques (Das et. al., 2021). The unified average changing intensity (UACI) and number of pixel change rate (NPCR) methodologies that we describe in our methodology have theoretical values of 99.6094% and 33.4635%, respectively. NPCR and UACI are often computed by below equations:

Table 4. Correlation Coefficient Values for RGB Images

Images	R-Channel	G-Channel	B-Channel
Horizontal direction			
Original Lena	0.9448	0.9322	0.9063
Encrypted Lena	-0.2977	-0.4167	-0.0779
Original Baboon	0.8959	0.8056	0.8784
Encrypted Baboon	-0.0577	0.0065	-0.0869
Vertical direction			
Original Lena	0.9705	0.9623	0.9431
Encrypted Lena	-0.0375	0.2209	0.0678
Original Baboon	0.8769	0.8316	0.8936
Encrypted Baboon	0.09350	-0.0035	0.1052
Diagonal direction			
Original Lena	0.9139	0.8952	0.8510
Encrypted Lena	0.0529	-0.1235	0.0019
Original Baboon	0.8635	0.7352	0.8427
Encrypted Baboon	-0.0879	0.0462	-0.0349

$$\mathrm{NPCR} = \frac{1}{HXW} \sum_{i=0}^{H-1} \sum_{j=0}^{W-1} D(i,j) \times 100\% \tag{3}$$

$$UACI = \frac{1}{HXW} \sum_{i=0}^{H-1} \sum_{j=0}^{W-1} \frac{|c_1(i,j) - c_2(i,j)|}{256} \times 100\% \tag{4}$$

where C_1 and C_2 are two images with the identical size $W \times H$, D (i, j) = 0 if (i, j) = (i, j). otherwise,

Table 5. NPCR and UACI Values for RGB Images

Image	NPCR			UACI		
	R	G	B	R	G	B
Lena	99.612	99.663	99.572	31.714	32.548	32.359
Baboon	99.582	99.636	99.621	29.691	29.153	31.576

D (i, j) = 1, The quality NPCR for 2 random photos is around 0.9961, whereas the quality UACI is approximately 0.3346. The NPCR and UACI of both the encrypted images are now calculated, and this procedure is repeated 1000 times for each sample image. The outcomes of these two values are displayed in the table below. We can then conclude that by implementing our suggested approach, we can success-fully defend against the differential assault.

D. Information Entropy Analysis

The property of an encryption method that displays the randomness of the image and measures the de-gree of image confusion is known as information entropy (Das et. al., 2019). The information entropy is calculated using the formula:

$$H(m) = \sum_{i=o}^{N} p(m_i) \log_2 \frac{1}{p(m_i)} \tag{5}$$

where N is the total number of symbols, m, mi, and p(mi) are symbols' probabilities, and s is the total number of symbols. For each random image with 128 X 128 colour levels, the optimal entropy should be H(m) = 8. If an algorithm generates an encrypted image with an entropy value that is close to 8, we

Table 6. The information entropy of the variant images

Images	Plain image			Encrypted image		
	R	G	B	R	G	B
Lena	7.5282	6.9849	6.6737	7.9812	7.9769	7.9785
Baboon	7.6563	7.3604	7.6692	7.9811	7.9753	7.9779

Table 7. Comparison table of correlation coefficient, NPCR and UACI of encrypted Lena image

Encryption algorithm	Correlation coefficient			measures	
	Horizontal	Vertical	Diagonal	NPCR (average)	UACI (average)
Proposed algorithm	-0.2977	-0.0375	0.0529	99.612	32.548
A.K.Das et.al. 2021	-0.0510	-0.0408	-0.0369	99.633	33.288
G.Ye et.al.2016	0.0088	-0.0087	-0.0060	99.61	33.48

may say that it is a good algorithm. Lena and Baboon's original and encrypted images both have an entropy value that is close to 8, proving that the source of the cypher image cannot be determined. The information entropy analysis of our encryption algorithm so indicates that it is successful.

The comparison of correlation coefficient, NPCR and UACI values with the present research has been shown in table VI. It has been seen that the proposed method is appreciable than another methods.

Strength of Proposed Scheme

The proposed bit shuffling and chaotic encryption scheme has been passed different cryptanalysis test like NPCR, UACI, histogram analysis, information entropy analysis, correlation coefficient etc. and the validity result shows the strength of the algorithm.

Pros and Cons

The secure encryption is the most powerful tool to communicate any message or text or signal in this digital era. So in this digital era it has been essential to cryptographic approach for secure the communicating data. The more complex algorithm like chaotic algorithm are suitable for these purpose. It has been noted that if algorithm is no such powerful, hackers may hack the data.

CONCLUSION

In this study the overall cryptography concept is discussed elaborately. The idea of cryptography is very old still it has significant impact in modern day technology. In various fields the cryptographic phenomena is used extensively. Some of the different algorithms used by scientist are discussed here with suitable example. The main focus of this chapter remains on the chaotic techniques using in encryption and decryption process. In a single sentence the definition of chaos is very hard but the explanation of it with natural example is very easy to understand. In the different field of real life chaos is used like mathematics, engineering, meteorology, economics, stock market, human body, social science and so on - the application is limitless. Although there are limitations in using chaos theory. The two major issues are relativity and uncertainty. Chaos can be bridge between many fields. We can proceed using observational data which are ignored because we think they are too erroneous in chaos. In our study the chaos is used to generate a random key which is used to do the encryption of an image i.e. to hide the original meaning of the image with a image with unrelated black and white pixel combination. The decryption of the encrypted image also done by the same key which is generated by chaotic algorithm.

This study uses MATLAB software to encrypt colour images using bit shuffle and magic key interaction. Here, two colour images of 128×128 pixels have been captured for the encryption and decryption processes. The suggested algorithm's validity and acceptability have been evaluated using a variety of security analyses, including NPCR, UACI, entropy analysis, correlation analysis, and histogram analysis, on the complete cryptographic process. Real-time cryptosystems can use the proposed encryption and decryption method.

FUTURE SCOPE

This method can be more secure for hyperchaotic and key generation with complex algorithm and encrypted the image or signal. It also implemented in prototype chip for real time communication.

REFERENCES

Akhshani, A., Akhavan, A., Mobaraki, A., Lim, S. C., & Hassan, Z. (2014). Pseudorandom random number generator based on quantum chaotic 242 map. *Communications in Nonlinear Science and Numerical Simulation, 19*, 101–111.

Alghamdi, Y., Munir, A., & Ahmad, J. (2022). A Lightweight Image Encryption Algorithm Based on Chaotic Map and Random Substitution. *Entropy, 24*, 1344.

Alvarez, G., & Li, S. (2006). Some basic cryptographic requirements for chaos-based cryptosystem. *International Journal of Bifurcation and Chaos in Applied Sciences and Engineering, 16*(8), 2129–2151. doi:10.1142/S0218127406015970

Alvarez, G., & Li, S. J. (2006). Some basic cryptographic requirements for chaos based cryptosystems. *International Journal of Bifurcation and Chaos in Applied Sciences and Engineering, 16*(08), 2129–2151. doi:10.1142/S0218127406015970

Amin, M., Faragallah, O. S., & Latif, A. A. (2009). Chaos-based hash function(CBHF) for cryptographic application. *Chaos, Solitons, and Fractals, 42*, 767.

Ariffin, M. R. K., & Abu, N. A. (2009). AA_-cryptosystem: A chaos based public key cryptosystem. *International Journal of Cryptology Research, 1*(2), 149–163.

Bai, E-W., Lonngren, K.E., & Uçar, A. (2005). Secure communication via multiple parameter modulation in a delayed chaotic system. *Chaos, Solitons & Fractals, February, 23*(3), 1071–1076.

Banerjee, S., & Ariffin, M. R. K. (2012, January). Chaos synchronization based data transmission with asymmetric encryption. *International Journal of Computers and Applications, 37*(12), 6–9.

Barakat, M. L., Mansingka, A. S., Radwan, A. G., & Salama, K. N. (2014, January). Hardware stream cipher with controllable chaos generator for colour image encryption. *IET Image Processing, 8*(1).

Behnia, S., Akhshania, A., Akhavanb, A., & Mahmodi, H. (2008). Chaotic cryptographic scheme based on composition maps. *International Journal of Bifurcation and Chaos in Applied Sciences and Engineering, 18*(1), 251–261. doi:10.1142/S0218127408020288

Benkouider, K. (2022). A New 5-D Multistable Hyperchaotic System With Three Positive Lyapunov Exponents: Bifurcation Analysis, Circuit Design, FPGA Realization and Image Encryption. *IEEE Access: Practical Innovations, Open Solutions, 10*, 90111–90132.

Benrhouma, O., Houcemeddine, H., & Safya, B. (2013). Security analysis and improvement of a partial encryption scheme. *Multimedia Tools and Applications, 74*(11), 3617–3634. doi:10.100711042-013-1790-4

Bergamo, P., D'Arco, P., De Santis, A., & Kocarev, L. (2005). Security of public-key cryptosystems based on chebyshev polynomials. *IEEE Transactions on Circuits and Systems I: Regular Papers, 52*(7), 1382–1393.

Bose, R. (2005, August). Novel public key encryption technique based on multiple chaotic systems. *Physical Review Letters, 95*, 098702.

Bose, R., & Pathak, S. (2006). A novel compression and encryption scheme using variable model arithmetic coding and coupled chaotic system. *IEEE Transactions on Circuits and Systems. I, Fundamental Theory and Applications*, *53*(4), 848–857. doi:10.1109/TCSI.2005.859617

Chong, K. Y., & Koshiba, T. (2007, September). More on Security of Public-Key Cryptosystems Based on Chebyshev Polynomials. *IEEE Transactions on Circuits and Wystems. II, Express Briefs*, *54*(9), 795–7747. doi:10.1109/TCSII.2007.900875

Das, A. K., Hazra, S., & Mandal, M. K. (2021). RGB image encryption using microcontroller ATMEGA 32. *Microsystem Technologies*, *21*, 409–417.

Das, A. K., & Mandal, M. K. (2019). *FPGA Based Chaotic Cryptosystem. In ICACCP-2019*. IEEE.

Diffie, W. F., & Hellman, M. E. (1976). New directions in cryptography. *IEEE Transactions on Information Theory*, *22*(10), 644–655.

Fengi, H. (1993). *The interpolating random spline cryptosystem and the chaotic-map public-key cryptosystem* [PhD thesis]. UMI Order No. GAX93-26596.

Fouda, J. S., Effa, J. V., Sabat, S. L., & Ali, M. (2014). A fast chaotic block cipher for image encryption. *Communications in Nonlinear Science and Numerical Simulation*, *19*, 578–588.

Fu, C., Meng, W., Zhan, Y., Zhu, Z., Lau, F. C. M., Tse, C. K., & Mae, H. (2013). An efficient and secure medical image protection scheme based on chaotic maps. *Computers in Biology and Medicine*, *43*(8), 1000–1010. doi:10.1016/j.compbiomed.2013.05.005 PMID:23816172

Gonzalez, J. A., & Pino, R. (1999). Random number generator based on unpredictable chaotic functions. *Computer Physics Communications*, *120*, 109–114.

Guan, P. (1987). Cellular automaton public key cryptosystem. *Complex Systems*, *1*, 51–57.

Guan, Z., Huang, F., & Guan, W. (2005). Chaos-based image encryption algorithm. *Physics Letters. [Part A]*, *346*(1–3), 153–157. doi:10.1016/j.physleta.2005.08.006

Habutu, T., Nishio, Y., Sasase, I., & Moris, S. (1990). A secret key cryptosystem using a chaotic map. *IEICE Trans.*, *73*(7), 1041–1044.

Hamdi & Boudriga. (2008). Four dimensional chaotic ciphers for secure image transmission. *IEEE Int. Conf. Multimedia and Expo.*, 437–440. doi:10.1109/ICME.2008.4607465

Houcemeddine, H., Rhouma, R., & Safya, B. (2013). Improvement of an image encryption algorithm based on hyper-chaos. *Telecommunication Systems*, *52*(2), 539–549.

Hu, H. P., Liu, L. F., & Ding, N. D. (2013). Pseudorandom sequence generator based on Chen chaotic system. *Computer Physics Communications*, *184*, 765–768.

Huang, Z. Q. (2011). A more secure parallel keyed hash function based on chaotic neural network. *Communications in Nonlinear Science and Numerical Simulation*, *16*, 3245–3256.

Huaping, L., Wang, S., & Gang, H. (2004). Pseudo-random number generator based on coupled map lattices. *International Journal of Modern Physics B*, *18*, 2409–2414.

Jiteurtragool, Ketthong, Wannaboon, & San-Um. (2013). A topologically simple keyed hash function based on circular chaotic sinusoidal map network. *2013 International Conference on Advanced Communication Technology*, 1089-1094.

Kanso, A. (2011, February). Self-shrinking chaotic stream ciphers. *Communications in Nonlinear Science and Numerical Simulation, 16*(2), 822–836.

Kanso, A., & Ghebleh, M. (2013). A fast and efficient chaos-based keyed hash function. *Communications in Nonlinear Science and Numerical Simulation, 18*, 109–123.

Kelber, K., & Schwarz, W. (2005). General design rules for chaos-based encryption systems. In *International symposium on nonlinear theory and its applications (NOLTA2005)*, Bruges, Belgium.

Kocarev, L., Halle, K. S., Eckert, K., Chua, L. O., & Parlitz, U. (1992). Experimental demonstration of secure communications via chaotic synchronization. *International Journal of Bifurcation and Chaos in Applied Sciences and Engineering, 2*(3), 709–713. doi:10.1142/S0218127492000823

Kocarev, L., & Lian, S. (2011). Chaos-Based Cryptography. Theory, Algorithms and Applications, Studies in Computational Intelligence, 354. doi:10.1007/978-3-642-20542-2

Kocarev, L., Makraduli, J., & Amato, P. (2005). Public-Key Encryption Based on Chebyshev Polynomials. *Circuits, Systems, and Signal Processing, 24*(5), 497–517.

Kocarev, L., & Tasev, Z. (2003). Public-key encryption based on chebyshev maps. *Circuits and Systems, 2003. ISCAS '03. Proceedings of the 2003 International Symposium on.*

Lai, Yang, & Liu. (2022). Design and realization of discrete memristive hyperchaotic map with application in image encryption. In *Chaos, Solitons and Fractals*. Elsevier.

Lawnik, M., Moysis, L., & Volos, C. (2022). Chaos-Based Cryptography: Text Encryption Using Image Algorithms. *Electronics, 11*, 3156.

Li, C., Arroyo, D., & Lo, K-T. (2010). Breaking a chaotic cryptographic scheme based on composition maps. *International Journal of Bifurcation and Chaos, 20*(8), 2561–2568.

Li, H. J., & Zhang, J. S. (2010). A novel chaotic stream cipher and its application to palmprint template protection. *Chinese Physics B, 19*(4), 040505.

Li, Y., Li, C., & Zhao, Y. (2022). Memristor-type chaotic mapping. *Chaos, 32*, 021104–021107.

Li, Y., Xiao, D., Deng, S., Han, Q., & Zhou, G. (2011). Parallel hash function construction based on chaotic maps with changeable parameters. *Neural Comput. Applic., 20*, 1305–1312.

Lima, J. B., Campello, R. M., & Panario, D. (2008). Security of public key cryptosystems based on Chebyshev polynomials over prime finite fields. *Proceedings of the IEEE International Symposium on Information Theory (ISIT'08)*, 1843-1847.

Liu, N. (2011). Pseudo-randomness and complexity of binary sequences generated by the chaotic system. *Communications in Nonlinear Science and Numerical Simulation, 16*, 761–768.

Long, M., & Wang, H. (2013, April-June). Collision analysis and improvement of a parallel hash function based on chaotic maps with changeable parameters. *International Journal of Digital Crime and Forensics, 5*(2), 23–34.

Maniccam, S. S., & Bourbakis, N. G. (2001). Lossless image compression and encryption using SCAN. *Pattern Recognition, 34*(6), 1229–1245. doi:10.1016/S0031-3203(00)00062-5

Masuda, N., Jakimoski, G., Aihara, K., & Kocarev, L. (2006, June). Chaotic Block Ciphers: From Theory to Practical Algorithms. *IEEE Trans. Circuits Syst. I. Fundam. Theory Appl., 53*(6), 1341–1352.

Mattews, R. (n.d.). On the derivation of a chaotic encryption algorithm. *Cryptologia, 13*(1), 29–42. doi:10.1080/0161118991863745

Norouzi, B., Mirzakuchaki, S., Seyedzadeh, S. M., & Mosavi, M. R. (2012). A simple, sensitive and secure image encryption algorithm based on hyper-chaotic system with only one round diffusion. *Multimedia Tools and Applications, 71*(3), 1469–1497. doi:10.100711042-012-1292-9

Oishi, S., & Inoue, H. (1982). Pscudo-Random Number Generators and Chaos. *Transactions of the Institute of Electronics and Communication Engineers of Japan, E65*(9), 534–554.

Pecora & Carroll. (1990). Synchronization in chaotic systems. *Physical Review Letters, 64*(8), 821-825.

Pisarchik, A. N., & Zanin, M. (2010). Chaotic map cryptography and security. Encryption: Methods, Software and Security, 1-28.

Ren, H., Wang, Y., Xie, Q., & Yang, H. (2009). A novel method for one-way hash function construction based on spatiotemporal chaos. *Chaos, Solitons, and Fractals, 42*, 2014–2022.

Shujun, L., Xuanqin, M., & Yuanlong, C. (2001). *Pseudo-random bit generator based on couple chaotic systems and its applications in stream-cipher cryptography.* Progress in Cryptology INDOCRYPT.

Stinson, D. R. (2009). *Cryptography: Theory and Practice.* CRC Press.

Stojanovski, T., & Kocarev, L. (2001). Chaos-based random number generators–Part I: Analysis. *IEEE Transactions on Circuits and Systems. I, Fundamental Theory and Applications, 48*, 281–288.

Stojanovski, T., Pihl, J., & Kocarev, L. (2001). Chaos-based random number generators–Part II: Practical realization. *IEEE Transactions on Circuits and Systems. I, Fundamental Theory and Applications, 48*, 382–385.

Tang, G., Wang, S., Lu, H., & Hu, G. (2003). Chaos-based cryptography incorporated with S-box algebraic operation. *Physics Letters [Part A], 318*(4–5), 388–398. doi:10.1016/j.physleta.2003.09.042

Tenny, R., & Tsimring, L. S. (2005). Additive mixing modulation for public key encryption based on distributed dynamics. *IEEE Transactions on Circuits and Systems I: Regular Papers, 52*(3), 672 – 679.

Tenny, R., Tsimring, L. S., Larson, L., & Abarbanel, H. D. (2003). Using distributed nonlinear dynamics for public key encryption. *Physical Review Letters, 90*(4), 047903.

Wang, Gong, Zhan, & Lai. (2005). Public-key encryption based on generalized synchronization of coupled map lattices. *Chaos, 15*(2), 1–8.

Wang, L., & Chen, Z. (2022). Hyperchaotic Image Encryption Algorithm Based on BD-Zigzag Transformation and DNA Coding. *LNEE, 961*, 667–677.

Wang, X. Y., & Qing, Y. (2009). A block encryption algorithm based on dynamic sequences of multiple chaotic systems. *Communications in Nonlinear Science and Numerical Simulation, 14*, 574–581.

Wei, Y., & Wei, P. (n.d.). Construct and analyzed K-hash function based on chaotic dynamica S-Boxes. *Applied Mechanics and Materials, 519-520*, 889–896.

Wong, K. (2003). A combined chaotic cryptographic and hashing scheme. *Physics Letters. [Part A], 307*, 292–298.

Xiao, D., Liao, X. F., & Wang, Y. (2009). Parallel keyed hash function based on chaotic neural network. *Neurocomputing, 72*, 2288–2296.

Xiao, D., Peng, W., Liao, X. F., & Xiang, T. (2010). Collision analysis of one kind of chaos-based hash function. *Physics Letters. [Part A], 374*, 1228–1231.

Xiao, D., Shih, F. Y., & Liao, X. F. (2010). A chaos-based hash function with both modification detection and localization capabilities. Communications in Nonlinear Science and Number Simulation, 15, 2254-2261.

Ye, G., & Huang, X. (2016). A feedback chaotic image encryption scheme based on both bit-level and pixel level. *Journal of Vibration and Control, 22*, 1171–1180.

Zhang, Guo, Xu, Zhu, & Yang. (2022). Hyperchaotic circuit design based on memristor and its application in image encryption. In *Microelectronic Engineering*. Elsevier.

Zhang, C., Chen, J., & Chen, D. (2022). Cryptanalysis of an Image Encryption Algorithm Based on a 2D Hyperchaotic Map. *Entropy, 24*, 1551.

Zhang, Y., Lin, X., & Wang, Q. (2011). Asymmetric cryptography algorithm with chinese remainder theorem. *Communication Software and Networks (ICCSN), 2011 IEEE 3rd International Conference on Communication and Software Networks*, 450–454.

Zhao, C., Wang, T., Wang, H., Du, Q., & Yin, C. (2023). A Novel Image Encryption Algorithm by Delay Induced Hyper-chaotic Chen System. *The Journal of Imaging Science and Technology*.

Chapter 12
An Image Steganography Approach Using Arnold Transformation

Solanki Pattanayak

Haldia Institute of Management, India

Sabyasachi Samanta

Haldia Institute of Technology, India

Dipankar Dey

https://orcid.org/0000-0003-4872-9901

Global Institute of Science and Technology, India

Abhijit Sarkar

Haldia Institute of Technology, India

Souvik Bhattacharyya

University Institute of Technology, Burdwan, India

ABSTRACT

Sleuthing images that conceal information has continuously been a stimulating and difficult problem in cyber security. Finding hidden data in nursing image is called steganalysis. In this chapter, the authors explore the method employed in the study. The investigational results are have included followed by a discussion with prospect analysis. Several 2×2 blocks are recycled to implant the data bits within the stego-image, and using the Arnold Map, four quadrants of the pixels of each block is selected to embed the data in nonlinear bit position. Different measures with the change of BPP (bits per pixel) are also worked out.

DOI: 10.4018/978-1-6684-7524-9.ch012

1. INTRODUCTION

With the progress of computer machinery in current years, information security is considered as one of the significant features in imminent information and communication technology. Cyber security has also become a trending security aspect in current days. Therefore, it's essential to take crucial measures to protect the confidential information. As a whole, confidential information can be secure by prevalent of two ways: by encryption or steganography. Cryptography encrypts stealthy messages to make them incomprehensible i.e. the encrypted message is visible to us but it's unexplainable to us. While steganography secrets the existence of the message through the carrier i.e. it covers the existence of secret messages (Setiadi, 2022).

Presently several methodologies that exist for finding of such concealed data bits within the form of information or images that largely need corporal inspection. During this model, some sensitive data has been embedded within Associate in nursing image, referred to as the stego-image and with none loss, extract constant data from that image, called the cover image(Rabie, 2021).

Steganography stands for the cleverness of concealing evidence in such a way that it prevent the uncovering of stealthy communications. It's originate from the Greek term for *"covered writing"*. It comprises a variety of dissimilar secret communication methodologies that conceal the existence of unrevealed messages. Steganography are classified into different types like, Text Steganography, Image Steganography, Audio Steganography, Video Steganography and Protocol Steganography. The image encryption method is utmost of the active ways to protect our privacy. The process of hiding a secret message inside the image has become widely used, due to weaknesses in the Human Visual System (HVS), as well as due to the reduced cost of storing and communicating the image (Subramanian et al., 2021; Wang, 2022).

Imaging steganography techniques can be divided into two cluster: Transform Domain and Spatial Domain Technique. The Transform domain technique embeds information into the frequency domain of the previously transformed image, while the spatial domain technique embeds the information directly into the pixel intensity (Ali et al., 2021). The spatial domain embedding technique is very common and informal to us in the field of steganography.

In terms of image hiding, we have noted that the original image without the secret message embedded is called the cover image or the carrier image, while the image resulting from the embedding of the secret message. The secret is called the hidden image. The secret message can be in the form of text, images, audio or video. After applying the steganography method, the output stego-image generated will look like the cover image.

There are reciprocal relationships between the requirements of cryptographic printing: capacity, robustness, and insensitivity (as in Fig. 1). Robustness refers to how much stego-image spoofing can withstand that an attacker cannot detect hidden data bits. Capacity indicates the volume of data bits that can be embedded in the cover medium lacking of damaging the integrity of the shield image. The most important requirement of a cryptographic recording system is insensitivity, since the strength of a cryptographic copy system dishonesties in its ability to remain ignored by human senses (like visual or audible). How to poise this three necessities in the fields of information hiding is an interesting question in current years (Sharmin et al., 2019; Kadhim, 2019).

The safekeeping of any steganography system be influenced by on the choice of pixels of embedding cover of the carrier. Pixels in the areas of texture and noise are a better choice for integration as they are challenging to any of the steganography model. Pixels in the edge area may be considered blaring

Figure 1. Triangle model of steganography

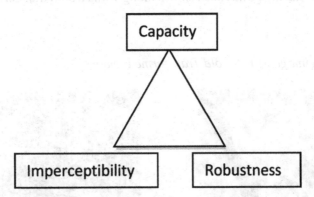

pixels, because their intensity is lower or higher than that of neighbouring or surrounding pixels, because of abrupt changes in the coefficient ascent. Because of these abrupt variations in statistical and image possessions, edges are very difficult to model compared to greater area pixels (Dadgostar et al., 2016).

Arnold transform is extensively used in information hiding like image stenography, authentication, and tamper detection, self-recovery and image cryptography algorithms. It's used as a scrambling step such that the number of repetitions is used as a strategy or key. But the limitation of the Arnold transformation is that it's only applicable to the square area or the block wise for the cover image.

Figure 2. Arnold transformation

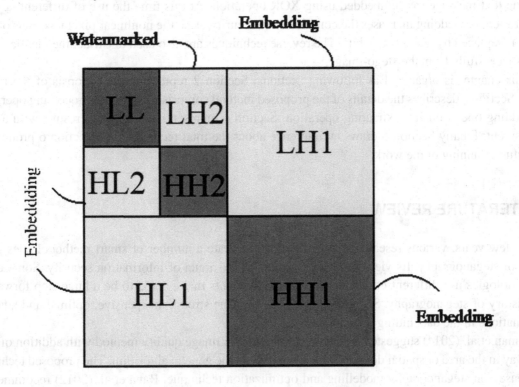

In Figure 3, original Lena image has been shown along with Arnold transformed image of Lena with $\omega \, {}^1\!/_4 \, 1$.

Figure 3. Original Lena image with Arnold Transformed image

Original Image   Transformed Image

Here, in our proposed scheme with a several number of 2×2 blocks are used to embed the data within the stego-image. Using the Arnold Map, we have select four quadrants of the pixels of each blocks throughout the image. Then using Chaotic Map, we have designed random secret key technique, after that the text messages are embedded using XOR operation. At this time the use of different key size for different embedding increases the complexity of security. Also the nonlinear pixel positions of each block is replaced by the message bits. The reverse techniques are also used to extract the identical message successfully from the stego-image.

This chapter is organized as following sections. Section 2 represents the synopsis of the related work. Section 3 describes the details of the proposed method comprising with pre-processing operation, embedding operation and extracting operation. Section 4 represents the tentative results with a petty assessment. Finally Section 5 draws an inference about the total technique and Section 6 pronounces the future planning of the work.

2. LITERATURE REVIEW

In last few years, various researchers have tried to integrate a number of smart methodologies in the arena of steganography. Its yield better attainments in the arena of information security. Some of the methodologies use different computer software implements that evicted to be a huge step forward in the history of steganography. Such algorithms can lead the strong, inexpensive, optimal and adaptive explanations in the data hiding difficulties.

Kanan et al. (2014) suggested a tuneable photographic image quality method with addition of lossless way in the area of spatial domain, which is based on the genetic algorithm. The proposed technique was based on steganography modelling and optimization technique. Rana et al. (2012) recommended an image encryption method, based on Kohonen neural network. El-Emam et al. (2015) proposed an intelligent three-phase steganography method, to hide data in colour images with indifferent properties. The projected algorithm efficiently embedded a large amount of data bits as of 12 BPP with an improved image superiority.

Nameer et al. (2013) proposed a covering method using an adaptive image filtering and segmentation method with the bit substitution on appropriate pixel positions. The key goal is to cover a huge volume of information through .bitmap type of images using the ultimate number of bits at each of the pixel positions. Later on, they proposed another smart method by using hybrid adaptive neural networks and with the modified adaptive genetic algorithm. Wu et al. (2005) also projected an image steganography based method on LSB substitution with Pixel Value Discrimination (PVD) method. In Fard et al. (2006), a scalable procedure was proposed to generate secure cryptographic encryption on JPEG images.

Chang et al. (2007) also presented a reversible cryptographic method that can competently rebuild the original image after extracting the embedded message with in it. This method can attain greater inerrability and reversibility in the field of image steganography. Furthermore in El-Emam et al. (2008), the authors presented a highly secure neural algorithm with a supplementary layer of safety. They introduced a neural network based learning system that augments the security against statistical and imaging attacks. Wang et al. (2010) demonstrated a hidden algorithm. Hare after embedding the secret data bits into the LSB positions of the carrier image, the cipher pixel values was modified by the genetic algorithm. That keeps the initials with their own indicators. The result also shows the effectiveness of the proposed algorithm against hidden analysis with better image quality.

Kunal Ashok Shinde et al. (2016) proposed a pixel intensity difference and LSB position based image steganography methodology. Depending on the flatter region and edges of the cover image, the sharper edge regions are used to hide the secret data into the cover images.

Aruna Malik et al. (2018) proposed the pixel intensity and secret message similarity based image steganography technique. They embedded the data bits into the LSB positions of the cover image depending on the intensity values of the pixels.

Shaowei Weng et al. (2019) proposed an improved pixel value assembling for adjustable data hiding through image. Dynamic IPVO RDH method, which compliantly modify the number of pixels in a block by classifying the local complexity into various levels. For highly correlated and smooth block progation nearly all of the pixels, except for one or two in the intermediate positions are convoluted in this embedding method.

Sadik Ali Al-Taweel et al. (2016) image within the image steganography technique using Arnold transform and LSB technique. The Arnold image transformation was demarcated by the coordinate point (w,h) to the unit square transform to other point. Minati Mishra et al. (2012) proposed an image steganography method with an improved Arnold's Cat Map practice. They uses the spatial domain based LSB substitution with Arnold's transform in two different segments to ensure the security.

Pratik D. Shah et al. (2021) proposed a secure massive capacity based image steganography method using the genetic algorithm. They also used the LSB based replacement steganography. The stealthy data is reshuffled and revised before embedding the data bits into the LSB positions of cover t image by using genetic algorithm.

Hanmin Ye et al. (2022) also proposed an image steganography technique based on Iimage interpolation and difference histogram shift methodologies. The pixel positions are selected by the double scrambling operation of random image block recombination and Arnold transform method. The chaotic sequence

Table 1. Comparative analysis of the reviewed related work

Sl. No.	Proposed By	Mechanism	Benefits/Features
1	Kanan et al. (2014)	Based on a genetic algorithm, a spatial domain technique for adjusting visual picture quality without sacrificing data (GA) is presented. The suggested method centres on recasting the steganography challenge as a search and optimization issue.	The suggested approach not only achieves high embedding capacity, but also improves the PSNR of the stego picture, in contrast to other prominent steganography algorithms.
2	Rana et al. (2012)	A novel kohonen neural network–based approach to high–capacity picture steganography is suggested. The absolute contrast sensitivity of the pixels in the cover picture is used to train the Kohonen network. A trained network sorts the pixels into several sensitivity categories.	Capacity and security are improved while maintaining an acceptable PSNR.
3	El-Emam et al. (2015)	To further enhance the data-hiding method in colour photos without being detected, a three-stage intelligent approach has been provided.	The suggested algorithm's output is capable of effectively embedding a huge amount of data, up to 12 bpp (bits per pixel), and while maintaining superior picture quality.
4	Nameer et al. (2013)	To effectively hide a large number of secret messages (Smsg) in colour photos, a novel steganography method is developed that combine's non-uniform adaptive image segmentation (NUAIS) with an intelligent computing approach.	As a result of the suggested method, its efficiency may be well masked. There are now four hidden bits each byte, resulting in higher picture quality.
5	Zhiyi Wang et al. (2022)	A unique technique is proposed for feature extraction in steganography, which makes use of the Transformer, with the goal of enhancing steganography's performance.	The Transformer outperforms the state-of-the-art deep learning models that were used for comparison.
6	Fard et al. (2005)	In order to create a safe steganographic encoding of JPEG pictures, a new GA evolutionary method is presented. OutGuess, the most secure steganographic scheme, is the basis of the steganography phase.	Underlying concept might be applied to other types of multimedia steganography as well.
7	Chang et al. (2007)	A new reversible steganographic technique is introduced that successfully restores the original picture after the removal of the hidden information.	Results of the experiments show that the suggested approach works well for BTC-compressed colour pictures and can incorporate more than three bits in each BTC-encoded block.
8	El-Emam et al. (2008)	To conceal a large quantity of data in a colour BMP picture, a novel Steganography technique based on a learning system is suggested.	Approach is capable of efficiently embedding a huge quantity of information up to 75% of the picture size (replace 18 bits for each pixel as a maximum) without sacrificing output quality.
9	Wang et al. (2010)	It is proposed that a new evolutionary algorithm-based steganography be used to guarantee protection against RS analysis.	The experimental findings prove the superior visual quality and resistance to steganalysis offered by the suggested method.
10	Kunal Ashok Shinde et al. (2016)	A new method, dubbed "Steganography," has been developed to protect sensitive information with a high level of security.	This method relies heavily on differences in pixel brightness as its primary input.
11	Aruna Malik et al. (2018)	To hide colour pictures more effectively, a novel strategy for improved image steganography is developed. The suggested method uses the cover image's pixel intensity and the similarity in hidden message to determine whether a message has been deciphered correctly.	The quality of the stego-image is enhanced as a result of the pre-processing, which drastically decreases the quantity of the secret data.
12	Shaowei Weng et al. (2019)	By categorising the local complexity into several levels, a dynamic IPVO RDH is proposed that can easily adjust the total amount of pixels in a given block.	Substantial experiments have shown that the suggested strategy is superior to the state-of-the-art approaches.

continued on following page

Table 1. Continued

Sl. No.	Proposed By	Mechanism	Benefits/Features
13	Sadik Ali Al-Taweel et al. (2016)	The combination of Least Significant Bit (LSB) steganography and Arnold's transformation algorithm ciphering is proposed as a unique approach for encrypting and concealing one picture inside another grey image file.	The technique is both secure and undetectable in grayscale photos.
14	Minati Mishra et al. (2012)	In this study, the information is embedded using the spatial domain LSB substitution technique, and security is provided by using Arnold's transform twice, once at the beginning and once at the end.	Results from testing and validation against a set of reference pictures demonstrate that the system is safe and has a high level of data concealing capabilities.
15	Pratik D. Shah et al. (2021)	The use of a genetic algorithm for covert data change based on high capacity picture steganography is proposed (GA). This novel method use LSB replacement steganography to conceal sensitive information.	The suggested method yields stego pictures with an average PSNR of 46.41 dB for 2 bit per pixel (bpp) data hiding capacity and 40.83 dB for 3 bpp data hiding capacity.
16	Hanmin Ye et al. (2022)	With the use of a novel interpolation picture and difference histogram shift, a reversible image steganography technique is developed for encrypted images.	According to the experiments, the embedding capacity has been significantly increased to the tune of 1,572,864 bits under the premise of guaranteeing information security and picture quality.
17	Manzoor Ahmad Lone et al. (2022)	Using the Arnold transform, a 3D logistic chaotic map with an XOR operation, and the affine hill cypher method in tandem, a new symmetric-key colour picture encryption strategy is suggested.	Suggested scheme's safety, efficiency, and efficacy have all been verified by extensive simulations of quality indicators and comparisons with current methods.
18	Ping Pan et al. (2022)	To address the issue of weak extraction capacity of steganographic pictures while under assault or interference, this work offers a double-matrix decomposition image steganography system with multi-region coverage.	Secret information is recovered from steganographic pictures assaulted by various image processing techniques, demonstrating the effectiveness of the suggested method's anti-attack capability.

is generated by logistic mapping and used as the diffusion sequence of the encryption algorithm. DNA encoding and intention are also performed to obtain the final encoded stego-image.

Manzoor Ahmad Lone et al. (2022) also proposed a colour image encryption based on symmetric keys. The encryption process also include Arnold transform, 3D chaotic map, XOR operation and affine hill cipher techniques for robust steganography technique.

Ping Pan et al. (2022) proposed a double-matrix decay of image steganography scheme. The cover image was transformed by using multi-wavelet transform. Also the hidden area of the cover image is also processed by Arnold transform, singular-value and Hessenberg decomposition. Zhiyi Wang et al. (2022) proposed an Image Steganography technique using Transformer and Recursive Permutation. The image encryption algorithm by using recursive permutation is used for more enhancement of purity through images.

Table 1 shows the comparison of different related work. Here we have proposed a steganographic algorithm that generates high-quality stego-images by statistical and visual resources with a high integration and low computational complexity. Our proposed scheme has been compared with other existing schemes where the built-in capacitance values, PSNR and SSIM, MSE give the best results.

3. PROPOSED WORK

In our proposed method, we have used steganography algorithm, which have been tested on different size of text messages vs different dimension of images. To implement this proposed work we have taken changed size of standard gray scale images such as LENA, PEPPER, MONALISHA, BOAT and other images. The size of the images have taken with the dimension of 512×512 or 256×256 or 128×128. To protect our scheme we have designed different size of secret keys (n) with respect to different size of text message and standard images. Here logistic map has been used to generate random numbers which help us to embedding text message inside the image. The Arnold transformation are also used to select the random pixels location (X, Y) throughout the carrier image. Yet again the image also has been separated into several blocks, each of size (2×2) and have embedded the text message inside the analogous blocks of it. The embedding capacities of the messages are defined as in Table 1. In our proposed method we have put our best effort to minimized the MSE value and maximize the PSNR value, so that we can generate the alike stego-image. Here Fig. 4 displays the strategy of our proposed steganography method.

Figure 4. Flow diagram for proposed steganography scheme

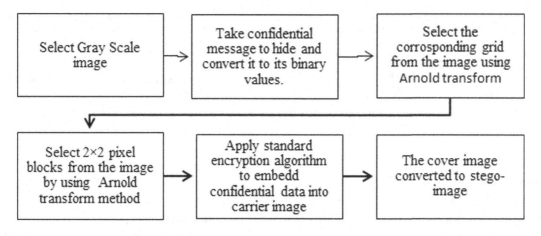

i) Pre-Processing Operation

This steganography algorithm has been tested on different sizes of text messages vs. different size of cover images. As we have used the 2×2 pixel blocks from the image by using Arnold transform method. That different blocks have been targeted to embed the data to the entire image. To implement this programs secure system, different secret keys (numerical value n) are designed according to multiple sizes of text messages and sizes of images. Secret keys, different sized text messages and different image sizes were mentioned as in Table 2.

In this section we have focused on the different parameters that are used in our proposed scheme.

Table 2. Payload and secret key

Size of the Text Message in Bytes (m)	Image Size and Secret keys
	128x128
500	3
1000	3
2000	9

ii) Logistic

For generating the random number of secret keys, a Chaotic Map has been implemented in this scheme. Here, the Chaotic Map generates the random number sequences. There are different types of Chaotic Maps such as Logistic Map, Arnold Map etc. Here, we have used Logistic Map to generate random sequence. The equation 2 shows the mathematical expression for the Logistic Map.

$$X_{i+1} = 3.5 \times X_i \times (1 - X_i) \tag{2}$$

iii) Arnold Map

This is also known as chaotic function or Arnold Map. Using this function, the standard image is scrambled. In our work, the Arnold Transformation is used to choose the pixel position in a nonlinear way of the image. The inverse function is also used to reorder the pixel positions into its original format. The equation 3 of the Arnold Map is described below:

$$\begin{pmatrix} x' \\ y' \end{pmatrix} = \begin{pmatrix} 1 & 1 \\ 1 & 2 \end{pmatrix} \times \begin{pmatrix} x \\ y \end{pmatrix} \% 511 + 1 \tag{3}$$

iv) Background Process

In our proposed system, we divided the image into grid of size $w \times col$, where (*row,col*) will be the size of the image. Next we have divided the image (2×2) several blocks. Suppose the co-ordinate of the each block becomes ((x-1), (y+1)); ((x-1), (y-1)) along (x_{axis}) and ((x+1), (y+1)); ((x+1), (y-1)) along (y_{axis}) and the centre of the blocks becomes (x, y). These points are used to implement eight neighbourhoods of the pixels. Then Arnold Map are used to select randomly one pixel of the block out of the eight pixels and perform the bitwise XOR operation in the following way and store the results (x–1), (y+1)position. The following equation 1 defines how to secret text embedded into the pixel.

$$img_{x+1,y+1} = img_{x,y} \oplus img_{x+1,y} \oplus p_k \oplus r \tag{4}$$

Figure 5. LENA image divided into grids

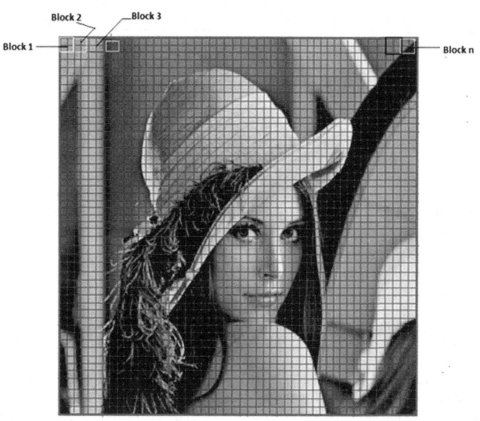

Figure 6. (2×2) image block

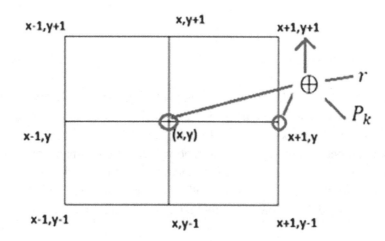

$$img_{x+1,y+1} = img_{x,y} \oplus img_{x+1,y} \oplus P_k \oplus r$$

The Figure 4 and Figure 5 below described the graphical overview of the proposed method.

v) Algorithm for Encoding Process

Following the steps are described for the steganography algorithm for (A) with embedding algorithm and (B) with extraction algorithm:

Input: A grayscale image size of (512×512)or (256×256) or (128×128), secret keys, (m,n,key) and different size of text messages.

Output: Stego-Image

A) Embedding Operation:

Step 1: Determine the value of n with respect to different size of the text message m (different values of n is given in Table 1).

Step 2: Initialize parameter $q=m/(row\times col\times 100)$.

Step 3: Store the value of n inside an image such as $img_{row,col}=n$.

Here text message P has been embedded inside the image $img_{i,j}$

$$\left(X',Y'\right) = arnold\left(i,j\right)$$

$$img_{x+1,y+1} = img_{x,y} \oplus img_{x+1,y} \oplus p_k \oplus r$$

where

$X= 2,4,6, \ldots, row$ (5)

And $Y= 2,4,5, \ldots, col$

And $r=\%253+1$

Step 4: Select random pixel based on Arnold Map.

Step 5: Calculate the values:

$$X_{i+1} = 3.5 \times X_i \times (1-X_i), \text{ for } i=1,2,3,\ldots,m$$

where m is the entire amount of text.

$q=m/(row \times col \times 100) \in (0,1)$

Used to embed text messages in images.

Step 6: Using the encryption algorithm, the textual content message P_k is embedded inner photo $img_{i,j}$.
Step 7: Construct the stego-image $C_{i,j}$.
Step 8: Stop.

B) Extraction Operation

Step 1: Proceed with the stego-image and choice the pixel positions from the image.

Step 2: Perform the Arnold Map Transform operation to select the embedded pixel and bit positions of the image.

$(X', Y') = arnold(X,Y)$

$p_k = img_{x,y} \oplus img_{x+1,y} \oplus img_{x+1,y+1} \oplus r,$

where

$X = 2,4,6, \ldots, row$ (6)

And $Y = 2,4,6, \ldots, col$

and $r = \%253+1$

Step 3: Store the data bits to an array and reform it to its original content.
Step 4: Stop.

4. PERFORMANCE ANALYSIS

Here we have accomplished the tentative result to validate the supremacy of the proposed steganography method. By embedding the maximum number of data bits to the different pixel positions, i.e. as Bits per Pixel (BPP), we have measured the embedded capacity or payload. The expression is defined as follows:

$$BPP = \frac{maximum embedding bits}{row \times col}$$ (7)

Figure 7: Experimental Results using grayscale image

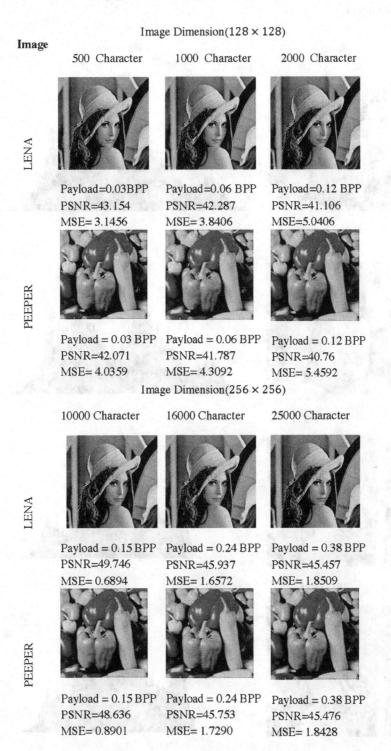

Figure 8. Histogram of PEPPER & LENA (Gray Scale, 128x128) as Cover and Stego-Image after Embedding 500 Characters

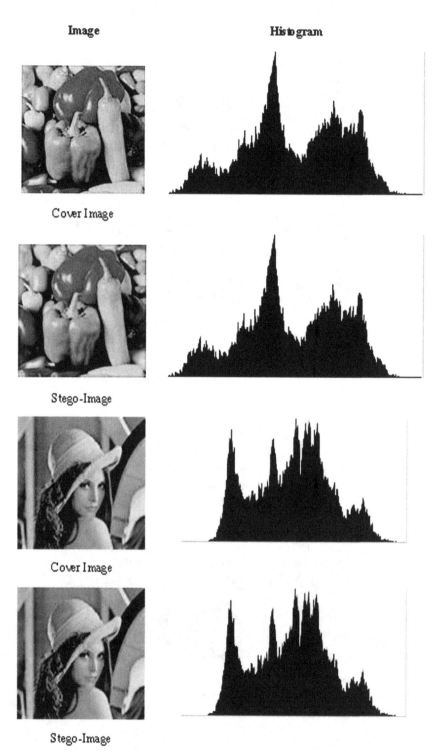

Where *row* and *col* respectively, are the height and width of the cover image.

The superiority of a stego-image is measured from two perspectives. The first is the Peak Signal-to-Noise Ratio (PSNR), used to calculate the variance between the cover image and the stego-image. Second, the superiority of any stego-image is compared to the cover image, seen by the Human Visual System (HSV) as MSE. The PSNR and MSE is defined as:

$$PSNR = \frac{10.log_{10}(255 \times 255)}{MSE} db \qquad (8)$$

$$MSE = \frac{1}{MN} \sum_{i=1}^{M}\sum_{j=1}^{N} \left(img_{i,j} - C_{i,j}\right)^2 \qquad (9)$$

The more PSNR value represents the best quality of the proposed algorithm. The smallest of MSE value is indicates a low error rate. In MSE, $C_{i,j}$ is the stego-image and $img_{i,j}$ is the original image. As a result of comparison, it was found that the proposed method exposed the best PSNR value.

To conduct our experiments, we used, respectively, (512×512), (256×256), (128×128) of LENA and PEPPER Gray scale images. Fig. 6 shows to compare our results with previous studies.

Steganography using Arnold Transformation is habitually used for image embedding with in the cover image. Here we have embedded more number of data bits than the embedding image information. Fig. 7 shows the superiority for PSNR of our proposed method over other existing techniques like PVD, GLM, and Mid Position Value (MPV) techniques. Fig. 8 shows the superiority for SSIM of our proposed method

Figure 9. PSNR comparison of proposed method with others

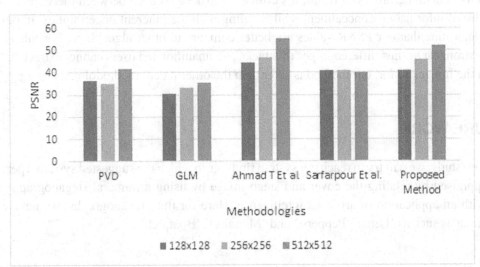

Figure 10. SSIM comparison of proposed method with others

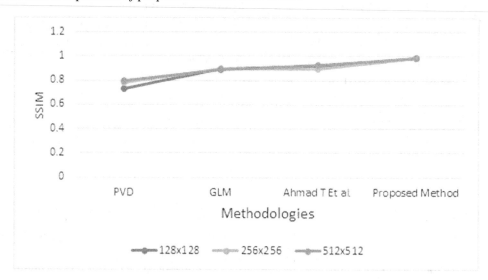

over other existing techniques like PVD, GLM, Ahmed T Et al., and MPV. Our proposed method performs better than the other for SSIM but for the case of PSNR it performs overall better than the others.

5. CONCLUSION

The practise of using an image to mask evidence though it, is known as image steganography. Steganography approaches strive to rise the volume of transformed media as well as the stego-object's toughness in inconsistency of passive and critical attacks. Furthermore, steganography tries to strengthen the quietness of the secret communication implanted in a stego-object. On the other hand the image steganography is apprehensive with hazard. As a result, it's critical to strike a balance between these three objectives in the realm of information concealment while dealing with the inherent uncertainties. In our chapter, we have determine that our PSNR values are better compare to other algorithms. For this reason this method is strongest against different types of attacks and unauthorised users cannot extract confidential data from the image. So for, our method is safer than the other recent methodologies.

6. FUTURE WORK

In our future study, we will try to reach our system findings in which the suggested system's performance will be appraised by relating the cover and stego-image by using a numeral steganography measure metrics with an application of artificial intelligence. Here for this steganography, we have employed standard images such as 'Lena,' 'Peppers,' and 'Monalisa' 'Boat,' etc.

REFERENCES

Ali, S., Husain, M., & Mahmoud, A. (2018). Image in image Steganography Technique based on Arnold Transform and LSB Algorithms. In International Journal of Computer Applications (Vol. 181, Issue 10, pp. 32–39). Foundation of Computer Science. doi:10.5120/ijca2018917652

Chang, C.-C., Lin, C.-Y., & Fan, Y.-H. (2008). Lossless data hiding for color images based on block truncation coding. In Pattern Recognition (Vol. 41, Issue 7, pp. 2347–2357). Elsevier BV. doi:10.1016/j.patcog.2007.12.009

Dadgostar, H., & Afsari, F. (2016). Image steganography based on interval-valued intuitionistic fuzzy edge detection and modified LSB. In *Journal of Information Security and Applications* (Vol. 30, pp. 94–104). Elsevier BV., doi:10.1016/j.jisa.2016.07.001

Ehsan Ali, U. A. M.., Ali, E., Sohrawordi, M., & Sultan, M. N. (2021). A LSB Based Image Steganography Using Random Pixel and Bit Selection for High Payload. In International Journal of Mathematical Sciences and Computing (Vol. 7, Issue 3, pp. 24–31). MECS Publisher. doi:10.5815/ijmsc.2021.03.03

El-Emam, N. N. (2008). Embedding a Large Amount of Information Using High Secure Neural Based Steganography Algorithm. *World Academy of Science, Engineering and Technology, International Journal of Computer, Electrical, Automation, Control and Information Engineering, 2,* 3806–3817.

El-Emam, N. N., & Al-Diabat, M. (2015). A novel algorithm for colour image steganography using a new intelligent technique based on three phases. In *Applied Soft Computing* (Vol. 37, pp. 830–846). Elsevier BV. doi:10.1016/j.asoc.2015.08.057

El-Emam, N. N., & AL-Zubidy, R. A. S. (2013). New steganography algorithm to conceal a large amount of secret message using hybrid adaptive neural networks with modified adaptive genetic algorithm. In *Journal of Systems and Software* (Vol. 86, Issue 6, pp. 1465–1481). Elsevier BV.

Fard, A. M., Akbarzadeh-T, M.-R., & Varasteh-A., F. (2006). A New Genetic Algorithm Approach for Secure JPEG Steganography. In *2006 IEEE International Conference on Engineering of Intelligent Systems. 2006 IEEE International Conference on Engineering of Intelligent Systems.* IEEE. 10.1109/ICEIS.2006.1703168

Kadhim, I. J., Premaratne, P., Vial, P. J., & Halloran, B. (2019). Comprehensive survey of image steganography: Techniques, Evaluations, and trends in future research. In *Neurocomputing* (Vol. 335, pp. 299–326). Elsevier BV. doi:10.1016/j.neucom.2018.06.075

Kanan, H. R., & Nazeri, B. (2014). A novel image steganography scheme with high embedding capacity and tunable visual image quality based on a genetic algorithm. In Expert Systems with Applications (Vol. 41, Issue 14, pp. 6123–6130). Elsevier BV. doi:10.1016/j.eswa.2014.04.022

Lin, W., Zhu, X., Ye, W., Chang, C.-C., Liu, Y., & Liu, C. (2022). An Improved Image Steganography Framework Based on Y Channel Information for Neural Style Transfer. In C.-L. Chen (Ed.), *Security and Communication Networks* (Vol. 2022, pp. 1–12). Hindawi Limited. doi:10.1155/2022/2641615

Lone, M. A., & Qureshi, S. (2022). RGB image encryption based on symmetric keys using Arnold transform, 3D chaotic map and affine hill cipher. In *Optik* (Vol. 260, p. 168880). Elsevier BV. doi:10.1016/j.ijleo.2022.168880

Malik, A., Kumar, R., & Singh, S. (2018). A New Image Steganography Technique Based on Pixel Intensity and Similarity in Secret Message. In *2018 International Conference on Advances in Computing, Communication Control and Networking (ICACCCN). 2018 International Conference on Advances in Computing, Communication Control and Networking (ICACCCN).* IEEE. 10.1109/ICACCCN.2018.8748668

Mishra, M., Ranjan Routray, A., & Kumar, S. (2012). High Security Image Steganography with Modified Arnold's Cat Map. In International Journal of Computer Applications (Vol. 37, Issue 9, pp. 16–20). Foundation of Computer Science. doi:10.5120/4636-6685

Mukherjee, S., Roy, S., & Sanyal, G. (2018). Image Steganography Using Mid Position Value Technique. In Procedia Computer Science (Vol. 132, pp. 461–468). Elsevier BV. doi:10.1016/j.procs.2018.05.160

Pan, P., Wu, Z., Yang, C., & Zhao, B. (2022). Double-Matrix Decomposition Image Steganography Scheme Based on Wavelet Transform with Multi-Region Coverage. In Entropy (Vol. 24, Issue 2, p. 246). MDPI AG. doi:10.3390/e24020246

Rabie, T., Baziyad, M., & Kamel, I. (2021). Secure high payload steganography: A model-based approach. In *Journal of Information Security and Applications* (Vol. 63, p. 103043). Elsevier BV. doi:10.1016/j.jisa.2021.103043

Rana, A., Sharma, N., & Kaur, A. A. (2012). Image Steganography Method Based on Kohonen Neural Network. Academic Press.

Safarpour, M., & Charmi, M. (2016). *Capacity Enlargement Of The PVD Steganography Method Using The GLM Technique* (Version 1). arXiv. doi:10.48550/ARXIV.1601.00299

Setiadi, D. R. I. M. (2022). Improved payload capacity in LSB image steganography uses dilated hybrid edge detection. In Journal of King Saud University - Computer and Information Sciences (Vol. 34, Issue 2, pp. 104–114). Elsevier BV. doi:10.1016/j.jksuci.2019.12.007

Shah, P. D., & Bichkar, R. S. (2021). Secret data modification based image steganography technique using genetic algorithm having a flexible chromosome structure. In Engineering Science and Technology, an International Journal (Vol. 24, Issue 3, pp. 782–794). Elsevier BV. doi:10.1016/j.jestch.2020.11.008

Sharmin, F., & Ibrahim, M. (2019). Image Steganography using Combined Nearest and Farthest Neighbors Methods. In International Journal of Advanced Computer Science and Applications (Vol. 10, Issue 11). The Science and Information Organization. doi:10.14569/IJACSA.2019.0101129

Shinde, K. A., Gandhi, O. R., & Langute, S. R. Adaptive Image Steganography using Pixel Intensity Difference. *Proceedings of International Conference on Computing, Communication and Energy Systems (ICCCES-16) In Association with IET, UK & Sponsored by TEQIP- In Association with IET, UK & Sponsored by TEQIP-II.*

Subramanian, N., Elharrouss, O., Al-Maadeed, S., & Bouridane, A. (2021). Image Steganography: A Review of the Recent Advances. In IEEE Access (Vol. 9, pp. 23409–23423). Institute of Electrical and Electronics Engineers (IEEE). doi:10.1109/ACCESS.2021.3053998

Wang, J., Jiang, W., Xu, H., Wu, X., & Kim, J. (2022). Image encryption based on Logistic-Sine self-embedding chaotic sequence. In *Optik* (Vol. 271, p. 170075). Elsevier BV. doi:10.1016/j.ijleo.2022.170075

Wang, S., Yang, B., & Niu, X. (2010). A Secure Steganography Method based on Genetic Algorithm. *J. Inf. Hiding Multim. Signal Process.*, *1*, 28–35.

Wang, Z., Zhou, M., Liu, B., & Li, T. (2022). Deep Image Steganography Using Transformer and Recursive Permutation. In Entropy (Vol. 24, Issue 7, p. 878). MDPI AG. doi:10.3390/e24070878

Weng, S., Shi, Y., Hong, W., & Yao, Y. (2019). Dynamic improved pixel value ordering reversible data hiding. In *Information Sciences* (Vol. 489, pp. 136–154). Elsevier BV. doi:10.1016/j.ins.2019.03.032

Wu, H.-C., Wu, N.-I., Tsai, C.-S., & Hwang, M.-S. (2005). Image steganographic scheme based on pixel-value differencing and LSB replacement methods. In IEE Proceedings - Vision, Image, and Signal Processing (Vol. 152, Issue 5, p. 611). Institution of Engineering and Technology (IET). doi:10.1049/ip-vis:20059022

Ye, H., Su, K., Cheng, X., & Huang, S. (2022). Research on reversible image steganography of encrypted image based on image interpolation and difference histogram shift. In IET Image Processing (Vol. 16, Issue 7, pp. 1959–1972). Institution of Engineering and Technology (IET). doi:10.1049/ipr2.12461

Chapter 13
Machine Learning–Based Algorithms Towards Crop Recommendation Systems

Soumya Roy

Haldia Institute of Technology, India

Yuvika Vatsa

Haldia Institute of Technology, India

Moumita Sahoo

Haldia Institute of Technology, India

Somak Karan

Haldia Institute of Technology, India

ABSTRACT

Technology is now playing a critical role in many industries to overcome challenges and get better and optimum results. The farming industry in India significantly affects the country's economy. The agricultural sector continues to employ half of the nation's workforce. The majority of agricultural activities in the nation still use outdated methods, and technical advancement is modest. Effective technology can be applied to this industry to maximize yield and minimize difficulties. Thus, based on the weather, moisture, and season, the machine learning-based farming solution may provide a crop recommendation system that aids farmers in selecting the appropriate crop to sow in their field. This work used six classifiers to recommend best fitted crop depending on soil as well as environmental parameters. It has been observed that the highest accuracy score has been achieved by Naïve Bayes followed by SVM – SVC, decision tree, KNN, SVM – NuSVC, and logistic regression classifier.

DOI: 10.4018/978-1-6684-7524-9.ch013

INTRODUCTION

In a country like India, where Farmers are called as FOOD PROVIDERS (ann-daata) and the land on which the crop is cultivated is considered as GODDESS, the inception of Machine Learning is indeed a boon. But on the other side, the farmers of our country are still practicing the traditional methods of farming due to lack of knowledge and money or the unawareness regarding the current technologies. Less expertise about soil textures, crops, yields, temperature, and irregular usage of pesticides, improper irrigation, erroneous harvesting and absence of information in regards to market trends results in the loss of poor farmers or adds up the extra cost. There are certain phases in agriculture and paucity of knowledge in each phase corresponds to some other hurdles or multiplies the old problems and consequently boosting up the farming cost. The growing population is also becoming a concern day by day and adding quantitative pressure to the agricultural sector. There are significant overall losses across the entire agricultural process, from crop selection to product sale. According to the proverb "Information is Power", farmers can take better decisions and tackle crop related problems very easily by keeping traces of information regarding the crops, weather and market (Arah et al., 2015; Liakos et al., 2018; Prange, 2012; Sharma et al., 2021; Suchithra and Pai, 2019). The Government is also lending a helping hand by introducing various schemes such as NeGPA (National e-governance plan in agriculture), e-NAM (National Agriculture Market), under the 'DIGITAL AGRICULTURE MISSION 2021-25, aiming towards increase in production and income of the farmers as well as enhancing the efficiency of the agriculture sector as a whole.

Machine Learning (ML) with high-performance data computation has emerged to provide a number of new opportunities for analyzing and measuring data-intensive operations across many industries. From product recommendation to crop recommendation, Machine learning has paved its way so far. Many companies across industries are leveraging these technologies to get ahead. A few years back, no expert could think of such an innovation which can make strenuous things effortless. As if all the process is done in just a snap! Machine Learning is a tool that permits the system to learn and improve automatically based on earlier experiences. The first and foremost objective of Machine Learning is to allow the system to learn automatically without any human intervention.

Now-a-days, there has been an abundant involvement of Machine Learning in the Agriculture sector. All the three phases of agriculture namely, pre-harvesting (Arah et al., 2015; Liakos et al., 2018; Morellos et al., 2016; Sharma et al., 2021; Yang et al., 2019), harvesting (Altaheri et al., 2019; Hossain et al., 2019; Kirk et al., 2020; Kushtrim et al., 2019; Onishi et al., 2019) and post harvesting (Ireri et al., 2019; Jr Piedad et al., 2018; Ohali et al., 2011; Sofu et al., 2016; Ucat and Dela Cruz, 2019), can be monitored through different algorithms. Currently, machine learning solutions are basically focused on tackling discrete problems. Nevertheless, with time and additional incorporation of data analysis, automated data recording and decision making with interrelated systems would change the traditional farming practices which in result, would be able to hype the production levels and quality of the products. Agricultural machine learning, for instance, is not a mysterious trick or magic, but a set of well-defined models that collect specific data and apply specific algorithms to achieve expected results. In our paper we have included various machine learning algorithms to get the desired result and found out which algorithm is more effective by comparing the respective accuracies.

LITERATURE REVIEW

Moraye et al. (2021) described a crop prediction using Random Forest algorithm for major cities in Maharashtra State in which a 10-fold cross-validation technique was used. They tried to establish a meaningful relation between the climate and the yield of the crop for helping the farmers to make a right decision according to a particular climate or climate change that which crop needs to plant based on that particular climate. In this model, a random forest algorithm of 20 decision trees was trained. The 10-fold cross-validation technique gave an accuracy of 87%.

Khanal et al. (2018) described a method rooted on remotely sensed data and machine learning algorithms to depict different soil characteristics and corn harvest at a local base. The algorithms mainly covered are Random forest, Neural Network, Support vector Machine, Gradient boosting model, Cubist. The sensed data evaluation is done using root mean square and accuracy.

An ELM (extreme learning machine) model based on artificial intelligence is proposed by Kouadio et al. (2018) for prediction of coffee harvest for small farms. It affirmed that for the extracting features, the ELM models are more effective than MLR (multiple linear regression) and RF (random forest) models. This ELM model has also been compared with various other machine learning models and claimed its superiority in effectiveness from others.

Garanayak et al. (2021) utilized machine learning techniques to construct and develop a recommendation model that will generate recommendations for crops based on geological and climatic variables. The dataset for the five different crops, including rice, ragi, gramme, potato, and onion, has been taken into account when designing the recommendation crop system. The dataset for these five crops is first preprocessed, and multiple regression techniques are then employed to forecast the accuracy, including support vector regression, decision tree regression, random forest regression, and linear regression prediction. In order to provide the ultimate accuracy, the majority voting (MV) approach has been used as a combination strategy. The final accuracy calculated using the aforementioned methods is 94.78%.

Kumar et al. (2018) studied about how sugarcane crop datasets may be used for data analytics. Three datasets are available: the soil dataset, the rainfall dataset, and the yield dataset. These datasets contain numerous parameters that can be used to determine the health of crops and to separate the data into different classes using supervised learning techniques on datasets gathered from the agriculture domain. This system is equipped to carry out both classification and regression. The data is divided into three classes (low, mid, and high) in the classification step, while the real cost of yield production is estimated in the regression step. To train and construct a model, we used three important supervised learning algorithms, including KNN, SVM, and LS-SVM.

Renuka and Terdal (2019) applied three different supervised learning methods, including SVM, KNN, and decision trees and studied the guidance on how to use the set of sugar cane crop data to analyse data. It used three types of datasets: soil, rainfall, and crop production. This data set is made up of a number of parameters that can be used to determine the status of crops and to conduct supervisory training on data sets gathered from the agriculture domain to categorise information into different categories. The 80% input data was used to train those algorithms and 20% data was used as the test dataset used to test them. The algorithms' outcomes were evaluated based on accuracy and mean square error. The decision tree method provides greater accuracy of 99% and also has a very low mean square error.

Singh et al. (2017) proposes a method for predicting the category of the yield based on the status of macronutrients and micronutrients in a dataset using various machine learning approaches. The Krishi Bhawan (Talab-Tillo) Jammu dataset used for crop yield prediction was obtained. Macro-nutrients (ph,

Oc, Ec, N, P, K, S) and Micro-nutrients (Zn, Fe, Mn, Cu) found in samples taken from various parts of the Jammu District are the parameters included in the data. Different machine learning algorithms like KNN, Naïve Bayes and Decision Tree classifiers are used to forecast the yield category. The Naïve Bayes classifier shows the highest accuracy of about 97.80%.

Doshi et al. (2018) put forward a crop recommendation system based the crop suitability and rainfall predictors. The rainfall prediction is done by Linear Regression algorithm model that displays a span of 12 months rainfall in several states. The monthly rainfall prediction data was then fed into the machine model that then provided the best suitable crop which can grow in that condition. The other Supervised Learning algorithms are compared and found out that the neural network proposition has a 91% accuracy outcome.

Kumar et al. (2020) shows how different data mining approaches are used to increase accuracy. The dataset includes variables such as temperature, rainfall, humidity, and pH. A massive number of decision trees are created in a training scenario, and the outcome or output is divided using the number of classes. To compare the two and choose the best one, this paper also uses a decision tree classifier. They forecasted the outcome using supervised learning techniques. To train the model, they contrasted Random Forest and Decision Tree.

Patil et al. (2020) introduces a classifier-based efficient crop recommendation system. Decision Tree and KNN, two ML classification algorithms, were compared in this work. The data set consists of productivity, meteorological, and soil factors. Algorithms for machine learning are used to compute in this research. This paper compared the two algorithms separately without combining them. This is an example of a recommendation system that uses the author-appropriate classifiers.

Priya et al. (2018) focuses mainly on supervised learning techniques like decision tree and random forest classifiers. The datasets in this case include more than half of the records in the datasets and include rainfall, precipitation, production, temperature, and a variety of decision trees. Following classification, decision trees are applied to the remaining records in order to boost accuracy. We learned from this paper that to assemble a decision tree, the RF method may produce more accurate and better results.

Thilakarathne et al. (2022) have build their recommendation platform as a cloud-based service. They have compared five predictive ML algorithms: K-Nearest Neighbors (KNN), Decision Tree (DT), Random Forest (RF), Extreme Gradient Boosting (XGBoost), and Support Vector Machine (SVM). They hope to provide precision farming solutions that are free and open source, as this will promote the growth and adoption of these solutions over time.

In order to determine which algorithm was more effective at forecasting the best fitted crop, Sundari et al. (2022) compared various machine learning methods. When comparing entropy calculation, precision, recall, F1 Score, sensitivity, specificity, and machine learning algorithm approach, they have taken into account the best fitting algorithm technique that has the best accuracy.

To address the farmers' conundrum, Bouni et al. (2022) introduced a deep reinforcement learning (DRL)-based crop classification system for precision agriculture selection. Advanced agriculture methods based on DRL reduce undesirable options and increase crop production.

METHODOLOGY

Dataset

The datasets of various crops are prepared from the government website and kaggle. The dataset have total 22 classes. They are Apple, banana, blackgram, chickpea, coconut, coffee, cotton, grapes, jute, kidneybeans, lentil, maize, mango, mothbeans, mungbean, muskmelon, orange, papaya, pigeonpeas, pomegranate, rice and watermelon. Each class has 7 features: N, P, K, Temperature, Humidity, pH and Rainfall. The correlation between each feature is represented as a Heat Map (see Figure 1).

Splitting of Training and Testing Dataset

A Machine Learning process initiates with collecting an abundant amount of data regarding different crops and preparing the dataset of all required parameters. Then the stored data is grouped in sets and processed using the processor during which the unwanted noise is removed. The processed data is divided and grouped in the form of Testing Data and Training data (as pre-processed data). The Test data is processed along with the raw data which in turn gives an output which is again stored to the training data. The final dataset is fed into the Machine Model for it to learn and acknowledge from it. This work considered 70% of the total data as a training set and rest 30% as the test set.

Machine Learning Based Algorithms

Before picking the method to apply, evaluation should be conducted to see which one is the best suited for the particular dataset. Basically, we test different models to address optimization problems when working on a machine learning problem with a given dataset. Here, using the help of accuracy score and confusion matrix, we will compare a few Classification models:

- Support Vector Machine
- Decision Tree
- Naive Bayes
- KNN
- Logistic Regression

Support Vector Machine

SVM (Support Vector Machine) is a supervised machine learning approach that is employed for binary classification issues. The goal of this approach is to draw a hyperplane in an N-dimensional space that clearly classifies the data points, where N is the number of features that will be included in the dataset. Any number of hyperplanes may be drawn, but the algorithm's primary aim is to locate the plane with the largest margin, or the greatest separation between the data points of the features being plotted. The classification will be more accurate, the more away it is. The larger margin could be achieved using support vectors. Any change or modification in the support vectors may result in change in position of

Figure 1. Heat Map among different features of the selected dataset

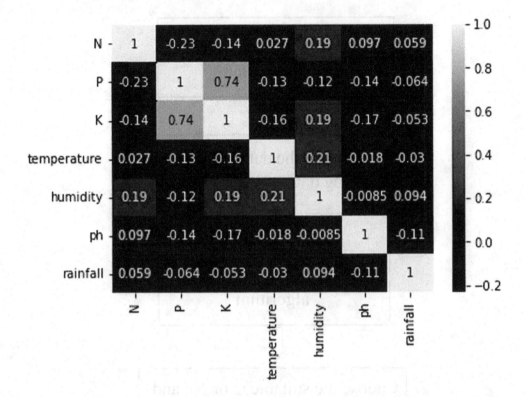

hyperplane. There are mainly two type classifiers present under the SVM namely, SVC, NuSVC. Figure 2 shows the algorithmic flow diagram of SVM.

SVC (Support Vector Classifier): The goal of the SVC classifier is to create optimal lines or decision boundaries that can divide the n-dimensional space into classes so that new data points can be easily placed in the correct category in the future. This optimal decision boundary is called a hyperplane. SVC selects extrema/vectors to create hyperplanes.

Some important hyperparameters used in SVC are as follows:

- Kernel: A kernel function is a technique for taking data as input and converting it into the format needed for data processing. The Support Vector Machine's set of mathematical functions, which offer a window for data manipulation, lead to the introduction of the "kernel." In order to convert non-linear decision surfaces into linear equations in a higher dimensional space, the kernel function, in general, transforms the training data set. Returns essentially the dot product in standard feature dimensions between two spots.
- Gamma: The gamma parameter defines how far the influence of a single training sample extends. A low value means "far" and a high value means "near". A low gamma value results in a less accurate model, the same as a high gamma value. It is the median value of gamma that provides a model with good decision limits.
- C parameter: The C parameter is a regularization parameter used to set the tolerance of the model, allowing misclassification of data points to reduce generalization error. The higher the value of C,

Figure 2. The algorithmic flow diagram of SVM

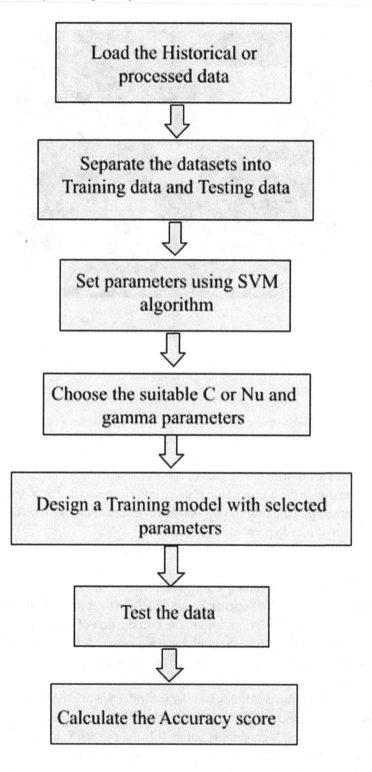

the lower the tolerance, and the maximum span classifier being trained. Smaller values of C are more tolerant to misclassification, and soft-tailed classifiers are trained, which are more generalized than max-tailed classifiers. The C value controls the misclassification penalty. A large value of C results in a high misclassification penalty, and a low value of C results in a low misclassification penalty. The larger the value of C, the smaller the acceptable margin if the decision functions can classify all training points better. The model may overfit the training dataset. Lower C gives more degrees of freedom, making the decision function easier at the expense of training accuracy.

- Degree: It is the degree of the polynomial kernel function ('poly') and is ignored by all other kernels. The default value is 3.

NuSVC: The nu-support vector classifier is used to classify binary and multiclass support vectors just like SVC. If you look closely, there is no major difference between SVC and NuSVC except a few sets of parameters and subsequently different mathematical calculations and formulations. NuSVC has a parameter that controls the number of support vectors.

- Nu: The nu parameter serves as a lower and upper bound for the proportion of samples that are support vectors and samples that are on the incorrect side of the hyperplane, respectively. The nu value can be anywhere beween 0 and 1 but the default one is considered as 0.1.

Decision Tree

The decision tree classifier uses the greedy approach. It is a supervised learning algorithm where attributes and class labels are represented by a tree. Decision trees are primarily used to train a training prototype that can be used to forecast the class or value of the target variables (training data). Decision nodes and leaves are two different categories that can be used to categorise decision trees. The eventual consequence or outcome is leaves. The edges descending from each node in the tree represent one of the potential solutions for the test case, and each node itself serves as a test case for a certain attribute. For each subtree formed from the new nodes, this recursive procedure is repeated. Figure 3 shows the algorithmic flow diagram of Decision Tree. Some important hyperparameters used in Decision Tree are as follows:

- Criterion: This setting determines how impurities of the separation are measured. The default is gini, but you can also use entropy as a measure for impurities.
- Max depth: This determines the maximum depth of the tree. Default value is none. This often leads to overfitting of decision trees. The depth parameter is one way to order the tree or constrain how it grows to prevent overfitting.
- Splitter: Decision trees locate features to split in this way. The algorithm chooses the optimum split for each node by default, taking into account all features. Any subset of characteristics is taken into account if the splitter random parameter is specified. On the features in any arbitrary subset, a split is built up. The max_features argument specifies the size of the random subset.

Figure 3. The algorithmic flow diagram of Decision Tree

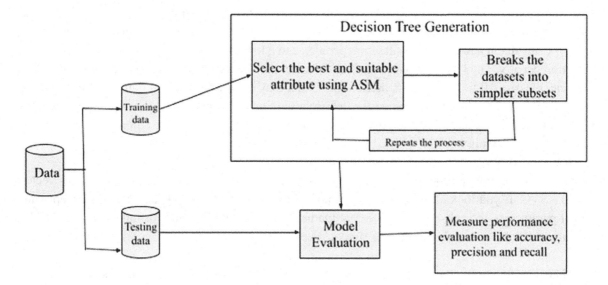

Naive Bayes

Naive Bayes classifier comes under probabilistic machine learning, which means that it predicts the output on the basis of the probability of features. In this classifier, the classification is done based on the Bayes theorem. It is commonly used where the large datasets are involved. The common principle of this algorithm is that every pair of features being classified is independent of each other. For instance, if a vegetable is recognised on the basis of color and shape, a white and spherical one would be named as potato. Naive Bayes classifier is considered as one of the simple and most effective classifiers that can make fast predictions. In this classification, we have to find the probability of an output with some given observed features. The usual method of the training step is a hectic work, but it can be simpler by using some assumptions. This is where the "naive" in Naive Bayes enters in: with some naive or random assumptions about the generative model for each outcome, we can easily predict the rough approximation of the same generative model. Figure 4 shows the algorithmic flow diagram of Naive Bayes.

KNN (K-Nearest Neighbors)

Unlike the above classifier, KNN is a non-parametric algorithm. It is also known as the Lazy Learner algorithm as it does not act immediately. In the training duration, it stores the values of the dataset and then after classification takes action on the dataset. It checks the new data by taking the previous dataset as reference and then classifies them accordingly. It is considered as one of the simplest classifiers used based on Supervised Learning Technique. With the help of KNN, it's easy to identify a new character or category. In KNN, firstly one has to select the number of neighbors (k) followed by calculating the Euclidean distance between them and get the nearest neighbors. Then, one can sum up the number of datasets in each k neighbors and allocate the new data points to that category for which the number of the neighbors are maximum. Figure 5 shows the algorithmic flow diagram of KNN. Some important hyperparameters used in KNN are as follows:

- N neighbors: Number of neighbors to use by.
- Leaf Size: The balance between the cost of node traversal and the cost of a brute-force distance estimate is effectively adjusted by the leaf size, which regulates the minimum number of points in a given node. This may impact how quickly the tree is built and queried as well as how much memory is needed to store the tree.
- p: p is the power parameter for Minkowski metric. For manhattan distance, p=1 and for euclidean distance, p=2.

Figure 4. The algorithmic flow diagram of Naive Bayes

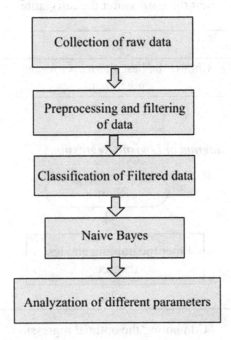

Logistic Regression

Logistic regression is a supervised machine learning algorithm that carries out binary classification tasks by estimating the likelihood of an action, occurrence, or observation. This model only produces dichotomous results with the options yes/no or 0/1 or true/false.

Logical regression divides the data into separate classes and examines the relationship between one or more independent variables. It is frequently used in predictive modelling, where algorithms calculate the likelihood that a given incident falls into a given category.

For example, 0 - indicates a negative class. 1 - Indicates a positive class. Logistic regression is commonly used for binary classification problems where the outcome variable represents one of two categories (0 and 1). Figure 6 shows the algorithmic flow diagram of Logistic Regression.

Figure 5. The algorithmic flow diagram of KNN

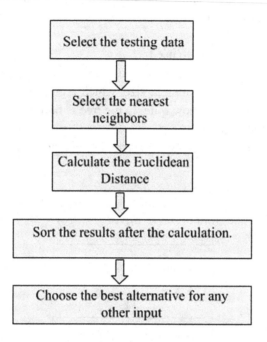

Figure 6. The algorithmic flow diagram of Logistic Regression

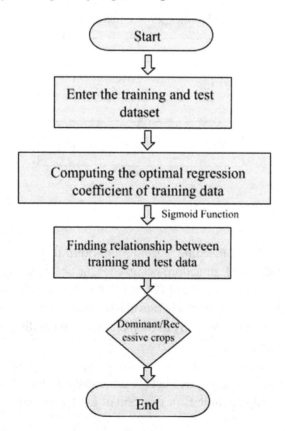

Hyperparameters Tuning Using Grid Search

Model parameters known as hyperparameters have values predetermined before training. The simplest hyperparameter tuning algorithm is grid search. In essence, it separates the lattices that make up the hyperparameter domain. Then, utilise cross-validation to determine some important performance indicators after attempting each combination of values in this grid. The ideal mixture of hyperparameter values is the location on the grid where cross-validation maximises the mean. Grid search is a thorough technique that takes into account every possible combination in order to locate the domain's top points. But the process is quite slow. It takes time and might occasionally be challenging to check each room combination individually. Every grid point needs n-fold cross-validation, which calls for n training steps. Figure 7 shows the algorithmic flow diagram of Grid Search.

Figure 7. The algorithmic flow diagram of Grid Search

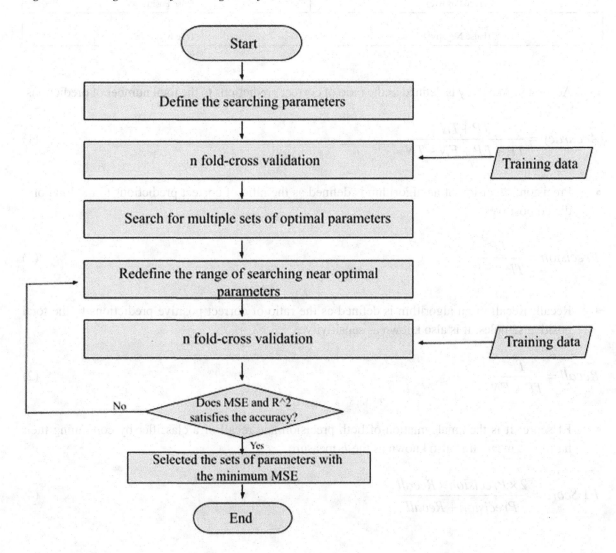

Performance Evaluation Parameter

The Performance standards of an algorithm are evaluated using Confusion Matrix, Accuracy, Precision, Recall, F1 score and Support.

Confusion Matrix: Confusion matrix is basically a performance measurement criterion for machine learning algorithms. We take the preprocessed data and fed it into the best model of ours and get the outcomes. But who would check the effectiveness of the model? Well, that's where Confusion matrix steps in. In the Confusion matrix, the output can have two or more classes defined. The confusion matrix with 4 different and combined predicted and real values is represented in Table 1.

Table 1. Confusion Matrix

TP (True Positive)	FP (False Positive)
FN (False Negative)	TN (True Negative)

- Accuracy: Accuracy is defined as the ratio of correct predictions to the total number of predictions.

$$Accuracy = \frac{TP + TN}{TP + FP + FN + TN} \tag{1}$$

- Precision: Precision of an algorithm is defined as the ratio of correct predictions to the total predicted positives.

$$Precision = \frac{TP}{TP + FP} \tag{2}$$

- Recall: Recall of an algorithm is defined as the ratio of correct positive predictions to the total positive samples. It is also known as sensitivity.

$$Recall = \frac{TP}{TP + FN} \tag{2}$$

- F1 score: It is the amalgamation of both precision and recall of a classifier by combining their harmonic mean. It is also known as the *F* measure.

$$F1\ Score = \frac{2 \times Precision \times Recall}{Precision + Recall} \tag{4}$$

- Support: Support is defined as the total number of actual predictions happening of the class in the given dataset. Support has a fixed value, it does not change with models, instead it diagnoses the evaluation process throughout.

RESULT ANALYSIS

To accurately estimate the yields of 22 distinct crops i.e. Apple, banana, blackgram, chickpea, coconut, coffee, cotton, grapes, jute, kidneybeans, lentil, maize, mango, mothbeans, mungbean, muskmelon, orange, papaya, pigeonpeas, pomegranate, rice and watermelon, this work have applied a variety of machine learning models, including Support Vector Classifier, Nu-Support Vector Classifier, Decision Tree Classifier, Naïve Bayes Classifier, KNN Classifier and Logistic Regression Classifier etc. Data exploration was the first step in order to understand the relationships between the variables and create the best model possible. The training phase and the test phase are the two phases of the suggested model. This work used 70% of the data for the dataset's training and the remaining 30% for testing. The Grid Search technique is used to tune the hyperparameters of the above said classifiers to get better accuracy. To evaluate best fitted model for crop recommendation system, different performance evaluators are used like accuracy score, confusion matrix, precision, recall, f1-score, support etc.

The Support Vector Machine is checked using both the SVC and NuSVC classifier with some selected hyperparameter like kernel, gamma, C, degree and Nu (for NuSVC). The Grid Search method gives the tuned parameter range of those selected hyperparameters like kernel = radial basis function ('rbf'), gamma = (0.0005:0.0015), C = (0:2), degree = 1 (as rbf kernel is used) and nu (for NuSVC) = (0.005:0.015). The confusion matrix and other performance evaluation parameters of these two classifiers are listed in Table 2.

The Decision Tree classifier is used in this work with some selected hyperparameters like criterion, max_depth and splitter. The Grid Search method returns the tuned parameter like criterion = 'gini', max_depth = (9:13), splitter = 'best'. The confusion matrix and other performance evaluation parameters are listed in Table 2.

The KNN classifier with some selected hyperparameter like n_neighbors, leaf_size, p is also evaluated with the same dataset. The Grid Search method gives the tuned parameter range of those selected hyperparameters like n_neighbors = (1:5), leaf_size = (1:3) and p = (1:2). The confusion matrix and other performance evaluation parameters are listed in Table 2.

Lastly, this work tested Logistic Regression and Naïve Bayes classifiers. The confusion matrix and other performance evaluation parameters of these two classifiers are listed in Table 2.

It has been clearly observed that the Naïve Bayes classifier gives highest accuracy score followed by SVM – SVC, Decision tree, KNN, SVM – NuSVC and lastly Logistic Regression algorithm. The accuracy score of all those classifiers is summarized in Figure 8. The accuracy of this work is also compared with other related work and represented in Figure 9. It has been observed that Renuka and Terdal (2019) and Kulkarni got the accuracy of more than 99% using Decision Tree and Naïve Bayes classifier respectively. The performance of this work is well comparable with the other related works and also produces a good accuracy score.

Figure 8. Accuracy score of different classifier with tuned parameter

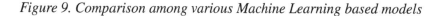

Figure 9. Comparison among various Machine Learning based models

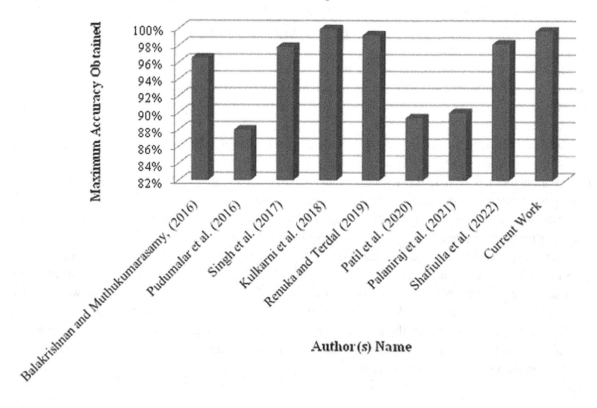

CONCLUSION

The major focus of this work is to motivate our farmers to rely on modern technologies rather than traditional practices. It is very pertinent for the farmers to trust in newer technologies since it will make their lives easier. Growing a crop involves a great deal of knowledge and insight into many different aspects,

Table 2. Performance Evaluation of different classifier

Confusion Matrix	Crop	Precision	Recall	F1-Score	Support
SVM – SVC					
(29 0 0 0 0 0 0 0 0 0 0 0 0 0 0 0 0 0 0 0 0 0)	Apple	1.00	1.00	1.00	29
(0 28 0 0 0 0 0 0 0 0 0 0 0 0 0 0 0 0 0 0 0 0)	banana	1.00	1.00	1.00	28
(0 0 31 0 0 0 0 0 0 0 0 0 0 0 0 0 0 0 0 0 0 0)	blackgram	1.00	1.00	1.00	31
(0 0 0 30 0 0 0 0 0 0 0 0 0 0 0 0 0 0 0 0 0 0)	chickpea	1.00	1.00	1.00	30
(0 0 0 0 30 0 0 0 0 0 0 0 0 0 0 0 0 0 0 0 0 0)	coconut	1.00	1.00	1.00	30
(0 0 0 0 0 34 0 0 0 0 0 0 0 0 0 0 0 0 0 0 0 0)	coffee	1.00	1.00	1.00	34
(0 0 0 0 0 0 31 0 0 0 0 0 0 0 0 0 0 0 0 0 0 0)	cotton	1.00	1.00	1.00	31
(0 0 0 0 0 0 0 30 0 0 0 0 0 0 0 0 0 0 0 0 0 0)	grapes	1.00	0.97	1.00	30
(0 0 0 0 0 0 0 0 33 0 0 0 0 0 0 0 1 0 0 0 0 0)	jute	0.89	1.00	0.93	34
(0 0 0 0 0 0 0 0 0 33 0 0 0 0 0 0 0 0 0 0 0 0)	kidneybeans	1.00	1.00	1.00	33
(0 0 0 0 0 0 0 0 0 0 22 0 0 0 0 0 0 0 0 0 0 0)	lentil	1.00	1.00	1.00	22
(0 0 0 0 0 0 0 0 0 0 0 34 0 0 0 0 0 0 0 0 0 0)	maize	1.00	1.00	1.00	34
(0 0 0 0 0 0 0 0 0 0 0 0 22 0 0 0 0 0 0 0 0 0)	mango	1.00	1.00	1.00	22
(0 0 0 0 0 0 0 0 0 0 0 0 0 33 0 0 0 0 0 0 0 0)	mothbeans	1.00	1.00	1.00	33
(0 0 0 0 0 0 0 0 0 0 0 0 0 0 24 0 0 0 0 0 0 0)	mungbean	1.00	1.00	1.00	24
(0 0 0 0 0 0 0 0 0 0 0 0 0 0 0 29 0 0 0 0 0 0)	muskmelon	1.00	1.00	1.00	29
(0 0 0 0 0 0 0 0 0 0 0 0 0 0 0 0 31 0 0 0 0 0)	orange	1.00	1.00	1.00	31
(0 0 0 0 0 0 0 0 0 0 0 0 0 0 0 0 0 31 0 0 0 0)	papaya	0.97	1.00	0.98	31
(0 0 0 0 0 0 0 0 0 0 0 0 0 0 0 0 0 0 25 0 0 0)	pigeonpeas	1.00	1.00	1.00	25
(0 0 0 0 0 0 0 0 0 0 0 0 0 0 0 0 0 0 0 34 0 0)	pomegranate	1.00	1.00	1.00	34
(0 0 0 0 0 0 0 4 0 0 0 0 0 0 0 0 0 0 0 0 31 0)	rice	1.00	0.89	0.94	35
(0 0 0 0 0 0 0 0 0 0 0 0 0 0 0 0 0 0 0 0 0 30)	watermelon	1.00	1.00	1.00	30
SVM – NuSVC					
(29 0 0 0 0 0 0 0 0 0 0 0 0 0 0 0 0 0 0 0 0 0)	Apple	1.00	1.00	1.00	29
(0 28 0 0 0 0 0 0 0 0 0 0 0 0 0 0 0 0 0 0 0 0)	banana	1.00	1.00	1.00	28
(0 0 31 0 0 0 0 0 0 0 0 0 0 0 0 0 0 0 0 0 0 0)	blackgram	1.00	1.00	1.00	31
(0 0 0 30 0 0 0 0 0 0 0 0 0 0 0 0 0 0 0 0 0 0)	chickpea	1.00	1.00	1.00	30
(0 0 0 0 29 0 0 0 0 0 0 0 0 0 0 0 0 1 0 0 0 0)	coconut	1.00	0.97	0.98	30
(0 0 0 0 0 33 0 0 0 0 0 0 0 0 0 0 0 1 0 0 0 0)	coffee	1.00	0.97	0.99	34
(0 0 0 0 0 0 31 0 0 0 0 0 0 0 0 0 0 0 0 0 0 0)	cotton	1.00	1.00	1.00	31
(0 0 0 0 0 0 0 30 0 0 0 0 0 0 0 0 0 0 0 0 0 0)	grapes	1.00	1.00	1.00	30
(0 0 0 0 0 0 0 0 26 0 0 0 0 0 0 0 0 2 1 0 5 0)	jute	0.90	0.76	0.83	34
(0 0 0 0 0 0 0 0 0 32 0 0 0 0 0 0 0 1 0 0 0 0)	kidneybeans	1.00	0.97	0.98	33
(0 0 0 0 0 0 0 0 0 0 21 0 0 1 0 0 0 0 0 0 0 0)	lentil	1.00	0.95	0.98	22
(0 0 0 0 0 0 0 0 0 0 0 34 0 0 0 0 0 0 0 0 0 0)	maize	0.97	1.00	1.00	34
(0 0 0 0 0 0 0 0 0 0 0 0 22 0 0 0 0 0 0 0 0 0)	mango	1.00	1.00	1.00	22
(0 0 0 0 0 0 0 0 0 0 0 0 0 33 0 0 0 0 0 0 0 0)	mothbeans	0.97	1.00	0.99	33
(0 0 0 0 0 0 0 0 0 0 0 0 0 0 23 0 0 0 1 0 0 0)	mungbean	1.00	0.96	0.98	24
(0 0 0 0 0 0 0 0 0 0 0 0 0 0 0 29 0 0 0 0 0 0)	muskmelon	1.00	1.00	1.00	29
(0 0 0 0 0 0 0 0 0 0 0 0 0 0 0 0 31 0 0 0 0 0)	orange	1.00	1.00	1.00	31
(0 0 0 0 0 0 0 0 0 0 0 0 0 0 0 0 0 29 2 0 0 0)	papaya	0.91	0.94	0.92	31
(0 0 0 0 0 0 0 0 0 0 0 0 0 0 0 0 0 0 25 0 0 0)	pigeonpeas	0.74	1.00	0.85	25
(0 0 0 0 0 0 0 0 0 0 0 0 0 0 0 0 0 0 0 34 0 0)	pomegranate	1.00	1.00	1.00	34
(0 0 0 0 0 0 0 0 3 0 0 0 0 0 0 0 1 2 0 29 0)	rice	0.85	0.83	0.84	35
(0 0 0 0 0 0 0 0 0 0 0 0 0 0 0 0 0 0 0 0 0 30)	watermelon	1.00	1.00	1.00	30

continued on following page

Table 2. Continued

Confusion Matrix	Crop	Precision	Recall	F1-Score	Support
Decision Tree					
(29 0 0 0 0 0 0 0 0 0 0 0 0 0 0 0 0 0 0 0 0 0)	Apple	1.00	1.00	1.00	29
(0 28 0 0 0 0 0 0 0 0 0 0 0 0 0 0 0 0 0 0 0 0)	banana	1.00	1.00	1.00	28
(0 0 30 0 0 0 0 0 0 0 0 1 0 0 0 0 0 0 0 0 0 0)	blackgram	0.97	0.97	0.97	31
(0 0 0 30 0 0 0 0 0 0 0 0 0 0 0 0 0 0 0 0 0 0)	chickpea	1.00	1.00	1.00	30
(0 0 0 0 30 0 0 0 0 0 0 0 0 0 0 0 0 0 0 0 0 0)	coconut	1.00	1.00	1.00	30
(0 0 0 0 0 34 0 0 0 0 0 0 0 0 0 0 0 0 0 0 0 0)	coffee	1.00	1.00	1.00	34
(0 0 0 0 0 0 31 0 0 0 0 0 0 0 0 0 0 0 0 0 0 0)	cotton	1.00	1.00	1.00	31
(0 0 0 0 0 0 0 30 0 0 0 0 0 0 0 0 0 0 0 0 0 0)	grapes	1.00	1.00	1.00	30
(0 0 0 0 0 0 0 0 34 0 0 0 0 0 0 0 0 0 0 0 0 0)	jute	0.87	1.00	0.93	34
(0 0 0 0 0 0 0 0 0 33 0 0 0 0 0 0 0 0 0 0 0 0)	kidneybeans	1.00	1.00	1.00	33
(0 0 0 0 0 0 0 0 0 0 22 0 0 0 0 0 0 0 0 0 0 0)	lentil	1.00	1.00	1.00	22
(0 0 1 0 0 0 0 0 0 0 0 33 0 0 0 0 0 0 0 0 0 0)	maize	0.97	0.97	0.97	34
(0 0 0 0 0 0 0 0 0 0 0 0 22 0 0 0 0 0 0 0 0 0)	mango	1.00	1.00	1.00	22
(0 0 0 0 0 0 0 0 0 0 0 0 0 33 0 0 0 0 0 0 0 0)	mothbeans	1.00	1.00	1.00	33
(0 0 0 0 0 0 0 0 0 0 0 0 0 0 24 0 0 0 0 0 0 0)	mungbean	1.00	1.00	1.00	24
(0 0 0 0 0 0 0 0 0 0 0 0 0 0 0 29 0 0 0 0 0 0)	muskmelon	1.00	1.00	1.00	29
(0 0 0 0 0 0 0 0 0 0 0 0 0 0 0 0 31 0 0 0 0 0)	orange	1.00	1.00	1.00	31
(0 0 0 0 0 0 0 0 0 0 0 0 0 0 0 0 0 31 0 0 0 0)	papaya	1.00	1.00	1.00	31
(0 0 0 0 0 0 0 0 0 0 0 0 0 0 0 0 0 0 25 0 0 0)	pigeonpeas	1.00	1.00	1.00	25
(0 0 0 0 0 0 0 0 0 0 0 0 0 0 0 0 0 0 0 34 0 0)	pomegranate	1.00	1.00	1.00	34
(0 0 0 0 0 0 0 5 0 0 0 0 0 0 0 0 0 0 0 30 0)	rice	1.00	0.86	0.92	35
(0 0 0 0 0 0 0 0 0 0 0 0 0 0 0 0 0 0 0 0 0 30)	watermelon	1.00	1.00	1.00	30
Naïve Bayes					
(29 0 0 0 0 0 0 0 0 0 0 0 0 0 0 0 0 0 0 0 0 0)	Apple	1.00	1.00	1.00	29
(0 28 0 0 0 0 0 0 0 0 0 0 0 0 0 0 0 0 0 0 0 0)	banana	1.00	1.00	1.00	28
(0 0 31 0 0 0 0 0 0 0 0 0 0 0 0 0 0 0 0 0 0 0)	blackgram	1.00	1.00	1.00	31
(0 0 0 30 0 0 0 0 0 0 0 0 0 0 0 0 0 0 0 0 0 0)	chickpea	1.00	1.00	1.00	30
(0 0 0 0 30 0 0 0 0 0 0 0 0 0 0 0 0 0 0 0 0 0)	coconut	1.00	1.00	1.00	30
(0 0 0 0 0 34 0 0 0 0 0 0 0 0 0 0 0 0 0 0 0 0)	coffee	1.00	1.00	1.00	34
(0 0 0 0 0 0 31 0 0 0 0 0 0 0 0 0 0 0 0 0 0 0)	cotton	1.00	1.00	1.00	31
(0 0 0 0 0 0 0 30 0 0 0 0 0 0 0 0 0 0 0 0 0 0)	grapes	1.00	1.00	1.00	30
(0 0 0 0 0 0 0 0 34 0 0 0 0 0 0 0 0 0 0 0 0 0)	jute	0.94	1.00	0.97	34
(0 0 0 0 0 0 0 0 0 33 0 0 0 0 0 0 0 0 0 0 0 0)	kidneybeans	1.00	1.00	1.00	33
(0 0 0 0 0 0 0 0 0 0 22 0 0 0 0 0 0 0 0 0 0 0)	lentil	1.00	1.00	1.00	22
(0 0 0 0 0 0 0 0 0 0 0 34 0 0 0 0 0 0 0 0 0 0)	maize	1.00	1.00	1.00	34
(0 0 0 0 0 0 0 0 0 0 0 0 22 0 0 0 0 0 0 0 0 0)	mango	1.00	1.00	1.00	22
(0 0 0 0 0 0 0 0 0 0 0 0 0 33 0 0 0 0 0 0 0 0)	mothbeans	1.00	1.00	1.00	33
(0 0 0 0 0 0 0 0 0 0 0 0 0 0 24 0 0 0 0 0 0 0)	mungbean	1.00	1.00	1.00	24
(0 0 0 0 0 0 0 0 0 0 0 0 0 0 0 29 0 0 0 0 0 0)	muskmelon	1.00	1.00	1.00	29
(0 0 0 0 0 0 0 0 0 0 0 0 0 0 0 0 31 0 0 0 0 0)	orange	1.00	1.00	1.00	31
(0 0 0 0 0 0 0 0 0 0 0 0 0 0 0 0 0 31 0 0 0 0)	papaya	1.00	1.00	1.00	31
(0 0 0 0 0 0 0 0 0 0 0 0 0 0 0 0 0 0 25 0 0 0)	pigeonpeas	1.00	1.00	1.00	25
(0 0 0 0 0 0 0 0 0 0 0 0 0 0 0 0 0 0 0 34 0 0)	pomegranate	1.00	1.00	1.00	34
(0 0 0 0 0 0 0 2 0 0 0 0 0 0 0 0 0 0 0 33 0)	rice	1.00	0.94	0.97	35
(0 0 0 0 0 0 0 0 0 0 0 0 0 0 0 0 0 0 0 0 0 30)	watermelon	1.00	1.00	1.00	30

continued on following page

Table 2. Continued

Confusion Matrix	Crop	Precision	Recall	F1-Score	Support
KNN					
(29 0 0 0 0 0 0 0 0 0 0 0 0 0 0 0 0 0 0 0 0 0)	Apple	1.00	1.00	1.00	29
(0 28 0 0 0 0 0 0 0 0 0 0 0 0 0 0 0 0 0 0 0 0)	banana	1.00	1.00	1.00	28
(0 0 31 0 0 0 0 0 0 0 0 0 0 0 0 0 0 0 0 0 0 0)	blackgram	0.97	1.00	0.98	31
(0 0 0 30 0 0 0 0 0 0 0 0 0 0 0 0 0 0 0 0 0 0)	chickpea	1.00	1.00	1.00	30
(0 0 0 0 30 0 0 0 0 0 0 0 0 0 0 0 0 0 0 0 0 0)	coconut	1.00	1.00	1.00	30
(0 0 0 0 0 34 0 0 0 0 0 0 0 0 0 0 0 0 0 0 0 0)	coffee	1.00	1.00	1.00	34
(0 0 0 0 0 0 31 0 0 0 0 0 0 0 0 0 0 0 0 0 0 0)	cotton	0.97	1.00	0.98	31
(0 0 0 0 0 0 0 30 0 0 0 0 0 0 0 0 0 0 0 0 0 0)	grapes	1.00	1.00	1.00	30
(0 0 0 0 0 0 0 0 30 0 0 0 0 0 0 0 0 0 0 0 4 0)	jute	0.94	0.88	0.91	34
(0 0 0 0 0 0 0 0 0 33 0 0 0 0 0 0 0 0 0 0 0 0)	kidneybeans	1.00	1.00	1.00	33
(0 0 0 0 0 0 0 0 0 0 21 0 0 1 0 0 1 0 0 0 0 0)	lentil	0.91	0.95	0.93	22
(0 0 0 0 0 0 1 0 0 0 0 33 0 0 0 0 0 0 0 0 0 0)	maize	1.00	0.97	0.99	34
(0 0 0 0 0 0 0 0 0 0 0 0 22 0 0 0 0 0 0 0 0 0)	mango	1.00	1.00	1.00	22
(0 0 1 0 0 0 0 0 0 0 2 0 0 30 0 0 0 0 0 0 0 0)	mothbeans	0.97	0.91	0.94	33
(0 0 0 0 0 0 0 0 0 0 0 0 0 0 24 0 0 0 0 0 0 0)	mungbean	1.00	1.00	1.00	24
(0 0 0 0 0 0 0 0 0 0 0 0 0 0 0 29 0 0 0 0 0 0)	muskmelon	1.00	1.00	1.00	29
(0 0 0 0 0 0 0 0 0 0 0 0 0 0 0 0 31 0 0 0 0 0)	orange	1.00	1.00	1.00	31
(0 0 0 0 0 0 0 0 0 0 0 0 0 0 0 0 0 31 0 0 0 0)	papaya	1.00	1.00	1.00	31
(0 0 0 0 0 0 0 0 0 0 0 0 0 0 0 0 0 0 25 0 0 0)	pigeonpeas	1.00	1.00	1.00	25
(0 0 0 0 0 0 0 0 0 0 0 0 0 0 0 0 0 0 0 34 0 0)	pomegranate	1.00	1.00	1.00	34
(0 0 0 0 0 0 0 0 2 0 0 0 0 0 0 0 0 0 0 0 33 0)	rice	0.89	0.94	0.92	35
(0 0 0 0 0 0 0 0 0 0 0 0 0 0 0 0 0 0 0 0 0 30)	watermelon	1.00	1.00	1.00	30
Logistic Regression					
(29 0 0 0 0 0 0 0 0 0 0 0 0 0 0 0 0 0 0 0 0 0)	Apple	1.00	1.00	1.00	29
(0 28 0 0 0 0 0 0 0 0 0 0 0 0 0 0 0 0 0 0 0 0)	banana	0.97	1.00	0.98	28
(0 0 28 0 0 0 0 0 0 0 0 0 3 0 0 0 0 0 0 0 0 0)	blackgram	0.85	0.90	0.88	31
(0 0 0 30 0 0 0 0 0 0 0 0 0 0 0 0 0 0 0 0 0 0)	chickpea	1.00	1.00	1.00	30
(0 0 0 0 30 0 0 0 0 0 0 0 0 0 0 0 0 0 0 0 0 0)	coconut	1.00	1.00	1.00	30
(0 0 0 0 0 34 0 0 0 0 0 0 0 0 0 0 0 0 0 0 0 0)	coffee	1.00	1.00	1.00	34
(0 0 0 0 0 0 29 0 0 0 2 0 0 0 0 0 0 0 0 0 0 0)	cotton	0.94	0.94	0.94	31
(0 0 0 0 0 0 0 30 0 0 0 0 0 0 0 0 0 0 0 0 0 0)	grapes	1.00	1.00	1.00	30
(0 0 0 0 0 0 0 0 31 0 0 0 0 0 0 0 3 0 0 0 0)	jute	0.91	0.91	0.91	34
(0 0 0 0 0 0 0 0 0 33 0 0 0 0 0 0 0 0 0 0 0 0)	kidneybeans	1.00	1.00	1.00	33
(0 0 0 0 0 0 0 0 0 0 22 0 0 0 0 0 0 0 0 0 0 0)	lentil	0.92	1.00	0.96	22
(0 1 1 0 0 0 2 0 0 0 0 30 0 0 0 0 0 0 0 0 0 0)	maize	0.94	0.88	0.91	34
(0 0 0 0 0 0 0 0 0 0 0 0 22 0 0 0 0 0 0 0 0 0)	mango	1.00	1.00	1.00	22
(0 0 4 0 0 0 0 0 0 0 1 0 0 25 2 0 0 0 1 0 0 0)	mothbeans	0.86	0.76	0.81	33
(0 0 0 0 0 0 0 0 0 0 0 1 0 0 23 0 0 0 0 0 0 0)	mungbean	0.92	0.96	0.94	24
(0 0 0 0 0 0 0 0 0 0 0 0 0 0 0 29 0 0 0 0 0 0)	muskmelon	1.00	1.00	1.00	29
(0 0 0 0 0 0 0 0 0 0 0 0 0 0 0 0 31 0 0 0 0 0)	orange	1.00	1.00	1.00	31
(0 0 0 0 0 0 0 0 0 0 0 1 0 0 0 0 0 30 0 0 0 0)	papaya	0.91	0.97	0.94	31
(0 0 0 0 0 0 0 0 0 0 0 0 0 0 0 0 0 0 25 0 0 0)	pigeonpeas	0.96	1.00	0.98	25
(0 0 0 0 0 0 0 0 0 0 0 0 0 0 0 0 0 0 0 34 0 0)	pomegranate	1.00	1.00	1.00	34
(0 0 0 0 0 0 0 0 3 0 0 0 0 0 0 0 0 0 0 0 32 0)	rice	1.00	0.91	0.96	35
(0 0 0 0 0 0 0 0 0 0 0 0 0 0 0 0 0 0 0 0 0 30)	watermelon	1.00	1.00	1.00	30

such as the contents of the soil, the temperature of the place, the pH of the soil, etc. The machine learning based algorithm is a boon to our agricultural field and the farmers. By advising the best crop while bearing several features in mind, the solution will help farmers to increase agricultural productivity, decrease soil degradation in cultivated fields, and reduce fertilizer consumption in crop production. This would offer a thorough forecast based on geographic, environmental, and economic factors.

This work used total 6 classifiers to recommend best fitted crop depending on soil as well as environmental parameters. It has been observed that the highest accuracy score has been achieved by Naïve Bayes followed by SVM – SVC, Decision tree, KNN, SVM – NuSVC and Logistic Regression classifier. These different accuracies would provide an ample amount of choices to farmers for better crop selection. Future this work can be extended by appling some more crop recomondation algorithm using machine learning as well as deep learning based approaches to select the best algorithm. Also a hardware sytem can be developed and merged with this to make it handy to the common farmers.

REFERENCES

Altaheri, H., Alsulaiman, M., & Muhammad, G. (2019). Date fruit classification for robotic harvesting in a natural environment using deep learning. *IEEE Access: Practical Innovations, Open Solutions*, 7, 117115–117133. doi:10.1109/ACCESS.2019.2936536

Arah, I. K., Amaglo, H., Kumah, E. K., & Ofori, H. (2015). Preharvest and postharvest factors affecting the quality and shelf life of harvested tomatoes: A mini review. *International Journal of Agronomy*, 6, 1–6. doi:10.1155/2015/478041

Balakrishnan, N., & Muthukumarasamy, G. (2016). Crop Production-Ensemble Machine Learning Model for Prediction. *International Journal of Computer Science and Software Engineering*, 5, 148–153.

Bouni, M., Hssina, B., Douzi, K., & Douzi, S. (2022). Towards an Efficient Recommender Systems in Smart Agriculture: A deep reinforcement learning approach. *Procedia Computer Science*, 203, 825–830. doi:10.1016/j.procs.2022.07.124

Doshi, Z., Nadkarni, S., Agrawal, R., & Shah, N. (2018). AgroConsultant: Intelligent Crop Recommendation System Using Machine Learning Algorithms. *Proc. of Fourth International Conference on Computing Communication Control and Automation*. 10.1109/ICCUBEA.2018.8697349

Garanayak, M., Sahu, G., Mohanty, S. N., & Jagadev, A. K. (2021). Agricultural Recommendation System for Crops Using Different Machine Learning Regression Methods. *International Journal of Agricultural and Environmental Information Systems*, 12(1), 12. doi:10.4018/IJAEIS.20210101.oa1

Hossain, M. S., Al-Hammadi, M., & Muhammad, G. (2019). Automatic fruit classification using deep learning for industrial applications. *IEEE Transactions on Industrial Informatics*, 15(2), 1027–1034. doi:10.1109/TII.2018.2875149

Ireri, D., Belal, E., Okinda, C., Makange, N., & Ji, C. (2019). A computer vision system for defect discrimination and grading in tomatoes using machine learning and image processing. *Artificial Intelligence in Agriculture*, 2, 28–37. doi:10.1016/j.aiia.2019.06.001

Jr Piedad, E., Larada, J. L., Pojas, G. J., Vithalie, L., & Ferrer, V. (2018). Postharvest classification of banana (Musa acuminata) using tier-based machine learning. *Postharvest Biology and Technology*, 145, 93–100. doi:10.1016/j.postharvbio.2018.06.004

Khanal, S., Fulton, J., Klopfenstein, A., Douridas, N., & Shearer, S. (2018). Integration of high resolution remotely sensed data and machine learning. *Computers and Electronics in Agriculture*, *153*, 213–225. doi:10.1016/j.compag.2018.07.016

Kirk, R., Cielniak, G., & Mangan, M. (2020). L*a*b*Fruits: A Rapid and Robust Outdoor Fruit Detection System Combining Bio-Inspired Features with One-Stage Deep Learning Networks. *Sensors (Basel)*, *20*(1), 275. doi:10.339020010275 PMID:31947829

Kouadio, L., Deo, R. C., Byrareddy, V., Adamowski, J. F., Mushtaq, S., & Nguyen, V. P. (2018). Artificial intelligence approach for the prediction of Robusta coffee yield using soil fertility properties. *Computers and Electronics in Agriculture*, *155*, 324–338. doi:10.1016/j.compag.2018.10.014

Kulkarni, N. H., Srinivasan, G. N., Sagar, B. M., & Cauvery, N. K. (2018). Improving Crop Productivity Through A Crop Recommendation System Using Ensembling Technique. *Proc. of 3rd International Conference on Computational Systems and Information Technology for Sustainable solutions*, 114–119. 10.1109/CSITSS.2018.8768790

Kumar, A., Kumar, N., & Vats, V. (2018). Efficient crop yield prediction using machine learning algorithms. *International Journal of Research in Engineering and Technology*, *05*, 3151–3159.

Kumar, Y. J. N., Spandana, V., Vaishnavi, V. S., Neha, K., & Devi, V. G. R. R. (2020). Supervised Machine learning Approach for Crop Yield Prediction in Agriculture Sector. *Proc. of 5th International Conference on Communication and Electronics Systems*, 736-741. 10.1109/ICCES48766.2020.9137868

Kushtrim, B., Demetrio, P., Alexandra, B., Brunella, M., & Grappa, C. (2019). Single-shot convolution neural networks for real-time fruit detection within the tree. *Frontiers in Plant Science*, *10*, 611. doi:10.3389/fpls.2019.00611 PMID:31178875

Liakos, K. G., Busato, P., Moshou, D., Pearson, S., & Bochtis, D. (2018). Machine learning in agriculture: A review. *Sensors (Basel)*, *18*(8), 1–29. doi:10.339018082674 PMID:30110960

Moraye, K., Pavate, A., Nikam, S., & Thakkar, S. (2021). Crop Yield Prediction Using Random Forest Algorithm for Major Cities in Maharashtra State. *International Journal of Innovative Research in Computer Science & Technology*, *9*(2), 40–44. doi:10.21276/ijircst.2021.9.2.7

Morellos, A., Pantazi, X., Moshou, D., Alexandridis, T., Whetton, R., Tziotzios, G., Wiebensohn, J., Bill, R., & Mouazen, A. M. (2016). Machine learning based prediction of soil total nitrogen, organic carbon and moisture content by using VIS-NIR spectroscopy. *Biosystems Engineering*, *152*, 104–116. doi:10.1016/j.biosystemseng.2016.04.018

Ohali, Y. A. (2011). Computer vision based date fruit grading system: design and implementation. *Journal of King Saud University - Computer and Information Sciences*, *23*, 29-36.

Onishi, Y., Yoshida, T., Kurita, H., Fukao, T., Arihara, H., & Iwai, A. (2019). An automated fruit harvesting robot by using deep learning. *ROBOMECH Journal*, *6*(1), 13. doi:10.118640648-019-0141-2

Palaniraj, A., Balamurugan, A. S., Durga Prasad, R., & Pradeep, P. (2021). Crop and Fertilizer Recommendation System using Machine Learning. *International Research Journal of Engineering and Technology*, *8*, 319–323.

Patil, A., Kokate, S., Patil, P., Panpatil, V., & Sapkal, R. (2020). Crop Prediction using Machine Learning Algorithms. *International Journal of Advancements in Engineering & Technology*, *1*, 1–8.

Patil, P., Panpatil, V., & Kokate, S. (2020). Crop Prediction System using Machine Learning Algorithms. *International Research Journal of Engineering and Technology*, *7*, 748–753.

Prange, R. K. (2012). Pre-harvest, harvest and post-harvest strategies for organic production of fruits and vegetables. *Acta Horticulturae*, (933), 43–50. doi:10.17660/ActaHortic.2012.933.3

Priya, P., Muthaiah, U., & Balamurugan, M. (2018). Predicting yield of the crop using machine learning algorithm. *International Journal of Engineering Sciences & Research Technology*, *7*, 1–7.

Pudumalar, S., Ramanujam, E., Rajashree, R. H., Kavya, C., Kiruthika, T., & Nisha, J. (2016) Crop Recommendation System for Precision Agriculture. *Proc. of Eighth International Conference on Advanced Computing*, 32 – 36.

Renuka, & Terdal, D. S. (2019). Evaluation of Machine learning algorithms for Crop Yield Prediction. *International Journal of Engineering and Advanced Technology*, *8*(6), 4082–4086. doi:10.35940/ijeat. F8640.088619

Shafiulla, S., Shwetha, R. B., Ramya, O. G., Pushpa, H., & Pooja, K. R. (2022). Crop Recommendation using Machine Learning Techniques. *International Journal of Engineering Research & Technology (Ahmedabad)*, *10*, 199–201.

Sharma, A., Jain, A., Gupta, P., & Chowdary, V. (2021). Machine learning applications for precision agriculture: A comprehensive review. *IEEE Access: Practical Innovations, Open Solutions*, *9*, 4843–4873. doi:10.1109/ACCESS.2020.3048415

Singh, V., Sarwar, A., & Sharma, V. (2017). Analysis of soil and prediction of crop yield (Rice) using Machine Learning approach. *International Journal of Advanced Research in Computer Science*, *8*, 1254–1259.

Sofu, M. M., Er, O., Kayacan, M. C., & Cetisli, B. (2016). Design of an automatic apple sorting system using machine vision. *Computers and Electronics in Agriculture*, *127*, 395–405. doi:10.1016/j.compag.2016.06.030

Suchithra, M. S., & Pai, M. L. (2019). Improving the prediction accuracy of soil nutrient classification by optimizing extreme learning machine parameters. *Information Processing in Agriculture*, *7*(1), 72–82. doi:10.1016/j.inpa.2019.05.003

Sundari, V., Anusree, M., Swetha, U., & Divya Lakshmi, R. (2022). Crop recommendation and yield prediction using machine learning algorithms. *World Journal of Advanced Research and Reviews*, *14*(3), 452–459. doi:10.30574/wjarr.2022.14.3.0581

Thilakarathne, N. N., Bakar, M. S. A., Abas, P. E., & Yassin, H. (2022). A Cloud Enabled Crop Recommendation Platform for Machine Learning-Driven Precision Farming. *Sensors (Basel)*, *22*(16), 6299. doi:10.339022166299 PMID:36016060

Ucat, R. C., & Dela Cruz, J. C. (2019). Postharvest grading classification of cavendish banana using deep learning and tensorflow. *Proc. of International Symposium on Multimedia and Communication Technology*, 1-6. 10.1109/ISMAC.2019.8836129

Yang, M., Xu, D., Chen, S., Li, H., & Shi, Z. (2019). Evaluation of machine learning approaches to predict soil organic matter and pH using vis-NIR spectra. *Sensors (Basel)*, *19*(2), 263–277. doi:10.339019020263 PMID:30641879

Chapter 14
House Rent Prediction Using Ensemble–Based Regression With Real–Time Data

Kuntal Mukherjee
Haldia Institute of Technology, India

Syed Saif Ahmed
Haldia Institute of Technology, India

Mohammad Aasif
Haldia Institute of Technology, India

Sumana Kundu
Dr. B.C. Roy Engineering College, India

Soumen Ghosh
 https://orcid.org/0000-0002-6931-840X
Haldia Institute of Technology, India

ABSTRACT

Finding a house for rent in a new city within the budget is a major issue especially for new college students and employees. In this scenario, an effective house rent prediction algorithm will be extremely beneficial. The rent for a house is affected by certain aspects such as number of rooms, distance from the market, region, availability of transport, and many more. With the help of different machine learning algorithms, the authors try to analyze, predict, and visualize the rent of a house. In this chapter, the authors have implemented multiple linear regression models and other ensemble learning methods like Adaboost regressor, random forest regressor, gradient boost regressor, and XGboost regressor to tune the overall model performance. The authors self-surveyed data set contains records of a city in West Bengal, India. So far, almost no work has been done in this context for Haldia. The authors' proposed house rent prediction model predicts rent with an accuracy of 98.20%.

DOI: 10.4018/978-1-6684-7524-9.ch014

INTRODUCTION

House rent prediction refers to the notion of calculating rent of a house using various techniques. It helps the student to find proper rent of a house in a particular region.

It is very difficult to accurately predict the house rent using any machine learning model because the rent of a house depends on many factors like region, market, time to college, playground, food stalls, period of time, shared room, single room, floor of the house and many other factors.

There are several machine learning algorithms to solve the house rent prediction problem. The models that can be used in the above said problem are linear regression, random forest regression, Adaboost, Gradient boost regression, XGboost regressor. Linear regression model is the most frequently used machine learning algorithm, because linear regression is a long-established statistical procedure, the procedure of linear regression models is well understood and can be trained very quickly. Random forest regression is an ensemble of decision trees. This means that many trees are constructed in a certain random order. Each of these trees makes their own individual predictions. These predictions are then averaged to produce a single result. In adaboost regressor, predictions are made by calculating the weighted average of the weak classifiers and the predictions are made within the range of -1.0 to +1.0. Gradient boosting often provides predictive accuracy that cannot be tampered. Lots of flexibility can be optimized on different loss functions and provides several hyper parameter tuning options that can make the function fit very flexible. XGBoost also known as Extreme Gradient Boosting is very efficient, accurate and feasible. It has both a linear model solver and tree learning algorithm. So, its capacity of performing parallel computation in a single machine is fast. The authors will explain the above mentioned machine learning algorithms in detail later.

The chapter concentrates on predicting the rent of houses in Haldia using the author's own collected dataset. The remainder of the paper is categorized as listed. Section (II) consists of a literature survey. Section (III) consists of the methodology part which includes data collection, data exploration, data preprocessing and data cleaning. After that the authors went for a model selection where the authors explored many models and then selected the best fit. Section (IV) comprises result and analysis of the data collected and in this section the authors compare different types of algorithms and decide which is working best with this dataset. Section (V) consists of the conclusion and the future scope of the author's model.

LITERATURE SURVEY

Many researchers already developed various traditional systems or models for house rent prediction; few of them are mentioned below.

Y. Tang et al. (2018) predicted house prices using ensemble learning algorithms. In this paper they used bagging and random forest algorithms to establish a model to predict house price. M. Ahtesham et al. (2020) had worked on House Price Prediction using Machine Learning Algorithm - The Case of Karachi City, Pakistan. The authors got an idea of machine learning algorithms that are used to construct their project namely Gradient Boost and XGBoost. They get an accuracy of 98% in their prediction model. S. Lu et al. (2017) had worked on a Hybrid Regression Technique for House Prices Prediction, they created the model with limited data and features. The application of a hybrid Lasso and Gradient boosting regression model to predict individual house price gives precise results. Going through the research paper of Z. Zhang et al. (2021), the authors learn how to solve house price predictions problems using decision tree methods. Y. Chen et al. (2021) worked on House Price Prediction in which they used Linear Regression (LR), Bayesian, Backpropagation neural network (BPN), Support Vector Machine (SVM), Deep Neural Network (DNN) to predict house price. C. Zhan et al. (2020) worked on the House Price Prediction using deep learning, where they use BPNN (Backpropagation Neural Network) and CNN (Convolutional Neural Network) out of which CNN shows the best prediction effects. K. Zhang et al. (2019) worked on the topic of House Rental prediction in China under which they use a combination of two different machine learning models namely XGBoost and CatBoost. Using these two algorithms they manage to get a small RMSE value. Y. Ming et al. (2020) worked on Chengdu housing rental data. They used Random Forest Regressor, XGBoost and Light GBM to predict house rent. They got their best prediction accuracy of 0.85 on XGBoost model through parameter adjustment. A. Verma et al. (2022) worked on the topic of House Price Prediction in India . They have used machine learning algorithms to predict the price of the house. Q. Truong et al. (2020) worked on "Housing Price in Beijing" dataset and applied ensemble techniques but using the stack generalization method had resulted in lowest RMSE value. C. Fan et al. (2018) have used data pre-processing, feature engineering and regression approach to solve house price prediction problem. Phan (2018) has worked on historical property transactions in Australia to discover useful model for house buyers and sellers, they have used stepwise support vector machines for their dataset. Raga Madhuri et al. (2019) involved regression techniques like Multiple linear, Ridge, LASSO, Elastic Net, Gradient boosting and AdaBoost Regression. The authors had tried to find the best amongst them. B. Sivasankar et al. (2020) had used Lasso Regression, Ridge Regression, Ada-Boost Regression, XGBoost Regression, Decision Tree Regression, Random Forest Regression approaches for their problem and had taken the one that give the lowest RMSE value according to their dataset.

METHODOLOGY

The authors conducted a survey using google form for the collection of the data. After acquiring a permissible amount of data, the authors started the data cleaning process as the data contains many outliers and missing values. At the stage of data preprocessing the authors decided to convert categorical data into numerical data for analysis. After conducting the analysis, the authors draw the insights from the data. On the basis of the analysis the authors select their machine learning model and then the authors deploy the model (Refer to Fig. 1).

Data Collection and Exploration

Data Collection

Data collection for Haldia House Rent was gathered through surveys among students living in different locations and in different residences in Haldia, West Bengal. Now for survey there were two methods:

1.   Survey Manually (traditional Survey Processes)
2.   Survey with e-forms (Survey Monkey, Google Forms, Microsoft Forms)

The authors have chosen Google Forms for the survey purpose.

Figure 1. Block diagram of proposed system

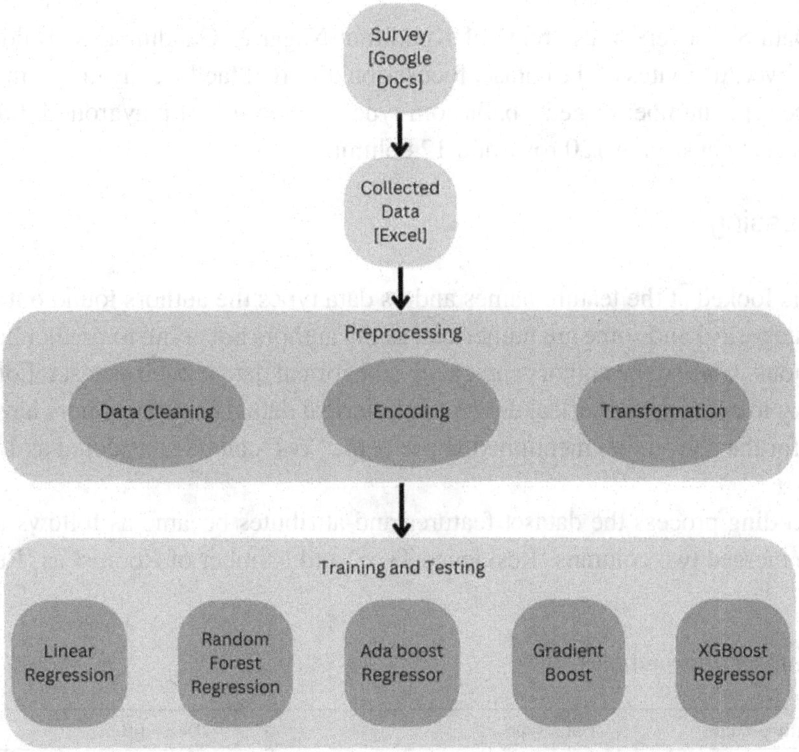

The dataset includes different features which are potentially impacting the house rents in Haldia Area. The collected dataset includes 13 features as mentioned in Table 1.

Table 1. Data collection information

	Feature Name	Data Type	Description
1.	Residence Type	Categorical	Type of a Residence (e.g., Single Room, Shared Room, Flat etc.)
2.	Number of Rooms	Numerical	If Residence type is flat then number of rooms in it
3.	Bathroom Type	Categorical	Type of Bathroom (e.g., shared, personal)
4.	Attached Kitchen	Categorical	If Kitchen is attached or not
5.	Number of Beds	Numerical	Number of beds in a residence.
6.	Shopping Mall Availability	Categorical	If Shopping mall is available or not in locality
7.	Rate Transport	Numerical	Transportation rating based on user experience
8.	Medical shop Availability	Categorical	If Medical shop is available or not in locality
9.	No of Hotels in area	Numerical	No of Hotels in that area
10.	Transport time to Market	Numerical	Transportation time from Room to Market
11.	Transport time to college	Numerical	Transport time from room to college.
12.	Available Playground	Categorical	If Playground is available or not
13.	House Rent	Numerical	Rent of the House

Data Exploration

The collected Data Set covers house rents of Khudiram Nagar & Gandhinagar, Haldia where mostly college students live. Attributes of the dataset focuses on different facilities available in the rented house such as residence type, number of beds, bathroom type, availability of playground, hotel facilities etc. The collected dataset consists of 120 rows and 12 columns.

Data Preprocessing

When the authors looked at the feature names and its data types the authors found out that some of the data types are categorical and some are numerical, as the authors are going to predict house rents which will be a continuous value so the authors can't keep categorical data in their dataset. For this the authors have to find a way to convert categorical data into numerical data. Here the authors have used encoding and fuzzy logic for the conversion mentioned above (e.g., 'Yes' can be considered as 1 and 'No' can be considered as 0)

After the encoding process the dataset features and attributes became as follows in Table 2. Here the authors have merged two columns 'Residence Type' and Number of Rooms' as 'Residence score'.

Table 2. Final dataset information

	Feature Name	**Data Type**	**Description**
1.	Residence Score	Numerical	Score a Residence based on its type (e.g Single Room, Shared Room, Flat etc.)
3.	Bathroom TScore	Numerical	Score of a Bathroom based on its type (e.g: shared, personal)
4.	Attached Kitchen	Numerical	If Kitchen is attached or not
5.	Number of Beds	Numerical	Number of beds in a residence.
6.	Shopping Mall Availability	Numerical	If Shopping mall is available or not in locality
7.	Rate Transport	Numerical	Transportation rating based on user experience
8.	Medical shop Availability	Numerical	If Medical shop is available or not in locality
9.	No. of Hotels in area	Numerical	No of Hotels in that area
10.	Transport time to Market	Numerical	Transportation time from Room to Market
11.	Transport time to college	Numerical	Transport time from room to college.
12.	Available Playground	Numerical	If Playground is available or not
13.	House Rent	Numerical	Rent of the House

Missing Data and Outlier Treatment

After Data Preprocessing Phase next problem that the authors have encountered is

1.   Missing Values in the Dataset
2.   Outliers in the Data

The authors know that if their dataset includes missing values, it cannot be used to feed a model, so it's necessary to treat missing values, when it comes to outliers, outliers can heavily impact the overall prediction of the model in a negative way, which will highly degrade overall models' accuracy. According to the problem scenario the author decided to replace the missing value with the mode value of that feature. In some cases, the authors have used their practical business knowledge to replace the incorrect data.

For example: Like, rent for a single room, attached bathroom, without kitchen cannot be greater than 4000 ₹ in Haldia region.

Model Selection

The goal is to predict house rent, the authors know house rent is a continuous value. To predict continuous value the authors have to apply regression models, the authors have various regression models available, to find the best fit model for their dataset the authors have to go with the hit and trial method, which includes applying all the machine learning algorithms one by one and pick up the best one which gives lowest RMSE value (Root Mean Squared Error) and high R^2 values.

During this process the authors have implemented Linear regression as well as Ensemble learning algorithms with their dataset. Algorithm names are listed below:

1. Linear Regression Model
2. Random Forest Regressor Model
3. Gradient Boost Regressor Model
4. Adaboost Regressor Model
5. Xgboost Regressor Model

Linear Regression Model

Linear Regression is a simple statistical approach to find a linear relationship between independent and dependent variables. Based on which model draws a line which will best fit the data

The mathematics behind this is,

$$y = mx+c \tag{1}$$

Here, y is the dependent variable
  m is the linear regression coefficient
  x is the independent variable
  c is the constant value

Random Forest Regressor Model

Random Forest falls under supervised Machine Learning. It's an ensemble learning method (bagging) which works by generating lots of decision trees and outputting the mean/mode of prediction of individual trees. It can solve both classification and regression problems. (Refer to Fig. 2)

Figure 2. Random forest regressor model

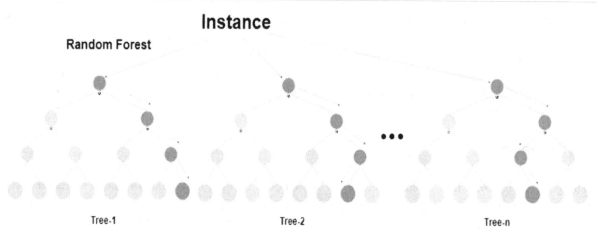

Gradient Boost Regressor Model

Gradient Boost algorithm can be used not only in regression cases but also in classification cases. When it is used as a regressor model the cost function is MSE (Mean Squared Error), Some properties of this algorithm that differs it from adaboost is the authors cannot define the base estimator here, for Gradient Boost the base estimator is always **decision stumps.**

$$S = \sum_{i=1}^{N}(x_i, y_i)\, h(x) = h_1(x) + h_2(x) + \ldots + h_n(x) \qquad (2)$$

Where $h_1(x) = \sum_{i=1}^{N}(x_i, y_i)$

$h_2(x) = \sum_{i=1}^{n}\left((x_i, y_i) - h_1(x_i)\right)$

Adaboost Regressor Model

Concept of Adaboost algorithm revolves around creating weak learners and combining them to form a strong learner. The whole process is carried out by specifying the number of estimators, learning rate and creating stumps, giving them weight and in each iteration mostly the wrongly predicted data are selected and fed to new models.

Initialize the observation weights $w_i = \dfrac{1}{n}$, i $=1,2,3\ldots..$N

 For m $=1$ to M:

1.   Fitting a classifier $G_m(x)$ to the training data using w_i

2.   2. Compute αm with the help offer rm

$$Output = G(x) = sign\left[\sum_{m=1}^{M} \alpha_m \, G_m(x)\right] \tag{3}$$

XGboost Regressor Model

Xgboost has built in regularization features (Ridge Regression & Lasso Regression) which prohibits the model from overfitting, at the same time it uses multiple CPU cores to execute Parallel Processing. Xgboost has in-built data validation capacity and it can also handle missing data. In Gradient Boosting Algorithm it stops tree pruning when it encounters negative loss, but in Xgboost, algorithm make splits up to the max depth and doesn't stop until it reaches the max depth specified and then prunes the tree. So the authors can see XGboost algorithm is a more regularized version of Gradient Boost Algorithm.

After applying all the machine learning algorithms one by one the authors have found out that the xgboost regressor model with specific parameters works best with their dataset (Refer to Fig 3).

$L(\Phi)$ is objective function

$$L(\theta) = \sum l(\hat{y_i}, y_i)\sum \Omega(f_k) \tag{4}$$

Where $\sum l(\hat{y_i}, y_i)$ is a loss function and $\sum \Omega(f_k)$ is a regularization.

Figure 3. Code block for xgboost

XGboost regressor model

```
[161] model5=XGBRegressor(
                  max_depth=8,
                  learning_rate=.1,
                  min_child_weight =15,
                  n_estimators=100)
      model5.fit(x_train,y_train,early_stopping_rounds=10,eval_set=[(x_test,y_test)])
```

IV. RESULT AND ANALYSIS

Splitting the Dataset into Training and Testing

In this phase the authors have splitted their dataset into two parts

1. Train Data
2. Test Data

Train Data

The Training Dataset is a subset of the whole dataset. The authors use this train data to train the machine learning models. Machine learning models use this train data to predict continuous values based on given conditions or parameters. With each iteration the training data will be different. The authors have used 90% of the data for training purposes.

Figure 4. Residence score vs. total rent

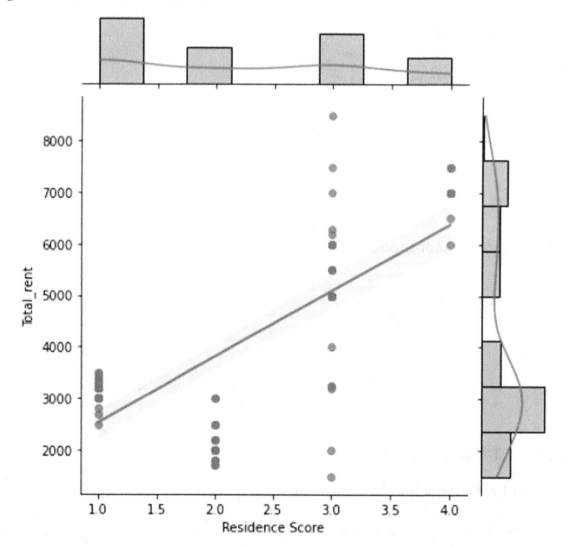

Test Data

Test data is a subset of the dataset. The authors didn't use this dataset for training purposes. For this dataset the predictor and predicted variables values both are known but supply only the predictor variable values to the model, based on which model will predict the predicted variables value. By this the authors can compare the actual result and the predicted result, and can assess models' accuracy. With each iteration the testing data will be different.

The authors have used 10% of their data set for evaluation purposes.

To implement train & test process in their dataset the authors have used pythons train_test_split() function with random_state=1

To check the flow of the data and relation in between them the authors have plotted seaborn graphs which depicts how change in one variable(feature) is affecting the other.

Figure 5. Bathroom score vs. total rent

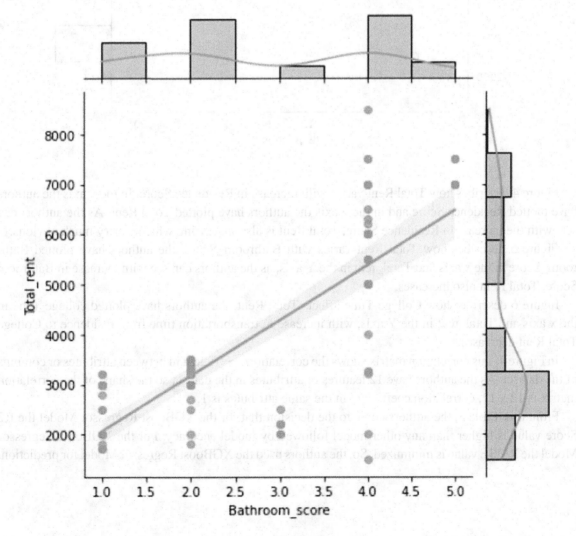

Figure 6. College time vs. total rent

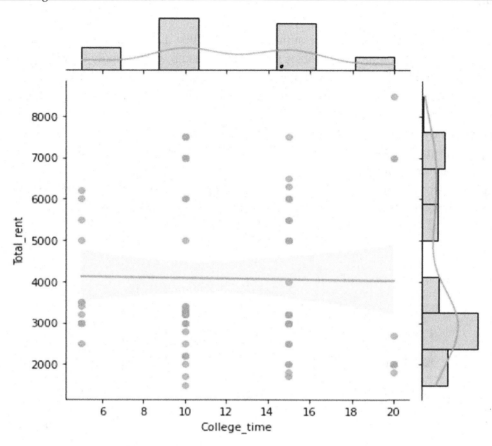

Figure 4 describes how Total Rent varies with increase in Residence Score. In the x axis the authors have plotted Residence Score and in the y axis the authors have plotted Total Rent. As the authors can see, with the increase in Residence Score, Total Rent is also increasing which is very much obvious.

Figure 5 describes how Total Rent varies with Bathroom_Score, the authors have plotted Bathroom_Score in the x axis and Total_rent in the Y axis, as the authors can see with increase in Bathroom Score, Total Rent also increases.

Figure 6 describes how College Time affects Total Rent, the authors have plotted college_time in the x axis and Total_rent in the Y axis, with increase in transportation time from residence to College Total Rent decreases.

In Figure 7, this correlation matrix shows the correlation coefficient in between attributes or columns of the dataset. As the authors have 12 features or attributes in the dataset so the shape of the correlation matrix is 12 x 12, correlation coefficient in the same attributes is 1.

From this Table 3, the authors come to the decision that for the XGBoost Regressor Model the R2 Score value is higher than any other model followed by model accuracy. For the XGBoost Regressor Model the RMSE value is minimized. So, the authors used the XGBoost Regressor Model for prediction.

Figure 7. Correlation matrix for Haldia house rent dataset

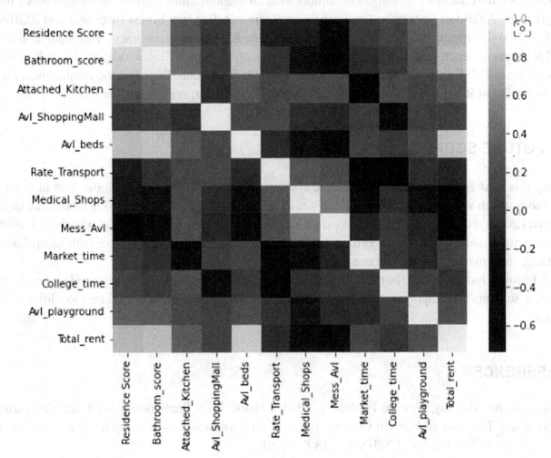

Table 3. Model performance metrics

	Model Name	R2 Score	RMSE Value	Cross Val Score	Model Accuracy
1.	Linear Regression	0.694	971.25	0.7157	75.71%
2.	AdaBoost Regressor	0.9197	534.88	0.8624	92.63%
3.	Gradient Boost Regressor	0.979	277.58	0.90	98.01%
4.	Random Forest Regressor	.9813	228.68	0.8843	98.15%
5.	XGBoost Regressor	0.9813	271.33	0.8907	98.20%

V. CONCLUSION

In order to find a house for rent, a house rent prediction model would be useful. As machine learning algorithms are considered to be efficient, the authors set up a house rent prediction model based on a few machine learning algorithms. The dataset used for this model was a self-surveyed dataset collected by the authors. In preprocessing of data, the authors encoded the required features of the dataset and then transformed the dataset for training. The authors tried different machine learning models namely Linear Regression, AdaBoost Regressor, Gradient Boost Regressor, Random Forest Regressor and XGBoost Regressor and compared them. The authors calculated the RMSE score, accuracy, cross validation score and R2 score for each mode. After comparing, as the authors came to know that, XGBoost Regressor has the least RMSE value compared to all models used in prediction. Based on the results, the authors chose XGBoost Regressor for their rent prediction model as it outperformed other models.

VI. FUTURE SCOPE

Using this model, a new student or employee coming to Haldia may be able to predict rent in different localities which will help them in finding a house for rent within their budget. This model can be improved later to give more facilities to the user. The created website out of this model will show available rooms within their budget and according to their specifications like distance from college/workplace, distance from market, and many more.

A business model can also be made out of this idea in which a website can be designed for connecting the new students and employees who have minimal knowledge about rent in different localities within Haldia.

REFERENCES

Ahtesham, M., Bawany, N. J., & Fatima, K. (2020). House Price Prediction using Machine Learning Algorithm - The Case of Karachi City, Pakistan. *21st International Arab Conference on Information Technology (ACIT)*, 1-5. 10.1109/IDAP.2018.8620781

Chen, Y., Xue, R., & Zhang, Y. (2021). House price prediction based on machine learning and deep learning methods. *2021 International Conference on Electronic Information Engineering and Computer Science (EIECS)*, 699-702. 10.1109/MLBDBI54094.2021.00059

Fan, C., Cui, Z., & Zhong, X. (2018). House Prices Prediction with Machine Learning Algorithms. *Proceedings of the 2018 10th International Conference on Machine Learning and Computing ICMLC 2018*, 6-10. 10.1145/3195106.3195133

Lu, S., Li, Z., Qin, Z., Yang, X., & Goh, R. S. M. (2017). A hybrid regression technique for house prices prediction. *2017 IEEE International Conference on Industrial Engineering and Engineering Management (IEEM)*, 319-323. 10.1109/IEEM.2017.8289904

Ming, Y., Zhang, J., Qi, J., Liao, T., Wang, M., & Zhang, L. (2020). Prediction and Analysis of Chengdu Housing Rent Based on XGBoost Algorithm. *ICBDT 2020: 2020 3rd International Conference on Big Data Technologies*, 1-5.10.1145/3373509.3373578

Phan, T. D. (2018). Housing Price Prediction Using Machine Learning Algorithms: The Case of Melbourne City, Australia. *2018 International Conference on Machine Learning and Data Engineering (ICMLDE) 2018*, 35-42. 10.1109/iCMLDE.2018.00017

Raga Madhuri, C. R., Anuradha, G., & Vani Pujitha, M. (2019). House Price Prediction Using Regression Techniques: A Comparative Study. *2019 International Conference on Smart Structures and Systems (ICSSS)*, 1-5. 10.1109/ICSSS.2019.8882834

Sivasankar, B., Ashok, A. P., Madhu, G., & Fousiya, S. (2020). House Price Prediction. *International Journal on Computer Science and Engineering*, 8(7), 98–102.

Tang, Y., Qiu, S., & Gui, P. (2018). Predicting Housing Price Based on Ensemble Learning Algorithm. *International Conference on Artificial Intelligence and Data Processing (IDAP)*, 1-5. 10.1109/IDAP.2018.8620781

Truong, Q., Nguyen, M., Dang, H., & Mei, B. (2020). Housing Price Prediction via Improved Machine Learning Techniques. *Procedia Computer Science*, *174*, 433–442. doi:10.1016/j.procs.2020.06.111

Verma, A., Nagar, C., Singhi, N., Dongariya, N., & Sethi, N. (2022). Predicting House Price in India Using Linear Regression Machine Learning Algorithms. *Conference: 2022 3rd International Conference on Intelligent Engineering and Management (ICIEM)*, 917-924. 10.1145/3373509.3373578

Zhan, C., Wu, Z., Liu, Y., Xie, Z., & Chen, W. (2020). Housing prices prediction with deep learning: an application for the real estate market in Taiwan. *2020 IEEE 18th International Conference on Industrial Informatics (INDIN)*, 719-724. 10.1109/INDIN45582.2020.9442244

Zhang, K., & Liu, N. (2019). House Rent Prediction Based on Joint Model. *ICCPR '19: 2019 8th International Conference on Computing and Pattern Recognition*, 507–511. 10.1145/3373509.3373578

Zhang, Z. (2021). Decision Trees for Objective House Price Prediction. *2021 3rd International Conference on Machine Learning, Big Data and Business Intelligence (MLBDBI)*, 280-283. 10.1109/MLBDBI54094.2021.00059

KEY TERMS AND DEFINITIONS

Adaboost: It is also known as Adaptive boost is a technique in Machine learning used as an ensemble method.

Gradient Boost: It is a machine learning algorithm which relies on the intuition that the best possible next model, when combined with the previous models, minimizes the overall prediction error.

R2 Score: It is a statistical measure in a regression model that determines the proportion of variance in the dependent variable that can be explained by the independent variable.

Random Forest: It is a machine learning algorithm which is used to solve regression and classification problems.

Real-Time Data: It is the information that is delivered immediately after collection.

Regression: It is a supervised machine learning technique which is used to predict continuous values. Loss function is being calculated using Gradient Descent Algorithm.

RMSE (Root Mean Square Error): It is a frequently used measure of the differences between values (sample or population values) predicted by a model.

XGBoost: It stands for Extreme Gradient Boosting, is scalable, distributed gradient boosted decision tree machine learning library.

Chapter 15

A Survey on Energy–Efficient Routing in Wireless Sensor Networks Using Machine Learning Algorithms

Prasenjit Dey

Coochbehar Government Engineering College, India

Arnab Gain

Coochbehar Government Engineering College, India

ABSTRACT

Wireless sensor network (WSN) consists of sparsely distributed, low energy, and bandwidth sensor nodes that collect sensed data. In WSNs, these data are initially converted from analog to digital signals and transmitted to base stations. Routing in WSNs is the process of determining the most efficient path for data transmission among various sensor nodes. In routing, small sensor nodes use limited network bandwidth and energy to capture and transmit a limited amount of data. However, with the advancement of big data and IoT, large-scale sensors are used to route massive amounts of data. Routing with this huge data consumes a lot of network bandwidth and energy and thus reduces the lifespan of the network. Thus, for energy-efficient routing (EER), there is a need for data optimization that can be achieved by many machine learning (ML) algorithms. Many researchers have devised various noteworthy works related to ML to have an EER in WSNs. This chapter reviews the existing ML-based routing algorithms in WSNs.

1 INTRODUCTION

Wireless Sensor Network (WSN) is a collection of distributed sensor nodes that monitor and/or track physical situations or circumstances (Yick et al., 2008). Recently, wireless sensor networks have grown in popularity among researchers due to advancement of Micro-Electro-Mechanical Systems (MEMS) technology. The deployment of WSNs involves many challenges, including design and implementation,

DOI: 10.4018/978-1-6684-7524-9.ch015

data fusion and aggregation, Energy Efficient Routing (EER) and clustering, localization, scheduling, quality of service (QoS), security, etc., due to less processing power, low storage capability, limited network bandwidth, limited battery power, etc. (Bhanderi et al., 2014). These limitations also affect the lifespan of a WSN if the routing algorithms are not implemented efficiently. EER in WSNs is an important concern nowadays because the energy usage and the latency in sending data to the sink node are the key problems in WSNs (Ghosh et al., 2020).

The energy-efficient routing depends on the design and development of the network as well as routing protocols. According to (Akkaya et al., 2005), there are three different routing techniques: proactive, reactive, and hybrid. The proactive technique uses static routing tables for periodic data redistribution and keeps routing tables correct and consistent across all sensor nodes in the network. In the reactive technique, the routes are found on-demand when a node wants to deliver a packet. This protocol considers a minimum number of needed hops to reach the destination. The hybrid technique combines the proactive and reactive techniques. When routing within a cluster, proactive routing is employed, and when routing between clusters, reactive routing is used. Thus, various routing protocols are implemented that effectively utilize the sensor nodes' limited energy. Most of the routing techniques leverage clusters to prolong network life and deliver energy savings, e.g., Low Energy Adaptive Clustering Hierarchy (LEACH), Threshold sensitive Energy Efficient sensor Network (TEEN), and Power-Efficient GAthering in Sensor Information Systems (PEGASIS). Hierarchical clustering is observed as an efficient method for EER (Bhanderi et al., 2014). However, large-scale sensor node deployment in WSNs invariably introduces enormous data into the network that needs to be processed, sent, and received. The limited energy and bandwidth of the sensors prevent the processing and transmission of this vast data. Therefore, the QoS of routing in WSNs can be improved either by using a vast amount of energy in the network or by minimizing the amount of data exchange. As the first solution is infeasible; therefore, the focus must be on the second solution, i.e., data optimization and distribution. For this purpose, machine learning (ML) techniques are be applied in WSNs. The ML algorithms helps to find the correlation among the data obtained by sensor nodes, which can help in reducing the size of actual data without losing any vital information. Evolutionary algorithms, fuzzy logic, neural networks, swarm intelligence, reinforcement learning, and ensemble learning are typical ML algorithms used in WSNs (Kulkarni et al., 2010). Below we have analyzed the advantages and disadvantages of ML algorithms for EER in WSNs.

1.1 Advantages and Limitations of Machine Learning in WSN

One of the main advantage of ML algorithms is that they efficiently use the distributive nature of WSNs when performing the data exchanges (Ghosh et al., 2020). This improves the network traffic in WSNs and in consequence helps to achieve EER. ML algorithms are capable of identifying faulty sensor nodes present in the network in run time (Lavanya et al., 2021), which improve the fault tolerance capability of the WSNs. Moreover, for the selection of cluster centers various ML algorithms are used that have shown better performance compared to traditional clustering methods (Venkataramana et al., 2019). Furthermore, when using WSN to track and monitor unsafe and inaccessible regions like coalmines, forest fires, etc., anything may occur at any time. Therefore, the initial setups should be capable of adapting to changing circumstances. Application of ML in these kinds of systems is crucial since ML algorithms are capable of adapting themselves to newly obtained knowledge. ML is employed to design WSNs so that the network can learn the structure and pattern on its own and adapt to such constantly changing environments.

However, there have been found some drawbacks of the ML algorithms in EER, which are as follows. The ML algorithms are data dependent and the performance of the algorithms depends on the number of training data samples, which may not be available all the time. Similarly, many ML algorithms need huge training time, which increase the latency in the WSNs. In a dynamic network scenario, the WSN architecture may not have ample time to train an ML algorithm; therefore, the applied ML algorithm must have less training time to perform efficiently. When dealing with big data, ML algorithms follow slow convergence to obtain the optimal routing path and, therefore, may degrade the performance.

This review chapter is structured as follows. The background of EER protocols in WSN and the different factors that impacted the creation of EER protocol are discussed in Section 2. In Section 3, reviews of several ML methods for EER in WSN are covered. The conclusion and the future direction of development in EER employing ML techniques are presented in Section 4.

2 BACKGROUND

According to (Sohraby et al., 2007), the energy-consuming stages in WSN are sensing, processing and communication. The energy-consuming operations in sensing are sampling, analog to digital conversion, modulation, and sense operations e.g., periodic, sleep/wake, etc. Energy-consuming operations in the processing are sensor controlling, protocol communication, and data processing. Energy usage during the communication stage is influenced by the distance between source and destination nodes as well as the data communication path between them. The objective of routing protocol is to find a minimum energy route from a source node to a sink node which in consequence expands the network lifetime. For communication between two sensors, the energy usage for data transmission (E_t) and receiving (E_r) is given below (Yan et al., 2013):

$$E_t = E_{dis_t}.n + \alpha.d^\gamma \tag{1}$$

$$E_{dis_t} = V.I \, / \, n_{rate}$$

$$E_r = E_{dis_r}.n \tag{2}$$

where E_{dis_t} and E_{dis_r} are respectively the energy dissipated to operate the transmitter and receiver. n is the number of transmitted data bits, α is the amplification coefficient that satisfies the minimum bit error rate at the receiver end, d is the distance between two sensors, and γ is an environmental parameter of wireless transmission. E_{dis_t} depends on voltage (V), current (I), and data transmission rate (n$r_{ate)}$.

The design of an EER protocol in WSNs faces many challenges. These challenges are related to the factors like, node deployment, node-link heterogeneity, radio medium, coverage, QoS, network dynamics, scalability, fault tolerance, etc. Based on any specific application, node deployment can be either deterministic or randomized, affecting a routing protocol's energy efficiency. Similarly, a WSN may consist of different types of heterogeneous sensor nodes, and this node-link heterogeneity affects EER. Radio medium of transmission also plays a vital role in energy consumption in WSNs. One approach to

MAC design for sensor networks in multi-hop WSNs is to employ TDMA-based protocols, which consume less energy than contention-based protocols like CSMA. The energy usage of the routing protocol depends on the network coverage area. QoS is also an important performance factor in WSNs. The data must be transferred within a predetermined timeframe.

Nevertheless, the preservation of energy, which is directly related to network lifetime, is viewed in some applications as being comparatively more significant than the caliber of the data conveyed. To fulfill this criterion, routing methods that are energy conscious are needed. Again, the data in WSNs may come from different sources, and aggregating these data from various sources is essential for WSNs. However, if this data aggregation is not done efficiently, it may consume much energy and reduce the lifetime of the network. In a dynamic environment where sensor nodes are mobile, the network consumes more energy than the stationary network. Energy usage of a WSN increases with the size of the network, hence affected by scalability. A fault-tolerant WSN, where the performance of the network does not degrade drastically on the failure of a few sensor nodes, consumes more energy (Bhanderi et al., 2014).

3 LITERATURE SURVEY

Machine learning has been used in various WSN routing protocols and applications. Here, ML algorithms used for EER protocols are categorized into: evolutionary algorithm, fuzzy logic system, artificial neural networks, swarm intelligence, reinforcement learning and ensemble learning. Depiction of hierarchy of various ML algorithms, which are used for EER, is given in figure 1. A few of these algorithms are discussed below.

Figure 1. Hierarchy of different ML based EER algorithms in WSN

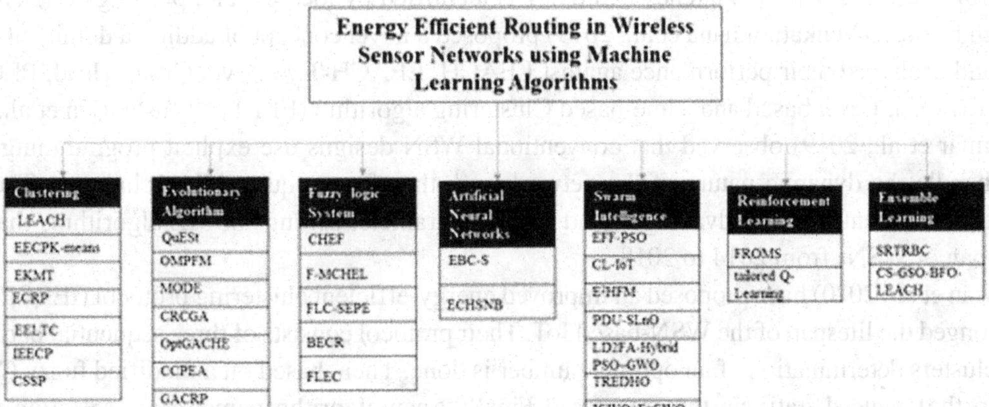

Energy Efficient Routing in Wireless Sensor Networks using Machine Learning Algorithms

Clustering	Evolutionary Algorithm	Fuzzy logic System	Artificial Neural Networks	Swarm Intelligence	Reinforcement Learning	Ensemble Learning
LEACH	QuESt	CHEF	EBC-S	EFF-PSO	FROMS	SRTRBC
EECPK-means	OMPFM	F-MCHEL	ECHSNB	CL-IoT	tailored Q-Learning	CS-GSO-BFO-LEACH
EKMT	MODE	FLC-SEPE		E²HFM		
ECRP	CRCGA	BECR		PDU-SLnO		
EELTC	OptGACHE	FLEC		LD2FA-Hybrid PSO-GWO		
IEECP	CCPEA			TREDHO		
CSSP	GACRP			IGWO+ExGWO		

3.1 Clustering

In an energy-constrained network, it is not an efficient approach to send data from each node to other nodes. It is more cost-effective to send data from each node to its local aggregator, called Cluster Head

(CII), who then transmits the information to the target node after aggregating all the data it has acquired from its cluster nodes. The goal is to group together related nodes in a WSN. Thus, the cluster-based routing is an effective way to cut down on energy use. In literature, LEACH is a popular energy-saving routing protocol in WSNs (Heinzelman et al., 2000). Many authors compare their routing methods with LEACH to assess their method's efficiency.

(El Mezouary et al., 2015) have proposed a new method based on the k-means clustering to create energy-aware clusters in WSNs. The authors have sought to enhance the clustering process by choosing those nodes as CHs that are at center and having energy at high level. Their efforts have decreased energy usage and increased the sensor network's lifespan. An Energy Efficient Clustering Protocol based on K-means (EECPK-means) has been implemented in (Ray et al., 2016). In this paper, for improving initial centroid selection procedure, midpoint algorithm has been utilized. Their method has balanced clusters by using residual energy as a parameter along with Euclidean distances. Their method has used the conventional k-means algorithm to choose CHs effectively. Simulation result have shown that their proposed approach were able to balance the CHs' workload, increase the network's lifespan, and reduce the energy consumption. An Energy efficient K-Means clustering Technique (EKMT) has been introduced in (Jain et al., 2018). By decreasing the sum of the squared distances between the closest cluster centers and member nodes, this approach has identified the CH. The CH has been re-chosen on the basis of the shortest distance between the base station (BS) and the newly discovered CHs. This effort has been done to increase the energy effectiveness of this process. Saleh et al. implemented a novel method to address the energy problems in WSNs in (Saleh et al., 2018). In order to reduce the amount of energy used during transmission, their approach has utilized a quaternary transceiver in configuration of a sensor node. Their study also suggests that if Neural Network Static Random Access Memory (NN-SRAM) is used in a system based on clusters, the overall energy used for data dissemination during storage and transmission is reduced. (Vimalapriya et al., 2019) have proposed Energy-Centric Route Planning (ECRP), a two-step ML technique to test node adaptability based on packet acceptance capability, latency, and energy. Here, the refurbished route with less latency and delay is identified by locating and pruning deficient nodes with high latency. (Venkataramana et al., 2019) proposed a novel concept of adding a dominant node in WSNs and evaluated their performance against LEACH, LEACH-Two Level Group Head, PEGASIS, Energy-Efficient Level based and Time-based Clustering algorithm (EELTC) (Tashtarian et al., 2007), etc. (Kumar et al., 2019) observed that conventional WSN designs use explicit programming, which cannot handle the dynamic nature of the network and, therefore, require ML techniques. They have discussed the advantages, disadvantages, and various parameter settings of ML algorithms that affect the lifespan of WSNs from 2014 to 2018.

(Hassan et al., 2020) have proposed an improved energy-efficient clustering protocol (IEECP) which has prolonged the lifespan of the WSN-based IoT. Their protocol consists of three sequential parts. First, for the clusters determination of an optimal number is done. Then, based on a modified fuzzy C-means algorithm the balanced-static clusters are formed. Finally, a new algorithm named as CH selection-rotation algorithm (CHSRA) is proposed which integrates two mechanisms: the back-off timer mechanism to select the CH and rotation mechanism for CH rotation. It is proven experimentally that, in performance, IEECP is better than an existing protocol named by EECPK-Means. According to the mathematical model proposed by them, the total energy consumption for K cluster or E_{Total} is:

$$E_{Total} = 2NLE_{elec} + NL\varepsilon_{fs}\left(\frac{1.262}{2\pi}\cdot\frac{M^2}{K}\right) + NLE_{AD} + KL\varepsilon_{fs}d_{BS}^2$$

where, the terms are explained in (Hassan et al., 2020).

(Al-Kaseem et al., 2021) have proposed a technique, which follows four procedures. Initially, they have partitioned the sensing field into equal regions based on number of mobile sinks. Then, they have introduced Stable Election Algorithm (SEA) to minimize the message exchange between sensor nodes and CHs. Then they have proposed a sojourn location determination algorithm to find the best position for the sinks. Finally, they have utilized Ant Colony Optimization (ACO), Genetic Algorithm (GA), and Simulated Annealing (SA) and evaluated the route of mobile sink. Their approach has succeeded to prolong network lifespan up to 66% and 48% compared to LEACH and TEEN respectively. The authors in (Rawat et al., 2022) have proposed Cluster based Sleep Scheduling Protocol (CSSP). In order to minimize the consumption of energy, their approach chooses the sleep and active nodes by employing a Particle Swarm Optimization (PSO) based sleep scheduling technique, which uses the distance to neighbors, remaining energy of nodes, and coverage neighbor as parameters. To form the clusters with energy-efficient CHs, their scheme selects the most energy-efficient sensor node as a CH on the basis of probability which considers the initial energy and remaining energy of nodes. As a result, the proposed scheme has shown effectiveness regarding energy-efficiency.

3.2 Evolutionary Algorithm (EA)

To solve routing problems in WSNs, various researchers have implemented EA. On the basis of Multi-Objective Genetic Algorithm (MOGA) a protocol named QoS-based energy-efficient sensor routing (QuESt) has been presented in (Saxena et al., 2009). This protocol has reduced energy usage though they have not considered data fusion and localization scenarios. A routing protocol has been implemented for a two-tier sensor network in (Bari et al., 2009). This protocol has used the GA to schedule the data collection of relay nodes, which lowers energy usage. Based on the evolutionary clustering approach used in WSNs, the cluster-based routing algorithm has been developed in (Zhou et al., 2010). The algorithm has been utilized to quickly re-cluster and re-select CHs to balance energy usage and prolong lifespan of the WSNs. (Banimelhem et al., 2014) have reduced the distance between BSs and CHs by determining new locations of the CHs in every round by utilizing GA. They have shown that their method is more energy efficient than LEACH method. By using a collection of low-level heuristics as building blocks to produce high heuristics, a set of random networks with different features have been constructed for training, and a GA has been used to create heuristics that have been more effective (Zhong et al., 2019). The proposed framework has prolonged the network lifetime by applying these heuristics in a greedy scheme.

For both single-path and multi-path routing problems, the authors (Xue et al., 2006) introduced a Multi-Objective Differential Evolution (MODE) method, which discovers a collection of Pareto optimal paths with regard to these objectives. The algorithm's applicability to dispersed underwater networks with both stationary and moving sensor nodes is being evaluated. With this method, a number of candidate routes are generated, each indicating a potential trade-off between energy consumption and latency for communication connectivity.

Data fusion is another technique used to enhance the data quality and energy efficiency in WSNs. The authors in (Pinto et al., 2013) proposed a genetic approach to implement parallel data fusion techniques. The capability to autonomously change the transmission rate of specific sensor nodes in response to the dynamic topology in dense WSNs exemplifies the novelty and significance of the study. However, they have not tested their model to optimize other parameters, such as evolution and checkpoint interval. (Nandan et al., 2021) have proposed Optimized Genetic Algorithm for Cluster Head Election (OptGACHE) to address the shortcomings regarding limited power in case of Internet of Things-enabled WSN. They have proposed a GA that elects CH incorporating four criteria: i) node density; ii) distance; iii) energy, and iv) heterogeneous node's capability. With the help of these criteria, they have performed EER by following ways: utilization of node's energy in systematic way in the cluster, inter-cluster distance optimization, hop count reduction, highly capable cluster head selection and cutting down transmission energy. (Yang et al., 2021) have proposed a new Cloned Chaotic Parallel Evolution Algorithm (CCPEA) and established a clustering model with low energy. They have defined a clone operator that increases population diversity to find the global optimal solution of High-Density Wireless Sensor Networks (HDWSNs). They have considered each solution as a chromosome, select a particular chromosome with low fitness value, then performed crossover and mutation onto it. Fitness function proposed by them is:

$$Fit(Q) = \sum_{n=1}^{N} \left(Cost_{sent} + Cost_{received} \right)$$

Where Q represents an individual, N is number of sensor nodes and they have proposed:

i) $Cost_{sent}(b,l) = E_{elec}.b + \varepsilon a_{mpb}.ln$
ii) $Cost_{received}(b) = E_{elec}.b$

Here, $Cost_{sent}$ represents the consumed energy when the sensor node sends b bits of data to receiving node and distance between two nodes is l; the electronic energy parameter and the power amplification parameter are represented by E_{elec} and εa_{mp} respectively. According to the communication environment quality, value of n *is* determined. $Cost_{received}$ represents communication energy required for a sensor to receive b *bits* energy.

(Chu-hang et al., 2022) have proposed a GA based annulus-sector Clustering Routing Protocol (GACRP). The circular network in GACRP has been split into sectors that are the same size for every annulus. Calculating the network's minimum energy consumption yields the number of sectors. The best node in each annulus-sector, which forms a cluster, has been chosen to serve as the CH. The optimum routing path for every CH has also been determined using a new fitness function that has taken energy and load balance into consideration, and an adaptive round time has also been computed to retain the clusters together. Han et al. have proposed energy-aware and trust-based adaptive GA called TAGA to defend against regular routing attacks, specific trust attacks and to cut down the energy used for data transmission (Han et al., 2022). To choose the secure CHs, they have constructed the comprehensive trust values on the basis of nodes' direct trust values and indirect trust values. Direct trust values are calculated using adaptive penalty factors and volatilization factors. Filtering procedures are designed to construct indirect trust values. Besides choosing best CHs regarding security and energy usage, their work has found out the safest and most energy efficient path as routing for the CHs.

3.3 Fuzzy Logic System (FLS)

(Alkesh et al., 2011) have proposed a FLS inference mechanism regarding movement strategy for a dynamic BS in a predefined cross path. They have considered the case where the BS moves in a path, which is predefined, based on the closeness of highest priority CH. In order to set a priority for each CH, they have developed a Fuzzy Inference System (FIS) that has considered two parameters: (i) residual energy and (ii) distance from BS. By simulation they have demonstrated that their work has more lifetime than LEACH with stationary BS. The result also shows that network lifetime is maximum in case of dynamic BS without any predefined path, but in reality, it is very difficult for BS to move over the entire field due to obstacles. In future, they have intended to apply type-2 fuzzy system for better network lifetime.

Fuzzy based Master Cluster Head Election Leach protocol (F-MCHEL) (Sharma et al., 2012), a development over Cluster Head Election mechanism utilizing Fuzzy logic (CHEF), has implemented fuzzy rules on the basis of energy and closeness. Based on these, a Master Cluster Head (MCH) i.e. the CH with maximum residual energy has been chosen to gather the data and transfer it to the BS. In this way their work has promoted the network efficiency. The Fuzzy Logic Control based Enhanced SEP (FLC-SEPE), proposed by (Mani et al., 2013), has been used to modify the existing Enhanced Stable Election Protocol (ESEP) based on fuzzy logic control and it has minimized energy consumption required by sensor nodes while optimizing its utilization. The authors in (Jaradat et al., 2013) have proposed an energy-efficient cross-layer routing protocol using FLS that receives input from different layers, such as physical, MAC, and network. To determine the next hop of the relay node toward the sink node, the authors have taken into consideration three factors: link quality, remaining battery capacity, and transmission capabilities of nodes within the local communication range. The implemented routing system uses a self-adaptive framework based on a fuzzy logic algorithm that adjusts in response to changing quantifiable factors. Their approach focuses on the overall network longevity while considering scalability and self-learning. The authors in (Rabelo et al., 2013) estimated the quality of routes in directed diffusion routing protocol using FLS. They have considered three evaluation metrics: message delay to the sink node, time of death, and packet loss rate of the first sensor node. They have used the ACO method to modify the rule base of the FIS. In (Nayak et al., 2015), Nayak et al. have introduced a routing protocol based on fuzzy inference engine that has proved its energy efficiency while prioritizing the selection of the Super Cluster Head (SCH) on the basis of distance, energy, and centrality of CH. (Nayak et al., 2017) have used an interval Type-2 Fuzzy Logic model to increase network lifetime in WSNs. (Zhao et al., 2018) have developed a Balanced Energy Consumption Routing (BECR) to enhance the network's lifetime. The authors have divided the nodes into clusters using fuzzy C means clustering, and the node in the center of each cluster has served as CH. The FLS proposed by them, has chosen the alternate node as the cluster head on a rotational basis when a CH's energy drops down. The authors (Preeth et al., 2018) have used adaptive Fuzzy multi-criteria decision-making strategy to create an Energy Efficient Clustering and Immune-Inspired Routing (FEEC-IIR) protocol. Their goal is to choose the CH based on the QoS parameters (packet delivery ratio, packet loss ratio, jitter, bit error rate (BER), throughput, etc.), node location and power usage. However, they were unable to locate any high residual energy optimal path for multi-hop inter-cluster communication that would lengthen the network's life.

Nowadays, WSNs are used for IoT systems that require an enhanced QoS (Thangaramya et al., 2019) Moreover, the energy needed for communication in IoT-based sensor networks poses a significant challenge to prevent significant packet loss or drop, quick energy depletion, and inequity across the network, which would reduce node performance and lengthen packet delivery time. For this purpose, the authors have proposed a neuro-fuzzy rule based cluster formation and routing protocol that shows better energy usage and network life expectancy than LEACH, Fuzzy Logic Cluster Formation Protocol (FLCFP), and Hybrid Energy-Efficient Distributed clustering (HEED) routing protocol. However, their models assume that all the nodes in the network are trustful which may not be practical in real-world scenario. The authors of (Baradaran et al., 2020) have proposed High-Quality Clustering Algorithm (HQCA) and selected optimal CH based on FLS and various criteria i.e. the maximum and minimum energy in each cluster, the residual energy, and the maximum and minimum distances between the nodes in each cluster and the BS. According to simulation results, their method improves the consumption of energy and lifespan of the network. To perform clustering for mobile sink in homogeneous wireless sensor networks, (Verma et al.,2020) have introduced Fuzzy Logic based Effective Clustering (FLEC). They have not only utilized the concept of average threshold and average energy based probability to select appropriate CHs, but also they have included CHs' average energy in fuzzy descriptors to make proper super CH. As per simulation results, FLEC outperforms over LEACH.

3.4 Artificial Neural Networks (ANNs)

In (Branch et al., 2013), Branch et al. have used k-Nearest Neighbour (k-NN) algorithm, where a missed data of any sensor node is replaced by the average value of observations given by the k number of nearest neighbours to that particular node. However, this has the downside of requiring a significant amount of memory to store and track each reading for all network nodes. Alsheikh et al. have reviewed different ML algorithms used to solve various problems of WSNs from 2002 to 2013 (Alsheikh et al., 2014). They have observed that ML enhances the ability of WSNs to adapt to the dynamic environments. They have also provided a comparative study to help researchers find suitable ML solutions for their specific application challenges. As the energy efficiency of WSNs depends on the route of data communication (Singh et al., 2017), the authors have estimated the optimal data route using different ML techniques, i.e., MLP, RBFN, Bayes Network, Naive Bayes classifier and C4.5 Decision Tree (DT) that receives the inputs from a fuzzy inference system. Their study evaluates that the C4.5 DT is best for estimating the link cost of data routing.

(Fadlullah et al., 2017) have compiled many applications of deep learning in WSN. They have observed that deep learning-based network traffic control algorithms are helpful in data optimization. They have also performed a case study on deep learning-based routing in WSN and demonstrated that deep learning-based routing works better than conventional routing methods. Ali et al. observed that in large-scale networks, when the LEACH routing protocol is used, the quick draining of energy of sensor nodes causes black holes in the network (Ali et al., 2019). These black holes create data redundancy in WSN and affects the routing cost. They have improved the data redundancy in WSN by adding mean and the minimum distance methods in LEACH protocol. Further, they have also proposed a Cyclic Neural Network (CNN) based data fusion algorithm to reduce data redundancy of the sensor nodes. (Mehmood et al., 2020) have presented an ELDC, or energy-efficient and resilient routing method for WSNs, based on ANN. To improve the network's dependability and environmental adaptability, this technique has trained the network using a sizable data set that covers almost all scenarios. Additionally, it has used a group-based technique, where groups may be of different sizes, to enhance the lifetime of the entire network. They have applied back propagation learning algorithm to enable a smart, efficient, and robust group organization by providing efficient threshold values for choosing a group's chief node as well as a CH. Due of this, the proposed solution by authors has proven energy-efficient and has the ability to increase the lifespan of sensor nodes.

Self-Organizing Maps (SOM) is one kind of ANN that has been created utilising unsupervised learning to decrease the dimensionality of data. Patra et al. (Patra et al., 2011), have built efficient topologies using a SOM. These efficient topologies have reduced the energy consumption efficiently while routing in WSNs. An unsupervised neural network for routing in WSNs named by Adaptive Resonance Theory (ART1) has been presented in (Mittal et al., 2014). Their study has extended the lifespan of the network by using a number of techniques, such as a least CH distance, a CH rotation system, CH election on the basis of ART1, and load balance cost functions.

In (Jafarizadeh et al.,2017, Kazemeyni et al.,2014, Liu et al.,2014), a few Naive Bayes (NB) routing strategies for WSNs have been described. Kazemeyni et al. in (Kazemeyni et al., 2014) have employed a Bayesian learning technique to select the best routing path by utilizing a previous knowledge of the nodes' motion patterns. They have developed a formal model of the learning-based routing protocol that has worked with both centralised and decentralised infrastructures and they have shown experimentally that the approach for decentralised infrastructures is twice as energy-efficient as the centralised infrastructures. Authors of (Liu et al., 2014) have described a new adaptive method, which has combined routing and data collection. This method has been built on a Bayesian compressed sensing framework, which has improved energy efficiency. (Jafarizadeh et al., 2017) have proposed Efficient Cluster Head Selection using Naïve Bayes classifier (ECHSNB), which has extended the network's lifespan by determining the CH node optimally.

3.5 Swarm Intelligence (SI)

In order to find the best inter-cluster routing path for the improvement of network lifespan, (Chen et al., 2010) used PSO. They have created an EER algorithm based on clusters that consider both energy efficiency and energy balance to increase network longevity. Clusters are generated by utilizing a local competition mechanism, and each cluster's energy consumption is balanced in each round. (Li et al., 2013) proposed an Adaptive Energy Efficient Clustering Routing Protocol (AECRP) for WSN using a particle swarm clustering algorithm and inter-cluster routing algorithm that takes energy conservation, load balancing, and dependable transmission into account. The research work in (Kuila et al., 2014) has given formulations of the issues regarding prolonging lifetime of WSNs using Linear/Nonlinear Programming (LP/NLP). They have followed two proposed techniques on the basis of PSO. To show superiority of the algorithm implemented in terms of usage of energy, rigorous testing and comparison with the existing algorithms have been conducted. The work proposed in (Arora et al., 2017) has used the concept of a neural network in the selection process of CHs and Hybrid ACO/PSO approach to find the shortest route. According to results, the proposed technique has helped to improve energy efficiency and optimised the network lifetime. SI has been used in (Gavali et al., 2022) to offer a unique routing technique for data transmission that is both energy and QoS-efficient between the underwater sensor node and the surface sink and called it Energy Optimization using the Routing Optimization (EORO) protocol. For Underwater WSN (UWSN) data delivery, they have designed Effective Fitness Function-based PSO (EFF-PSO) to choose the best forwarder node. To reduce energy consumption of each forwarder node, EFF-PSO has used four parameters for fitness computation; those parameters are residual energy, packet transmission ability, node connectivity, and distance.

(Gui et al., 2017) performed a survey on various SI-based routing protocols in WSNs. They have also presented the properties of fission-fusion social structure-based Spider Monkey Optimization (SMO) and Termite Colony Optimization (TCO)-based clustering in WSN for future directions. ACO has been used in the research work in (Sun et al., 2017) for routing the data packet while taking into consideration a number of component, such as the transmission distance for node communication, direction for transmission, and residual energy. This method identified the most energy-efficient route between the source node and the destination.

(Lavanya et al., 2021) have developed a novel Energy-Efficient Heterogeneous Fault Management (E²HFM) strategy by utilizing three appropriate diagnosis algorithms to handle hardware, software, and time-based faults in IoT based WSN (IWSN). After these heterogeneous faults have been classified by a new Tuned Support Vector Machine (TSVM) classifier, the tuning parameters have been optimized through Hierarchy based Grasshopper Optimization Algorithm (HGOA). Due to this approach, the energy consumption has uniformly been distributed over all of the sensor nodes, which has provided energy-efficiency. The shortcoming of their work is that mobility approach in IWSN and recovery mechanism have not been addressed by their work. (Yadav et al., 2021) have proposed an algorithm named as Particle Distance Updated Sea Lion Optimization (PDU-SLnO) algorithm, which combines the concept of Sea Lion Optimization (SLnO) and PSO algorithm, selects CH considering energy, QoS, delay and distance, and improves the network lifespan by reducing energy consumption. To utilize the energy with efficiency, (Prithi et al., 2021) has proposed an approach named as Learning Dynamic Deterministic Finite Automata-hybrid PSO–Grey Wolf Optimizer (LD²FA-Hybrid PSO–GWO). Here LD²FA finds out the available route and Hybrid PSO–GWO finds the optimal route among the available routes. Artificial Bee Colony (ABC) has been proposed in (Thekiya et al.,2022), where the authors have chosen CH based on various clustering factors which includes CH energy balancing, CH load balancing, energy GINI coefficient, and intra and inter-cluster distance. Then utilizing ACO, they have routed data from CH to BS and thus, their work has optimized cluster selection, which has improved the network lifespan. In order to incorporate the problems regarding obtaining a route with minimum energy consumption, Christopher et al. have proposed a Three Way Point Rule based Fusion of Earthworm and Deer Hunt Optimization Routing (TREDHO) in (Christopher et al., 2022). The model proposed by them has included two stages: the setup stage and the communication stage. The setup stage consists of two phases: the phase for network structure and the node movement phase. They have divided network structure into small triangles in the first phase. Then on the next phase they have established route connection on the basis of movement of nodes and some random parameters. In the communication stage, they have applied three waypoint rules in the combination of EarthWorm and Deer Hunt optimization (EW-DHO) algorithm and chosen the optimal route for packet transmission. Their work has been proven more effective than all the modern methods with regard to the aspects including latency, maximization of throughput, packet delivery ratio (PDR), quality of connection, minimization of energy usage, and lifespan of the WSNs. To find out optimal path in WSN, (Seyyedabbasi et al., 2023) have proposed two new energy-efficient routing methods based on Incremental Grey Wolf Optimization (I-GWO) and Expanded Grey Wolf Optimization (Ex-GWO) algorithms. To increase lifespan and minimize traffic, the proposed methods have considered residual energy, traffic, buffer size, distance, and hop size and defined a fitness function and has determined the next hop. They have established a network system by implementing their proposed method in simulation environment and outperformed the other methods i.e. GA Based Routing (GAR), ABC Based routing (ABCbased), Multi-Agent Protocol based on ACO (MAP-ACO), and WSN based on Grey Wolf Optimizer (GWO-WSN) algorithms by choosing most suitable WSN with better lifetime. In order to calculate the cost between two sensor nodes (suppose i and j), the fitness function or *Cost*$_{i,j}$ designed by them is:

$$\mathrm{Cos}\,t_{i,j} = \left(c_1 d_{i,j}\right) + \left(c_2 H_j\right) + \left(c_2\,\frac{ValidTraffic}{T_{i,j}}\right) + \left(c_3\,\frac{E_{initial}}{E_j}\,\frac{BufferCapacity}{B_j}\right)$$

Where, the terms are defined in (Seyyedabbasi et al., 2023).

3.6 Reinforcement Learning (RL)

(Dong et al., 2007) have proposed a geographic routing strategy based on RL for Ultra-Wide Band (UWB) sensor networks. In order to take node energy and network lifespan into account and boost network robustness and longevity, they presented a comprehensive reward function. This function has considered routing failure, delay, energy of the nodes and lifespan of the network. This reward function has looked into these four scenarios regarding routing: (1) next hop is not the sink, (2) next hop is the sink, (3) next hop is not found, and (4) next hop is found but it has low energy. Their RL algorithm has performed better than Greedy Perimeter Stateless Routing (GPSR) in terms of number of packets sent, delivery ratio, average delay and network lifetime. A tailored Q-Learning method for energy-efficient routing has been built in (Sharma et al., 2012). However, their method produces the same simulation result as Q-learning method in Network Simulator version 2. Sharawi et al. surveyed different soft computing methods for EER in WSN (Sharawi et al.,2013). They have found that RL is best among other soft computing based routing protocols due to its less memory usage, less power consumption, high flexibility, and robustness.

3.7 Ensemble Learning (EL)

There are several applications of EL approach for EER in WSN. In order to optimize LEACH protocol, (Xie et al., 2019) have proposed an improved EL, which has performed coupling on the basis of Cuckoo Search algorithm (CS), Glowworm Swarm Optimization (GSO), and Bacterial Foraging Optimization (BFO). This proposed work (CS-GSO-BFO-LEACH) finds out the best sensor node in the cluster with the help of this EL. As a result, energy consumption is reduced greatly and the network life cycle is prolonged. For effective routing in WSN, (Sridhar et al, 2022) have proposed Softmax-Regressed-Tanimoto-Reweight-Boost-Classification (SRTRBC) based EL technique. This technique has two steps: route path construction and congestion-aware Multiple-Input Multiple-Output (MIMO) routing. In the first step, softmax regression is used to determine energy efficiency of the sensor node by analyzing residual energy level. In the second step, the proposed technique selects the optimal route based bandwidth capability and buffer space using Tanimoto Reweight Boost Classification.

Table 1. Comparison study mentioning algorithm used, benefits, features, drawback

Name	algorithm used	benefits	features	drawbacks
LEACH	Clustering	Energy-saving, ease of configuration	• Uses localized coordination • Incorporates data fusion	• Random and uneven distribution of CHs.
IEECP	Clustering	Better clustering structure, energy efficiency	• Forms mathematical model for determining optimal number of clusters • Uses modified fuzzy C-means algorithm • Balances communication distance among the CHs	• Not concerned about random initial selection of CH
OMPFM (Al-Shalabi et al., 2019)	EA	Energy efficiency	• Selects the efficient CH based on energy level • Finds out the optimal multi-hop path from CH to BS	• Time consuming
CRCGA (Wang et al., 2020).	EA	Simultaneously finds the optimal route and the best CH	• Combines three functions—clustered node maintenance, route determination, and cluster maintenance	• Not presented for dynamic WSNs
CHEF (Kim et al., 2008)	FLS	Reduces the clustering overhead and energy usage	• Selects CH based on node's remaining energy and sum of distances from other nodes in cluster. • CH collects and aggregates data from other nodes in cluster and then transmits to BS	• Approach is not done in heterogeneous sensor nodes
FLEC	FLS	Energy efficiency, better throughput	• CHs selection is based on average threshold and average energy, • SCH selection approach using fuzzy inference rule	• Not performed on heterogeneous WSN
EBC-S (Enami et al., 2010)	ANN	Prolonged network lifespan,	• Forms cluster of nodes based on level of energy and node coordinates • CH collects data from member node in the cluster and aggregates it and then send to the BS	• Not considered multi-hoping routing protocols • Not considered parameters except level of energy and sensor node coordinates for clustering
ECHSNB	ANN	Improved lifetime, flexible in choosing CH in WSN	• NB technique is used • Considers two parameters: (i) sum of Euclidean distances between member nodes and CH, (ii) node's residual energy	• Not performed on dynamic sensor nodes
CL-IoT (Mahajan et al., 2021)	SI	Energy-efficient, less communication overhead	• Divides WSNs by using a cross-layer-based clustering among network, physical and MAC layer • Uses ACO with a unique function for probabilistic decision rule as a fitness function	• Not considered the scenarios like simulation time, farm size, data rate and security
IGWO+ExGWO	SI	Very less energy consumption, optimal path between any two nodes	• Defines a fitness function considering residual energy, traffic, buffer size, distance, and hop size, • Implemented IGWO and Ex-GWO	• Not performed on heterogeneous sensor nodes
FROMS (Förster et al., 2008)	RL	Improved energy efficiency,better delivery rate in different network scenarios	• Implemented multicast routing protocol based on reinforcement learning	• Not considered mobile sink
CS-GSO-BFO-LEACH	EL	Even distribution of CH in cluster, enhanced network lifetime	• Performs coupling on the basis CS, GSO, and BFO	• Hard to learn

4 CONCLUSION

This chapter has described numerous algorithms used to make safe, energy-efficient routing algorithms for WSNs utilizing ML, one of the newest technologies available today. It has been shown that by enhancing the network's intelligence and effectiveness, ML techniques can improve the overall performance of WSNs. This chapter will fulfill the need to understand the recent technologies related to WSN, which will eventually offer future directions to the new researchers of this domain.

From literature, it has been observed that EA, FLS and SI based algorithms perform better regarding EER compared to other algorithms. Moreover, algorithms designed by combining more than one swarm intelligences as well as swarm intelligences based on fuzzy logic and fuzzy logic based evolutionary algorithm are better than approaches taken by only fuzzy logic or swarm intelligences or evolutionary algorithms. In future direction, we suggest to use multiple ML algorithm in combination to achieve the best performance with respect to EER in WSNs.

REFERENCES

Akkaya, K., & Younis, M. (2005). A survey on routing protocols for wireless sensor networks. *Ad Hoc Networks*, *3*(3), 325–349. doi:10.1016/j.adhoc.2003.09.010

Al-Kaseem, B. R., Taha, Z. K., Abdulmajeed, S. W., & Al-Raweshidy, H. S. (2021). Optimized energy–efficient path planning strategy in WSN with multiple Mobile sinks. *IEEE Access: Practical Innovations, Open Solutions*, *9*, 82833–82847. doi:10.1109/ACCESS.2021.3087086

Al-Shalabi, M., Anbar, M., Wan, T. C., & Alqattan, Z. (2019). Energy efficient multi-hop path in wireless sensor networks using an enhanced genetic algorithm. *Information Sciences*, *500*, 259–273. doi:10.1016/j.ins.2019.05.094

Ali, B., Mahmood, T., Abbas, M., Hussain, M., Ullah, H., Sarker, A., & Khan, A. (2019). LEACH robust routing approach applying machine learning. *IJCSNS*, *19*(6), 18–26.

Alkesh, A., Singh, A. K., & Purohit, N. (2011, June). A moving base station strategy using fuzzy logic for lifetime enhancement in wireless sensor network. In *2011 International Conference on Communication Systems and Network Technologies* (pp. 198-202). IEEE. 10.1109/CSNT.2011.49

Alsheikh, M. A., Lin, S., Niyato, D., & Tan, H. P. (2014). Machine learning in wireless sensor networks: Algorithms, strategies, and applications. *IEEE Communications Surveys and Tutorials*, *16*(4), 1996–2018. doi:10.1109/COMST.2014.2320099

Arora, P. (2017, July). Enhanced NN based RZ leach using hybrid ACO/PSO based routing for WSNs. In *2017 8th International Conference on Computing, Communication and Networking Technologies (ICCCNT)* (pp. 1-7). IEEE.

Banimelhem, O., Mowafi, M., Taqieddin, E., Awad, F., & Al Rawabdeh, M. (2014, August). An efficient clustering approach using genetic algorithm and node mobility in wireless sensor networks. In *2014 11th international symposium on wireless communications systems (ISWCS)* (pp. 858-862). IEEE. 10.1109/ISWCS.2014.6933473

Baradaran, A. A., & Navi, K. (2020). HQCA-WSN: High-quality clustering algorithm and optimal cluster head selection using fuzzy logic in wireless sensor networks. *Fuzzy Sets and Systems*, *389*, 114–144. doi:10.1016/j.fss.2019.11.015

Bari, A., Wazed, S., Jaekel, A., & Bandyopadhyay, S. (2009). A genetic algorithm based approach for energy efficient routing in two-tiered sensor networks. *Ad Hoc Networks*, *7*(4), 665–676. doi:10.1016/j.adhoc.2008.04.003

Bhanderi, M., & Shah, H. (2014). Machine learning for wireless sensor network: A review, challenges and applications. *Adv. Electron. Electr. Eng*, *4*, 475–486.

Branch, J. W., Giannella, C., Szymanski, B., Wolff, R., & Kargupta, H. (2013). In-network outlier detection in wireless sensor networks. *Knowledge and Information Systems*, *34*(1), 23–54. doi:10.100710115-011-0474-5

Chen, Y. P., & Chen, Y. Z. (2010, July). A novel energy efficient routing algorithm for wireless sensor networks. In *2010 International Conference on Machine Learning and Cybernetics* (Vol. 2, pp. 1031-1036). IEEE. 10.1109/ICMLC.2010.5580625

Christopher, V. B., Sajan, R. I., Akhila, T. S., & Kavitha, M. J. (2022). A QoS Aware Three Way Point Rule based Fusion of Earth Worm and Deer Hunt Optimization Routing in Wireless Sensor Network. *Wireless Personal Communications*, 1–23.

Chu-hang, W., Xiao-li, L., You-jia, H., Huang-shui, H., & Sha-sha, W. (2022). An Improved Genetic Algorithm Based Annulus-Sector Clustering Routing Protocol for Wireless Sensor Networks. *Wireless Personal Communications*, *123*(4), 3623–3644. doi:10.100711277-021-09306-1

Dong, S., Agrawal, P., & Sivalingam, K. (2007, November). Reinforcement learning based geographic routing protocol for UWB wireless sensor network. In *IEEE GLOBECOM 2007-IEEE Global Telecommunications Conference* (pp. 652-656). IEEE. 10.1109/GLOCOM.2007.127

El Mezouary, R., Choukri, A., Kobbane, A., & El Koutbi, M. (2015, September). An energy-aware clustering approach based on the K-means method for wireless sensor networks. In *International Symposium on Ubiquitous Networking* (pp. 325-337). Springer.

Enami, N., & Moghadam, R. A. (2010). Energy based clustering self organizing map protocol for extending wireless sensor networks lifetime and coverage. *Canadian Journal on Multimedia and Wireless Networks*, *1*(4), 42–54.

Fadlullah, Z. M., Tang, F., Mao, B., Kato, N., Akashi, O., Inoue, T., & Mizutani, K. (2017). State-of-the-art deep learning: Evolving machine intelligence toward tomorrow's intelligent network traffic control systems. *IEEE Communications Surveys and Tutorials*, *19*(4), 2432–2455. doi:10.1109/COMST.2017.2707140

Förster, A., Murphy, A. L., Schiller, J., & Terfloth, K. (2008, October). An efficient implementation of reinforcement learning based routing on real WSN hardware. In *2008 IEEE International Conference on Wireless and Mobile Computing, Networking and Communications* (pp. 247-252). IEEE. 10.1109/WiMob.2008.99

Gavali, A. B., Kadam, M. V., & Patil, S. (2022). Energy optimization using swarm intelligence for IoT-Authorized underwater wireless sensor networks. *Microprocessors and Microsystems*, *93*, 104597. doi:10.1016/j.micpro.2022.104597

Ghosh, A., Ho, C. C., & Bestak, R. (2020). Secured energy-efficient routing in wireless sensor networks using machine learning algorithm: Fundamentals and applications. *Deep Learning Strategies for Security Enhancement in Wireless Sensor Networks*, 23-41.

Gui, T., Ma, C., Wang, F., & Wilkins, D. E. (2016, March). Survey on swarm intelligence based routing protocols for wireless sensor networks: An extensive study. In *2016 IEEE international conference on industrial technology (ICIT)* (pp. 1944-1949). IEEE.

Han, Y., Hu, H., & Guo, Y. (2022). Energy-Aware and Trust-Based Secure Routing Protocol for Wireless Sensor Networks Using Adaptive Genetic Algorithm. *IEEE Access: Practical Innovations, Open Solutions*, *10*, 11538–11550. doi:10.1109/ACCESS.2022.3144015

Hassan, A. A. H., Shah, W. M., Habeb, A. H. H., Othman, M. F. I., & Al-Mhiqani, M. N. (2020). An improved energy-efficient clustering protocol to prolong the lifetime of the WSN-based IoT. *IEEE Access: Practical Innovations, Open Solutions*, *8*, 200500–200517. doi:10.1109/ACCESS.2020.3035624

Heinzelman, W. R., Chandrakasan, A., & Balakrishnan, H. (2000, January). Energy-efficient communication protocol for wireless microsensor networks. In *Proceedings of the 33rd annual Hawaii international conference on system sciences* (pp. 10-pp). IEEE. 10.1109/HICSS.2000.926982

Jafarizadeh, V., Keshavarzi, A., & Derikvand, T. (2017). Efficient cluster head selection using Naïve Bayes classifier for wireless sensor networks. *Wireless Networks*, *23*(3), 779–785. doi:10.100711276-015-1169-8

Jain, B., Brar, G., & Malhotra, J. (2018). EKMT-k-means clustering algorithmic solution for low energy consumption for wireless sensor networks based on minimum mean distance from base station. In *Networking communication and data knowledge engineering* (pp. 113–123). Springer. doi:10.1007/978-981-10-4585-1_10

Jaradat, T., Benhaddou, D., Balakrishnan, M., & Al-Fuqaha, A. (2013, July). Energy efficient cross-layer routing protocol in wireless sensor networks based on fuzzy logic. In *2013 9th International Wireless Communications and Mobile Computing Conference (IWCMC)* (pp. 177-182). IEEE. 10.1109/IWCMC.2013.6583555

Kazemeyni, F., Owe, O., Johnsen, E. B., & Balasingham, I. (2014). Formal Modeling and analysis of learning-based routing in mobile wireless sensor networks. In *Integration of Reusable Systems* (pp. 127–150). Springer. doi:10.1007/978-3-319-04717-1_6

Kim, J. M., Park, S. H., Han, Y. J., & Chung, T. M. (2008, February). CHEF: cluster head election mechanism using fuzzy logic in wireless sensor networks. In *2008 10th international conference on advanced communication technology* (Vol. 1, pp. 654-659). IEEE. 10.1109/ICACT.2008.4493846

Kuila, P., & Jana, P. K. (2014). Energy efficient clustering and routing algorithms for wireless sensor networks: Particle swarm optimization approach. *Engineering Applications of Artificial Intelligence*, *33*, 127–140. doi:10.1016/j.engappai.2014.04.009

Kulkarni, R. V., Forster, A., & Venayagamoorthy, G. K. (2010). Computational intelligence in wireless sensor networks: A survey. *IEEE Communications Surveys and Tutorials*, *13*(1), 68–96. doi:10.1109/SURV.2011.040310.00002

Kumar, D. P., Amgoth, T., & Annavarapu, C. S. R. (2019). Machine learning algorithms for wireless sensor networks: A survey. *Information Fusion*, *49*, 1–25. doi:10.1016/j.inffus.2018.09.013

Lavanya, S., Prasanth, A., Jayachitra, S., & Shenbagarajan, A. (2021). A Tuned classification approach for efficient heterogeneous fault diagnosis in IoT-enabled WSN applications. *Measurement*, *183*, 109771. doi:10.1016/j.measurement.2021.109771

Li, T., Ruan, F., Fan, Z., Wang, J., & Kim, J. U. (2015, October). An improved PEGASIS protocol for wireless sensor network. In *2015 3rd international conference on computer and computing science (COMCOMS)* (pp. 16-19). IEEE. 10.1109/COMCOMS.2015.20

Li, X., Gang, W., Zongqi, L., & Yanyan, Z. (2013, May). An energy-efficient routing protocol based on particle swarm clustering algorithm and inter-cluster routing algorithm for WSN. In *2013 25th Chinese control and decision conference (CCDC)* (pp. 4029-4033). IEEE. 10.1109/CCDC.2013.6561655

Liu, Z., Zhang, M., & Cui, J. (2014). An adaptive data collection algorithm based on a Bayesian compressed sensing framework. *Sensors (Basel)*, *14*(5), 8330–8349. doi:10.3390140508330 PMID:24818659

Mahajan, H. B., Badarla, A., & Junnarkar, A. A. (2021). CL-IoT: Cross-layer Internet of Things protocol for intelligent manufacturing of smart farming. *Journal of Ambient Intelligence and Humanized Computing*, *12*(7), 7777–7791. doi:10.100712652-020-02502-0

Mani, M., & Sharma, A. K. (2013, August). Modified approach for routing and clustering in sensor network using fuzzy logic control. In *2013 Sixth International Conference on Contemporary Computing (IC3)* (pp. 102-107). IEEE. 10.1109/IC3.2013.6612170

Mehmood, A., Lv, Z., Lloret, J., & Umar, M. M. (2020). ELDC: An artificial neural network based energy-efficient and robust routing scheme for pollution monitoring in WSNs. *IEEE Transactions on Emerging Topics in Computing*, *8*(1), 106–114. doi:10.1109/TETC.2017.2671847

Mittal, M., & Kumar, K. (2014, November). Network lifetime enhancement of homogeneous sensor network using ART1 neural network. In *2014 International Conference on Computational Intelligence and Communication Networks* (pp. 472-475). IEEE. 10.1109/CICN.2014.110

Nandan, A. S., Singh, S., Kumar, R., & Kumar, N. (2021, August). An optimized genetic algorithm for cluster head election based on movable sinks and adjustable sensing ranges in IoT-based HWSNs. *IEEE Internet of Things Journal*, *9*(7), 5027–5039. doi:10.1109/JIOT.2021.3107295

Nayak, P., & Devulapalli, A. (2015). A fuzzy logic-based clustering algorithm for WSN to extend the network lifetime. *IEEE Sensors Journal*, *16*(1), 137–144. doi:10.1109/JSEN.2015.2472970

Nayak, P., & Vathasavai, B. (2017). Energy efficient clustering algorithm for multi-hop wireless sensor network using type-2 fuzzy logic. *IEEE Sensors Journal*, *17*(14), 4492–4499. doi:10.1109/JSEN.2017.2711432

Patra, C., Chattopadhyay, M., Bhaumik, P., & Roy, A. G. (2011, February). Using self organizing map in wireless sensor network for designing energy efficient topologies. In *2011 2nd International Conference on Wireless Communication, Vehicular Technology, Information Theory and Aerospace & Electronic Systems Technology (Wireless VITAE)* (pp. 1-6). IEEE. 10.1109/WIRELESSVITAE.2011.5940819

Pinto, A. R., Montez, C., Araújo, G., Vasques, F., & Portugal, P. (2014). An approach to implement data fusion techniques in wireless sensor networks using genetic machine learning algorithms. *Information Fusion*, *15*, 90–101. doi:10.1016/j.inffus.2013.05.003

Preeth, S. K., Dhanalakshmi, R., Kumar, R., & Shakeel, P. M. (2018). An adaptive fuzzy rule based energy efficient clustering and immune-inspired routing protocol for WSN-assisted IoT system. *Journal of Ambient Intelligence and Humanized Computing*, 1–13. doi:10.100712652-018-1154-z

Rabelo, R. A., Sobral, J. V., Araujo, H. S., Baluz, R. A., & Holanda Filho, R. (2013, June). An approach based on fuzzy inference system and ant colony optimization for improving the performance of routing protocols in Wireless Sensor Networks. In *2013 IEEE Congress on Evolutionary Computation* (pp. 3244-3251). IEEE. 10.1109/CEC.2013.6557967

Rawat, P., & Chauhan, S. (2022). Particle swarm optimization based sleep scheduling and clustering protocol in wireless sensor network. *Peer-to-Peer Networking and Applications*, *15*(3), 1417–1436. doi:10.100712083-022-01307-6

Ray, A., & De, D. (2016). Energy efficient clustering protocol based on K-means (EECPK-means)-midpoint algorithm for enhanced network lifetime in wireless sensor network. *IET Wireless Sensor Systems*, *6*(6), 181–191. doi:10.1049/iet-wss.2015.0087

Saleh, N., Kassem, A., & Haidar, A. M. (2018). Energy-efficient architecture for wireless sensor networks in healthcare applications. *IEEE Access: Practical Innovations, Open Solutions*, *6*, 6478–6486. doi:10.1109/ACCESS.2018.2789918

Saxena, N., Roy, A., & Shin, J. (2009). QuESt: A QoS-based energy efficient sensor routing protocol. *Wireless Communications and Mobile Computing*, *9*(3), 417–426. doi:10.1002/wcm.546

Seyyedabbasi, A., Kiani, F., Allahviranloo, T., Fernandez-Gamiz, U., & Noeiaghdam, S. (2023). Optimal data transmission and pathfinding for WSN and decentralized IoT systems using I-GWO and Ex-GWO algorithms. *Alexandria Engineering Journal*, *63*, 339–357. doi:10.1016/j.aej.2022.08.009

Sharawi, M., Saroit, I. A., El-Mahdy, H., & Emary, E. (2013). Routing wireless sensor networks based on soft computing paradigms: Survey. *International Journal on Soft Computing Artificial Intelligence and Applications (Commerce, Calif.)*, *2*(4), 21–36. doi:10.5121/ijscai.2013.2403

Sharma, T., & Kumar, B. (2012). F-MCHEL: Fuzzy based master cluster head election leach protocol in wireless sensor network. *International Journal of Computer Science and Telecommunications*, *3*(10), 8–13.

Sharma, V. K., Shukla, S. S. P., & Singh, V. (2012, December). A tailored Q-Learning for routing in wireless sensor networks. In *2012 2nd IEEE International Conference on Parallel, Distributed and Grid Computing* (pp. 663-668). IEEE.

Sohraby, K., Minoli, D., & Znati, T. (2007). *Wireless sensor networks: technology, protocols, and applications*. John Wiley & Sons. doi:10.1002/047011276X

Sridhar, V., & Rao, R. (2022). A machine learning-based intelligence approach for multiple-input/multiple-output routing in wireless sensor networks. *Mathematical Problems in Engineering*, *2022*, 1–13. doi:10.1155/2022/6391678

Sun, Y., Dong, W., & Chen, Y. (2017). An improved routing algorithm based on ant colony optimization in wireless sensor networks. *IEEE Communications Letters*, *21*(6), 1317–1320. doi:10.1109/LCOMM.2017.2672959

Tashtarian, F., Haghighat, A. T., Honary, M. T., & Shokrzadeh, H. (2007, September). A new energy-efficient clustering algorithm for wireless sensor networks. In *2007 15th International Conference on Software, Telecommunications and Computer Networks* (pp. 1-6). IEEE.

Thangaramya, K., Kulothungan, K., Logambigai, R., Selvi, M., Ganapathy, S., & Kannan, A. (2019). Energy aware cluster and neuro-fuzzy based routing algorithm for wireless sensor networks in IoT. *Computer Networks*, *151*, 211–223. doi:10.1016/j.comnet.2019.01.024

Thekiya, M. S., & Nikose, M. D. (2022). Energy efficient clustering routing protocol using novel admission allotment scheme (AAS) based intra-cluster communication for Wireless Sensor Network. *International Journal of Information Technology*, 1-10.

Venkataramana, S., Sekhar, B. V. D. S., Deshai, N., Chakravarthy, V. V. S. S. S., & Rao, S. K. (2019, May). Efficient time reducing and energy saving routing algorithm for wireless sensor network. *Journal of Physics: Conference Series*, *1228*(1), 012002. doi:10.1088/1742-6596/1228/1/012002

Verma, A., Kumar, S., Gautam, P. R., Rashid, T., & Kumar, A. (2020). Fuzzy logic based effective clustering of homogeneous wireless sensor networks for mobile sink. *IEEE Sensors Journal*, *20*(10), 5615–5623. doi:10.1109/JSEN.2020.2969697

Vimalapriya, M. D., Vignesh, B. S., & Sandhya, S. (2019). *Energy-Centric Route Planning using Machine Learning Algorithm for Data Intensive Secure Multi-Sink Sensor Networks*. International Journal of Innovative Technology and Exploring Engineering.

Wang, C., Liu, X., Hu, H., Han, Y., & Yao, M. (2020). Energy-efficient and load-balanced clustering routing protocol for wireless sensor networks using a chaotic genetic algorithm. *IEEE Access: Practical Innovations, Open Solutions*, *8*, 158082–158096. doi:10.1109/ACCESS.2020.3020158

Xie, P., Lv, M., & Zhao, J. (2020). An improved energy-low clustering hierarchy protocol based on ensemble algorithm. *Concurrency and Computation*, *32*(7), e5575. doi:10.1002/cpe.5575

Xue, F., Sanderson, A., & Graves, R. (2006, April). Multi-objective routing in wireless sensor networks with a differential evolution algorithm. In *2006 IEEE International Conference on Networking, Sensing and Control* (pp. 880-885). IEEE.

Yadav, R. K., & Mahapatra, R. P. (2022). Hybrid metaheuristic algorithm for optimal cluster head selection in wireless sensor network. *Pervasive and Mobile Computing*, *79*, 101504. doi:10.1016/j.pmcj.2021.101504

Yan, R., Sun, H., & Qian, Y. (2013). Energy-aware sensor node design with its application in wireless sensor networks. *IEEE Transactions on Instrumentation and Measurement, 62*(5), 1183–1191. doi:10.1109/TIM.2013.2245181

Yang, R., Xu, M., & Zhou, J. (2021). Clone Chaotic Parallel Evolutionary Algorithm for Low-Energy Clustering in High-Density Wireless Sensor Networks. *Scientific Programming, 2021*, 1–13. doi:10.1155/2021/6630322

Yick, J., Mukherjee, B., & Ghosal, D. (2008). Wireless sensor network survey. *Computer Networks, 52*(12), 2292–2330. doi:10.1016/j.comnet.2008.04.002

Zhao, X., Wei, Z., Cong, Y., & Yin, B. (2018, December). A balances energy consumption clustering routing protocol for a wireless sensor network. In *2018 IEEE 4th Information Technology and Mechatronics Engineering Conference (ITOEC)* (pp. 521-527). IEEE. 10.1109/ITOEC.2018.8740385

Zhong, J., Huang, Z., Feng, L., Du, W., & Li, Y. (2019). A hyper-heuristic framework for lifetime maximization in wireless sensor networks with a mobile sink. *IEEE/CAA Journal of Automatica Sinica, 7*(1), 223-236.

Zhou, R., Chen, M., Feng, G., Liu, H., & He, S. (2010, August). Genetic clustering route algorithm in WSN. In *2010 Sixth International Conference on Natural Computation* (Vol. 8, pp. 4023-4026). IEEE. 10.1109/ICNC.2010.5584826

Compilation of References

Ahmed, J. A., & Wesam, M. A. (2012). Image Retrieval Based on Content Using Color Feature. *International Scholarly Research Notices*, *2012*, 1–11.

Ahtesham, M., Bawany, N. J., & Fatima, K. (2020). House Price Prediction using Machine Learning Algorithm - The Case of Karachi City, Pakistan. *21st International Arab Conference on Information Technology (ACIT)*, 1-5. 10.1109/IDAP.2018.8620781

Akhshani, A., Akhavan, A., Mobaraki, A., Lim, S. C., & Hassan, Z. (2014). Pseudorandom random number generator based on quantum chaotic 242 map. *Communications in Nonlinear Science and Numerical Simulation*, *19*, 101–111.

Akkaya, K., & Younis, M. (2005). A survey on routing protocols for wireless sensor networks. *Ad Hoc Networks*, *3*(3), 325–349. doi:10.1016/j.adhoc.2003.09.010

Albayati, H., Kim, S. K., & Rho, J. J. (2020). Accepting financial transactions using blockchain technology and cryptocurrency: A customer perspective approach. *Technology in Society*, *62*, 101320. doi:10.1016/j.techsoc.2020.101320

Alexakis, E. B., & Armenakis, C. (2020). Evaluation of unet and unet++ architectures in high resolution image change detection applications. *ISPRS – International Archives of the Photogrammetry, Remote Sensing and Spatial Information Sciences*. . doi:10.5194/isprs-archives-XLIII-B3-2020-1507-2020

Alghamdi, Y., Munir, A., & Ahmad, J. (2022). A Lightweight Image Encryption Algorithm Based on Chaotic Map and Random Substitution. *Entropy*, *24*, 1344.

Ali, B., Mahmood, T., Abbas, M., Hussain, M., Ullah, H., Sarker, A., & Khan, A. (2019). LEACH robust routing approach applying machine learning. *IJCSNS*, *19*(6), 18–26.

Alistar, M., Pop, P., & Madsen, J. (2016, May). Synthesis of Application-Specific Fault-Tolerant Digital Microfluidic Biochip Architectures. *IEEE Transactions on Computer-Aided Design of Integrated Circuits and Systems*, *35*(5), 764–777. doi:10.1109/TCAD.2016.2528498

Al-Jaroodi, J., & Mohamed, N. (2019). Blockchain in industries: A survey. *IEEE Access: Practical Innovations, Open Solutions*, *7*, 36500–36515. doi:10.1109/ACCESS.2019.2903554

Al-Kaseem, B. R., Taha, Z. K., Abdulmajeed, S. W., & Al-Raweshidy, H. S. (2021). Optimized energy–efficient path planning strategy in WSN with multiple Mobile sinks. *IEEE Access: Practical Innovations, Open Solutions*, *9*, 82833–82847. doi:10.1109/ACCESS.2021.3087086

Alkesh, A., Singh, A. K., & Purohit, N. (2011, June). A moving base station strategy using fuzzy logic for lifetime enhancement in wireless sensor network. In *2011 International Conference on Communication Systems and Network Technologies* (pp. 198-202). IEEE. 10.1109/CSNT.2011.49

Al-Shalabi, M., Anbar, M., Wan, T. C., & Alqattan, Z. (2019). Energy efficient multi-hop path in wireless sensor networks using an enhanced genetic algorithm. *Information Sciences*, *500*, 259–273. doi:10.1016/j.ins.2019.05.094

Alsheikh, M. A., Lin, S., Niyato, D., & Tan, H. P. (2014). Machine learning in wireless sensor networks: Algorithms, strategies, and applications. *IEEE Communications Surveys and Tutorials*, *16*(4), 1996–2018. doi:10.1109/COMST.2014.2320099

Altaheri, H., Alsulaiman, M., & Muhammad, G. (2019). Date fruit classification for robotic harvesting in a natural environment using deep learning. *IEEE Access: Practical Innovations, Open Solutions*, *7*, 117115–117133. doi:10.1109/ACCESS.2019.2936536

Alvarez, G., & Li, S. (2006). Some basic cryptographic requirements for chaos-based cryptosystem. *International Journal of Bifurcation and Chaos in Applied Sciences and Engineering*, *16*(8), 2129–2151. doi:10.1142/S0218127406015970

Amin, M., Faragallah, O. S., & Latif, A. A. (2009). Chaos-based hash function(CBHF) for cryptographic application. *Chaos, Solitons, and Fractals*, *42*, 767.

Ana, B. M., Javaid, U., Valdés, G., Nguyen, D., Desbordes, P., Macq, B., Willems, S., Vandewinckele, L., Holmström, M., Löfman, F., Michiels, S., Souris, K., Sterpin, E., & Lee, J. A. (2021). Artificial intelligence and machine learning for medical imaging: A technology review. *Physica Medica*, *83*, 242–256. https://doi.org/10.1016/j.ejmp.2021.04.016

Anthony, L. (2017). *A Novel Mathematical Framework for the Analysis of Neural Networks*. http://hdl.handle.net/10012/12173

Anum, K., Irfan, M., Moin, A., Rho, S., & Maqsood, M. (2020). An Efficient Liver Tumor Detection using Machine Learning. *2020 International Conference on Computational Science and Computational Intelligence (CSCI)*. DOI 10.1109/CSCI51800.2020.00130

Arah, I. K., Amaglo, H., Kumah, E. K., & Ofori, H. (2015). Preharvest and postharvest factors affecting the quality and shelf life of harvested tomatoes: A mini review. *International Journal of Agronomy*, *6*, 1–6. doi:10.1155/2015/478041

Ariffin, M. R. K., & Abu, N. A. (2009). AA_-cryptosystem: A chaos based public key cryptosystem. *International Journal of Cryptology Research*, *1*(2), 149–163.

Arora, P. (2017, July). Enhanced NN based RZ leach using hybrid ACO/PSO based routing for WSNs. In *2017 8th International Conference on Computing, Communication and Networking Technologies (ICCCNT)* (pp. 1-7). IEEE.

Aurangzeb, A. M., Eckert, C., Teredesai, A., & McKelvey, G. (2018), Interpretable Machine Learning in Healthcare. *ACM International Conference on Bioinformatics, Computational Biology and Health Informatics*, 559-560.

Bai, E-W., Lonngren, K.E., & Uçar, A. (2005). Secure communication via multiple parameter modulation in a delayed chaotic system. *Chaos, Solitons & Fractals, February*, *23*(3), 1071–1076.

Baird, L., Harmon, M., & Madsen, A. P. (2020). *Hedera: A Public Hashgraph Network & Governing Council* [white paper]. Retrieved November 2022: https://hedera.com/hh_whitepaper_v2.1-20200815.pdf

Balakrishnan, N., & Muthukumarasamy, G. (2016). Crop Production-Ensemble Machine Learning Model for Prediction. *International Journal of Computer Science and Software Engineering*, *5*, 148–153.

Bamakan, S. M. H., Motavali, A., & Bondarti, A. B. (2020). A survey of blockchain consensus algorithms performance evaluation criteria. *Expert Systems with Applications*, *154*, 113385. doi:10.1016/j.eswa.2020.113385

Banerjee, S., & Ariffin, M. R. K. (2012, January). Chaos synchronization based data transmission with asymmetric encryption. *International Journal of Computers and Applications*, *37*(12), 6–9.

Banimelhem, O., Mowafi, M., Taqieddin, E., Awad, F., & Al Rawabdeh, M. (2014, August). An efficient clustering approach using genetic algorithm and node mobility in wireless sensor networks. In *2014 11th international symposium on wireless communications systems (ISWCS)* (pp. 858-862). IEEE. 10.1109/ISWCS.2014.6933473

Baradaran, A. A., & Navi, K. (2020). HQCA-WSN: High-quality clustering algorithm and optimal cluster head selection using fuzzy logic in wireless sensor networks. *Fuzzy Sets and Systems*, *389*, 114–144. doi:10.1016/j.fss.2019.11.015

Barakat, M. L., Mansingka, A. S., Radwan, A. G., & Salama, K. N. (2014, January). Hardware stream cipher with controllable chaos generator for colour image encryption. *IET Image Processing*, *8*(1).

Bari, A., Wazed, S., Jaekel, A., & Bandyopadhyay, S. (2009). A genetic algorithm based approach for energy efficient routing in two-tiered sensor networks. *Ad Hoc Networks*, *7*(4), 665–676. doi:10.1016/j.adhoc.2008.04.003

Bas, H. M., Hugo, V. D., Kuijf, H. J., Gilhuijs, K. G. A., & Viergever, M. A. (2022). Explainable artificial intelligence (XAI) in deep learning-based medical image analysis. *Medical Image Analysis*, *79*. doi:10.1016/j.media.2022.102470

Behnia, S., Akhshania, A., Akhavanb, A., & Mahmodi, H. (2008). Chaotic cryptographic scheme based on composition maps. *International Journal of Bifurcation and Chaos in Applied Sciences and Engineering*, *18*(1), 251–261. doi:10.1142/S0218127408020288

Benkouider, K. (2022). A New 5-D Multistable Hyperchaotic System With Three Positive Lyapunov Exponents: Bifurcation Analysis, Circuit Design, FPGA Realization and Image Encryption. *IEEE Access: Practical Innovations, Open Solutions*, *10*, 90111–90132.

Benrhouma, O., Houcemeddine, H., & Safya, B. (2013). Security analysis and improvement of a partial encryption scheme. *Multimedia Tools and Applications*, *74*(11), 3617–3634. doi:10.100711042-013-1790-4

Bergamo, P., D'Arco, P., De Santis, A., & Kocarev, L. (2005). Security of public-key cryptosystems based on chebyshev polynomials. *IEEE Transactions on Circuits and Systems I: Regular Papers, 52*(7), 1382 –1393.

Bhanderi, M., & Shah, H. (2014). Machine learning for wireless sensor network: A review, challenges and applications. *Adv. Electron. Electr. Eng*, *4*, 475–486.

Bhatnagar, S., Gill, L., & Ghosh, B. (2020). Drone Image Segmentation Using Machine and Deep Learning for Mapping RaisedBog Vegetation Communities. *Remote Sensing*, *12*, 2602. doi:10.3390/rs12162602

Bhishman, D. (2020). Image Filtering -Techniques, Algorithm and Applications. *GIS Science Journal*, *7*(11), 940–975.

Bose, R. (2005, August). Novel public key encryption technique based on multiple chaotic systems. *Physical Review Letters*, *95*, 098702.

Bose, R., & Pathak, S. (2006). A novel compression and encryption scheme using variable model arithmetic coding and coupled chaotic system. *IEEE Transactions on Circuits and Systems. I, Fundamental Theory and Applications*, *53*(4), 848–857. doi:10.1109/TCSI.2005.859617

Bouni, M., Hssina, B., Douzi, K., & Douzi, S. (2022). Towards an Efficient Recommender Systems in Smart Agriculture: A deep reinforcement learning approach. *Procedia Computer Science*, *203*, 825–830. doi:10.1016/j.procs.2022.07.124

Boycov, Y., & Funka-Lea, G. (2006, November). Graph cuts and efficient ND image segmentation. *International Journal of Computer Vision*, *70*(2), 109–131.

Branch, J. W., Giannella, C., Szymanski, B., Wolff, R., & Kargupta, H. (2013). In-network outlier detection in wireless sensor networks. *Knowledge and Information Systems*, *34*(1), 23–54. doi:10.100710115-011-0474-5

Cakir, F., He, K., Xia, X., Kulis, B., & Sclaroff, S. (2019). Deep metric learning to rank. In Proceedings of the IEEE/ CVF conference on computer vision and pattern recognition (pp. 1861-1870). IEEE.

Canziani, A., Paszke, A., & Culurciello, E. (2016). *An analysis of deep neural network models for practical applications.* arXivpreprint arXiv:1605.07678.

Chen, Li, & Hua. (2022). Retinex Low-Light Image Enhancement Network based on Attention Mechanism. *Multimedia Tools Application.* . doi:10.1007/s11042-022-13411-z

Chen, Y., Xue, R., & Zhang, Y. (2021). House price prediction based on machine learning and deep learning methods. *2021 International Conference on Electronic Information Engineering and Computer Science (EIECS)*, 699-702. 10.1109/ MLBDBI54094.2021.00059

Chen, Y. P., & Chen, Y. Z. (2010, July). A novel energy efficient routing algorithm for wireless sensor networks. In *2010 International Conference on Machine Learning and Cybernetics* (Vol. 2, pp. 1031-1036). IEEE. 10.1109/IC-MLC.2010.5580625

Chen, Z., Teng, D. H.-Y., Wang, G. C.-J., & Fan, S.-K. (2011). Droplet routing in high-level synthesis of configurable digital microfluidic biochips based on microelectrode dot array architecture. *Journal of BioChips*, *5*(4), 343–352. doi:10.100713206-011-5408-5

Chong, K. Y., & Koshiba, T. (2007, September). More on Security of Public-Key Cryptosystems Based on Chebyshev Polynomials. *IEEE Transactions on Circuits and Wystems. II, Express Briefs*, *54*(9), 795–7747. doi:10.1109/ TCSII.2007.900875

Christopher, V. B., Sajan, R. I., Akhila, T. S., & Kavitha, M. J. (2022). A QoS Aware Three Way Point Rule based Fusion of Earth Worm and Deer Hunt Optimization Routing in Wireless Sensor Network. *Wireless Personal Communications*, 1–23.

Chu-hang, W., Xiao-li, L., You-jia, H., Huang-shui, H., & Sha-sha, W. (2022). An Improved Genetic Algorithm Based Annulus-Sector Clustering Routing Protocol for Wireless Sensor Networks. *Wireless Personal Communications*, *123*(4), 3623–3644. doi:10.100711277-021-09306-1

Çiçek, Ö., Abdulkadir, A., Lienkamp, S. S., Brox, T., & Ronneberger, O. (2016). 3D U-Net: learning dense volumetric segmentation from sparse annotation. In *International conference on medical image computing and computer assisted intervention 2016 Oct 17* (pp. 424-432). Springer.

Çiçek, Ö., Abdulkadir, A., Lienkamp, S., & Brox, T. (2016). 3D U-Net: Learning Dense Volumetric Segmentationfrom parse Annotation. In S. Ourselin, L. Joskowicz, M. Sabuncu, G. Unal, & W. Wells (Eds.), Medical Image Computing and Computer-Assisted Intervention: Vol. 9901. MICCAI 2016. MICCAI 2016. Lecture Notes in Computer Science. Springer. https://doi.org/10.1007/978-3-319-46723-8_49.

Das, A. K., Hazra, S., & Mandal, M. K. (2021). RGB image encryption using microcontroller ATMEGA 32. *Microsystem Technologies*, *21*, 409–417.

Das, A. K., & Mandal, M. K. (2019). *FPGA Based Chaotic Cryptosystem. In ICACCP-2019.* IEEE.

Datta, S., Joshi, B., Ravindran, A., & Mukherjee, A. (2009). Efficient parallel testing and diagnosis of digital microfluidic biochips. *ACM Journal on Emerging Technologies in Computing Systems*, *5*(2), 10. doi:10.1145/1543438.1543443

Davids, D. (2008). A fault detection and diagnosis technique for digital Microfluidic biochips. *IEEE International Mixed-Signal, Sensor and Systems Test Workshop.* 10.1109/IMS3TW.2008.4581597

Day, A. L., & Livingstone, H. A. (2001, October). Chronic and acute stressors among military personnel: Do coping styles buffer their negative impact on health? *Journal of Occupational Health Psychology*, *6*(4), 348.

Deepa, N., Pham, Q. V., Nguyen, D. C., Bhattacharya, S., Prabadevi, B., Gadekallu, T. R., Maddikunta, P. K. R., Fang, F., & Pathirana, P. N. (2022). A survey on blockchain for big data: Approaches, opportunities, and future directions. *Future Generation Computer Systems, 131*, 209–226. doi:10.1016/j.future.2022.01.017

Deng, J., Feng, J., Li, Z., Sun, Z., & Jia, K. (2020). Unet-based for Photoacoustic Imaging Artifact Removal. In *Imaging and Applied Optics Congress*. Optica Publishing Group.

Dhanachandra, N., Manglem, K., & Chanu, Y. J. (2015, January 1). Image segmentation using K-means clustering algorithm and subtractive clustering algorithm. *Procedia Computer Science, 54*, 764–771.

Diffie, W. F., & Hellman, M. E. (1976). New directions in cryptography. *IEEE Transactions on Information Theory, 22*(10), 644–655.

Ding, Z. (2017). Research of improved particle swarm optimization algorithm. *AIP Conference Proceedings, 1839*, 020148. doi:10.1063/1.4982513

Dong, H., Yang, G., Liu, F., Mo, Y., & Guo, Y. (2017). Automatic brain tumor detection and segmentation using U-Net based fully convolutional networks. In *Annual conference on medical image understanding and analysis* (pp. 506-517). Springer.

Dong, S., Agrawal, P., & Sivalingam, K. (2007, November). Reinforcement learning based geographic routing protocol for UWB wireless sensor network. In *IEEE GLOBECOM 2007-IEEE Global Telecommunications Conference* (pp. 652-656). IEEE. 10.1109/GLOCOM.2007.127

Doshi, Z., Nadkarni, S., Agrawal, R., & Shah, N. (2018). AgroConsultant: Intelligent Crop Recommendation System Using Machine Learning Algorithms. *Proc. of Fourth International Conference on Computing Communication Control and Automation*. 10.1109/ICCUBEA.2018.8697349

Du, X.F., Wang, J.S., & Sun, W.Z. (2021). UNet retinal blood vessel segmentation algorithm based on improved pyramidpooling method and attention mechanism. *Phys Med Biol., 66*(17). doi:10.1088/1361-6560/ac1c4c

El Ioini, N., & Pahl, C. (2018, October). A review of distributed ledger technologies. In *OTM Confederated International Conferences "On the Move to Meaningful Internet Systems"* (pp. 277-288). Springer. 10.1007/978-3-030-02671-4_16

El Mezouary, R., Choukri, A., Kobbane, A., & El Koutbi, M. (2015, September). An energy-aware clustering approach based on the K-means method for wireless sensor networks. In *International Symposium on Ubiquitous Networking* (pp. 325-337). Springer.

Elsayed, G., Kornblith, S., & Le, Q. V. (2019). Saccader: Improving accuracy of hard attention models for vision. *Advances in Neural Information Processing Systems, 2019*, 32.

Enami, N., & Moghadam, R. A. (2010). Energy based clustering self organizing map protocol for extending wireless sensor networks lifetime and coverage. *Canadian Journal on Multimedia and Wireless Networks, 1*(4), 42–54.

Erickson, B. J. (2017). Machine learning for medical imaging. *Radiographics, 37*, 505–515.

Essa, Z. M., Zainab, M., & Al-Jamal, A. N., Abood, Z. M., & Essa, D. M. (2020). Marker Controlled Watershed Method for Magnification Materials. *Journal of Green Engineering, 10*(9), 6261–6270.

Fadlullah, Z. M., Tang, F., Mao, B., Kato, N., Akashi, O., Inoue, T., & Mizutani, K. (2017). State-of-the-art deep learning: Evolving machine intelligence toward tomorrow's intelligent network traffic control systems. *IEEE Communications Surveys and Tutorials, 19*(4), 2432–2455. doi:10.1109/COMST.2017.2707140

Fan, C., Cui, Z., & Zhong, X. (2018). House Prices Prediction with Machine Learning Algorithms. *Proceedings of the 2018 10th International Conference on Machine Learning and Computing ICMLC 2018*, 6-10. 10.1145/3195106.3195133

Fengi, H. (1993). *The interpolating random spline cryptosystem and the chaotic-map public-key cryptosystem* [PhD thesis]. UMI Order No. GAX93-26596.

Feng, J., Deng, J., Li, Z., Sun, Z., Dou, H., & Jia, K. (2020). End-to-end Res-Unet based reconstruction algorithm for photoacoustic imaging. *Biomedical Optics Express*, *11*, 5321–5340.

Feng, Q., He, D., Zeadally, S., Khan, M. K., & Kumar, N. (2019). A survey on privacy protection in blockchain system. *Journal of Network and Computer Applications*, *126*, 45–58. doi:10.1016/j.jnca.2018.10.020

Ferreira, J. J., & Monteiro, M. S. (2020). *What Are People Doing About XAI User Experience? A Survey on AI Explainability Research and Practice. In Design, User Experience, and Usability. Design for Contemporary Interactive Environments*. Springer.

Fiebelkorn, I. C., Saalmann, Y. B., & Kastner, S. (2020). Functional specialization in the attention network. *Annual Review of Psychology*, *71*(221).

Förster, A., Murphy, A. L., Schiller, J., & Terfloth, K. (2008, October). An efficient implementation of reinforcement learning based routing on real WSN hardware. In *2008 IEEE International Conference on Wireless and Mobile Computing, Networking and Communications* (pp. 247-252). IEEE. 10.1109/WiMob.2008.99

Fouda, J. S., Effa, J. V., Sabat, S. L., & Ali, M. (2014). A fast chaotic block cipher for image encryption. *Communications in Nonlinear Science and Numerical Simulation*, *19*, 578–588.

Fu, Zeng, Huang, Zhang, & Ding. (2016). A Weighted Variational Model for Simultaneous Reflectance and Illumination Estimation. In *Proceedings of the IEEE conference on computer vision and pattern recognition* (pp. 2782-2790). 10.1109/CVPR.2016.304

Fu, C., Meng, W., Zhan, Y., Zhu, Z., Lau, F. C. M., Tse, C. K., & Mae, H. (2013). An efficient and secure medical image protection scheme based on chaotic maps. *Computers in Biology and Medicine*, *43*(8), 1000–1010. doi:10.1016/j.compbiomed.2013.05.005 PMID:23816172

Fu, X., Wang, H., & Shi, P. (2021). A survey of Blockchain consensus algorithms: Mechanism, design and applications. *Science China. Information Sciences*, *64*(2), 1–15. doi:10.100711432-019-2790-1

Gao, W., Hatcher, W. G., & Yu, W. (2018, July). A survey of blockchain: Techniques, applications, and challenges. In *2018 27th international conference on computer communication and networks (ICCCN)* (pp. 1-11). IEEE.

Gao, Z. M., & Zhao, J. (2019). An Improved Grey Wolf Optimization Algorithm with Variable Weights. *Computational Intelligence and Neuroscience*. doi:10.1155/2019/2981282

Garanayak, M., Sahu, G., Mohanty, S. N., & Jagadev, A. K. (2021). Agricultural Recommendation System for Crops Using Different Machine Learning Regression Methods. *International Journal of Agricultural and Environmental Information Systems*, *12*(1), 12. doi:10.4018/IJAEIS.20210101.oa1

Gavali, A. B., Kadam, M. V., & Patil, S. (2022). Energy optimization using swarm intelligence for IoT-Authorized underwater wireless sensor networks. *Microprocessors and Microsystems*, *93*, 104597. doi:10.1016/j.micpro.2022.104597

Gayem, Q., Liu, H., Richardson, A., & Burd, N. (2009). Builtin test solutions for the electrode structures in bio-fluidic microsystems. *Proc. ETS*, 73-78.

Ghaderi, S., Ghaderi, K., & Ghaznavi, H. (2021). Using Marker-Controlled Watershed Transform to Detect Baker's Cyst in Magnetic Resonance Imaging Images: A Pilot Study. *Journal of Medical Signals and Sensors*, *12*(1), 84–89. https://doi.org/10.4103/jmss.JMSS_49_20

Ghosh, A., Ho, C. C., & Bestak, R. (2020). Secured energy-efficient routing in wireless sensor networks using machine learning algorithm: Fundamentals and applications. *Deep Learning Strategies for Security Enhancement in Wireless Sensor Networks*, 23-41.

Gilpin, L. H. (2018). Explaining explanations: An overview of interpretability of machine learning. In *2018 IEEE 5th InternationalConference on data science and advanced analytics* (pp. 80–89). DSAA.

Girisha, S., Pai, M. M. M., & Pai, R. (2019). Performance Analysis of Semantic Segmentation Algorithms for Finely Annotated New UAV Aerial Video Dataset (ManipalUAVid). *IEEE Access: Practical Innovations, Open Solutions*, *7*, 136239–136253. doi:10.1109/ACCESS.2019.2941026

Gonczol, P., Katsikouli, P., Herskind, L., & Dragoni, N. (2020). Blockchain implementations and use cases for supply chains-a survey. *IEEE Access: Practical Innovations, Open Solutions*, *8*, 11856–11871. doi:10.1109/ACCESS.2020.2964880

Gonzalez, J. A., & Pino, R. (1999). Random number generator based on unpredictable chaotic functions. *Computer Physics Communications*, *120*, 109–114.

Guan, P. (1987). Cellular automaton public key cryptosystem. *Complex Systems*, *1*, 51–57.

Guan, Z., Huang, F., & Guan, W. (2005). Chaos-based image encryption algorithm. *Physics Letters. [Part A]*, *346*(1–3), 153–157. doi:10.1016/j.physleta.2005.08.006

Gui, T., Ma, C., Wang, F., & Wilkins, D. E. (2016, March). Survey on swarm intelligence based routing protocols for wireless sensor networks: An extensive study. In *2016 IEEE international conference on industrial technology (ICIT)* (pp. 1944-1949). IEEE.

Gu, J., Wang, Z., Kuen, J., Ma, L., Shahroudy, A., Shuai, B., Liu, T., Wang, X., Wang, G., Cai, J., & Chen, T. (2018, May 1). Recent advances in convolutional neural networks. *Pattern Recognition*, *77*, 354–377.

Guo, Li, & Ling. (2017, February). LIME: Low-Light Image Enhancement via Illumination Map Estimation. IEEE Transactions on Image Processing, 26(2), 982-993. doi:10.1109/TIP.2016.2639450

Guo, X., & Hu, Q. (2023). Low-light Image Enhancement via Breaking Down the Darkness. *International Journal of Computer Vision*, *131*(1), 48–66. doi:10.100711263-022-01667-9

Gu, Z., Cheng, J., Fu, H., Zhou, K., Hao, H., & Zhao, Y. (2019). Context encoder network for 2D medical image segmentation. *IEEE Transactions on Medical Imaging*, *38*(10), 2281–2292.

Habutu, T., Nishio, Y., Sasase, I., & Moris, S. (1990). A secret key cryptosystem using a chaotic map. *IEICE Trans.*, *73*(7), 1041–1044.

Hai, J., Xuan, Z., Yang, R., Hao, Y., Zou, F., Lin, F., & Han, S. (2023). R2rnet: Low-light image enhancement via real-low to real-normal network. *Journal of Visual Communication and Image Representation*, *90*, 103712. doi:10.1016/j.jvcir.2022.103712

Hamdi & Boudriga. (2008). Four dimensional chaotic ciphers for secure image transmission. *IEEE Int. Conf. Multimedia and Expo.*, 437–440. doi:10.1109/ICME.2008.4607465

Hamdi, A., Shaban, K., Erradi, A., Mohamed, A., Rumi, S.K., & Salim, F.D. (2022). Generative adversarial networks for spatio-temporal data: A survey. *ACM Transactions on Intelligent Systems and Technology, 13*(2), 1-25.

Hanumantharaju, Ravishankar, Rameshbabu, & Manjunath Aradhya. (2013). Novel Full-Reference Color Image Quality Assessment Based on Energy Computation in the Wavelet Domain. *Journal of Intelligent Systems, 22*(2). 155-177.doi.org/10.1515/jisys-2012-0026

Han, Y., Hu, H., & Guo, Y. (2022). Energy-Aware and Trust-Based Secure Routing Protocol for Wireless Sensor Networks Using Adaptive Genetic Algorithm. *IEEE Access: Practical Innovations, Open Solutions, 10*, 11538–11550. doi:10.1109/ACCESS.2022.3144015

Hassan, A. A. H., Shah, W. M., Habeb, A. H. H., Othman, M. F. I., & Al-Mhiqani, M. N. (2020). An improved energy-efficient clustering protocol to prolong the lifetime of the WSN-based IoT. *IEEE Access: Practical Innovations, Open Solutions, 8*, 200500–200517. doi:10.1109/ACCESS.2020.3035624

Hassan, H. A., & Zellagui, M. (2017). Application of Grey Wolf Optimizer Algorithm for Optimal PowerFlow of Two-Terminal HVDC Transmission System. *Advances in Electrical and Electronic Engineering., 15*(5), 701–712.

Heinzelman, W. R., Chandrakasan, A., & Balakrishnan, H. (2000, January). Energy-efficient communication protocol for wireless microsensor networks. In *Proceedings of the 33rd annual Hawaii international conference on system sciences* (pp. 10-pp). IEEE. 10.1109/HICSS.2000.926982

Heming, J. (2019). Multilevel Thresholding Segmentation for Color Image UsingModified Moth-Flame Optimization. *IEEE Access: Practical Innovations, Open Solutions, 7*, 44097–44134.

Hossain, M. S., Al-Hammadi, M., & Muhammad, G. (2019). Automatic fruit classification using deep learning for industrial applications. *IEEE Transactions on Industrial Informatics, 15*(2), 1027–1034. doi:10.1109/TII.2018.2875149

Houcemeddine, H., Rhouma, R., & Safya, B. (2013). Improvement of an image encryption algorithm based on hyper-chaos. *Telecommunication Systems, 52*(2), 539–549.

Hou, Y., Gao, H., Wang, Z., & Du, C. (2022, May 17). Improved Grey Wolf Optimization Algorithm and Application. *Sensors (Basel), 22*(10), 3810. doi:10.339022103810

Hu, J., Shen, Li., Albanie, S., Sun, G., & Wu, E. (2017). *Squeeze-and-excitation networks.* arXiv:1709.01507

Huang, H. C., Chuang, Y. Y., & Chen, C. S. (2011, September 29). Multiple kernel fuzzy clustering. *IEEE Transactions on Fuzzy Systems, 20*(1), 120–134.

Huang, Z. Q. (2011). A more secure parallel keyed hash function based on chaotic neural network. *Communications in Nonlinear Science and Numerical Simulation, 16*, 3245–3256.

Huaping, L., Wang, S., & Gang, H. (2004). Pseudo-random number generator based on coupled map lattices. *International Journal of Modern Physics B, 18*, 2409–2414.

Hu, H. P., Liu, L. F., & Ding, N. D. (2013). Pseudorandom sequence generator based on Chen chaotic system. *Computer Physics Communications, 184*, 765–768.

Huimin, H., Lin, L., Tong, R., Hu, H., Zhang, Q., Iwamoto, Y., Han, X., Chen, Y., & Wu, J. (2020). UNet3+: A Full-Scale Connected UNet for Medical Image Segmentation.. *ICASSP 2020 - 2020 IEEE International Conference on Acoustics, Speech and Signal Processing (ICASSP)*: 1055-1059.

Ireri, D., Belal, E., Okinda, C., Makange, N., & Ji, C. (2019). A computer vision system for defect discrimination and grading in tomatoes using machine learning and image processing. *Artificial Intelligence in Agriculture, 2*, 28–37. doi:10.1016/j.aiia.2019.06.001

Jafarizadeh, V., Keshavarzi, A., & Derikvand, T. (2017). Efficient cluster head selection using Naïve Bayes classifier for wireless sensor networks. *Wireless Networks*, 23(3), 779–785. doi:10.100711276-015-1169-8

Jain, B., Brar, G., & Malhotra, J. (2018). EKMT-k-means clustering algorithmic solution for low energy consumption for wireless sensor networks based on minimum mean distance from base station. In *Networking communication and data knowledge engineering* (pp. 113–123). Springer. doi:10.1007/978-981-10-4585-1_10

Jaradat, T., Benhaddou, D., Balakrishnan, M., & Al-Fuqaha, A. (2013, July). Energy efficient cross-layer routing protocol in wireless sensor networks based on fuzzy logic. In *2013 9th International Wireless Communications and Mobile Computing Conference (IWCMC)* (pp. 177-182). IEEE. 10.1109/IWCMC.2013.6583555

Jayapal, C., Sekar, N., Sekar, R., & Suresh, R. (2020, October). Secured Voting Using Blockchain. In *2020 IEEE 5th International Conference on Computing Communication and Automation (ICCCA)* (pp. 177-184). IEEE. 10.1109/ICCCA49541.2020.9250859

Jebrail, M. J., Bartsch, M. S., & Patel, K. D. (2012, July). Digital microfluidics: A versatile tool for applications in chemistry, biology, and medicine. *Lab on a Chip*, 12(14), 5452–2463. doi:10.1039/c2lc40318h PMID:22699371

Jetley, S., Lord, N. A., Lee, N., & Torr, P. H. S. (2018). Learn to pay attention. *International Conference on Learning Representations*. https://openreview.net/forum?id=HyzbhfWRW

Jin, W., Li, X., & Hamarneh, G. (2022). Evaluating Explainable AI on a Multi-Modal Medical Imaging Task: Can Existing Algorithms Fulfill Clinical Requirements? Association for the Advancement of Artificial Intelligence, 1-9.

Jiteurtragool, Ketthong, Wannaboon, & San-Um. (2013). A topologically simple keyed hash function based on circular chaotic sinusoidal map network. *2013 International Conference on Advanced Communication Technology*, 1089-1094.

Jobson, D. J., Rahman, Z., & Woodell, G. A. (1997, July). A Multiscale Retinex for Bridging the gap between Color images and the human observation of scenes. *IEEE Transactions on Image Processing*, 6(7), 965–976. doi:10.1109/83.597272 PMID:18282987

Jr Piedad, E., Larada, J. L., Pojas, G. J., Vithalie, L., & Ferrer, V. (2018). Postharvest classification of banana (Musa acuminata) using tier-based machine learning. *Postharvest Biology and Technology*, 145, 93–100. doi:10.1016/j.postharvbio.2018.06.004

Kanso, A. (2011, February). Self-shrinking chaotic stream ciphers. *Communications in Nonlinear Science and Numerical Simulation*, 16(2), 822–836.

Kanso, A., & Ghebleh, M. (2013). A fast and efficient chaos-based keyed hash function. *Communications in Nonlinear Science and Numerical Simulation*, 18, 109–123.

Kapdi, R., & Raval, M. (2020). Brain Tumor Segmentation and Survival Prediction. *Lecture Notes in Computer Science*, 11992, 338–348. doi:10.1007/978-3-030-46640-4_32

Kazemeyni, F., Owe, O., Johnsen, E. B., & Balasingham, I. (2014). Formal Modeling and analysis of learning-based routing in mobile wireless sensor networks. In *Integration of Reusable Systems* (pp. 127–150). Springer. doi:10.1007/978-3-319-04717-1_6

Kelber, K., & Schwarz, W. (2005). General design rules for chaos-based encryption systems. In *International symposium on nonlinear theory and its applications (NOLTA2005)*, Bruges, Belgium.

Kerkhoff, H. G. (2007). Testing of microelectronic-biofluidic systems. *IEEE Design & Test of Computers*, 24(1), 72–82. doi:10.1109/MDT.2007.28

Khanal, S., Fulton, J., Klopfenstein, A., Douridas, N., & Shearer, S. (2018). Integration of high resolution remotely sensed data and machine learning. *Computers and Electronics in Agriculture*, *153*, 213–225. doi:10.1016/j.compag.2018.07.016

Khelifi, L., & Mignotte, M. (2017, November 1). EFA-BMFM: A multi-criteria framework for the fusion of colour image segmentation. *Information Fusion*, *38*, 104–121.

Kim, J. M., Park, S. H., Han, Y. J., & Chung, T. M. (2008, February). CHEF: cluster head election mechanism using fuzzy logic in wireless sensor networks. In *2008 10th international conference on advanced communication technology* (Vol. 1, pp. 654-659). IEEE. 10.1109/ICACT.2008.4493846

Kimmel, Elad, Shaked, Keshet, & Sobel. (2003). A Variational Framework for Retinex. International Journal of Computer Vision, 52(1), 7–23.

Kirk, R., Cielniak, G., & Mangan, M. (2020). L*a*b*Fruits: A Rapid and Robust Outdoor Fruit Detection System Combining Bio-Inspired Features with One-Stage Deep Learning Networks. *Sensors (Basel)*, *20*(1), 275. doi:10.339020010275 PMID:31947829

Kocarev, L., & Lian, S. (2011). Chaos-Based Cryptography. Theory, Algorithms and Applications, Studies in Computational Intelligence, 354. doi:10.1007/978-3-642-20542-2

Kocarev, L., & Tasev, Z. (2003). Public-key encryption based on chebyshev maps. *Circuits and Systems, 2003. ISCAS '03. Proceedings of the 2003 International Symposium on.*

Kocarev, L., Halle, K. S., Eckert, K., Chua, L. O., & Parlitz, U. (1992). Experimental demonstration of secure communications via chaotic synchronization. *International Journal of Bifurcation and Chaos in Applied Sciences and Engineering*, *2*(3), 709–713. doi:10.1142/S0218127492000823

Kocarev, L., Makraduli, J., & Amato, P. (2005). Public-Key Encryption Based on Chebyshev Polynomials. *Circuits, Systems, and Signal Processing*, *24*(5), 497–517.

Kouadio, L., Deo, R. C., Byrareddy, V., Adamowski, J. F., Mushtaq, S., & Nguyen, V. P. (2018). Artificial intelligence approach for the prediction of Robusta coffee yield using soil fertility properties. *Computers and Electronics in Agriculture*, *155*, 324–338. doi:10.1016/j.compag.2018.10.014

Krig, S. (2014). Image Pre-Processing. In Computer Vision Metrics. Apress. https://doi.org/10.1007/978-1-4302-5930-5_2.

Kuila, P., & Jana, P. K. (2014). Energy efficient clustering and routing algorithms for wireless sensor networks: Particle swarm optimization approach. *Engineering Applications of Artificial Intelligence*, *33*, 127–140. doi:10.1016/j.engappai.2014.04.009

Kulkarni, N. H., Srinivasan, G. N., Sagar, B. M., & Cauvery, N. K. (2018). Improving Crop Productivity Through A Crop Recommendation System Using Ensembling Technique. *Proc. of 3rd International Conference on Computational Systems and Information Technology for Sustainable solutions*, 114 – 119. 10.1109/CSITSS.2018.8768790

Kulkarni, R. V., Forster, A., & Venayagamoorthy, G. K. (2010). Computational intelligence in wireless sensor networks: A survey. *IEEE Communications Surveys and Tutorials*, *13*(1), 68–96. doi:10.1109/SURV.2011.040310.00002

Kumar, A., Kumar, N., & Vats, V. (2018). Efficient crop yield prediction using machine learning algorithms. *International Journal of Research in Engineering and Technology*, *05*, 3151–3159.

Kumar, D. P., Amgoth, T., & Annavarapu, C. S. R. (2019). Machine learning algorithms for wireless sensor networks: A survey. *Information Fusion*, *49*, 1–25. doi:10.1016/j.inffus.2018.09.013

Kumar, Y. J. N., Spandana, V., Vaishnavi, V. S., Neha, K., & Devi, V. G. R. R. (2020). Supervised Machine learning Approach for Crop Yield Prediction in Agriculture Sector. *Proc. of 5th International Conference on Communication and Electronics Systems*, 736-741. 10.1109/ICCES48766.2020.9137868

Kushtrim, B., Demetrio, P., Alexandra, B., Brunella, M., & Grappa, C. (2019). Single-shot convolution neural networks for real-time fruit detection within the tree. *Frontiers in Plant Science*, *10*, 611. doi:10.3389/fpls.2019.00611 PMID:31178875

Lai, Yang, & Liu. (2022). Design and realization of discrete memristive hyperchaotic map with application in image encryption. In *Chaos, Solitons and Fractals*. Elsevier.

Lai, K. Y.-T., Yang, Y.-T., Wang, G., Lu, Y.-W., & Lee, C.-Y. (2013). A digital microfluidic processor for biomedical applications. *Signal Processing Systems (SiPS)*, 54-58. 10.1109/SiPS.2013.6674480

Lambin, P., & Leijenaar, R. T. H. (2017). Radiomics: The bridge between medical imaging and personalized medicine. *Nature Reviews. Clinical Oncology*, *14*, 749–762.

Lambin, P., & Rios, V. E. (2021). Radiomics: Extracting more information from medical images using advanced feature analysis. *European Journal of Cancer (Oxford, England)*, *48*, 441–446.

Land, E. (1977, December). The Retinex Theory of Color Vision. *Scientific American*, *236*(6), 108–128. doi:10.1038cientificamerican1277-108 PMID:929159

Laurent, A., Brotcorne, L., & Fortz, B. (2022). Transactions fees optimization in the Ethereum blockchain. *Blockchain: Research and Applications*, 100074.

Lavanya, S., Prasanth, A., Jayachitra, S., & Shenbagarajan, A. (2021). A Tuned classification approach for efficient heterogeneous fault diagnosis in IoT-enabled WSN applications. *Measurement*, *183*, 109771. doi:10.1016/j.measurement.2021.109771

Lawnik, M., Moysis, L., & Volos, C. (2022). Chaos-Based Cryptography: Text Encryption Using Image Algorithms. *Electronics*, *11*, 3156.

LeCun, Y., & Bengio, Y. (1998). Convolutional networks for images, speech, and time-series. The handbook of brain theory and neural networks, 255–258.

Lee, S., Soak, S., Oh, S., Pedrycz, W., & Jeo, M. (2008). Modified binary particle swarm optimization. *Progress in Natural Science, 18*(9), 1161-1166. doi:10.1016/j.pnsc.2008.03.018

Le, H. T., & Hien, P. (2018). Brain tumour segmentation using U-Net based fully convolutional networks and extremely randomized trees. *Vietnam Journal of Science, Technology and Engineering*, *60*, 19–25. doi:10.31276/VJSTE.60(3).19

Li, C., Arroyo, D., & Lo, K-T. (2010). Breaking a chaotic cryptographic scheme based on composition maps. *International Journal of Bifurcation and Chaos, 20*(8), 2561–2568.

Li, Guo, Sun, & Sun. (2022). A Low-Illuminance Image Enhancement Method in YUV Color Space. *14th International Conference on Measuring Technology and Mechatronics Automation (ICMTMA)*, 286-291. 10.1109/ICMTMA54903.2022.00062

Li, T., Ruan, F., Fan, Z., Wang, J., & Kim, J. U. (2015, October). An improved PEGASIS protocol for wireless sensor network. In *2015 3rd international conference on computer and computing science (COMCOMS)* (pp. 16-19). IEEE. 10.1109/COMCOMS.2015.20

Li, X., Gang, W., Zongqi, L., & Yanyan, Z. (2013, May). An energy-efficient routing protocol based on particle swarm clustering algorithm and inter-cluster routing algorithm for WSN. In *2013 25th Chinese control and decision conference (CCDC)* (pp. 4029-4033). IEEE. 10.1109/CCDC.2013.6561655

Liakos, K. G., Busato, P., Moshou, D., Pearson, S., & Bochtis, D. (2018). Machine learning in agriculture: A review. *Sensors (Basel)*, *18*(8), 1–29. doi:10.339018082674 PMID:30110960

Li, C., Guo, C., Han, L., Jiang, J., Cheng, M.-M., Gu, J., & Loy, C. C. (2022, December 1). Low-Light Image and Video Enhancement using Deep Learning: A Survey. *IEEE Transactions on Pattern Analysis and Machine Intelligence*, *44*(12), 9396–9416. Advance online publication. doi:10.1109/TPAMI.2021.3126387 PMID:34752382

Li, C., Guo, J., Porikli, F., & Pang, Y. (2018). LightenNet: A convolutional neural network for weakly illuminated image enhancement. *Pattern Recognition Letters*, *104*, 15–22. doi:10.1016/j.patrec.2018.01.010

Li, C., Wang, X., Eberl, S., Fulham, M., Yin, Y., Chen, J., & Fang, D. D. (2013). A Likelihood and Local Constraint Level Set Model for Liver Tumor Segmentation from CT Volumes. *IEEE Transactions on Biomedical Engineering*, *60*(10), 2967–2977. doi:10.1109/TBME.2013.2267212 PMID:23771304

Li, H. J., & Zhang, J. S. (2010). A novel chaotic stream cipher and its application to palmprint template protection. *Chinese Physics B*, *19*(4), 040505.

Li, M., Liu, J., Yang, W., Sun, X., & Guo, Z. (2018, February). Structure-Revealing Low-Light Image Enhancement via Robust Retinex Model. *IEEE Transactions on Image Processing*, *27*(6), 2828–2841. doi:10.1109/TIP.2018.2810539 PMID:29570085

Lima, J. B., Campello, R. M., & Panario, D. (2008). Security of public key cryptosystems based on Chebyshev polynomials over prime finite fields. *Proceedings of the IEEE International Symposium on Information Theory (ISIT'08)*, 1843-1847.

Liu, D., Soran, B., Petrie, G., & Shapiro, L. (2012). *A Review of Computer Vision Segmentation Algorithms*. Academic Press.

Liu, H., Ruan, Z., Zhao, P., Dong, C., Shang, F., Liu, Y., Yang, L., & Timofte, R. (2022). Video Super-Resolution based on Deep Learning: A Comprehensive Survey. *Artificial Intelligence Review*, *55*(8), 5981–6035. doi:10.100710462-022-10147-y

Liu, N. (2011). Pseudo-randomness and complexity of binary sequences generated by the chaotic system. *Communications in Nonlinear Science and Numerical Simulation*, *16*, 761–768.

Liu, X., Deng, Z., & Yang, Y. (2019). Recent progress in semantic image segmentation. *Artificial Intelligence Review*, *52*, 1089–1106. https://doi.org/10.1007/s10462-018-9641-3

Liu, X., Ma, W., Ma, X., & Wang, J. (2023). LAE-Net: A locally-adaptive embedding network for low-light image enhancement. *Pattern Recognition*, *133*, 109039. doi:10.1016/j.patcog.2022.109039

Liu, Z., Zhang, M., & Cui, J. (2014). An adaptive data collection algorithm based on a Bayesian compressed sensing framework. *Sensors (Basel)*, *14*(5), 8330–8349. doi:10.3390140508330 PMID:24818659

Li, X., Wenhua, Q., Xu, D., & Liu, C. (2021). Image Segmentation Based on Improved Unet. *Journal of Physics: Conference Series*, *1815*, 012018. doi:10.1088/1742-6596/1815/1/012018

Li, Y., Li, C., & Zhao, Y. (2022). Memristor-type chaotic mapping. *Chaos*, *32*, 021104–021107.

Li, Y., Xiao, D., Deng, S., Han, Q., & Zhou, G. (2011). Parallel hash function construction based on chaotic maps with changeable parameters. *Neural Comput. Applic.*, *20*, 1305–1312.

Li, Z., Dinh, T. A., Ho, T.-Y., & Chakrabarty, K. (2014). Reliability-Driven Pipelined Scan-Like Testing of Digital Microfluidic Biochips. *Proc. of IEEE 23rd Asian Test Symposium*, 57-62. 10.1109/ATS.2014.22

Long, M., & Wang, H. (2013, April-June). Collision analysis and improvement of a parallel hash function based on chaotic maps with changeable parameters. *International Journal of Digital Crime and Forensics*, 5(2), 23–34.

Lu, S., Li, Z., Qin, Z., Yang, X., & Goh, R. S. M. (2017). A hybrid regression technique for house prices prediction. *2017 IEEE International Conference on Industrial Engineering and Engineering Management (IEEM)*, 319-323. 10.1109/IEEM.2017.8289904

Maesa, D. D. F., & Mori, P. (2020). Blockchain 3.0 applications survey. *Journal of Parallel and Distributed Computing*, 138, 99–114. doi:10.1016/j.jpdc.2019.12.019

Magadza, T., & Viriri, S. (2021). Deep Learning for Brain Tumor Segmentation: A Survey of State-of-the-Art. *Journal of Imaging*, 7(19), 1–22. https://doi.org/10.3390/jimaging7020019

Mahajan, H. B., Badarla, A., & Junnarkar, A. A. (2021). CL-IoT: Cross-layer Internet of Things protocol for intelligent manufacturing of smart farming. *Journal of Ambient Intelligence and Humanized Computing*, 12(7), 7777–7791. doi:10.100712652-020-02502-0

Maier, A., Syben, C., Lasser, T., & Riess, C. (2018). A gentle introduction to deep learning in medical image processing. *Zeitschrift fur Medizinische Physik*, 29(2), 86–101. https://doi.org/10.1016/j.zemedi.2018.12.003

Mani, M., & Sharma, A. K. (2013, August). Modified approach for routing and clustering in sensor network using fuzzy logic control. In *2013 Sixth International Conference on Contemporary Computing (IC3)* (pp. 102-107). IEEE. 10.1109/IC3.2013.6612170

Maniccam, S. S., & Bourbakis, N. G. (2001). Lossless image compression and encryption using SCAN. *Pattern Recognition*, 34(6), 1229–1245. doi:10.1016/S0031-3203(00)00062-5

Marmanis, D., Datcu, M., Esch, T., & Stilla, U. (2015, December 1). Deep learning earth observation classification using ImageNet pretrained networks. *IEEE Geoscience and Remote Sensing Letters*, 13(1), 105–109.

Masuda, N., Jakimoski, G., Aihara, K., & Kocarev, L. (2006, June). Chaotic Block Ciphers: From Theory to Practical Algorithms. *IEEE Trans. Circuits Syst. I. Fundam. Theory Appl.*, 53(6), 1341–1352.

Mattews, R. (n.d.). On the derivation of a chaotic encryption algorithm. *Cryptologia*, 13(1), 29–42. doi:10.1080/0161118991863745

Mayle, n. 2020. Blockchain based Communication Architectures with Applications to Private Security Networks (No. Sand-2020-12719r). Univ. of New Mexico.

Mehmood, A., Lv, Z., Lloret, J., & Umar, M. M. (2020). ELDC: An artificial neural network based energy-efficient and robust routing scheme for pollution monitoring in WSNs. *IEEE Transactions on Emerging Topics in Computing*, 8(1), 106–114. doi:10.1109/TETC.2017.2671847

Ming, Y., Zhang, J., Qi, J., Liao, T., Wang, M., & Zhang, L. (2020). Prediction and Analysis of Chengdu Housing Rent Based on XGBoost Algorithm. *ICBDT 2020: 2020 3rd International Conference on Big Data Technologies*, 1-5. 10.1145/3373509.3373578

Min, H. (2019). Blockchain technology for enhancing supply chain resilience. *Business Horizons*, 62(1), 35–45. doi:10.1016/j.bushor.2018.08.012

Mirjalili, S., Mirjalili, S.M., & Lewis, A. (2014). Grey Wolf Optimizer. *Advances in Engineering Software, 69*, 46-61. https://www.sciencedirect.com/science/article/pii/S0965997813001853

Mitra, D. (2008). Accelerated functional testing of digital microfluidic biochips. *IEEE Asian Test Symposium*, 295-300.

Mittal, A., Soundararajan, R., & Bovik, A. C. (2012). Making a Completely Blind Image Quality Analyzer. *IEEE Signal Processing Letters, 20*(3), 209–212. doi:10.1109/LSP.2012.2227726

Mittal, M., & Kumar, K. (2014, November). Network lifetime enhancement of homogeneous sensor network using ART1 neural network. In *2014 International Conference on Computational Intelligence and Communication Networks* (pp. 472-475). IEEE. 10.1109/CICN.2014.110

Molnar, C. (2020). *Interpretable Machine Learning, A Guide for Making Black Box Models Explainable.* Leanpub.

Monrat, A. A., Schelén, O., & Andersson, K. (2019). A survey of blockchain from the perspectives of applications, challenges, and opportunities. *IEEE Access: Practical Innovations, Open Solutions, 7*, 117134–117151. doi:10.1109/ACCESS.2019.2936094

Moraye, K., Pavate, A., Nikam, S., & Thakkar, S. (2021). Crop Yield Prediction Using Random Forest Algorithm for Major Cities in Maharashtra State. *International Journal of Innovative Research in Computer Science & Technology, 9*(2), 40–44. doi:10.21276/ijircst.2021.9.2.7

Morellos, A., Pantazi, X., Moshou, D., Alexandridis, T., Whetton, R., Tziotzios, G., Wiebensohn, J., Bill, R., & Mouazen, A. M. (2016). Machine learning based prediction of soil total nitrogen, organic carbon and moisture content by using VIS-NIR spectroscopy. *Biosystems Engineering, 152*, 104–116. doi:10.1016/j.biosystemseng.2016.04.018

Morra, L., Delsanto, S., &Correale, L. (2019). *Artificial Intelligence in Medical Imaging.* . doi:10.1201/9780367229184

Mukherjee, G., Chatterjee, A., & Tudu, B. (2022). Identification of the types of disease for tomato plants using a modified gray wolf optimization optimized MobileNetV2 convolutional neural network architecture driven computer vision framework. *Concurrency and Computation: Practice and Experience, 34*.

Mustaffa, Z., Sulaiman, H. M., Yusob, B., & Ernawan, F. (2016). Integration of GWO-LSSVM for time series predictive analysis. *4th IET Clean Energy and Technology Conference (CEAT 2016)*, 1-5. doi: 10.1049/cp.2016.1360

Nandan, A. S., Singh, S., Kumar, R., & Kumar, N. (2021, August). An optimized genetic algorithm for cluster head election based on movable sinks and adjustable sensing ranges in IoT-based HWSNs. *IEEE Internet of Things Journal, 9*(7), 5027–5039. doi:10.1109/JIOT.2021.3107295

Nayak, P., & Devulapalli, A. (2015). A fuzzy logic-based clustering algorithm for WSN to extend the network lifetime. *IEEE Sensors Journal, 16*(1), 137–144. doi:10.1109/JSEN.2015.2472970

Nayak, P., & Vathasavai, B. (2017). Energy efficient clustering algorithm for multi-hop wireless sensor network using type-2 fuzzy logic. *IEEE Sensors Journal, 17*(14), 4492–4499. doi:10.1109/JSEN.2017.2711432

Negi, G., Kumar, A., Pant, S., & Ram, M. (2021). GWO: A review and applications. *Int J Syst Assur Eng Manag, 12*, 1–8. doi:10.1007/s13198-020-00995-8

Nguyen, G. T., & Kim, K. (2018). A survey about consensus algorithms used in blockchain. *Journal of Information Processing Systems, 14*(1), 101-128.

Nida, M., & Zaitouna, M. J. (2015). Survey on Image Segmentation Techniques. *Procedia Computer Science, 65*, 797–806. doi:10.1016/j.procs.2015.09.027

Noh, H., You, T., Mun, J., & Han, B. (2017). Regularizing deep neural networks by noise: Its interpretation and optimization. *Advances in Neural Information Processing Systems, 2017*, 30.

Noor, N. M. (2018). *IOP Conference Series. Earth and Environmental Science*, 169.

Norouzi, B., Mirzakuchaki, S., Seyedzadeh, S. M., & Mosavi, M. R. (2012). A simple, sensitive and secure image encryption algorithm based on hyper-chaotic system with only one round diffusion. *Multimedia Tools and Applications, 71*(3), 1469–1497. doi:10.100711042-012-1292-9

Ohali, Y. A. (2011). Computer vision based date fruit grading system: design and implementation. *Journal of King Saud University - Computer and Information Sciences, 23*, 29-36.

Oishi, S., & Inoue, H. (1982). Pscudo-Random Number Generators and Chaos. *Transactions of the Institute of Electronics and Communication Engineers of Japan, E65*(9), 534–554.

Onishi, Y., Yoshida, T., Kurita, H., Fukao, T., Arihara, H., & Iwai, A. (2019). An automated fruit harvesting robot by using deep learning. *ROBOMECH Journal, 6*(1), 13. doi:10.118640648-019-0141-2

Palaniraj, A., Balamurugan, A. S., Durga Prasad, R., & Pradeep, P. (2021). Crop and Fertilizer Recommendation System using Machine Learning. *International Research Journal of Engineering and Technology, 8*, 319–323.

Pandey,P., Pallavi,S.,&Chandra,S., (2019). Pragmatic Medical Image Analysis and Deep Learning: An Emerging Tren. *Advancement of Machine Intelligence in Interactive Medical Image Analysis*, 1–18.. doi:10.1007/978-981-15-1100-4_1,2019

Patil, A., Kokate, S., Patil, P., Panpatil, V., & Sapkal, R. (2020). Crop Prediction using Machine Learning Algorithms. *International Journal of Advancements in Engineering & Technology, 1*, 1–8.

Patil, P., Panpatil, V., & Kokate, S. (2020). Crop Prediction System using Machine Learning Algorithms. *International Research Journal of Engineering and Technology, 7*, 748–753.

Patra, C., Chattopadhyay, M., Bhaumik, P., & Roy, A. G. (2011, February). Using self organizing map in wireless sensor network for designing energy efficient topologies. In *2011 2nd International Conference on Wireless Communication, Vehicular Technology, Information Theory and Aerospace & Electronic Systems Technology (Wireless VITAE)* (pp. 1-6). IEEE. 10.1109/WIRELESSVITAE.2011.5940819

Pecora & Carroll. (1990). Synchronization in chaotic systems. *Physical Review Letters, 64*(8), 821-825.

Pegado, R., Ñaupari, Z., Molina, Y., & Castillo, C. (2019). Radial distribution network reconfiguration for power losses reduction based on improved selective BPSO. *Electric Power Systems Research, 169*, 206-213. doi:10.1016/j.epsr.2018.12.030

Phan, T. D. (2018). Housing Price Prediction Using Machine Learning Algorithms: The Case of Melbourne City, Australia. *2018 International Conference on Machine Learning and Data Engineering (ICMLDE) 2018*, 35-42. 10.1109/iCMLDE.2018.00017

Pinto, A. R., Montez, C., Araújo, G., Vasques, F., & Portugal, P. (2014). An approach to implement data fusion techniques in wireless sensor networks using genetic machine learning algorithms. *Information Fusion, 15*, 90–101. doi:10.1016/j.inffus.2013.05.003

Pisarchik, A. N., & Zanin, M. (2010). Chaotic map cryptography and security. Encryption: Methods, Software and Security, 1-28.

Pizer, Amburn, Austin, Cromartie, Geselowitz, Greer, Romeny, Zimmerman, & Zuiderveld. (1987). Adaptive Histogram Equalization and Its Variations. *Computer Vision, Graphics, and Image Processing, 39*(3), 355-368,

Pollack, M. G., Fair, R. B., & Shenderov, A. D. (2000). Electrowetting-based actuation of liquid droplets for microfluidic applications. *Applied Physics Letters*, *77*(11), 1725–1726. doi:10.1063/1.1308534

Prange, R. K. (2012). Pre-harvest, harvest and post-harvest strategies for organic production of fruits and vegetables. *Acta Horticulturae*, (933), 43–50. doi:10.17660/ActaHortic.2012.933.3

Preeth, S. K., Dhanalakshmi, R., Kumar, R., & Shakeel, P. M. (2018). An adaptive fuzzy rule based energy efficient clustering and immune-inspired routing protocol for WSN-assisted IoT system. *Journal of Ambient Intelligence and Humanized Computing*, 1–13. doi:10.100712652-018-1154-z

Priyanka, P., Garg, R., Pathak, P., Trivedi, A., & Raj, A. (2020). Image Processing Using Machine Learning. *International Journal of Scientific Development and Research*, *5*(9), 471–477.

Priya, P., Muthaiah, U., & Balamurugan, M. (2018). Predicting yield of the crop using machine learning algorithm. *International Journal of Engineering Sciences & Research Technology*, *7*, 1–7.

Pudumalar, S., Ramanujam, E., Rajashree, R. H., Kavya, C., Kiruthika, T., & Nisha, J. (2016) Crop Recommendation System for Precision Agriculture. *Proc. of Eighth International Conference on Advanced Computing*, 32 – 36.

Puttagunta, M., & Ravi, S. (2021). Medical image analysis based on deep learning approach. *Multimed Tools Appl*, *80*, 24365–24398. doi:10.1007/s11042-021-10707-4

Puttagunta, M., & Ravi, S. (2021). Medical image analysis based on deep learning approach. *Multimedia Tools and Applications*, *80*, 24365–24398. https://doi.org/10.1007/s11042-021-10707-4

Qian, S., Shi, Y., Wu, H., Liu, J., & Zhang, W. (2022). An Adaptive Enhancement Algorithm Based on Visual Saliency for Low Illumination Images. *Applied Intelligence*, *52*(2), 1770–1792. doi:10.100710489-021-02466-4

Rabelo, R. A., Sobral, J. V., Araujo, H. S., Baluz, R. A., & Holanda Filho, R. (2013, June). An approach based on fuzzy inference system and ant colony optimization for improving the performance of routing protocols in Wireless Sensor Networks. In *2013 IEEE Congress on Evolutionary Computation* (pp. 3244-3251). IEEE. 10.1109/CEC.2013.6557967

Raga Madhuri, C. R., Anuradha, G., & Vani Pujitha, M. (2019). House Price Prediction Using Regression Techniques: A Comparative Study. *2019 International Conference on Smart Structures and Systems (ICSSS)*, 1-5. 10.1109/ICSSS.2019.8882834

Ranschaert, E. R., Morozov, S., & Algra, P. R. (2019). *Artificial Intelligence in Medical Imaging: Opportunities, Applications and Risks*. Springer. doi:10.1007/978-3-319-94878-2

Rao & Chen. (2012). A Survey of Video Enhancement Techniques. *Multimedia Signal Processing*, *3*(1), 71–99.

Rawat, P., & Chauhan, S. (2022). Particle swarm optimization based sleep scheduling and clustering protocol in wireless sensor network. *Peer-to-Peer Networking and Applications*, *15*(3), 1417–1436. doi:10.100712083-022-01307-6

Ray, A., & De, D. (2016). Energy efficient clustering protocol based on K-means (EECPK-means)-midpoint algorithm for enhanced network lifetime in wireless sensor network. *IET Wireless Sensor Systems*, *6*(6), 181–191. doi:10.1049/iet-wss.2015.0087

Ren, H., Wang, Y., Xie, Q., & Yang, H. (2009). A novel method for one-way hash function construction based on spatiotemporal chaos. *Chaos, Solitons, and Fractals*, *42*, 2014–2022.

Renuka, & Terdal, D. S. (2019). Evaluation of Machine learning algorithms for Crop Yield Prediction. *International Journal of Engineering and Advanced Technology*, *8*(6), 4082–4086. doi:10.35940/ijeat.F8640.088619

Ren, W., Liu, S., Ma, L., Xu, Q., Xu, X., Cao, X., Du, J., & Yang, M. H. (2019). Low-light image enhancement via a deep hybrid network. *IEEE Transactions on Image Processing*, 28(9), 4364–4375. doi:10.1109/TIP.2019.2910412 PMID:30998467

Risius, M., & Spohrer, K. (2017). A blockchain research framework. *Business & Information Systems Engineering*, 59(6), 385–409. doi:10.100712599-017-0506-0

Rizal Batubara, F., Ubacht, J., & Janssen, M. (2019, June). Unraveling transparency and accountability in blockchain. In *Proceedings of the 20th annual international conference on digital government research* (pp. 204-213). 10.1145/3325112.3325262

Saleh, N., Kassem, A., & Haidar, A. M. (2018). Energy-efficient architecture for wireless sensor networks in healthcare applications. *IEEE Access: Practical Innovations, Open Solutions*, 6, 6478–6486. doi:10.1109/ACCESS.2018.2789918

Saxena, N., Roy, A., & Shin, J. (2009). QuESt: A QoS-based energy efficient sensor routing protocol. *Wireless Communications and Mobile Computing*, 9(3), 417–426. doi:10.1002/wcm.546

Schneider, Keszocze, Stoppe, & Drechsler. (2017). Effects of Cell Shapes on the Routability of Digital Microfluidic Biochips. *Design Automation and Test in Europe Conference*, 1627-1630.

Seyyedabbasi, A., Kiani, F., Allahviranloo, T., Fernandez-Gamiz, U., & Noeiaghdam, S. (2023). Optimal data transmission and pathfinding for WSN and decentralized IoT systems using I-GWO and Ex-GWO algorithms. *Alexandria Engineering Journal*, 63, 339–357. doi:10.1016/j.aej.2022.08.009

Shafiulla, S., Shwetha, R. B., Ramya, O. G., Pushpa, H., & Pooja, K. R. (2022). Crop Recommendation using Machine Learning Techniques. *International Journal of Engineering Research & Technology (Ahmedabad)*, 10, 199–201.

Sharawi, M., Saroit, I. A., El-Mahdy, H., & Emary, E. (2013). Routing wireless sensor networks based on soft computing paradigms: Survey. *International Journal on Soft Computing Artificial Intelligence and Applications (Commerce, Calif.)*, 2(4), 21–36. doi:10.5121/ijscai.2013.2403

Sharma, V. K., Shukla, S. S. P., & Singh, V. (2012, December). A tailored Q-Learning for routing in wireless sensor networks. In *2012 2nd IEEE International Conference on Parallel, Distributed and Grid Computing* (pp. 663-668). IEEE.

Sharma, A., Jain, A., Gupta, P., & Chowdary, V. (2021). Machine learning applications for precision agriculture: A comprehensive review. *IEEE Access: Practical Innovations, Open Solutions*, 9, 4843–4873. doi:10.1109/ACCESS.2020.3048415

Sharma, T., & Kumar, B. (2012). F-MCHEL: Fuzzy based master cluster head election leach protocol in wireless sensor network. *International Journal of Computer Science and Telecommunications*, 3(10), 8–13.

Shen, L., Yue, Z., Feng, F., Chen, Q., Liu, S., & Ma, J. (2017). *Msr-net: Low-light image enhancement using deep convolutional network*. arXiv preprint arXiv:1711.02488.

Shi, J., & Malik, J. (2000, August). Normalized cuts and image segmentation. *IEEE Transactions on Pattern Analysis and Machine Intelligence*, 22(8), 888–905. doi:10.1109/34.868688

Shin, H. C., Roth, H., Gao, M., Lu, L., Xu, Z., Nogues, I., Yao, J., Mollura, D., & Summers, R. (2016). Deep convolutional neural networks for computer-aided detection: CNN architectures, dataset characteristics and transfer learning. *IEEE Transactions on Medical Imaging*, 35(5).

Shujun, L., Xuanqin, M., & Yuanlong, C. (2001). *Pseudo-random bit generator based on couple chaotic systems and its applications in stream-cipher cryptography*. Progress in Cryptology INDOCRYPT.

Shukla, V., & Noohul, B. B. (2014). Diagonal Testing in Digital Microfluidics Biochips Using MEDA Based Approach. *Proc. of 5th IEEE International Conference of Intelligent and Advanced Systems*, 469-474.

Shukla, V., & Noohul, B. B. (2016). Fault Modeling and Simulation of MEDA based Digital Microfluidics Biochips. *Proc. of 29th IEEE International Conference on VLSI Design*.

Shukla, V., Noohul, B. Z. A., Hussin, F. A., & Zwolinski, M. (2013). On Testing of MEDA Based Digital Microfluidics Biochips. *5th IEEE Asia Symposium on Quality Electronic Design*, 60-65. 10.1109/ASQED.2013.6643565

Singh, K., Kapoor, R., & Sinha, S. K. (2015, October). Enhancement of Low Exposure Images via Recursive Histogram Equalization Algorithms. *Optik (Stuttgart)*, *126*(20), 2619–2625. doi:10.1016/j.ijleo.2015.06.060

Singh, R., Wu, W., Wang, G., & Kalra, M. K. (2020). Artificial intelligence in image reconstruction: The change is here. *Physica Medica*, *79*, 113–125. doi:10.1016/j.ejmp.2020.11.012 PMID:33246273

Singh, V., Sarwar, A., & Sharma, V. (2017). Analysis of soil and prediction of crop yield (Rice) using Machine Learning approach. *International Journal of Advanced Research in Computer Science*, *8*, 1254–1259.

Sivagami, M., & Revathi, T. (2003). Marker Controlled Watershed Segmentation Using Bitplane Slicing. *International Journal of Image Processing and Vision Science*, *1*(3), 179–183. doi:10.47893/IJIPVS.2013.1033

Sivasankar, B., Ashok, A. P., Madhu, G., & Fousiya, S. (2020). House Price Prediction. *International Journal on Computer Science and Engineering*, *8*(7), 98–102.

Sofu, M. M., Er, O., Kayacan, M. C., & Cetisli, B. (2016). Design of an automatic apple sorting system using machine vision. *Computers and Electronics in Agriculture*, *127*, 395–405. doi:10.1016/j.compag.2016.06.030

Sohraby, K., Minoli, D., & Znati, T. (2007). *Wireless sensor networks: technology, protocols, and applications*. John Wiley & Sons. doi:10.1002/047011276X

Sridhar, V., & Rao, R. (2022). A machine learning-based intelligence approach for multiple-input/multiple-output routing in wireless sensor networks. *Mathematical Problems in Engineering*, *2022*, 1–13. doi:10.1155/2022/6391678

Stinson, D. R. (2009). *Cryptography: Theory and Practice*. CRC Press.

Stojanovski, T., & Kocarev, L. (2001). Chaos-based random number generators–Part I: Analysis. *IEEE Transactions on Circuits and Systems. I, Fundamental Theory and Applications*, *48*, 281–288.

Stojanovski, T., Pihl, J., & Kocarev, L. (2001). Chaos-based random number generators–Part II: Practical realization. *IEEE Transactions on Circuits and Systems. I, Fundamental Theory and Applications*, *48*, 382–385.

Su, Ozev, & Chakrabarty. (2006). Concurrent testing of digital microfluidic based biochips. *ACM TODAES*, *11*(2).

Suchithra, M. S., & Pai, M. L. (2019). Improving the prediction accuracy of soil nutrient classification by optimizing extreme learning machine parameters. *Information Processing in Agriculture*, *7*(1), 72–82. doi:10.1016/j.inpa.2019.05.003

Su, F. (2003). Testing of droplet-based microelectrofluidic systems. *Proc. IEEE Int. Test Conf.*, 1192-1200.

Su, F., Ozev, S., & Chakrabarty, K. (2005). Ensuring the operational Health of droplet-based microelectrofluidic biosensor systems. *IEEE Sensors Journal*, *5*(4), 763–773. doi:10.1109/JSEN.2005.848127

Suganyadevi, S., Seethalakshmi, V., & Balasamy, K. (2022). A review on deep learning in medical image analysis. *International Journal of Multimedia Information Retrieval*, *11*, 19–38. https://doi.org/10.1007/s13735-021-00218-1

Sundari, V., Anusree, M., Swetha, U., & Divya Lakshmi, R. (2022). Crop recommendation and yield prediction using machine learning algorithms. *World Journal of Advanced Research and Reviews, 14*(3), 452–459. doi:10.30574/wjarr.2022.14.3.0581

Sun, Y., Dong, W., & Chen, Y. (2017). An improved routing algorithm based on ant colony optimization in wireless sensor networks. *IEEE Communications Letters, 21*(6), 1317–1320. doi:10.1109/LCOMM.2017.2672959

Tang, G., Wang, S., Lu, H., & Hu, G. (2003). Chaos-based cryptography incorporated with S-box algebraic operation. *Physics Letters [Part A], 318*(4–5), 388–398. doi:10.1016/j.physleta.2003.09.042

Tashtarian, F., Haghighat, A. T., Honary, M. T., & Shokrzadeh, H. (2007, September). A new energy-efficient clustering algorithm for wireless sensor networks. In *2007 15th International Conference on Software, Telecommunications and Computer Networks* (pp. 1-6). IEEE.

Tenny, R., & Tsimring, L. S. (2005). Additive mixing modulation for public key encryption based on distributed dynamics. *IEEE Transactions on Circuits and Systems I: Regular Papers, 52*(3), 672 – 679.

Tenny, R., Tsimring, L. S., Larson, L., & Abarbanel, H. D. (2003). Using distributed nonlinear dynamics for public key encryption. *Physical Review Letters, 90*(4), 047903.

Thangaramya, K., Kulothungan, K., Logambigai, R., Selvi, M., Ganapathy, S., & Kannan, A. (2019). Energy aware cluster and neuro-fuzzy based routing algorithm for wireless sensor networks in IoT. *Computer Networks, 151*, 211–223. doi:10.1016/j.comnet.2019.01.024

Thekiya, M. S., & Nikose, M. D. (2022). Energy efficient clustering routing protocol using novel admission allotment scheme (AAS) based intra-cluster communication for Wireless Sensor Network. *International Journal of Information Technology*, 1-10.

Thilakarathne, N. N., Bakar, M. S. A., Abas, P. E., & Yassin, H. (2022). A Cloud Enabled Crop Recommendation Platform for Machine Learning-Driven Precision Farming. *Sensors (Basel), 22*(16), 6299. doi:10.339022166299 PMID:36016060

Thompson, R. F., Valdes, G., Fuller, C. D., Carpenter, C. M., Morin, O., Aneja, S., Lindsay, W. D., Aerts, H. J. W. L., Agrimson, B., Deville, C. Jr, Rosenthal, S. A., Yu, J. B., & Thomas, C. R. Jr. (2018). Artificial intelligence in radiation oncology: A specialty-wide disruptive transformation? *Radiotherapy and Oncology: Journal of the European Society for Therapeutic Radiology and Oncology, 129*(3), 421–426. doi:10.1016/j.radonc.2018.05.030 PMID:29907338

Truong, Q., Nguyen, M., Dang, H., & Mei, B. (2020). Housing Price Prediction via Improved Machine Learning Techniques. *Procedia Computer Science, 174*, 433–442. doi:10.1016/j.procs.2020.06.111

Trusculescu, A. A., Manolescu, D., Tudorache, E., & Oancea, C. (2020, November). Deep learning in interstitial lung disease—How long until daily practice. *European Radiology, 30*(11), 6285–6292.

Tuyen, D. N., Tuan, T. M., Son, L. H., Ngan, T. T., Giang, N. L., Hieu, V. V., Gerogiannis, V. C., Tzimos, D., & Kanavos, A. (2021). A Novel Approach Combining Particle Swarm Optimization And Deep Learning for Flash Flood Detection from Satellite Images. *Mathematics, 9*, 2846. doi:10.3390/math9222846

Ucat, R. C., & Dela Cruz, J. C. (2019). Postharvest grading classification of cavendish banana using deep learning and tensorflow. *Proc. of International Symposium on Multimedia and Communication Technology*, 1-6. 10.1109/ISMAC.2019.8836129

Ulmas, P., & Liiv, I. (2020). *Segmentation of Satellite Imagery using U-Net Models for Land Cover Classification. ArXiv* abs/2003.02899.

Venkataramana, S., Sekhar, B. V. D. S., Deshai, N., Chakravarthy, V. V. S. S. S., & Rao, S. K. (2019, May). Efficient time reducing and energy saving routing algorithm for wireless sensor network. *Journal of Physics: Conference Series*, *1228*(1), 012002. doi:10.1088/1742-6596/1228/1/012002

Verma, A., Kumar, S., Gautam, P. R., Rashid, T., & Kumar, A. (2020). Fuzzy logic based effective clustering of homogeneous wireless sensor networks for mobile sink. *IEEE Sensors Journal*, *20*(10), 5615–5623. doi:10.1109/JSEN.2020.2969697

Vimalapriya, M. D., Vignesh, B. S., & Sandhya, S. (2019). *Energy-Centric Route Planning using Machine Learning Algorithm for Data Intensive Secure Multi-Sink Sensor Networks*. International Journal of Innovative Technology and Exploring Engineering.

Wang, F., Jiang, M., Qian, C., Yang, S., Cheng, L., Zhang, H., Wang, X., & Tang, X. (2017). Residual attention network for image classification. IEEE CVPR, 3156–3164.

Wang, Gong, Zhan, & Lai. (2005). Public-key encryption based on generalized synchronization of coupled map lattices. *Chaos, 15*(2), 1–8.

Wang, X., Girshick, R., Gupta, A., & He, K. (2017). *Non-local neural networks*. arXivpreprintarXiv:1711.07971

Wang, Z., Yin, Y., & Yin, R. (2022) Multi-tasking atrous convolutional neural network for machinery fault identification. *Int J Adv Manuf Technol*. doi:10.1007/s00170-022-09367-x

Wang, C., Liu, X., Hu, H., Han, Y., & Yao, M. (2020). Energy-efficient and load-balanced clustering routing protocol for wireless sensor networks using a chaotic genetic algorithm. *IEEE Access: Practical Innovations, Open Solutions*, *8*, 158082–158096. doi:10.1109/ACCESS.2020.3020158

Wang, C., Zhu, X., Hong, J. C., & Zheng, D. (2019). Artificial Intelligence in Radiotherapy Treatment Planning: Present and Future. *Technology in Cancer Research & Treatment*, *2019*(18). doi:10.1177/1533033819873922 PMID:31495281

Wang, G., & Teng, D. (2011). Digital Microfluidic Operations on Microfluidic Dot Array Architecture. *IET Nanobiotechnology*, *5*(4), 152–160. doi:10.1049/iet-nbt.2011.0018 PMID:22149873

Wang, G., Teng, D., Lai, Y.-T., Lu, Y.-W., Ho, Y., & Lee, C.-Y. (2014). Field-programmable lab-on-a-chip based on microelectrode dot array architecture. *IET Nanobiotechnology / IET*, *8*(3), 163–171. doi:10.1049/iet-nbt.2012.0043

Wang, J. S., & Li, S. X. (2019). An Improved Grey Wolf Optimizer Based on Differential Evolution and Elimination Mechanism. *Scientific Reports*, *9*(1), 7181. doi:10.103841598-019-43546-3 PMID:31073211

Wang, L., & Chen, Z. (2022). Hyperchaotic Image Encryption Algorithm Based on BD-Zigzag Transformation and DNA Coding. *LNEE*, *961*, 667–677.

Wang, M., Zhang, Q., Lam, S., Cai, J., & Yang, R. (2020). A Review on Application of Deep Learning Algorithms in External Beam Radiotherapy Automated Treatment Planning. *Frontiers in Oncology*, *10*, 580–919. doi:10.3389/fonc.2020.580919 PMID:33194711

Wang, T., Lei, Y., Fu, Y., Wynne, J. F., Curran, W. J., Liu, T., & Yang, X. (2021). A review on medical imaging synthesis using deep learning and its clinical applications. *Journal of Applied Clinical Medical Physics*, *22*(1), 11–36. doi:10.1002/acm2.13121 PMID:33305538

Wang, W., Wu, X., Yuan, X., & Gao, Z. (2020). An Experiment-Based Review of Low-Light Image Enhancement Methods. *IEEE Access: Practical Innovations, Open Solutions*, *8*, 87884–87917. doi:10.1109/ACCESS.2020.2992749

Wang, X. Y., & Qing, Y. (2009). A block encryption algorithm based on dynamic sequences of multiple chaotic systems. *Communications in Nonlinear Science and Numerical Simulation*, *14*, 574–581.

Wei, Y., & Wei, P. (n.d.). Construct and analyzed K-hash function based on chaotic dynamica S-Boxes. *Applied Mechanics and Materials, 519-520*, 889–896.

Wong, K. (2003). A combined chaotic cryptographic and hashing scheme. *Physics Letters. [Part A], 307*, 292–298.

Wu, G., Shao, X., Guo, Z., Chen, Q., Yuan, W., Shi, X., Xu, Y., & Shibasaki, R. (2018). Automatic Building Segmentation of Aerial imagery Using Multi-Constraint Fully Convolutional Networks. *Remote Sensing, 10*(3), 407. https://doi.org/10.3390/rs10030407

Xiangyi, Y., Tang, H., Sun, S., Ma, H., Kong, D., & Xie, X. (2021). AFTer-UNet: Axial Fusion Transformer UNet for Medical Image Segmentation. *2022 IEEE/CVF Winter Conference on Applications of Computer Vision (WACV)*, 3270-3280.

Xiao, D., Shih, F. Y., & Liao, X. F. (2010). A chaos-based hash function with both modification detection and localization capabilities. Communications in Nonlinear Science and Number Simulation, 15, 2254-2261.

Xiao, D., Liao, X. F., & Wang, Y. (2009). Parallel keyed hash function based on chaotic neural network. *Neurocomputing, 72*, 2288–2296.

Xiao, D., Peng, W., Liao, X. F., & Xiang, T. (2010). Collision analysis of one kind of chaos-based hash function. *Physics Letters. [Part A], 374*, 1228–1231.

Xie, P., Lv, M., & Zhao, J. (2020). An improved energy-low clustering hierarchy protocol based on ensemble algorithm. *Concurrency and Computation, 32*(7), e5575. doi:10.1002/cpe.5575

Xu & Sun. (2022). A Novel Variational Model for Detail-Preserving Low-Illumination Image Enhancement. *Signal Processing, 195*, 108468. ISSN0165-1684.doi.org/10.1016/j.sigpro.2022.108468

Xu, T., & Chakrabarty, K. (2007). Parallel scan-like test and multiple-Defect diagnosis for digital microfluidic biochips. IEEE Trans. Biomed.Circuits Syst., 1(2), 148–158. doi:10.1109/TBCAS.2007.909025

Xue, F., Sanderson, A., & Graves, R. (2006, April). Multi-objective routing in wireless sensor networks with a differential evolution algorithm. In *2006 IEEE International Conference on Networking, Sensing and Control* (pp. 880-885). IEEE.

Yadav, R. K., & Mahapatra, R. P. (2022). Hybrid metaheuristic algorithm for optimal cluster head selection in wireless sensor network. *Pervasive and Mobile Computing, 79*, 101504. doi:10.1016/j.pmcj.2021.101504

Yang, M., Xu, D., Chen, S., Li, H., & Shi, Z. (2019). Evaluation of machine learning approaches to predict soil organic matter and pH using vis-NIR spectra. *Sensors (Basel), 19*(2), 263–277. doi:10.339019020263 PMID:30641879

Yang, R., Xu, M., & Zhou, J. (2021). Clone Chaotic Parallel Evolutionary Algorithm for Low-Energy Clustering in High-Density Wireless Sensor Networks. *Scientific Programming, 2021*, 1–13. doi:10.1155/2021/6630322

Yan, R., Sun, H., & Qian, Y. (2013). Energy-aware sensor node design with its application in wireless sensor networks. *IEEE Transactions on Instrumentation and Measurement, 62*(5), 1183–1191. doi:10.1109/TIM.2013.2245181

Yao, W., Ye, J., Murimi, R., & Wang, G. (2021). *A survey on consortium blockchain consensus mechanisms.* arXiv preprint arXiv:2102.12058.

Ye, G., & Huang, X. (2016). A feedback chaotic image encryption scheme based on both bit-level and pixel level. *Journal of Vibration and Control, 22*, 1171–1180.

Yick, J., Mukherjee, B., & Ghosal, D. (2008). Wireless sensor network survey. *Computer Networks, 52*(12), 2292–2330. doi:10.1016/j.comnet.2008.04.002

Young, S. S., & Mohamed, Z.I.F. (2014). *Binary Particle Swarm Optimization (BPSO) Algorithm for Distributed Node Localization.* Trans Tech Publications Ltd. www.scientific.net/AMM.556-562.3666

Ypsilantis, P. P., & Montana, G. (2017). *Learning what to look in chest X-rays with a recurrent visual attention model.* arXivpreprint arXiv:1701.06452.

Zhan, C., Wu, Z., Liu, Y., Xie, Z., & Chen, W. (2020). Housing prices prediction with deep learning: an application for the real estate market in Taiwan. *2020 IEEE 18th International Conference on Industrial Informatics (INDIN),* 719-724. 10.1109/INDIN45582.2020.9442244

Zhang, Guo, Xu, Zhu, & Yang. (2022). Hyperchaotic circuit design based on memristor and its application in image encryption. In *Microelectronic Engineering.* Elsevier.

Zhang, Y., Lin, X., & Wang, Q. (2011). Asymmetric cryptography algorithm with chinese remainder theorem. *Communication Software and Networks (ICCSN), 2011 IEEE 3rd International Conference on Communication and Software Networks,* 450–454.

Zhang, C., Chen, J., & Chen, D. (2022). Cryptanalysis of an Image Encryption Algorithm Based on a 2D Hyperchaotic Map. *Entropy, 24,* 1551.

Zhang, L., Shen, J., & Zhu, B. (2021). View A research on an improved Unet-based concrete crack etectionalgorithm. *Structural Health Monitoring, 20*(4), 1864–1879. doi:10.1177/1475921720940068

Zhao, R., Yan, R., Chen, Z., Mao, K., Wang, P., & Gao, R.X. (2019). Deep learning and its applications to machine health monitoring. *Mechanical Systems and Signal Processing, 115,* 213-37.

Zhao, X., Wei, Z., Cong, Y., & Yin, B. (2018, December). A balances energy consumption clustering routing protocol for a wireless sensor network. In *2018 IEEE 4th Information Technology and Mechatronics Engineering Conference (ITOEC)* (pp. 521-527). IEEE. 10.1109/ITOEC.2018.8740385

Zhao, C., Wang, T., Wang, H., Du, Q., & Yin, C. (2023). A Novel Image Encryption Algorithm by Delay Induced Hyperchaotic Chen System. *The Journal of Imaging Science and Technology.*

Zhao, Z., Xiong, B., Wang, L., Ou, Q., Yu, L., & Kuang, F. (2021). Retinexdip: A unified deep framework for low-light image enhancement. *IEEE Transactions on Circuits and Systems for Video Technology, 32*(3), 1076–1088. doi:10.1109/TCSVT.2021.3073371

Zheng, Z., Xie, S., Dai, H. N., Chen, X., & Wang, H. (2018). Blockchain challenges and opportunities: A survey. *International Journal of Web and Grid Services, 14*(4), 352–375. doi:10.1504/IJWGS.2018.095647

Zhong, J., Huang, Z., Feng, L., Du, W., & Li, Y. (2019). A hyper-heuristic framework for lifetime maximization in wireless sensor networks with a mobile sink. *IEEE/CAA Journal of Automatica Sinica, 7*(1), 223-236.

Zhou, R., Chen, M., Feng, G., Liu, H., & He, S. (2010, August). Genetic clustering route algorithm in WSN. In *2010 Sixth International Conference on Natural Computation* (Vol. 8, pp. 4023-4026). IEEE. 10.1109/ICNC.2010.5584826

Zongwei, Z., Siddiquee, M. M. R., Tajbakhsh, N., & Liang, J. (2018). UNet++: A Nested U-Net Architecture for Medical Image Segmentation. *Deep Learning in Medical Image Analysis and Multimodal Learning for Clinical Decision Support: 4th International Workshop, DLMIA, and 8th International Workshop, ML-CDS, held in conjunction with MICCAI 2018,* 3-11.

About the Contributors

Santanu Koley earned his doctorate in philosophy in 2013 from CSJM University in Kanpur, Uttar Pradesh, India. He is currently employed as a professor in the computer science and engineering department at Haldia Institute of Technology in Haldia, West Bengal, India. In several AICTE-approved engineering institutions across India, he has more than seventeen years of teaching experience and more than sixteen years of research experience. In numerous national and international journals, conferences, books (written/edited), and book chapters, he has published more than forty research publications. He is currently conducting research in the fields of machine learning, cloud computing, digital image processing, and artificial intelligence.

Subhabrata Barman is an Assistant Professor with the Department of Computer Science & Engineering, Haldia Institute of Technology, West Bengal, India. His research interests are in the field of Wireless Networks, Computational Intelligence, Remote Sensing and Geo-Informatics, Parallel and Grid Computing. He has published research papers at various International and National Journals and Conferences. He is a Professional Member of IEEE, IACSIT, IAENG and a reviewer of International Journal of Wireless Networks (Springer).

Subhankar Joardar is presently Professor & Head in the Department of Computer Science and Engineering, Haldia Institute of Technology, Haldia-721657, India. He received his Ph.D degree from Birla Institute of Technology, Mesra, Ranchi, India in 2016. He did his masters (M. Tech and MCA) both from BIT, Mesra, Ranchi in 2009 and 2002 respectively. He has published more than 20 technical papers in the referred journals/conferences. He has served as Organizing Chair of international conference (ICITAM 2017). He is also Program Committee member of International Conferences (ICCDC 2019) and Program Chair (ISAI 2022). He is a member of Computer Society of India. His current research interests include Swarm intelligence, Routing in Mobile Ad Hoc Networks, Machine Learning.

* * *

Mohammad Aasif is currently pursuing his Bachelor of Technology in Computer Science & Engineering with specialization in Data Science from Haldia Institute of Technology. He is an aspiring data scientist and his field of interests are Machine Learning, Deep Learning, Neural Networks and Data Science. He likes to solve real life data science problems.

Pinaki Pratim Acharjya has completed his Doctorate of Philosophy in the year 2016 and presently he is working at Haldia Institute of Technology, Haldia, West Bengal India as a Professor in Computer Science and Engineering Department. He has more than thirteen years of research experience and more than fifteen years of teaching experience in various AICTE approved engineering colleges all over the India. He has published more than eighty research papers in various national and international Journal/ conferences. Presently he is doing research works in the areas of Digital Image Processing, Artificial Intelligence and Machine Learning.

Syed Saif Ahmed is a student at Haldia Institute of Technology currently pursuing Bachelor of Engineering Degree on Computer Science and Engineering with specialization in data science. He is an aspiring data scientist and his field of interests are Machine Learning, Data Analysis, Data Science, Deep learning and Neural Networks. He has a great interest in solving the real world issues with the help of the above mention field of interests.

Indrajit Banerjee received the Bachelor degree in Mechanical Engineering from Institute of Engineers, India, the Masters in Information Technology from Bengal Engineering and Science University, and the Ph.D. in Information Technology from Indian Institute of Engineering Science and Technology (IIEST), Shibpur, India. He is currently an associate professor in the Information Technology department at the Indian Institute of Engineering Science and Technology (IIEST), Shibpur, India. His research area includes Ad Hoc Network, with special interest in Wireless Sensor Network.

Swarnajit Bhattacharya is a student of Haldia Institute of Technology, Haldia, WB, India in the department of AEIE. His research interest is in the field of ML, DL, and IoT.

Arpitam Chatterjee did his PhD from Jadavpur University and is currently working as associate professor in Department of Printing Engineering, Jadavpur University. His research interests include digital image processing, computer vision, print and packaging process optimization, advertising and media research.

Anup Kumar Das received the Ph.D. degree in Physics from the NIT DURGAPUR, INDIA in 2022. He has been a Assistant Professor with the Dr. B. C. Roy Engineering College, Durgapur under Maulana Abul Kalam Azad University of West Bengal, India, since 2019. His current research interests include non dynamicas systems, chaotic signals, Cryptography, Secure Communication.

Sanjoy Das completed his B.E. from Regional Engineering College, Durgapur, M.E. from Bengal Engineering College, Howrah, Ph. D. from Bengal Engineering and Science University, Shibpur. Currently he is working as Senior Scientific Officer in Dept. of Engineering and Technological Studies, University of Kalyani. His research interests are Tribology and Optimization Techniques.

Prasenjit Dey received the B.Tech. degree in computer science and engineering from the West Bengal University of Technology, Kolkata, India, in 2010, and the M.Tech. degree in computer science and engineering from the National Institute of Technology Durgapur, Durgapur, India, in 2012. He was an Associate Innovator with Nivio Technologies, Gurgaon, India, in 2012. He was hardware graphics designer at Intel from 2017 to 2018. He received his Ph.D. degree in computer science and engineering from the

National Institute of Technology Durgapur, Durgapur, India, in 2018. He has joined the Cooch Behar Government Engineering College, Cooch Behar, India in 2018 and is currently working as an Assistant Professor in the Department of Computer Science. His current research interests include artificial neural networks, pattern recognition and machine learning. He has more than 10 research publications in internationally reputed journals, international edited books, and international IEEE conference proceedings. He served as a reviewer in several International conferences and also in several international editorial books. He also served as a reviewer in some reputed international journals, like, IEEE Transactions on Neural Networks and Learning Systems, IEEE Transactions on Systems, Man, and Cybernetics, IEEE Transactions on Artificial Intelligence, Applied Soft Computing, Elsevier, etc.

Krishna Gopal Dhal completed his B.Tech and M. Tech from Kalyani Government Engineering College, India. He received his Ph.D. in Engineering from University of Kalyani, West Bengal, India. Currently, he is working as Assistant Professor in the Department of Computer Science and Application, Midnapore College (Autonomous). His research interests are digital image Processing, Medical Imaging, and Nature inspired Optimisation Algorithms.

Arnab Gain has been appointed as Assistant Professor in Coochbehar Government Engineering College in the department of Computer Science and Engineering from 2018. He has served as Assistant Professor in B. P. Poddar Institute of Management and Technology in the department of Information Technology from 2016 to 2018. He has completed his M.E. degree in 2015 from Indian Institute of Engineering Science and Technology, Shibpur. He has completed his B.Tech degree in 2011 from The Government College of Engineering and Ceramic Technology, Kolkata. He has many research publications in various book chapters, and he has reviewed many research articles.

Soumen Ghosh is an Assistant Professor with the Department of Computer Science & Engineering (Data Science), Haldia Institute of Technology, West Bengal, India. His research interests are in the field of Machine Learning, Data Analysis, Data Mining, Cyber-Security. He has published research papers at various International and National Journals and Conferences and Book Chapters. Currently he is working in the area of ECG Signal data using Machine Learning. He is a Professional Member of Internet Society and also working as a reviewer of International book chapter.

Tarun Kumar Ghosh received his B.Tech. in Computer Science & Engineering from the University of Calcutta, India, M.E. in Computer Science & Technology from the B E College (DU) [now IIEST], Shibpur, Howrah, India and earned PhD in Computing from the University of Kalyani. He is currently a Professor in the Department of Computer Science & Engineering, Haldia Institute of Technology, West Bengal, India. His research interests include Grid Computing, Optimization, Computer Architecture, and Interconnection Networks. He is author of research studies published at national and international journals, conference proceedings as well as books published by Tata McGraw-Hill.

Priyatosh Jana is an Assistant Professor in the Department of CSE(Cyber Security) of Haldia Institute of Technology with more than 15 years of teaching experience. He is presently pursuing research work in the domain of Microfluidic Biochip. His research interests include Microfluidic Biochip, Cyber Security, IoT, Cryptography, Machine Learning, Deep Learning etc.

Sunanda Jana received her B.Tech. and M.Tech. degrees from Biju Patnaik University of Technology, Orissa, India, in 2007, and Berhampur University, Orissa, India, in 2010. Presently, she is working as an Assistant Professor at the Haldia Institute of Technology, West Bengal, India. Her research interests include the design and analysis of algorithms and network security.

Cynthia Jayapal is currently working as Professor in Department of Computer science and Engineering, Kumaraguru College of Technology, Coimbatore. She has completed her BE and ME in Computer Science Engineering and PhD from Anna university, Chennai. She has an experience of over 22 years in Industry and academia. She has over twenty five international journals, three book chapters and fifteen International conference publications to her credit. She has completed over fifteen certification courses from various international universities. She is member of ISTE and IET. She is recipient of various international awards. She has completed five consultancy projects for various industries and Government organizations. Her areas of interests include wired and wireless network protocols, VANET, IoT, Block chain and smart city applications.

Chandan Koner did his Ph .D. in CSE in 2012 from Jadavpur University. Now he is Professor and HOD of the CSE Department of Dr. B. C. Roy Engineering College, Durgapur. He has more than seventeen years of teaching experience in different engineering colleges. He is a Fellow of IETE, IE(I), South Asian Chamber of Scientific Research & Development, Nikhil Bharat Shiksha Parisad, Senior Member of ORSI, Member of CSI, ISTE, ISCA, IACSIT, Singapore, UACEE, Australia and IRSS, Canada. He is now working of HOD of CSE department at Dr B C Roy Engineering College.

Sumana Kundu worked as a Full time Research Scholar and received her PhD degree in Computer Science and Engineering (CSE) from National Institute of Technology (NIT), Durgapur, India in 2018. She received her M.Tech and B.E. degree in Computer Science and Engineering in 2010 and 2008 respectively. Currently, she is working as an Associate Professor in the department of Computer Science and Engineering (CSE) at Dr. B. C. Roy Engineering College, Durgapur, India. She has more than 12 years of Research and Teaching experiences. Her research interest includes – Machine Learning, Pattern recognition, Biometric identification, Image classification, Neural networks and Steganography.

Gopala Krishna M. T. has received his B. E degree from Bangalore University, M. Tech and Ph.D. degrees from Visvesvaraya Technological University, Belgaum, Karnataka, India in the year 2014. He is currently a Professor and Head of the Department of Artificial Intelligence and Machine Learning, SJB institute of Technology, Bengaluru, India. Main focus of his research interests consist mainly in the detection of moving objects in challenging environments. He have authored more than 50 papers in refereed international journals and conferences in the field of Background Modelling and foreground detection, Reviewer for many international journals.

Gitika Maity received her B. Tech and M. Tech in Computer Science Engineering and in Electronics and Communication Engineering respectively from Maulana Abul Kalam Azad University of Technology, West Bengal (formerly known as WBUT). She is currently a Lecturer in Computer Science and Technology at Dr. Meghnad Saha Institutte of Technology, Haldia, West Bengal, India. Her research interests are fault attack on AES algorithm, sensor network securities, cellular automata and machine learning.

Gunjan Mukherjee is currently working as the Assistant professor in the MCA Department in Regent Education and Research Foundation. He is pursuing his PhD from Jadavpur University on the application of machine learning in the field of agriculture. His research interests include the machine learning, computer vision, image processing and soft computing. Gunjan Mukherjee has completed his BSc in physics from Calcutta University, MCA from IGNOU and MTech from Calcutta University. He is the life member of CSI, ISOC and IAENG. He has published number of papers in different journals and international conferences of repute. Mr Mukherjee also guided many students of BTech and MCA in their project works. He also authored the school computer book series (class 3 to 10) under his sole authorship. He is currently attached to the reputed publishing house for publication of the question answer-based books for diploma and engineering level students. He has acted also as the reviewer for many technical books. Mr. Mukherjee worked as an Assistant teacher in Sree Aurobindo Institute of Education, as education officer in CSI, Kolkata chapter, as a senior faculty in NIT Ltd and as a lecturer in Calcutta Institute of Technology respectively. He also served as the visiting faculty in Aliha University and Techno India College.

Kuntal Mukherjee is currently pursuing bachelor's degree in engineering with Computer Science & Engineering (Data Science) from Haldia Institute of Technology. He is an aspiring Data Scientist, his filed of interests are Statistical Analysis, Deep Learning, Neural Networks, Cloud Architecture, Big Data & Machine Learning.

Sourav Paul is a research scholar at Swami Vivekananda Research Centre. He did his MSc and MTech from Calcutta University and IIT Kharagpur respectively.

Vishalakshi R. has completed Bachelors of Engineering (B.E) in Electronics and communication, Masters of Technology (M.Tech) in Digital Electronics from Visvesvaraya Technological University (VTU), Belgaum, Karnataka, India in the year 2005 and 2012, respectively and Pursuing Ph.D. in VTU under the guidance of Dr. M.T. Gopalakrishna on video enhancement technique. Her research interest is in different subjects like image and video processing, VLSI, CNN.

Hanumantha Raju received his B. E (Electronics and Communication Engineering) degree from Bangalore University in the year 2001, M. Tech (Digital Communication and Network Engineering) degree from Visvesvaraya Technological University (VTU), Belagavi in the year 2004, and Ph. D (VLSI Signal and Image Processing) degree from VTU, Belgaum, in the year, 2014. He is currently working as a Professor in the Department of ECE at BMS Institute of Technology and Management, Bengaluru, India. He has authored two books and 50 technical articles in refereed journals and proceedings such as IEEE, Intelligent Systems, Particle Swarm Optimization, etc. He is currently serving as a reviewer for IEEE Transaction on Industrial Electronics, Computers and Electrical Engineering Journal, Journal of Microscopy and Ultrastructure, etc. His research interests include Design of hardware architectures for signal and image processing algorithms, computer vision, Register Transfer Level (RTL) Verilog coding, synthesis and optimization of Integrated Circuits (ICs), FPGA/ASIC Design.

Soumya Roy is currently working in the department of Applied Electronics and Instrumentation Engineering, Haldia Institute of Technology as a capacity of Associate Professor. He awarded Ph.D (Engg.) degree from Jadavpur University on the year of 2021. He passed M.Tech examination in Instrumentation and Control Engineering from University of Calcutta on the year of 2014 with First Class Second position. He passed B.E. examination in Applied Electronics and Instrumentation Engineering from The University of Burdwan on the year of 2012 with First Class First position. His research interest is Instrumentation system designing and Signal Processing. He has published more than 24 research article including Patent, International Journals and Conferences. Currently, he is working on solar signal analysis, agricultural system modelling and designing, heath monitoring system etc.

Moumita Sahoo is currently working in the Applied electronics and instrumentation engineering department at Haldia Institute of Technology. She is holding a post of assistant professor in the same. Currently, she is pursuing her PhD research in medical image processing from Calcutta University. She has published 7 research articles including international journals and conferences till now.

Abhijit Sarkar is an Assistant Professor in the Department of CSE(Cyber Security) of Haldia Institute of Technology with more than 11 years of teaching experience. He is presently pursuing research work in the domain of Steganography. His research interests include Steganography, Cryptography, Machine Learning, Deep Learning, Cloud Computing etc. He has published several research papers in different Journals, International Conference Proceedings.

Anirban Sarkar is a dynamic, adaptable, and communicative person. Anirban enjoys using his skills to contribute to the exciting technological advances that happen every day around him. Anirban is a powerful force in the workplace or while learning new things and uses his positive attitude, tireless energy and self-motivated skills to encourage others to work hard and succeed. In his free time, Anirban likes to practice typing, watches Netflix and plays video games especially Call of Duty.

Minakshi Sarkar is currently pursuing PhD in Information Technology from Indian Institute of Engineering Science and Technology, Shibpur. She completed her M.Tech in Computer Science and Engineering from the Kalyani Government Engineering College, Nadia, West Bengal, India in 2017. She completed her B.Tech in Computer Science and Engineering from Guru Nanak Institute of Technology under Maulana Abul Kalam Azad University of Technology (Formerly known as West Bengal University of Technology), West Bengal, India in 2015. Her research interests include Image Steganography, IOT Security and Machine Learning. Presently, she is working as Assistant Professor in the department of CSE Data Science of Haldia Institute of Technology, Haldia, West Bengal.

Mrinmoy Sen received his B. Tech degree and M. Tech degree in Computer Science and Engineering from Maulana Abul Kalam Azad University of Technology, West Bengal (formerly known as WBUT) and National Institute of Technology, Durgapur respectively. He completed his Ph.D. in Information Technology from Indian Institute of Engineering Science and Technology (IIEST), Shibpur, India. He is currently an assistant professor in the department of Computer Science and Engineering at Haldia Institute of Technology, Haldia, India. His research interests are localization, deployment and mobility in Wireless Sensor Network.

J. Clement Sudhahar, MBA, Ph.D., is currently Professor and Head of the Department of Management Studies, Karunya School of Management, Karunya Deemed University, Coimbatore. He has over 30 years of experience. The first decade in Marketing Industry In companies including M&M. The next two decades in the Education industry as Faculty and Administrator, involving himself in Research and Consultancy. He has completed two applied research projects funded by ICSSR for the upliftment of the MSME sector. He has penned over 10 books and published over 80 articles with more than 1000 citations to his credit. He has also produced 14 PhDs in his thrust area of interest in Digital Branding and Marketing Analytics.

Bipan Tudu received his Ph.D. degree in the year 2011 from Jadavpur University, Kolkata, India. He is currently a Professor of Instrumentation and Electronics Engineering, Jadavpur University, Kolkata, India. His main research interest includes pattern recognition, artificial intelligence, machine olfaction, electronic tongue, QCM fabrication and utilization in diverse range of sensors, molecular imprinting technology, signal processing, image processing, and instrumentation development.

Tahamina Yesmin is a faculty member in Computer Science department at Haldia Institute of Management, Haldia. She has both industry and academic experiences. She worked for leading software development company's and also, she has academic experiences in school and college both. She is doing her PhD currently on Medical Image Processing. She has the ability and adaptable concept ability to include her industry experiences in her academic field to increase student's practical knowledge and improve students' concept regarding industry field. Her current research interests include Image Processing with different algorithms, Cyber Security and Data Analysis. She has published several research papers in various well cited National and International journals like UGG Approved (Grade A) on Image Processing, Cryptography steganography, Artificial Intelligence, Stress Management, Teaching Learning Approach and Audio Signal Processing also published various Book Chapters in Springer Nature. She has authored one Copyright file. She also presented various research papers at national and international conferences. She has the skilled in technology, programming and strong knowledge of practical works. She has collaborated actively with other researchers in several other disciplines of Computer Science, mainly Image Processing Algorithms and its Applications in the field of Medical Images. She particularly focused on how students can develop new applications and improve their knowledge on computer-based technologies and systems with new age technologies.

Index

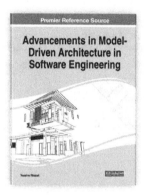

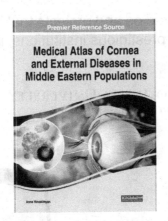

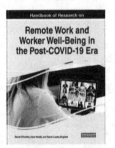